Presidents by Fate

Presidents by Fate

Nine Who Ascended through Death or Resignation

F. Martin Harmon

McFarland & Company, Inc., Publishers
Jefferson, North Carolina

LIBRARY OF CONGRESS CATALOGUING-IN-PUBLICATION DATA

Names: Harmon, F. Martin, 1951– author.
Title: Presidents by Fate : Nine Who Ascended through
Death or Resignation / F. Martin Harmon.
Description: Jefferson, North Carolina : McFarland & Company, Inc.,
Publishers, 2019 | Includes bibliographical references and index.
Identifiers: LCCN 2019028354 | ISBN 9781476677422 (paperback) |
ISBN 9781476636849 (ebook)
Subjects: LCSH: Presidents—Succession—United States—History—
Case studies. | Presidents—United States—Biography. |
Vice-Presidents—United States—Biography.
Classification: LCC E176.1 .H28 2019 | DDC 973.09/9—dc23
LC record available at https://lccn.loc.gov/2019028354

BRITISH LIBRARY CATALOGUING DATA ARE AVAILABLE

ISBN (print) 978-1-4766-7742-2
ISBN (ebook) 978-1-4766-3684-9

Front cover images: *clockwise from bottom left* Andrew Johnson,
between 1865 and 1870; John Tyler, between 1860 and 1865;
Calvin Coolidge, 1920; Harry S. Truman, 1945; Theodore Roosevelt,
1913; Lyndon B. Johnson, 1964; Gerald R. Ford, 1975;
Chester A. Arthur, 1882; Millard Fillmore, between 1850 and 1874
(Library of Congress); *background* © 2019 Shutterstock

Printed in the United States of America

*McFarland & Company, Inc., Publishers
Box 611, Jefferson, North Carolina 28640
www.mcfarlandpub.com*

In one of the most poignant and famous photographs from 20th century America, Lyndon Baines Johnson takes the presidential oath of office aboard Air Force One on the tarmac at Love Field in Dallas, Texas, following the assassination of President John F. Kennedy earlier that day—November 22, 1963. As with the three previous vice presidents who assumed the nation's highest office following the assassination of the president, the unique burden felt by Johnson that day consumed his thoughts, actions, and prayers for months to come.

In a lasting tribute to LBJ and the eight others who have shared the burden of replacing a suddenly deceased or disgraced president, this book is proudly dedicated to their remembrance—giving credit where credit is long overdue (LBJ Library photograph by Cecil Stoughton).

"It seems very unfortunate that in order to secure political preference, people are made vice president who were never intended, neither by party nor the Lord, to be president."—General George S. Patton (upon learning of Harry Truman's ascension to the White House in 1945)

Table of Contents

Part III. Their Burden:
Rankings, Similarities and Contrasts

Introduction

Common Bond, Shared Burden

Mention the names Tyler, Fillmore, Johnson, Arthur, Roosevelt, Coolidge, Truman, Johnson (again), and Ford, and most, if not all, Americans of reasonable age will identify them as some of our former presidents. Admittedly, this identification would probably come quicker if their order was reshuffled to list Roosevelt or Truman first, but sticking with their chronological order as before should nonetheless achieve the same result once the entire group has been revealed.

Regardless of their order, however, this particular group of former chief executives shares a much more significant characteristic than just the commonality of presidential leadership. As a group, theirs is the shared legacy of succession to the highest office in the land due to the death or failure of their predecessors by natural causes, assassination, or resignation (but not impeachment, at least not yet).

Theirs was the task of continuing democracy and ensuring leadership in the midst of tragedy by ascending to the White House without benefit of an election. Although previously raised to the second-highest office in the land through their own good works, political expediency, or even twists of fate, their ultimate ascendance to 1600 Pennsylvania Avenue came not by the electorate, but by their status as next in line during moments of national calamity.

For some, those moments were obviously not too large, while for others they would prove overwhelming. Some would rise to the occasion and some would not. Some would eventually be re-elected in their own right, while others would be voted out or lose the opportunity to run again. One or two would rise to the elite level of presidential legends, while at least three may always be rated among the worst of all time.

Despite varying degrees of ambition and readiness for the job, their success ratios could not be determined until their individual administrations were complete. Most had political enemies and a few skeletons or drawbacks rattling in their closets. With only two clear exceptions, most never wanted the job; but of those who did, all either grew into it or out of it with no single (or common) determining factor. Instead, like any historic sample (in this case, nearly one-seventh of our first 44 U.S. presidents), there were definite winners and losers, and examining the whys and why-nots reveals a great deal about our American experience for over 135 years.

From 1841, when Vice President John Tyler succeeded President William Henry Harrison, who died after only a month in office due to acute pneumonia, to 1976, when Gerald Ford lost his re-election bid to Jimmy Carter after succeeding the disgraced Richard Nixon due to scandal (now known as "Watergate") and resignation, our history of presidential ascension has been one of uncertainty. Never a sure thing, the road map for vice presidential succession to the presidency has proved uncertain, both to the ascending chief executives and to the country.

Following are the stories of America's nine accidental presidents. No revisionist history here—these nine men were all burdened by history in the same way. One of mankind's heaviest responsibilities was abruptly thrust upon them, and how each responded had a lot to due with American development in the two preceding centuries, as well as what we might expect in the rest of this one. Certain precedents have been established, political trends and similarities have reoccurred, and in a leadership landscape that's scrutinized (and vilified) more than ever, the certainty of history repeating itself in the lives of future accidental presidents is to be expected. After all, this is one burden of history that will never be easy.

Preface
A Unique Fraternity

Over 350 American history books crowd my bookshelves, remnants of a double major in history and journalism, 30-plus years as a member of the History Book Club, and a host of other nonfiction acquisitions. It's a sizable collection that now seems obsolete in the "Internet Age," but hopefully one I can bequeath to some appreciative descendant or library some day.

Already the author of four nonfiction books, each of which was written via special access to the subject matter, I found this one different. Instead of access, the motivation for this one was challenge, as in the challenge of tackling a unique historical theme that has not been adequately tackled before. Why they have rarely been considered as a group is hard to figure because the historical connection of nine U.S. presidents, all of whom were unexpectedly thrust into the office by death or resignation, is unmistakable. Each ascended to the nation's highest office through the demise of another, his predecessor, who personally selected him or at least acquiesced to his selection for valid, political reasons. Theirs is the unique role, at least in democratic circles, of advancing to the top rung of the republic without benefit of an election. It's a unique fraternity and worthy of examination.

This book is divided into three sections. The first details the basics of their individual careers. The longer, second section is a review of biographies about each one. The third offers a retrospective look at their common bonds and differences; their similar or dissimilar paths and results; and why some were successful and others not so much.

Two recognized presidential references were relied upon—*The Complete Book Of U.S. Presidents*, by William A. DeGregorio (Eighth Edition) and *Don't Know Much About the American Presidents*, by Kenneth C. Davis. Section two was built around the following presidential biographies: *John Tyler: The Accidental President*, by Edward P. Crapol; *Andrew Johnson: A Biography*, by Hans L. Trefousse; *Theodore Rex*, by Edmund Morris; *Coolidge*, by Amity Shlaes; *Truman*, by David McCullough; *The Passage of Power* and *Means of Ascent*, both part of *The Years of Lyndon Johnson*, by Robert A. Caro; and *Millard Fillmore*, by Paul Finkelman; *Chester Alan Arthur*, by Zachary Karabell; and *Gerald R. Ford*, by Douglas Brinkley, all part of The American Presidents Series. In addition, a bevy of other historical narratives from each of the American eras involved were utilized as supporting sources, with publication dates ranging from 1939 to 2018.

The comparisons and conclusions expressed in the third section were also based on numerous historic narratives and opinions, as well as history's tendency to repeat itself. Additional insights, assumptions, and reflections were possible as a result.

In time, other presidents are likely to join this select group, and given the partisan intensity of our country, new additions may come not so much by natural causes or an assassin's bullet, but as the result of scrutiny more intense than ever before; the sheer disdain and constant animosity of our two warring political parties; or even the willful lies, damaging dialogue, and dedicated wrongdoing (especially through social media) that threatens to become an accepted part of our discourse. Like Gerald Ford, our next accidental president may not follow a deceased predecessor. The American presidency has entered a new phase, to say the least, and accidental or otherwise, it may never be the same.

Prologue
Hometown Disappointment

My father grew up as part of a large, farm family near Greeneville, Tennessee, one of several mid-size towns that seem to mirror each other in the upper east corner of that state. Harmon remains a very common last name in that part of the country, with their residences dotting the countryside. While several of my father's brothers would remain farmers all their lives, at least two would work in town as a barber and newspaper-advertising salesman. The youngest of nine, my father was the only one to leave the area and attend college.

As a child, I can remember trips to Greene County to visit relatives, staying at the old home place, and excursions into town. A lover of history even at a young age, I was impressed by the fact that my father's hometown was also the home of an American president. What I eventually learned that was not so impressive, however, was this president's rank among our chief executives.

In fact, although he is still revered locally, it was disappointing to discover that Andrew Johnson, the tailor who had risen from poverty to become our 17th U.S. president, consistently ranked near the bottom in presidential ratings. Like most former presidents, his home and preserved tailor shop remain National Historic Sites in Greeneville, still visited by thousands each year, but his legacy, I learned, was not the glowing, iconic reputation of a Washington, Jefferson, Lincoln, or Roosevelt. Rather, I was faced with the reality that while he remained my father's hometown hero, he was not nearly so well regarded elsewhere and was very nearly relieved of his presidential duties in the midst of "Reconstruction," the period of reunification after the Civil War. Such animosity towards someone so close to home was ultimately a hard lesson to swallow, but also motivation to learn more about this fellow East Tennessean, the president who replaced Lincoln after he was assassinated in April 1865.

Who really was this obviously controversial replacement for one of our most sainted presidents, and how in the world was a Tennessean serving as Lincoln's vice president at the time the Civil War ended? With Tennessee one of 11 seceded Southern states, was it not a hard-to-believe, historical improbability that Lincoln's successor when the war ended was a Southern Democrat at a time when the Republican Party dominated Union and Northern decision-making? It didn't make sense.

Or, on the other hand, maybe it made perfect sense—at least to Lincoln. As I came to find out, Johnson had been the only Southern senator to remain in Congress when the war began. A staunch Unionist from the mountainous part of Tennessee who never wanted to follow the state's ruling (and slaveholding) planter class into secession, he was openly regarded as a traitor by most of the South. While hung in effigy in his own state, his actions gained heroic stature in the North, so much so, in fact, that when Lincoln was looking for a new running mate in 1864, legitimately concerned about his own re-election chances in the midst of a far longer and bloodier war than anyone had expected, it actually made sense for him to choose the loyal, Southern defector, who by that time was his military governor of re-conquered Tennessee. It was a politically expedient choice designed to influence votes and attitudes, especially in the less than certain "Border States" of Kentucky, Maryland, West Virginia, and Missouri.

Johnson was not, however, a popular choice among the Republican leadership, the so-called "Radical Republicans," and his place at the head of any post-war government was destined for trouble. Once the conciliatory (and suddenly revered) Lincoln was no longer alive, his successor would prove not nearly so adept at conciliation. Although an avowed Unionist, Johnson was also a confirmed Southern segregationist, especially with statements like, "This is a country for White men and, by God, as long as I am president it shall be a government for White men."

Located at the Andrew Johnson National Historic Site in Greeneville, Tennessee, this statue of the man who rose from uneducated poverty to become the nation's 17th president seems to convey a sense of determined achievement that unfortunately has not been his story handed down by history (photograph property of the author).

As a result, he would hinder Reconstruction as much by his appeasing, hands-off stance as his Radical Republican foes in Congress would stall its progress with their desire to force the reunited but unrepentant South to toe the line upon its re-entry to the nation, especially in regard to its suddenly freed former slaves—a situation, in other words, rife for the total breakdown that ultimately occurred between president and Congress at one of our nation's most important crossroads. As a result, it would take another 100 years to redress the resulting civil rights problems that were manifested at that time.

It would also result in Andrew Johnson avoiding congressional banishment by a single Senate vote and in his acquired epitaph as one of our most unsuccessful presidents. Burdened by history, I had to admit that my father's hometown hero had not measured up, but there had to be more to his story, just as there had to be for our other accidental presidents. What made Andrew Johnson an abject failure in the eyes of history, while Theodore Roosevelt has generally been considered a resounding success? After all, both followed assassins' bullets to the White House after being surprising selections for vice president by the Republican Party—the ruling party during both of their eras. What traits made one rise to a spot on Mount Rushmore alongside Washington, Jefferson, and Lincoln, while the other was almost fired? And what of our seven other accidental presidents, a total of nine thus far?

The first of those, John Tyler, was labeled "His Ascendency" when he followed the deceased William Henry Harrison only a month into office and basically established the tradition that a vice president elevated to the White House by death or wrongdoing would not be a temporary president subject to another election. Or what about a largely uneducated farm boy from Missouri, Harry Truman, the protégé of a corrupt political machine, who was able to successfully follow the tragic death of a legendary president and politician like Franklin Delano Roosevelt, while an equally lacking farmer's son from New York, Millard Fillmore, who also rose through political patronage, was unable to surpass even the inconsequential leadership of his predecessor, Zachary Taylor, a famous general with no previous political experience or apparent acumen for the job? Such are the questions to be considered for this select group of American heads of state. With something so obvious in common, what were the determining factors in their presidential successes and/or failures?

PART I

Their Careers: The Basics

1

John Tyler—
Establishing Precedent

"If the tide of defamation shall turn and my administration come to be praised, future vice presidents who succeed me may feel encouragement to pursue an independent course."

Coined the original accidental president by at least one of his biographers[1] and "His Ascendency" by contemporary detractors,[2] John Tyler of Virginia was the first vice president to ascend to the presidency through the death or resignation of the president. By and through him was the precedent established. What became known as "The Tyler Precedent," in fact, was the rightful and permanent ascension of elected American vice presidents to the station of presidential leadership upon the death in office of a sitting president.[3]

When 68-year-old William Henry Harrison (the "Tippecanoe" of "Tippecanoe and Tyler too" campaign fame) died of pneumonia only a month after taking the presidential oath in 1840, it was not a given that his vice president would automatically assume permanent residence in the White House. Even among leaders of the victorious Whig Party, which had come into existence two decades earlier as an offshoot of the National Republican Party and in response to the burgeoning influence of General Andrew Jackson and his elevation of the common man in national politics, the ascension of the Whigs' vice president, Tyler, was expected to be only temporary until Congress could vote on a permanent replacement.[4] After all, Tyler had previously aligned himself with the other party, the Democrats, before his recent conversion due to Jacksonian overreach, and his addition to the winning ticket was purely an act of sectional, vote-getting convenience—one of the earliest examples of American political expedience. Only by adhering to the party line laid out by longtime Senate icon Henry Clay of Kentucky would his Whig colleagues be interested in retaining him at the head of their first administration. It was that simple.[5]

But Tyler was not about to play along. Alerted to Harrison's grave illness days earlier, realizing there was no previously established precedent on presidential succession, and knowing the Constitution was rather ambiguous on the question, Tyler chose the loose interpretation and basically decided an ascending VP, like himself, should indeed become president outright. "By decisive, adroit political maneuvering during his first week in office," he made moot any objections and basically established unelected presidential succession in the event of death or resignation of a sitting U.S. president.[6]

Meanwhile, the Whigs' ascendance had been a long time coming. After Jackson's victory over the invading British at New Orleans in 1815, along with his previous successes in Southern Indian wars versus the Creeks and Seminoles, and his influential role in Spain's decision to cede Florida to the United States in 1819, "Old Hickory," as he became known, was a certified American celebrity. Although just a one-term senator from Tennessee, his anti-establishment views played well in an ever-expanding country tired of Eastern dominance in national affairs.[7] His loss in the presidential election of 1824, when none of the top three finishers received a majority in the Electoral College, forced the final decision into the House of Representatives. This was seen as a "corrupt bargain" between the eventual president, John Quincy Adams of Massachusetts, and the influential Clay, who allegedly threw his congressional support to Adams in exchange for being named secretary of state with the presumed status of next-in-line for the presidency four years later.[8]

Thus the groundwork was laid for a new political alignment between 1824 and 1828. It was an alignment, however, that would not lead to Clay's ascension to the presidency, but to consolidation of Jacksonian power. The Democrats would seize control of the executive branch for three straight elections, Jackson's two in 1828 and 1832, and one more by his vice president, Martin Van Buren, in 1836.[9] Van Buren, in fact, would be the only succeeding vice president to win a U.S. presidential election following the normal departure from office of his predecessor until George H. W. Bush successfully followed Ronald Reagan in 1988.[10]

As a result, one can imagine the great anticipation of the Whigs as they approached the election of 1840 and their best chance to end Jacksonian rule in the traditional ebb and flow of political fortunes and public approval. As so often happens, a sagging economy, courtesy of the Panic of 1837, and the breakup of what had been a successful coalition of Democratic voters in different sections of the country opened the door to the opposing party, and the Whigs were only too happy to finally take advantage. Adopting the winning philosophy of their opponents, the Whigs chose another well-known general (their own military hero, so to speak) as their standard bearer.

Regarded as the epitome of Southern distinction and refinement during his long political career, John Tyler of Virginia (portrait ca. 1860) would become the first U.S. vice president to ascend to the presidency through death or resignation (Library of Congress, Prints and Photographs Division—Reproduction Number USZ62-13010, Brady-Handy Collection).

Although descended from Virginia aristocrats, William Henry Harrison was known more as a leader of the Northwest Territory, an Indian fighter and territorial governor who had stabilized the country north of the Ohio River.[11] His career and successes had all come in the West of that era. As a result, when striving for political balance for their national ticket, it was no surprise the Whigs sought a Southerner for vice president.[12] Although a Border State slaveholder, Clay would never accept anything but the top of the ticket, so they turned instead to another famous Commonwealth family who had always been identified with Virginia. In fact, Tyler's father had been governor of the state and was Thomas Jefferson's roommate at the College of William & Mary.[13]

Little known outside of Virginia, where he had established his career as a multi-term member of the House of Burgesses before representing his state for five years in the House of Representatives, nine in the Senate, and two as governor, Tyler was first and foremost a states' rights advocate even with his conversion to the Whig Party.[14] The first president to be born after ratification of the U.S. Constitution, he also fathered more children than any other president, having had eight by his first wife, who died of a stroke during the first year of his presidency, and seven with his second.[15]

With Tyler sworn in as the tenth U.S. president at Brown's Hotel in Washington just two days after Harrison's death, it was assumed by one and all that he would pursue the wishes of his party and particularly its congressional leader, Clay, despite his earlier Democratic connections. Those ties had been prevalent during his earliest years in the Senate, when he opposed the administration of John Quincy Adams and its call for a national program of internal improvements. As a result, he joined the anti-administration forces of Jackson, who initially pleased Tyler as president by vetoing a re-charter of the national bank.[16]

During Jackson's second term, however, Tyler split with the popular president over the issue of nullification, when South Carolina, led by its firebrand senator, John C. Calhoun, actively advanced the idea of a state's right to "nullify" federal laws it did not agree with and to secede from the Union if forced to comply. The issue had come to a head over the so-called "Tariff of Abominations," which had been enacted under Adams and moderated by Jackson. It was a federal law the South Carolinians deemed intolerable and worthy of their Ordinance of Nullification, which declared the high tariff rates void in their state. To this doctrine and threat of secession, Jackson famously responded: "Disunion by armed force is treason. Are you ready to incur guilt? If you are, on the heads of the instigators be the dreadful consequences; on their heads the dishonor, but on yours may fall the punishment."

To this perceived threat of armed force, Tyler could not agree, instead seeking a middle of the road, states' rights position that opposed nullification but upheld a state's right of secession. His was the Senate's lone dissenting vote amidst a wave of abstentions to Jackson's Force Bill, which gave Jackson authority to use the Army if necessary to collect the tariff in South Carolina. That was the start of Tyler's drift to the Whigs, especially as he came to view Jackson as a would-be dictator.[17]

During the presidential campaign of 1836, Tyler supported Senator Hugh Lawson White of Tennessee but gradually became a proponent of Clay, Jackson's chief antagonist among the Whigs. After another failed attempt by Clay for the Whig nomination in 1840, Tyler, as already established, was offered the VP spot on the Harrison ticket despite his Democratic past.[18] Understanding that, it should not have been surprising to Clay and the other Whigs when he proved less than amenable to their desires once he assumed the presidency. But it was. That same year, congressional Whigs led by Clay sought to resurrect the national bank that had been abolished by Jackson, only to have Tyler fail to acquiesce to their wishes. Twice he vetoed renewal of the bank, and to protest this abandonment of Whig principles, most of the Cabinet he inherited from Harrison resigned, effectively leaving him a president without a party.[19]

Enraged by his actions, Clay and the most powerful Whigs called for his resignation, attempted to have him impeached, and even failed in their attempt to change the Constitution to allow a simple majority to override a presidential veto. Tyler, in fact, would veto a total of ten bills, totally frustrating the party that brought him to national power.[20] Among the legislation he did sign was the Preemption Act of 1841, which recognized squatters' rights and the right of purchase to anyone who settled and improved unsurveyed public land; the Webster-Ashburton Treaty that fixed the present boundary between the State of Maine and the Canadian province of New Brunswick; and the Treaty of Wanghia, which achieved United States access to Chinese trade.[21]

In addition, he lived through one of Washington's worst disasters, when he and other dignitaries were part of an excursion aboard the USS *Princeton* to witness the firing of a massive new cannon called "The Peacemaker." Fortunately for Tyler, he had gone below decks when, on the third firing of the gun, it exploded, killing, among others, Secretary of State Abel Upshur and former Congressman and current Secretary of the Navy Thomas Gilmer.[22]

In addition to establishing the precedent of presidential succession, however, the thing Tyler is most remembered for was the annexation of Texas. Although the Whig-dominated Senate at first refused to ratify the 1844 treaty that annexed the Lone Star Republic following its independence from Mexico, Tyler knew that with the election of his Democratic successor, James K. Polk, on a pro-annexation platform, public opinion would overwhelmingly endorse the addition and influence Congress to act. It was Tyler who signed the legislation before leaving office.[23] Texas joined Florida in officially becoming a state under Tyler's watch. Both entered the Union as slave states.[24]

Texas proved Tyler's last and most important battle with the Whig-dominated Congress. By circumventing the constitutional requirements for treaty ratification between the election and Polk's inauguration, he orchestrated a joint resolution, which required only a simple majority rather than the normal two-thirds of both Houses, a sly maneuver that ensured what most historians have agreed was his most significant presidential act. Nevertheless, his precedent-setting ascension would rate a close second, making his most lasting achievements on the way in and out of office.[25]

Needless to say, Tyler's independent approach stunned the Whigs, and none more so than Clay, who had fully expected his congressional colleague of 20 years to endorse the party's agenda for a bank and internal improvements. Clay misread Tyler's resolve to be his own man.[26] That was the start of a political feud that stalled the newly realized Whig momentum. It was also a harbinger of a crippled presidency resulting from all those vetoes (only one of which was overridden).[27] As a president without congressional backing, Tyler was destined to be a lame duck throughout his four years in office, without hope of re-election.[28]

Nearly 20 years later during the opening salvos of the Civil War, Tyler would take ironic pleasure in Virginia's adoption of the secession ordinance and early Confederate victories. His unexpected death less than a year later came in the Confederate capital, Richmond, as he was about to take a seat in the Confederate Congress. After a bout of nausea and dizziness, he fainted and died a short time later on January 18, 1862. The fact that his body lay in state in the Confederate capital draped by a Confederate flag ensured him a traitorous legacy in the North that would not fade for a half-century.[29]

2

Millard Fillmore—
Repeating History

"The government of the United States is a limited government and it is at all times a special duty to guard against infringement on the just rights of the states."

In some ways, the second accidental president was a lot like the first. Although not from a prominent family like John Tyler, Millard Fillmore rose to the nation's highest office by ascending the political ranks of his native state. He served three terms in the New York Assembly and four in the U.S. Congress before unsuccessfully running for governor and finishing his state service as comptroller, an important but hardly prestigious position. Like Tyler, he was selected by the Whig Party as a vice presidential running mate for a well-known general, Zachary Taylor, as a means of balancing the national ticket.[1]

Taylor's home was Kentucky, and he was famous for his successes in the War of 1812, the Black Hawk Indian War of 1832, the Second Seminole War of 1837–1840, and the Mexican War from 1846–1848.[2] With outgoing Democratic President James K. Polk, an avid expansionist, deciding to not seek re-election to a second term in 1848, Taylor became the first president elected without any government experience and totally on the strength of his military record. Labeled by his soldiers "Old Rough and Ready," he was a unique slaveholder who sided with the North more than the South, including opposition to the expansion of slavery into the new, Western territories.

Indeed, as the Compromise of 1850, the handiwork of Kentucky Senator Henry Clay, began to make its way through Congress as the last best hope of keeping the country together and avoiding a sectional war, Taylor openly opposed its Whig backers.[3] Theirs was a political stalemate, in fact, that continued until an extremely hot July day that same year, a day on which the president presided over the ceremonial laying of the cornerstone for the Washington Monument. Following patriotic speeches and big meals throughout the day, the 65-year-old Taylor developed acute gastroenteritis and shockingly died five days later from what most historians have deemed food poisoning or cholera. But regardless of what killed the 12th president less than two years into his term, the ascension of his vice president seemed eerily similar to what America had undergone with Harrison and Tyler less than a decade before.[4]

Into this breach, Fillmore, described as "handsome" and "persuasive in small groups," but "otherwise underwhelming," took over as the 13th president and immediately renewed efforts for Clay's Compromise. Having made known his feelings in favor of the legislation before Taylor died, President Fillmore's renewed endorsement, including not only California's admission as a free state but also the stricter fugitive slave component, was a welcome reprieve for Southerners. It was intended to better enforce the return of all runaway slaves to their Southern masters. At the same time, the borders for the slave state of Texas were to be redefined and its outstanding debts covered by the federal government. Also, New Mexico and Utah were to be added as new territories.[5] Fillmore's support for the fugitive slave portion of the bill, however, cost him in the court of public opinion in the North and essentially doomed any chance he had for re-election two years hence in 1852.[6]

Nevertheless, the Compromise of 1850 achieved its purpose, at least for the time being. It satisfied the North and appeased the increasingly belligerent South. But it also divided the Whigs and proved the ultimate demise of this short-lived American political party, as most Whigs would adopt the new Republican Party, which nominated the Western explorer John C. Fremont as its first presidential candidate in 1856 and the victorious Abraham Lincoln as its second in 1860.[7] Along with compromise, Fillmore's abbreviated administration of just 32 months accounted for additional Far East trade opportunities, as

Little known outside of his native New York at the time he became a vice presidential candidate, Millard Fillmore has remained nearly as historically anonymous after ascending to the presidency. Photograph by Mathew Brady, ca. 1855–1865 (Library of Congress, Prints and Photographs Division—Reproduction Number USZ62-13013).

he dispatched Commodore Matthew Perry to open relations with the reclusive island nation of Japan.[8]

After retiring to Buffalo, Fillmore endured the deaths of his first wife and daughter within the first 16 months after leaving office. Eventually recovered from the emotional strain of those events, he remarried and travelled extensively throughout the South, Midwest, and even Europe. Active in civic affairs for the remainder of his life and a willing presidential nominee of the fledgling anti–Catholic, anti–immigrant Know-Nothing Party in 1856, Fillmore came under renewed attack during the Civil War for his previous support of the compromise's fugitive slave legislation a decade earlier, as well as support for Democrat George McClellan in the 1864 presidential election against Lincoln. Following Lincoln's assassination in 1865, a mob even vandalized the exterior of Fillmore's home.[9]

Nonetheless, he continued to reside in Western New York and enjoyed excellent health until 1874, when he suffered a stroke at age 74 that rendered his left side paralyzed. A second stroke 13 days later ended whatever chance he had for recovery, and he died on March 8, 1874. In death, he would remain one of our least-known presidents, a politician with lofty ambitions who failed to inspire the masses and lacked the ability to see big-picture issues in a politically expedient way. But thanks to his support for the Compromise of 1850, the Civil War was postponed for a decade—a postponement that wishfully provided more time to peaceably iron out the sectional differences inherent in the continuation of slavery in the South, the troubling issue the nation's founders had originally compromised on for the sake of ratifying the Constitution.[10]

Upon assuming the presidency, in fact, Fillmore had premonitions of the bloodbath yet to come. With the lessening influence of the Whigs, something made clear by their rejection of him as a sitting president in order to nominate aging General Winfield Scott in 1852, as well as the birth of the Republicans and "Know-Nothings" four years later, Fillmore had predicted that if either a Democrat or Republican followed him into the White House, "civil war and anarchy would stare us in the face." That's one thing he got right.[11]

3

Andrew Johnson—
A Lack of Temperament

"Who then will govern? The answer must be man, for we have no angels in the shape of men."

The third of our accidental presidents, the one featured in this book's Prologue, had what at least one recent presidential historian has categorized as a lack of the temperament that would have been necessary to provide solutions in a land so obviously still divided by one of the bloodiest civil wars in world history.[1] Andrew Johnson, as already established, had the regrettable chore of following the man generally regarded as our greatest president, Abraham Lincoln. But Lincoln's elite status wasn't always so cut and dried. Indeed, before he was assassinated at Ford's Theater by the actor and Southern sympathizer John Wilkes Booth on April 14, 1865, Lincoln had at times been dismissed as uncouth and uncultured, assailed for most of his time in office, nearly denied renomination for a second term, and vilified throughout the South. Suddenly, immediately, he was martyred in death and elevated to American sainthood.[2] Ironically, Lincoln's presidential predecessor, James Buchanan, is as routinely ranked among the worst U.S. chief executives as Johnson is, in their positions on either side of the sainted "Honest Abe."[3]

But at least Buchanan never had to deal with the taint of impeachment. Most of the so-called "high crimes and misdemeanors" the House of Representatives charged Johnson with in 1868 had to do with his supposed violations of the Tenure of Office Act, a law Congress passed over his veto when he attempted to remove certain public officials, including Lincoln Cabinet members who supported the policies (and politics) of the Radical Republicans, who preferred a much stricter stance concerning the defeated Southern states as they returned to the Union than did President Johnson. One, Secretary of War Edwin Stanton, refused to relinquish his office at the War Department (even barricading himself inside) upon news of his dismissal by Johnson, claiming protection under the Tenure of Office Act until the charges against the president could be heard. But on May 16, 1868, Johnson was acquitted just one vote shy of the necessary two-thirds needed for conviction in the Senate, thus allowing him to finish his term.[4]

This narrowest of face-saving victories was the culmination of some of the most bitter years of executive-legislative dysfunction in our nation's history. Although a product of Lincoln's vote-getting election logic as vice president, Johnson's elevation to the presidency as a loyal "War Democrat" came at a time when most of the ruling Republicans were determined to humble the recalcitrant South upon its return to the national fold. On the other hand, Johnson envisioned a more lenient Reconstruction policy whereby full rights of citizenship were to be restored to individual Southerners willing to swear a simple oath of allegiance to the federal government and to any Southern states willing to draft new constitutions repudiating secession, slavery, and Confederate war debts. Once these objectives were accomplished, Southerners would be allowed to govern themselves and send men of their own choosing back to Congress.[5] As for the emancipated slaves, Johnson hoped for reconciliation and at least some recognition by their White Southern neighbors, including the enfranchisement of Black males who could read, something the vast majority of White Southerners were not ready to grant.[6]

Most Republicans in the North wanted to punish the South and prevent a resurgence of Southern Democratic power. As a counter-measure, Southern states enacted the so-called "Black Codes," whereby the former slaves could be denied voting rights at the state level; not be allowed to serve on juries or testify in court; and not be allowed to contract for labor on an equal basis to Whites (or, needless to say, marry a White person). For that reason, the Civil Rights Act of 1866 was designed to protect Black voting rights and was incorporated into the Fourteenth Amendment to the Constitution.[7]

As a result of all this legal maneuvering, the tension between Johnson and Congress was palpable. Twenty-nine times he exercised presidential vetoes, and 15 times those vetoes were overridden, resulting in the Freedman's Bureau Act of 1866, the District of Columbia Suffrage Act of 1867, and four Reconstruction Acts in 1867 and 1868. Led by Thaddeus Stevens of Pennsylvania in the House and Charles Sumner of Massachusetts in the Senate, Congress brought the Johnson administration to a standstill.[8] The harsh rhetoric Johnson had directed at the Southern planter class during the Civil War continued once he became president, but he took a more moderate tone towards the Southern states and their "common people." Congress, meanwhile, elected to maintain military control of the South even with the war over by leaving 20,000 troops in five military districts throughout the former Confederacy. This resulted in biracial legislatures in some Southern states, the revival of the Democratic Party, the emergence of the Ku Klux Klan, and all manner of beatings, lynchings, and other forms of racial intimidation throughout the region.[9]

The only Southern senator to remain at his post in Washington after 11 Southern states seceded from the Union, Tennessee's Andrew Johnson (photograph ca. 1874) would become the first vice president elevated to the White House by an assassin's bullet (Library of Congress Prints and Photographs Division—Reproduction Number USZ62-13017, Brady-Handy Collection).

A testament to the separation of power, Johnson's stubborn resolve to the point of inflexibility made the task of Reconstruction divisive and bitter. Lacking Lincoln's patience, sensitivity, and ability to work through issues, he was "the wrong man at the wrong time," something that may have been predetermined by

Johnson's lack of formal education, his ingrained sectional racism, and his lifelong aversion to the South's social pecking order.[10]

A tailor by trade and an alderman in his adopted home, Greeneville, Tennessee, Johnson had grown up fatherless and in poverty in Raleigh, North Carolina, before he and his brother were apprenticed and learned the tailor's trade. After crossing the mountains to open his own tailor shop at age 17, he took a liking to and exhibited a talent for politics. He eventually served two separate stints in the Tennessee House, one term as a state senator, ten years as a representative in the U.S. House, one four-year term as governor, and a five-year stretch as a U.S. senator from 1857 through 1862. With East Tennessee a largely pro–Union and non-slaveholding part of the state, Johnson had always been a pro–Union Democrat and, as previously noted, he became the only Southern senator to remain at his post in Washington when the Civil War began. With that background and status, he made an easy choice when Lincoln needed a military governor once Tennessee had been reconquered by the middle of the war, and he also made political sense when Lincoln was looking for a new vice presidential running mate in the critical presidential election of 1864. With the war finally going the Union's way and Lincoln's administration hanging in the balance, a pro–Union Southerner made sense, especially for an embattled president looking for validation at the ballot box and a path to reconciliation once the fighting was over.[11]

Rough around the edges and certainly not the patient peacemaker Lincoln probably would have been, Johnson's role in the Reconstruction era will always suffer by comparison. Obviously not a candidate for presidential re-election in 1868,[12] he returned to East Tennessee and made unsuccessful bids to return to the U.S. Senate in 1871 and the House in 1872 before finally being returned to the Senate in 1875. Shortly thereafter, however, he died at age 67 on July 31, 1875. His wife of 48 years died just six months later.[13]

4

Chester Alan Arthur— The Unlikeliest President

"Men may die, but the fabrics of our free institutions remain unshaken. No higher or more assuring proof could exist of the strength and permanence of popular government."

No president was ever more unlikely or ill-suited to gain that office than the fourth of our accidental ascendants, Chester Alan Arthur. His ascension to the presidency, in fact, was even questioned by political opponents because of his birthplace being near the Canadian border in rural Vermont. That made him the focus of the original "birther" controversy. Obviously if proven, the rumors that he had actually been born in Canada would have rendered him constitutionally ineligible for the White House.[1]

Regardless, little Vermont has always claimed him as one of its two native-son presidents, the other being Calvin Coolidge. Arthur was born and lived the first three years of his life in tiny Fairfield, in the upper northwest corner of the state, while Coolidge hailed from even tinier (and unincorporated) Plymouth Notch near the state's geographic center. Ironically, both would attain the nation's highest office by virtue of the death in office of their presidential predecessors.[2] One would be hard-pressed, however, to establish career similarities between Arthur and any other president. His only government job before ascending to the second-loftiest position in the land had been as a political appointee.[3]

Indeed, after starting his professional life as a schoolteacher and principal while earning his way to a law degree and admittance to the bar, Arthur became a junior partner in a New York City law firm. It was as an attorney and quartermaster for the New York State Militia during the Civil War that his political involvement began. That led to him being named to the executive committee of the local, New York City Republican Party and a close association with its conservative boss, Roscoe Conkling.[4]

Following a one-year stint as counsel for the city's tax commission, Arthur used that association to garner a plum appointment under President Ulysses Grant, the job of Collector of the Port of New York (1871–1876). Seventy-five percent of the nation's duties from ships landed within his jurisdiction, and he became the classic example of what was known as a political "spoilsman" and product of the "Spoils System" then in place throughout American government. Later he would back Conkling, his benefactor, at the 1876 Republican Convention, but when Rutherford B. Hayes became the nominee instead and ultimately president, Arthur became the subject of corruption charges as a result of the new administration's decision to target New York's lucrative customhouse for what presidential historians now agree was a symbolic reduction of its workforce by eliminating reputedly non-essential government jobs.[5]

In the interest of party unity, Arthur was offered another job, consul to France, but not wishing to give up his New York City lifestyle, Arthur refused the appointment and simply returned to his law practice in 1880. It was during this time that his wife tragically died of pneumonia at age 43. Indeed, he was still mourning her death when seemingly out of nowhere, the Republicans came calling later that year, seeking a vice presidential nominee from the party's conservative wing to run with moderate James Garfield of Ohio, who emerged as their compromise choice when Hayes did not seek re-election.[6]

A Civil War brigadier general and state senator even before the war's conclusion, Garfield had been a U.S. congressman for eight terms before emerging as the Republican's nominee in 1880. His opponent was an even better-known Union general, Winfield Scott Hancock, a hero of the decisive Battle of Gettysburg.[7]

In an extremely close election, the Garfield-Arthur ticket proved victorious even though the vice presidency would be Arthur's first elected office.[8] Then, in American history's second-most abbreviated administration, Garfield's presidency ended just six months after it began when a disgruntled, mentally disturbed office seeker, Charles Guiteau, shot the president in the back as he was waiting for a train. Garfield died two months later, the victim of a lack of modern sterilization procedures for his wounds and rampant infection. Suddenly (and some believed suspiciously), Chester Arthur was president.[9]

Because of the intense rivalry within the Republican Party at that time, a conflict between the conservatives (known as "Stalwarts") and moderates (so-called "Half-Breeds"), a shadow was cast over Arthur's ascension due to his earlier connections to Conkling's New York machine and especially because of Guiteau's delusional belief that he had saved the nation by eliminating Garfield and putting Arthur in charge.[10] Cynics among the general public even suspected a Stalwart conspiracy inspired by Conkling and designed to elevate Arthur to the White House.[11]

As a result, there was a caustic, rumor-filled national environment the day Arthur assumed the presidency, September 20, 1881. Garfield had expired the night before, and "when news of his death reached New York," so the story goes, reporters rushed to Arthur's home and found the vice president sitting

Despite never holding elected office before becoming vice president, Chester Alan Arthur (photograph 1882) would become president of the United States just six months later after the second of four U.S. presidential assassinations (Library of Congress Prints and Photographs Division—Reproduction Number USZ62-13021, C. M. Bell, photographer).

alone, sobbing like a child." A few hours later, Arthur was sworn into office by a state judge in his parlor.[12]

Actually, by the time Garfield's death finally occurred, Arthur had begun a transformation that few of his friends could believe. Although he would continue to aid Conkling's efforts to regain his old Senate seat, which he had resigned from in 1881, Arthur had begun to chart his own course without Conkling's input. As long as Garfield survived, he felt as though he was "standing not on a mountaintop but a precipice."[13] However, once the deed was done and Garfield's infection had taken its toll, Arthur, well aware of the opportunity suddenly thrust upon him and the fact that it never would have been conferred any other way, accepted his fate and professed to want nothing more than to be the president his predecessor would have been had he lived.[14]

Adjusting quickly from a chain-dependent spoilsman to civil service reformer, Arthur, who owed as much to the Spoils System as any American, turned his attention to reforming the very things that had made his predecessor a political target. The rampant political corruption and anarchy of the times that Garfield's death served to illuminate sparked outrage that could no longer be ignored, and the most unlikely president intended to do something about it.[15]

Naively, Conkling presumed that his political protégé would resume his conservative bidding even from the lofty realm of the White House, but to his surprise, Arthur not only refused but was offended by the presumption that he would. Powerless, Conkling faded from the political stage, while Arthur would become a respected leader with his presidency marked by unlikely achievement.[16]

As president, he signed the Pendleton Act of 1883, creating our modern civil service system. The law initiated open, competitive exams for government applicants; banned the practice of political contributions as a means of ensuring partisan jobs; curbed political nepotism; and eliminated addicts and alcoholics from government service.[17] He also created a tariff commission that resulted in a reduction of duties and initiated a tariff struggle that would continue along distinct party lines for decades.[18] And he vetoed a multi-million dollar bill for internal improvements that he considered "Pork Barrel Legislation," earning accolades for his protection of the Treasury.[19]

At the same time, he tempered the 20-year Chinese Exclusion Act by vetoing it before acquiescing and signing a law that did the same thing for ten years, an economically motivated mandate that reconfirmed America's ugly tendency for racism. The law was a response to the large number of Chinese who had migrated to the West Coast during the Gold Rush of the mid-1800s and the construction of a transcontinental railroad. However, as financial panics set in and wages fell after the Civil War, an increasing number of White Americans blamed the encroachment on the harder-working, lesser-paid Asian immigrants for the country's economic ills. Thus, "at the stroke of Chester Arthur's pen," according to one historian, a phenomenon that was previously unknown in America would grow in size and complexity ever afterward—illegal immigration.[20]

Nonetheless, Arthur's commitment to reform was obvious despite running up against an assertive Senate that had become, after the Civil War, what was termed the "Millionaires' Club." He instituted a long-overdue upgrade of the U.S. Navy and utilized the budget surplus to reduce the national debt.[21] He also officially opened the Brooklyn Bridge on May 24, 1883, and dedicated the Washington Monument on February 21, 1885, all while battling kidney failure from Bright's disease, which eventually led to a stroke that claimed his life November 18, 1886.[22]

His death followed the 1884 presidential election in which the Republicans, still split into Stalwart and Half-Breed factions, turned to the more charismatic Senator James G. Blaine over the still seemingly "illegitimate" Arthur and lost to the Democrat Grover Cleveland (the first Democratic president since before the Civil War). Needless to say, with his health failing, Arthur never pressed for a second term even with influential Americans like Mark Twain admitting: "I am but one in fifty-five million. Still, in the opinion of this one-fifty-fifth millionth of the country's population, it would be hard to better President Arthur's administration."[23]

5

Theodore Roosevelt— Never One Who Enjoyed It More

"The credit belongs to the man who is actually in the arena, whose face is marred by dust and sweat and blood."

Once aptly described as a "steam engine in trousers," nobody enjoyed being president more than Theodore Roosevelt, accidental or otherwise, and that goes doubly for most of the men suddenly thrust into the presidency by the death or malfeasance of their predecessors. A true force of nature who was nothing if not multi-faceted (and multi-tasked) when it came to his life and lifestyle, "Teddy" or TR, as he came to be known, even struggled to show the appropriate remorse when his predecessor, William McKinley, was shot in September of 1901 by an avowed anarchist and died eight days later.[1]

Finally located in the wilds of Maine atop a mountain, Vice President Roosevelt rushed to Buffalo to be at McKinley's side, but arrived too late and was immediately sworn in as the nation's youngest chief executive (age 42) in the parlor of a friend in that same Western New York city. In his prologue to *Theodore Rex*, Pulitzer Prize–winning Roosevelt biographer Edmund Morris touched on the restrained enthusiasm TR brought to his new job when he wrote, "He managed to look solemn, but his mind was seething with politics. 'I feel bully,' he would famously say upon awaking his first day as president." Whatever his previous roles, whether young and exuberant state assemblyman, aggressive New York City police commissioner, assertive assistant secretary of the Navy, self-made hero of the Spanish-American War, or confrontational New York governor turned vice presidential fill-in following the death of McKinley's original vice president, TR had always proven eager for the next challenge, and nothing about that would change once he became president.[2]

Despite an upper crust upbringing and sickly childhood, this Roosevelt was all about the strenuous life. An outdoorsman and advocate of all manner of manly activities, he loved hunting, the great outdoors, horseback riding, and any form of exercise.[3] But just as much, he loved being president, and he was good enough at it to change the dynamics of the job during his seven-plus years in office. Thus his legacy was more remarkable than most. In fact, without a war or some other national crisis during which he could provide leadership, and despite an ironic pledge he made to run for re-election only once, his tenure as president remains among the most memorable in American history.[4]

So how did this privileged scion of New York City society measure up? Any answer to that question must begin with his boundless energy. Never at a loss for causes that needed addressing, ideas that he wanted to pursue, and projects that he either initiated, consummated, or both, Teddy Roosevelt didn't waste any time. He built the previously unbuildable Panama Canal, still one of mankind's most important achievements; reinforced America's primacy in the Western Hemisphere and new status in the world through his "Big Stick" diplomacy; mediated an end to the Russo-Japanese War for which he won America's first Nobel Peace Prize; developed America's first anti-trust policy, reining in the monopoly and corporate greed of the late-19th century; preached and negotiated balance between management and labor through such actions as resolving the Anthracite Coal Strike of 1902; made the country healthier through such things as the Federal Meat Inspection and Pure Food and Drug Acts; initiated national conservation through such concepts as national forests, monuments, parks, and refuges; and even saved college football through a set of fundamental rules and the creation of the National Collegiate Athletic Association.[5]

Through constant action, it's safe to say, he got a lot done. And he did it all while authoring a prodigious, 30-plus books during a 60-year lifetime, maintaining a hectic travel and appearance schedule that had him crisscrossing the country via train numerous times, and remaining a much-involved head of household for one of America's youngest presidential families.[6] But he enjoyed being president and was determined to make a difference before handing over his presidential reins to a handpicked successor, the well-meaning William Howard Taft of Ohio. Unfortunately for the irrepressible Roosevelt, it was a succession he came to regret once he realized that many of the progressive ideals he had championed were being constrained by Taft at the behest of the more conservative Republican leadership TR had previously subdued.[7]

That, of course, led Roosevelt to his ill-fated try to regain the presidency in 1912 without benefit of the Republican nomination. Feeling that he and his progressive supporters had been robbed of the nomination by the much more conservative Republican leaders who favored Taft, they walked out of the convention and effectively split the party, giving the election to Woodrow Wilson and the Democrats. It was one of the most momentous elections in American history and a harbinger of the future, with Democrats claiming the more progressive (or liberal) approach to government and Republicans the more conservative mantra.[8]

Thus ended, once and for all, the political career of one of our most pop-

Theodore Roosevelt, pictured here in 1904, was America's youngest president when he ascended to the presidency, and he would remain among its most popular, as evidenced by his place on Mount Rushmore with Washington, Lincoln, and Jefferson (Library of Congress Prints and Photographs Division—Reproduction Number USZ62-7233).

ular presidents. In an era before approval ratings, is there any doubt Teddy Roosevelt would have probably set all-time highs at the time he dutifully left office in 1909, as he had pledged to do? He connected with the electorate as few before or since, and his enthusiasm for the job obviously had a lot to do with his all-time popularity.[9]

Although not president at the time, he survived an assassin's bullet while running for president again in 1912, despite delaying medical assistance for an hour in order to finish a speech.[10] Along with leading military charges in Cuba or big-game hunting in Africa and the American West, it was another example of his capacity for courage and lust for adventure, something that would again threaten his life two years later, when he and his second son, Kermit, were part of an expedition to explore a little-known tributary of the Amazon River.[11] Assailed by malarial fever and ravaged by infection from another wound suffered during their trek, he literally had to be carried out of the jungle to survive, but recurrences of both the malaria and infection would usher him towards an early death five years later, on January 6, 1919. Those maladies plus the loss of his youngest son, Quentin, during World War I sapped the energy that had always made him a driving force on the American stage. His wife, the second Mrs. Theodore Roosevelt, outlived him by 29 years.[12]

Chances are that if TR had run for another term in 1908, America's history in the 20th century might have been very different. For one thing, the Republican Party would have remained progressively oriented a while longer and may never have moved as much to the right and the conservative doctrines it mandates today.[13] But while the early departure of our most energetic president left an ideological void in one party, it never diminished the legacy of success TR had already achieved. His presidency marked the start of America's modern age.[14]

6

Calvin Coolidge—
Boom Times

"I favor the policy of economy, not because I wish to save money, but because I wish to save people."

Known as "Silent Cal" for his economy of words, Calvin Coolidge was also all about fiscal economy once he ascended to the White House upon the death in office of Warren G. Harding. Although our sixth accidental president, Coolidge did seem better prepared than some of his predecessors because of a more administrative background as a former mayor, lieutenant governor, and governor, all in Massachusetts.[1] It was as governor, in fact, that Coolidge attracted national attention and ultimately national acclaim when he backed Boston Mayor Andrew Peters and the city police commissioner in 1919 by sending troops to replace striking Boston policemen and upholding the commissioner's decision not to recognize their union or rehire strikers with the comment: "There is no right to strike against the public safety by anybody, anywhere, anytime."[2]

His unyielding stance earned enormous publicity and approval and made him a favorite of Republican voters, which he was when his home state made him a favorite-son candidate for president. Later, the national convention turned to him as its overwhelming favorite to assume the vice presidential role on a ticket with Harding, a polished, easygoing senator from Ohio who emerged as the Republicans' compromise choice for president in 1920.[3] As a result of their victory, Vice President Coolidge would spend his next several years presiding over the Senate and rarely involved in national issues. However, his role in the Washington shadows all changed on August 2, 1923, when Harding, while on a cross-country speaking tour to the Western U.S. dubbed the "Voyage of Understanding," developed severe indigestion. Felt at the time to be suffering food poisoning, he continued his journey to San Francisco, where his illness worsened with the onset of pneumonia, and he died five days later.[4]

Harding died as one of our most scandal-prone presidents, a factor that preceded and no doubt contributed to his undertaking the strenuous Western tour. His administration was rocked by corruption because of a Cabinet that included the most corrupt attorney general in American history, Harry Daugherty; an equally corrupt secretary of the interior, Albert Fall; and a disgraced secretary of the Navy, Edwin Denby; as well as the far-reaching (and locally named) "Teapot Dome" scandal, which involved illegal leases and bribes related to U.S. oil reserves in the West. Harding was also ridiculed over two extra-marital affairs, one with a neighbor's wife for about 15 years and the other with a hero worshiper about half his age. In death, there were even rumors that his wife had poisoned him after the extra-marital revelations surfaced, especially after she denied permission for an official autopsy. No such foul play was ever proven, however, and it was rarely believed. Still, it had to be refreshing to have the high-character, strait-laced Coolidge in the White House once the appropriate period of mourning for his deceased predecessor was over.[5]

After receiving a telegram about Harding's death, Coolidge was administered the oath of office by his 78-year-old father, a local notary, in the family farmhouse in Vermont by the light of a kerosene lamp.[6] From such quaint beginnings, Coolidge, the man of few words, would soon belie the era in which he led. After all, who would have predicted such a soft-spoken president in the midst of the "Roaring Twenties?" But with a rapidly recovering economy, Coolidge would win another full term in a landslide vote just one year later (1924) with the slogan "Keep Cool With Coolidge."[7]

It was an economic boom time, a period of innovation and transition to some amazing new consumer goods—such things as automobiles, radios, washing machines, and even airplanes—mass-produced products that transformed society and created the American middle class. Further spurring this economic surge were President Coolidge's tax-cutting measures. He would reduce four different kinds of taxes—income, inheritance, gift, and excise—much to the benefit of the wealthiest Americans, initiating the Republican belief in what has become known as "trickle down economics."[8] In freeing up funds for even more private investment, Coolidge contributed to dizzying speculation and bears what many historians consider some responsibility for the stock market crash of 1929, the opening salvo of the "Great Depression," which would follow his departure and haunt his successor, Herbert Hoover. From the "normalcy" promised by Harding to the boom times administered by Coolidge and the crash and burn of the Hoover administration, the Republican decade of the 1920s ended as a transitional experience for America following its first major foreign intervention in World War I.[9]

Luckily for Coolidge, he got out of the White House while the getting was good. Another Republican, Ronald Reagan, would resurrect his reputation half a century later (1981), when he stated, "You hear a lot of jokes about Silent Cal Coolidge. Well, the joke is on the people who make the jokes. We had probably the greatest growth and prosperity that we've ever known."[10]

Known as "Silent Cal" for his economy of words, Calvin Coolidge (photograph ca. 1919) is best remembered as America's thriftiest president for his efforts to cut taxes and avoid excess spending (Library of Congress Prints and Photographs Division—Reproduction Number DIG-ds-07523 [John H. Garo, photographer]).

The original opponent of what's been termed "big government," Coolidge's economic policies and low interest rates combined for what is now called a "bull market," sparking commercial giants like

General Motors. It was an era of "crony capitalism," which increased corruption through above-the-law commercialism in which representing a political constituency and corporate clients were often one and the same. Along with real estate, the speculative bubble of the Coolidge years was constantly growing and did burst once he was gone.[11]

Important legislation from the Coolidge years included the Immigration Act of 1924, which cut immigration quotas; the Veterans Bonus of the same year, which was passed over his veto and set the stage for the Bonus March of World War I veterans that helped undo the Hoover presidency eight years later; the Air Commerce Act of 1926, which placed civil administration under the Commerce Department for the first time; and the Kellogg-Briand Treaty of 1928, whereby 47 of the most modern and civilized nations renounced war in hopes of avoiding another worldwide conflict.[12]

Choosing to not seek re-election in 1928, Coolidge retired to Northampton, Massachusetts, where he authored his autobiography and magazine articles for the *Saturday Evening Post* and *Colliers*. Many have speculated that he chose not to run again in order to ensure his health and that of his wife; because as a tight-fisted economist, he realized that the next four years would require a less frugal chief executive; or because he was perceptive enough to foresee the coming economic difficulties and to protect his reputation for prosperity. Regardless, the timing seemed to reinforce his reputation for common sense. He died on January 5, 1933, at the age of 60. His wife outlived him by 24 years.[13]

7

Harry Truman—
Better Than Expected

"It is amazing what you can accomplish if you do not care who gets the credit."

When Harry Truman became president of the United States on April 12, 1945, "most Americans were in a state of shock." That's the way historian Kenneth Davis described the country's reaction to the death of Franklin D. Roosevelt and the sudden ascension of our seventh accidental president, Harry S. Truman, of Independence, Missouri, the last of our chief executives without a college education and someone who had failed in every financial or career endeavor he had tried up to that point, except the military and politics. Only in those two areas had this otherwise unsuccessful Midwestern farmer's son proven himself. Most people seriously doubted his ability to fill the shoes of the nation's longest serving and arguably most successful chief executive, FDR, especially with World War II still raging and the prospect of a very different world in its aftermath.[1]

With his humble beginnings and plainspoken personality, Truman just didn't seem presidential to a nation used to the "ebullient, charming, persuasive, gregarious" Roosevelt. It was like going from the imperial court to the courthouse square, and it seemed even more so when the new president's first official remarks included "Boys, if you ever pray, pray for me now. I don't know whether you have ever had a load of hay fall you, but when they told me yesterday what had happened [FDR's death from a cerebral hemorrhage], I felt like the moon, the stars, and the planets had all fallen on me."[2]

It was an honest reaction, but it was not the most confident start for a man who truly never wanted to be president—so much so, in fact, that he also never wanted to be vice president and tried to avoid it at all costs. Only when FDR shamed him into acceptance did Truman assume the second spot on the Dems' ticket, the spot formerly held by Henry A. Wallace, Roosevelt's choice during his third term and a man suddenly deemed too liberal by the party's rank-and-file, especially by the South.[3]

Despite intense personal reservations, including the mudslinging sure to come with a national campaign and the skeletons it might expose, Truman relented to being the Democrats' compromise choice, a moderate who had risen through suspect political ranks to personal success he had previously never enjoyed in (of all places) the U.S. Senate.[4] The fact was that Harry Truman had been the product of one of the most corrupt political machines of the era, the one run by Kansas City boss Thomas J. Pendergast, because his heroic leadership of a local World War I artillery company made him an attractive local candidate. With the backing of the "Pendergast Machine" and the support of area veterans, many of whom had served under him, Captain Truman was elected to a county judgeship from which he would advance to the county chief executive post four years later.[5]

In each of those roles, Truman proved an able administrator, curbing waste, improving roads, and building such things as a new hospital and courthouse, while doing so without any taint of Pendergast influence. His success within the Kansas City area was such that he earned statewide recognition, leading to back-to-back terms in the Senate regardless of the notion that his rapid rise had been due to the Pendergast Machine. It was an underlying notion that Truman worked hard to dispel. Nonetheless, his opponents labeled him "the senator from Pendergast," and for the rest of his life he was forced to maintain that Kansas City's notorious boss had never asked him to do anything unethical or dishonest.[6]

As a senator, he helped draft the Civil Aeronautics Act of 1938, regulating the fledgling airline industry for the first time, and the Transportation Act of 1940, strengthening the Interstate Commerce Commission. He also supported pro-labor legislation, an anti-lynching bill, an end to poll taxes, and the Fair Employment Practices Commission, becoming a fast-rising political star of the Democratic Party. His most visible contribution, however, was as chairman of a special committee to investigate the National Defense Program between 1941 and 1944, what became known as the "Truman Commission" that exposed billions of dollars of waste throughout the U.S. military-industrial complex.[7] It was his final senatorial star in a constellation leading to being singled out to replace Wallace on the 1944 Democratic ticket with the by-then ailing president. FDR's cardio issues were such that he never should have sought a fourth term, a fact overruled in his own mind by a desire to finish the ongoing global conflict he had become so much a part of heading into its final stages.[8]

A lightly-regarded senator from Missouri before becoming vice president, Harry Truman, pictured here in 1945, was faced with ending a world war and containing communist expansion when he succeeded America's longest-serving president (Library of Congress Prints and Photographs Division—Reproduction Number USZ62-117122).

Into this impending crisis of presidential succession stepped Harry Truman, unaware of just how sick FDR really was. Just 82 days after assuming his vice presidential role, he suddenly found himself president, much as our first accidental president, John Tyler, had upon the death of William Henry Harrison. The big difference—Truman was following a man who had been president longer than anyone (12-plus years) and in the midst of world war.[9]

While pledged to carry on Roosevelt's policies and initiatives, Truman seemed to rise to the challenge by establishing his own style, "the buck stops here" mantra first enunciated by a sign on his office desk. He would go on to establish his "Give 'em Hell, Harry" persona as a political campaigner and chief executive, a blunt way of expressing himself that reprimanded Republican rivals and roused the Democratic base, and somehow he managed to maintain the coalition of national supporters FDR had so successfully welded together. With a decidedly different style from his aristocratic predecessor, one of his earliest statements in the White House summed up his feelings about being there: "Within the first few months, I discovered that being president is like riding a tiger. A man has to keep riding or be swallowed."[10]

But swallowed he was not, becoming better than his detractors anticipated.[11] Among his first responsibilities in place of Roosevelt was the Potsdam Conference in Europe, alongside Great Britain's Winston Churchill and the Soviet Union's Joseph Stalin. It was a continuation of the series of "Big Three" conferences they had previously engaged in with FDR in the war's final two years, as Germany gradually succumbed to the Allies and focus shifted to Japan. Taking FDR's place on such a world stage, Truman warmed to the task, something made easier by finally learning of his predecessor's authorization of a secret weapon that could end the war. Although fearing its use might eventually endanger all mankind, Truman nevertheless authorized that two of these aptly named "atomic bombs" be dropped on the Japanese cities of Hiroshima and Nagasaki as a means of inducing the Japanese to surrender without having to spend more American lives on an invasion. Following the second bomb on August 9, 1945, Japan sued for peace, and the biggest and most costly war in human history finally came to a close.[12]

Another milestone of the Truman presidency was the trials at Nuremburg, Germany, of war criminals—surviving Nazi leaders of the global conflict they caused.[13] The Truman administration also oversaw the start of the United Nations, FDR's hopeful vision for avoiding future wars, and instituted the Truman Doctrine and Marshall Plan for European recovery. Named for his Secretary of State and former General George Marshall, the latter invested billions to rebuild Europe's Western democracies and involved a policy of "containment" to stem the obvious tide of communism being perpetuated by Stalin, a series of "police actions" that checked aggression but avoided another world war. The collapse of the Soviet Union in 1991 was Truman's vindication.[14]

His Point Four Program followed in 1949, marking the beginning of U.S. technical commitment to third world nations in Latin America, Asia, and Africa. In 1950, he opted for U.S. troops to contain communist aggression on the Korean Peninsula, when Soviet-backed North Korea invaded South Korea. Truman's commitment led to a United Nations mandate with American troops and those of other nations under the command of U.S. General Douglas MacArthur. The Korean War did not end until 1953, and not before the Communist Chinese entered the conflict to drive U.S. led forces back to the 38th parallel, the original (and still existing) line of demarcation on the peninsula between North and South Korea. Then, in a controversial and highly politicized decision, Truman removed the iconic and immensely popular MacArthur from command for insubordination after his repeated efforts to escalate the conflict with China, which could have sparked another world war.[15]

Still more important legislation of the Truman years included the Taft-Hartley Act, which passed over his veto and curbed labor rights. In addition, he signed the Housing Act of 1949 for urban renewal as part of his "Fair Deal," which increased the minimum wage, extended Social Security coverage, and desegregated the U.S. Armed Forces. But much of his hoped-for agenda failed to pass, including national health insurance and repeal of Taft-Hartley. Also under his watch, America's Central Intelligence Agency (CIA) was founded, development of a "hydrogen bomb" took place, and the Twenty-Second Amendment (1951) officially limited future presidents to two consecutive terms.[16]

Obviously a very contentious administration full of what one biographer has described as "more far-reaching decisions than any president before him," Truman not only surprised with his ability to step into FDR's shoes, but also with his ability to win re-election in 1948, one of the most surprising U.S. presidential verdicts ever. Despite being undermined by other candidates within his own party—Henry Wallace on the liberal "left," Strom Thurmond on the conservative "right"—Truman bettered the heavily favored Republican standard bearer, Thomas Dewey, the governor of New York making his second straight presidential run. Truman's upset shocked the nation but also set him up for four more years of declining approval ratings while struggling with a Republican Congress and committing U.S. troops to the ongoing conflict in Korea.[17]

After deciding to not seek re-election in 1952, Truman returned to Independence and enjoyed his post-presidential years away from the limelight before dying at age 88 on December 26, 1972. His wife, who loathed the role of First Lady, lived to 97—the longest of any presidential spouse.[18]

8

Lyndon B. Johnson—
Political Disciple

"There are no problems we cannot solve together and very few we can solve by ourselves."

Unlike some of our accidental presidents, no one should ever question Lyndon Baines Johnson's desire for the position or the power. From an early age, the political disciple that was LBJ was obvious to anyone and everyone who crossed his path from one election to the next. No one ever approached the political game with more ferocity than the six-foot-four, arm-twisting Texan from the Hill Country west of Austin.[1]

Once described as taking to politics like "mother's milk," Johnson's father and maternal grandfather had both been respected members of the state legislature, and by the time he was in college at Southwest Texas State, he was already exhibiting his political inclinations by joining the debate team, serving as campaign manager for the school's White Stars faction, and writing editorials for the campus newspaper. He was also elected president of the Press Club, a senior class legislator, and to the student council. And in 1928, he and some of his college friends "crashed" the Democratic National Convention in nearby Houston while directing the successful political campaign of a young aspirant to the State Senate, another harbinger of things to come.[2]

Later, after teaching school briefly, Johnson was able to study law at Georgetown University while serving on the Washington staff of Texas Congressman Richard Kleberg for three years. During that time, he was elected speaker of the "Little Congress," the unofficial name given an organization of congressional assistants. Following his marriage in 1934, he took a job as director of the National Youth Administration in Texas, which provided technical training and local public works jobs for young adults during the Great Depression.[3]

A young disciple of President Franklin Roosevelt and his "New Deal" initiatives of the 1930s, Johnson entered the political wars himself in 1937. As a candidate for Texas' Tenth District congressional seat in a special election, he bested a crowded field and headed back to Washington. It was his first of six straight two-year terms representing Austin and its environs, and he would make a name for himself with dam building and by bringing electricity to rural Central Texas.[4]

In 1941, he stepped up to a Senate race, which he narrowly lost in a disputed election to former Texas Governor Lee "Pappy" O'Daniel. In 1949, he ran again for the Senate against another former governor, Coke Stevenson, and this time he won in an equally disputed election by a mere 87 votes, earning the sarcastic nickname "Landslide Lyndon." Although controversial, his victory would provide the start for one of the most dynamic Senate careers ever, including becoming the youngest majority leader ever at age 46.[5]

Johnson exhibited unique parliamentary skills and a talent for achieving compromise to pass a significant amount of legislation during his 12 years of Senate leadership. It was said of him by a Senate colleague, "The senator from Texas is a genius in the art of the legislative process," and by taking care of the powerful oil and gas interests in his home state, achieving the extension of Social Security, and increasing the minimum wage, as well as his remarkable passage of 1957 and 1960 Civil Rights Acts despite being a Southerner, he secured star status in the Democratic Party and presidential potential in both 1956 and 1960.[6]

As a hard-to-elect Southerner, however, those chances eluded him both times. Instead, the Democrats turned to more liberal, Northern candidates—former Illinois governor Adlai Stevenson in 1956, who would lose a second straight presidential election to popular World War II icon Dwight Eisenhower, and young Massachusetts Senator John Kennedy in 1960, the charismatic son of one of the wealthiest men in America.[7] Like Johnson a former congressman (1947–1953) and fast-rising senator (1953–1961), Kennedy and his family brought a well-oiled organization to the Democratic nomination process and captured seven

From Senate majority leader to vice president to president, Lyndon Baines Johnson, pictured here in 1955, was at the pinnacle of American power for over 14 years and the chief executive who finally accomplished civil rights legislation (Library of Congress Prints and Photographs Division—Reproduction Number LC-U91-242-2).

straight primaries en route to the national convention, where he almost doubled Johnson on the first ballot and then surprised everyone by offering his vanquished rival the vice presidential spot on the ticket to improve his vote-getting chances in the South. Just as surprisingly, Johnson accepted the number two role for a winning combination that narrowly defeated Eisenhower's vice president and heir apparent, Richard Nixon, in the general election that fall.[8]

Although he did not get along well with the Kennedy insiders, including the president's brother, Attorney General Robert Kennedy, Johnson proved a loyal VP, serving as chairman of the National Aeronautics and Space Council, the Peace Corps Advisory Council, and the President's Committee on Equal Opportunity in addition to overseeing the Senate. He also undertook more than 30 international missions and tours for the Kennedy administration. In other words, although deeply disappointed that his pathway to the White House had been blocked by his younger Senate colleague, LBJ proved a good soldier and team player until that fateful day in his own home state (of all places) that thrust him back into the much larger role he had always envisioned for himself.[9]

That was the day, November 22, 1963, when John F. Kennedy became the fourth American president to die from an assassin's bullet and the first to be gunned down while riding in a motorcade. As with our prior presidential deaths in office, shock waves reverberated throughout the country and world, especially given the optimism and momentum the young JFK had generated in his three years of leadership. There followed the wild pursuit and apprehension of his apparent assailant, Lee Harvey Oswald, who would be mysteriously gunned down himself just a few days later in a police transfer worthy of the Keystone Cops and one that would leave the country embracing all kinds of conspiracy theories about the murder of a president.[10]

In the meantime, the VP who had been riding just two cars behind Kennedy in that same motorcade suddenly found himself sworn in as the new president, but not in a way for which he would have ever wished. Instead, with JFK's stunned widow and his own wife flanking him, Johnson took the oath of office aboard Air Force One on the Dallas Love Field tarmac (see Dedication Page) before returning to Washington.[11]

Like the fallen presidents before him, Kennedy's death inspired a period of mourning and ceremony, and like his accidental predecessors, Johnson accepted his new fate with respectful, determined commitment, rallying behind his fallen predecessor's unfinished agenda. In his first message to Congress four days later, Johnson pointed to at least two major tasks he would address moving forward. At the time, he said, "This nation will keep its commitments from South Vietnam to West Berlin. We have talked long enough in this country about equal rights. We have talked for one hundred years or more. It's time to write the next chapter and to write it in the books of law."[12]

Keeping that commitment to South Vietnam would, of course, prove a burden and blemish on the Johnson administration that will never go away. It overshadowed a series of major legislative accomplishments for which he has never garnered sufficient credit. In fact, while the brief administration of his predecessor was idealized as a three-year "Camelot" (after the mythological King Arthur's court), the Johnson years will forever be mired in the legacy of Vietnam, dimming for posterity his presidential triumphs that otherwise would have earned more eternal commendation. While the gloriously remembered Kennedy years were fraught with tensions, the Johnson years were more productive. LBJ's aggressive agenda included his "War on Poverty" initiative, passage of another Civil Rights Act in 1964 and milestone Voting Rights Act in 1965, the introduction of Medicare as part of Social Security, and our earliest environmental protection legislation, the Water Quality and Air Quality Acts of the mid 1960s.[13]

Instead of the legacy of hope he hoped to leave (like his political hero, FDR), LBJ's progressive accomplishments would be overshadowed by his build-up, cover-up, and prolonged prosecution of the Vietnam War, a conflict that offered no easy off-ramps or obvious means of victory. More than Truman's eventual stalemate in Korea, Vietnam became a dead end that Johnson would leave to his successor (Richard Nixon), amidst national outrage and with no resolution in sight. Weighed down by this unpopular military and political quagmire, historians have not had a chance to recognize what his Equal Opportunity Act, Immigration and Nationality Act, Work-Study Program, Work Experience Program, Head Start and Upward Bound Programs did for so many poor and disadvantaged Americans, or how the previously noted environmental acts finally curbed decades of industrial abuse of our air and waterways.[14]

In addition, Medicare became an insurance lifeline for the nation's senior citizens, something FDR's Social Security Act had not addressed, and Medicaid a life preserver for the disadvantaged of any age. Considered unaffordable entitlements by opponents before and ever since, they have nonetheless withstood the tests of time, now over a half-century, to the point of becoming accepted and non-negotiable parts of the American political land-scape.[15]

Given the domination of race in our national experience, however, it was Johnson's civil rights stance and action that would have topped his historical record had it not been for Vietnam. The fact that a Southern Democrat, a protégé of the "Solid South's" irre-deemable contingent of Senate guardians, who for decades filibustered their way to stoppage of any civil rights legislation, became the president who finally limited election discrimi-nation in the South should ensure LBJ a significant place in our racially charged history books. But with rampant, ongoing prejudice and generations of racial divide in this country, it also ensured an increase in political polarization to the point that our two major parties now regularly face off in a no-holds-barred game of lies, innuendo, and one-upsmanship that leaves little chance for compromise.[16]

From LBJ, then, one can track the development of "Red" and "Blue" states from coast to coast, with many in the South actually changing color at the time he was president. For what should have been better, but has too often been worse, American politics, in an ever-increasing media- and technology-driven age, has ever since entered a downward spiral of "them versus us" with an internal divide more threatening to the United States than any external nation, faction, or foe.[17]

With Johnson as president, the first African American Supreme Court justice, Thur-good Marshall, was appointed; the same court unanimously struck down any remaining state laws against inter-racial marriage; and Civil Rights Movement icon Martin Luther King was awarded the Nobel Peace Prize. The bottom line: racial hypocrisy, which had existed in America since the Declaration of Independence, all came full circle in a rush to judgment that has continued to reverberate to the present day.[18]

On March 31, 1968, in a surprise move that shocked the nation, LBJ announced that he would not seek re-election later that year, instead concentrating on the war and other polarizing issues that had limited his hoped for "Great Society" after being re-elected in a landslide over Republican firebrand Barry Goldwater four years earlier. It had to be a supremely disheartening moment for such a political disciple, someone who had always craved the reins of power, who relished adulation, and who wanted nothing more than to do as much good as possible for his "fellow Americans."

Without Vietnam, his time in office would have probably stretched to nine years, leav-ing him second all-time to FDR's 12-plus, but unwilling to face the animosity sure to come if he sought another term, Johnson retired to his Hill Country, where he died on his ranch on January 22, 1973, the victim of the heart trouble that had plagued him since 1955. His wife of 39 years outlived him by 34.[19]

9

Gerald Ford—
Restoration Project

"Our national nightmare is over. Our Constitution works. Our great republic is a government of laws and not of men."

No state of mourning greeted Gerald Ford's ascension to the presidency. Unlike our other accidental chief executives who were faced with the shocking deaths of their predecessors, his assumption of leadership was not brought on by the grave. While not having to deal with the suddenness of a presidential death, Ford's elevation to the nation's highest office was no less traumatic and occurred over a more prolonged period of time.[1]

Our ninth accidental president was, in fact, our first unelected vice president, the result of also being our first appointed VP under provisions of the Twenty-Fifth Amendment, which was added to the Constitution in 1967. Ford became the first replacement VP when he was appointed by President Richard Nixon to take the place of Spiro Agnew, who resigned from that post in 1973 as part of a negotiated legal settlement to avoid prosecution for tax evasion. As a result of that replacement, Ford also became the first replacement vice president to ascend to the presidency when Nixon was forced to resign in disgrace to avoid impeachment following the Watergate scandal and ensuing cover-up, both of which wrecked his second term.[2]

Thus did Gerald Ford replace the president (and friend) who had appointed him vice president eight months earlier, in an ironic twist of fate that would have lasting consequences for the successor. Obviously, Ford was the first and will, very probably, be the only person to replace both a sitting vice president and president, a dubious distinction less than a year apart but one this steady, unassuming Republican mainstay from Michigan was able to endure.

He needed to be that way—one of the presidency's true nice guys. No one had ever become president amidst more suspicion and anger over what had just transpired in the White House than Gerald Ford when he took the oath of office on August 9, 1974. Into this political cauldron that was unique in American history stepped a man with no frills and no presidential ambitions, a former college football star, honor student, male model, and Navy World War II veteran—a man who had been happy just to serve the people of his home state's Fifth District in the House of Representatives for 24 years (1949–1973), including the last eight as minority leader.[3]

A moderate conservative who first rose to prominence for his work on the Defense Appropriations Committee, Ford crossed party lines to support President Truman's Marshall Plan and repeatedly spoke up for Republican President Dwight Eisenhower and his more controversial vice president, "Dick" Nixon of California, whom he had gotten to know when they were both in the House. Later, as a member of the Warren Commission, he fully endorsed the determination that Lee Harvey Oswald acted alone in the assassination of President Kennedy. He opposed President Johnson's War on Poverty and the establishment of Medicare, and he consistently supported President Nixon's pursuit of "peace with honor" when it came to getting out of Vietnam.[4]

The only accidental president to ascend to that post for reasons other than the death of his predecessor, Gerald Ford, pictured here in 1974, had to move the country past the worst political scandal in modern history (Library of Congress Prints and Photographs Division—Reproduction Number DIG-ppmsca-08440 [James J. O'Halloran, photographer]).

Trusted by both Nixon and Democrats, he was no doubt the best available man to replace Agnew, and he accepted the VP appointment despite having to relinquish his personal dream of someday ascending to Speaker of the House once Republicans regained control of the lower chamber.[5] The day he took the VP oath of office, he also defended Nixon against charges of a Watergate cover-up, the start of an eight-month, downhill procession of events that led Ford to realize that Nixon's position in the scandal was indefensible and that he had no choice but to resign. In other words, like the other accidentals, Ford would be president, whether he wanted it or not.[6]

It was time spent adjusting to the task. When he finally did ascend to the White House, he remarked, "I believe that truth is the glue that holds government together, not only our government but civilization itself. That bond, though strained, is unbroken at home and abroad. In my public and private acts as your president, I expect to follow my instincts of openness and candor with full confidence that honesty is always the best policy."[7]

Such belief and reliance on being honest obviously came at just the right moment for a nation shaken by the dishonesty of the Nixon White House. "He [Ford] faced incredible challenges on a wide series of fronts: a nation still at war in Southeast Asia, an economic crisis brought on by the new Arab oil power, and an ugly, sour mood in the country brought on by Nixon's 'high crimes and misdemeanors,'" Kenneth Davis summarized in his *Don't Know Much About the American Presidents*.[8]

To confront and move past these issues and the cynicism that accompanied his ascension, Ford first stunned (and even angered) much of the nation by pardoning Nixon, believing it was time for the country to move on from Watergate. He also offered amnesty to the thousands of Vietnam draft dodgers if they were willing to swear an oath of allegiance (to the U.S.) and perform two years of community public service.[9] That same year, 1974, after Congress denied Ford's request for more aid to South Vietnam, he was relegated to being the president who ultimately had to accept communist victory and ascendancy in Southeast Asia.[10]

The next year, however, it could be said that he rebounded by overseeing the Helsinki Agreement, an understanding among 35 nations designed to ease long-standing East-West tensions in Europe; by signing four consumer bills passed by Congress to enable more equity in the marketplace; and by reluctantly allowing federal emergency credit to cash-strapped New York City, thus preventing the nation's largest city from financial default. In addition, he created the Energy Research and Development Administration in an effort to curb oil consumption; put into effect a campaign reform law designed to restrict individual contributions and influence in future presidential campaigns; extended the 1965 Voting Rights Act to include Spanish-speaking and other language minorities; and luckily, avoided two separate assassination attempts, ironically both by women, when the gun of the first misfired at close range and when the only shot of the second missed from 40 feet away.[11]

The very idea that Ford, a conciliator doing the best he could to move past partisan acrimony and the embarrassment of Watergate, could be the target of back-to-back assassination attempts revealed something of the unsettling times the nation had moved through and the total lack of confidence most Americans had in their elected officials. Once described by a Michigan senator as "a person virtually without enemies," he would have seemed the perfect replacement in a time of national distrust, but even he, as much a unifier as he had always been, could not escape would-be detractors in an age of dissatisfaction nurtured by rampant inflation.[12]

Although pocketbook issues went to the root of American dissatisfaction at the time and Ford had nothing to do with the illegalities of the politics that ushered him into the White House, his attempts to move the country past it all led him to seek re-election for a job he had never really wanted, had never campaigned for, and never had much chance to retain in 1976, beginning 30 points behind in the polls. Nevertheless, he closed the gap to a dead heat by election day before losing by just two percent of the vote to a previously little-known, former governor of Georgia, Jimmy Carter, a rival who would later become his very good friend.[13]

Ford's 29 months in office were the briefest of any of the nine accidental presidents, but he would also live longer than any former U.S. chief executive up to 2018, dying at age 93 on December 26, 2006. His wife would outlive him by five and a half years.[14]

PART II

Their Biographies: An In-Depth Review

10

Tyler, Texas and
Setting the Record Straight

"Tyler deserves the lasting gratitude of the country for arresting the dominant majority in Congress in their mad career."—James K. Polk, 1841

Tidewater, Virginia, the land between the James and Charles Rivers, was the home of America's first accidental president, John Tyler. It's also home to one of America's oldest colleges, a sanctuary of higher learning that has never had the notoriety of New England's Ivy League schools like Harvard and Yale, but a school with similar academic and historic credentials, the College of William & Mary. As a result, it seems only fitting that one of the best biographies on Tyler, a William & Mary grad, was written by William & Mary Professor Emeritus Edward Crapol in 2006. It was titled, in fact, *John Tyler, The Accidental President* and offered a very different take on our tenth president from most history books. In obvious agreement, another constitutionally motivated historian more recently wrote, "John Tyler is not a household name, but he should be."

The sixth of eight presidents born in The Commonwealth of Virginia, Tyler was an unlikely successor to the first Whig president, 68-year-old William Henry Harrison, another of those Virginians who died of natural causes (pneumonia) only a month into his presidency. Tyler was paired with Harrison on the Whig Party ticket of 1840 although his political career to that point had been as a devotee of the earliest Republicans, whose name turned to Democrats in the 19th century—the party of Thomas Jefferson and James Madison that would pass its legacy (if not its name) to the Democrats of Andrew Jackson and Martin Van Buren. Indeed, Tyler always considered himself an "anointed heir" of Virginia's presidential dynasty—the line of Jefferson, Madison, and James Monroe—particularly after he was called on to deliver The Commonwealth's official eulogy for Jefferson when the author of American independence died on the Fourth of July, 1826.[1] Tyler was governor of Virginia at the time, having always been a strong states' rights advocate and defender of what is now termed "White supremacy" before deciding to cast his political future with the Whigs.[2]

One Whig loyalist even portrayed Tyler as a "renegade Democrat without allegiance to Whig principals" during the 1840 campaign, a presidential race that made famous the political slogan Tippecanoe and Tyler too, referencing General Harrison's best-known victory in the Indian wars of the early Northwest and his Southern vice presidential running mate.[3] That would be just one of the stories addressed by Crapol while trying to adjust the Tyler narrative, casting him as a largely misunderstood chief executive deserving of more credit than he has generally received and a lot less derision.

Opening with Tyler's sudden ascension to the White House and the famous precedent he set for all succeeding VPs, Crapol approached his biography of Tyler in a very non-traditional, unchronological way. Along with his annexation of Texas, the precedent of vice presidential succession became what Tyler has been remembered for, a defining moment for American democracy.[4] For the entire Tyler story, however, read a little further into the book for the background of where he came from and how he got there by age 51. Unlike Harrison, whose legacy would span the Appalachians and attain its most enduring fame west of the mountains on America's first Northwestern frontier,[5] Tyler was a mainstay of Old Virginia, an entrenched blue blood whose father was part of the Revolutionary War generation and three times governor of the state. The elder John Tyler, a jurist and judge by trade, was a contemporary of Jefferson, Madison, and Monroe, and knew them all, so it's easy to see how any son of his would be imbued with a zeal and faith for what Crapol termed "the American republican experiment."[6]

The Tyler family estate was known as Greenway and consisted of two adjoining farms along the James River west of Williamsburg, the Virginia capital from 1699 to 1780 and home of the College of William & Mary. Approximately 40 slaves were kept at Greenway as Tyler grew up there and joined the social elite. As a student, he would have witnessed the so-called "Jeffersonians" in action, accomplishing the Louisiana Purchase, which added vast new territory in the West, setting the stage for expansion. It was a lesson that made a lasting impression on the young Tyler.[7]

At the same time, he grew up detesting the British, a feeling left over from his father's generation and nurtured by the War of 1812. After college and the opportunity to study law under former U.S. Attorney General Edmund Randolph, Tyler enjoyed a lucrative private practice as "an up-and-coming country lawyer" groomed for greatness in the political circles of his day. Indeed, at only 21 he was elected to the Virginia House of Delegates and married well, ensuring his social and economic standing in Virginia society, and positioning himself for a career in politics.[8]

Although Crapol advised that Tyler could be "calculating and devious," he always attempted to be high-minded in his political approach. The first challenge to his notion of what our national destiny should be came as a member of the Virginia delegation to the U.S. House of Representatives in 1819 and 1820. That's when debate intensified over whether Missouri should enter the Union as a free state or as one allowing slavery within its borders. Like many of his congressional colleagues, he considered the issue a threat to the Union while also being determined to promote the idea that territorial and commercial expansion could actually ease sectional differences.[9] By contrast, Illinois Congressman and eventual President Abraham Lincoln did not share Tyler's enthusiasm for territorial expansion because in his uniquely simplified manner of speaking, he did "not believe in enlarging our field, but in keeping our fences where they are and cultivating our current possession, making it [the] garden."[10]

When confronted by such opposing voices and the growing national focus on slavery, the institution and way of life he had grown up with, Tyler developed a ready answer. He called it "diffusion"—the theory that if slavery was allowed to spread all over the country, or at least into the new, Western territories, the slave population would thin so much that it could eventually become politically feasible to abolish it entirely in the South. In his mind, too much time and effort was being spent arguing over slavery expansion when, if left to its own course, slavery would die a natural death within a couple of generations.

Crapol reminded readers that this seemingly "cynical, self-serving doctrine" of Southern slaveholders like Tyler rationalized a gathering storm with logic they deemed "irrefutable" if only given a chance. Using states where slaves had previously been emancipated as examples, he contended that the scarcity of slaves in those places made it a no-brainer, while in the Deep South, where plantation production remained paramount to local economies, such objectives would constitute political suicide. As a result, admitting Missouri as a slave state and allowing slaveholders to migrate there like other U.S. citizens would support the necessary economic thinning of slavery. Meanwhile, Northern politicians cast this idea by Tyler and other Southerners as merely their realization of how divisive "chattel slavery" (human beings held as personal property) was going to remain for the foreseeable future.[11]

At about the same time, the young congressman from Virginia, who has been described "as a tall man with an angular face, aquiline nose, deep-set, thoughtful eyes, jug ears, and a wild shock of hair circling his brow,"[12] revealed his inbred opposition to anything British. He opposed protective tariffs while identifying Great Britain as the chief U.S. rival in the quest for global supremacy. "America is now the granary of the world," he declared in advocating free and unfettered trade.[13] Was this one of the earliest enunciations of the doctrine that would become "Manifest Destiny," the expansionist concept that would sweep the country before and after the Civil War? Undoubtedly it would become a recurring theme in the decades to come as a centerpiece of Tyler presidential ideology. However, a bout with ill health would end the congressional stage of his career in 1821, setting up a different stage for his successful return to politics in 1825 in the footsteps of his illustrious father—the Virginia Governor's Mansion.[14]

Branding himself an heir to Jefferson and an advocate of states' rights, Tyler continued up the Southern political ladder, being elected to the Senate in 1827 at age 37. By then he had already surpassed his father's legacy and positioned himself for a possible presidential run. But in the presidential campaign of 1828, he was forced to choose the lesser of two evils, supporting Andrew Jackson over incumbent John Quincy Adams. Opposed to Adams on the grounds that he was an isolationist, he also worried about Jackson's possible abuse of executive power, which was not a stretch given the Tennessean's impulsive reputation as a former duelist and military commander. Avenging his controversial election loss of 1824, which had been decided in the House of Representatives, Jackson was victorious.[15]

Meanwhile, Tyler continued to envision an America that extended to the Pacific and from there accessed the markets of the Orient. During the 1832 Nullification Crisis, which pitted John C. Calhoun at the head of the Southern nullifiers against a re-elected Jackson (once Calhoun's South Carolina delegation declared the federal tariffs of 1828 and 1832 null and void within their sovereign state boundaries),[16] Tyler rose to confront what he considered an even more ominous threat—the rise of abolitionist societies in the North. Primarily led by clergymen who inundated Congress with calls for the federal government to support anti-slavery measures, they flooded the mail with petitions touching off years of anti-abolition backlash and violence, especially in the South, as fears of racial inbreeding began to sweep the country. Some came to believe that the abolitionists were actually working for Great Britain, while Tyler, with his inbred bias, even suspected a British-led conspiracy to foment slave insurrection.[17]

In 1835, Tyler and a group of his local Williamsburg constituents went so far as to resolve that anti-slavery literature of any kind published inside Virginia should be regarded as treasonous and a punishable act. "Fortunately," Crapol interjected, "such high-handed and illegal proscriptions [to the First Amendment] were never carried out to stymie the anti-slavery movement," but the so-called "Williamsburg Resolution" illustrated the fervor with which Tyler viewed the abolitionist threat. Crapol also believed it "reflected his moral anxiety about slavery."[18] At the same time, Calhoun in the Senate and fellow South Carolinian James Hammond in the House sponsored legislation to quiet the Northern abolitionists by denying them the right to petition Congress, an undemocratic idea that bothered Tyler and one he predicted would be "counterproductive" by ceding "the moral and constitutional high ground."[19]

But before he could vote against the legislation, Tyler resigned from the Senate because he refused to go along with instructions from the Virginia legislature to vote for the censure of Jackson over the president's withholding of documents related to his defunding of the Second Bank of the United States. That was something the Whig-controlled and business-oriented Congress was much opposed to, but something Jackson's populist supporters could easily rally around. In fact, the legislature's public condemnation of the popular president helped his Democratic Party take over the congressional halls in the midterm elections of 1834.[20]

Tyler was proven right about both. In addition to censure hurting the Whig Party a lot more than it hurt Jackson, Calhoun's so-called "gag rule" made martyrs of the abolitionists in the North and further stimulated Northern feelings against slavery.[21] Unlike two of his closest friends and advisers, Professor Beverly Tucker of William & Mary and Judge Abel Upshur, what worried Tyler most about the increasing anti-slavery sentiment was Southern outrage and calls to dissolve the Union because of it.[22] Tucker actually forecast the creation of a separate Southern confederacy (17 years before it happened) in a novel he wrote, while Upshur, Tyler's future secretary of the Navy (and later secretary of state), became "an ardent defender of the South's system of human bondage," calling it "essential to White freedom" and a guarantee of "republican equality" for all White men. Upshur's was a "master race" mentality that blurred class lines and appealed to non-slaveholders in the South as well as the Southern "slaveocracy." Tyler sided with Upshur over the more radical Tucker. That was the safer of two paths for a Southern politician with any national aspirations in the mid–1830s.[23]

Although still a committed Unionist and devout believer in the nation's continental destiny, Tyler knew the need to "exorcise the spirit of sectional feeling" and even said so at a patriotic gathering in Yorktown, Virginia, in October 1837. At the same time, he seemed unable to understand contradictions in some of his ideological stances. Crapol noted that despite Tyler's global mission for America, he held firm to the Jeffersonian ideal of limited government, especially at the federal level. His biographer also brought out Tyler's fleeting support for the idea of foreign colonization of America's African Americans, possibly as a follow-up to his diffusion advocacy. The Abolitionist Movement's disdain for the possible annexation of Texas also angered Tyler, especially when the Northerners so anxious about the possibility of Texas being carved into several slave-holding states (with representation in Congress for each), were the same people advocating for recognition of the Black Republic of Haiti in the Caribbean (1838–1839). Evidently, to him and most Southern slaveholders, recognizing a nation of free Blacks so close to home was somehow dangerous to their own way of life.[24]

Such realities, however, actually hid what Crapol termed the Tyler family's "moral aversion to the buying and selling of human beings," which was illustrated by his father's 1787 vote against the Constitution "because of the clause that allowed for the continuation of the slave trade for twenty years," and the younger Tyler's introduction of a new legal code five decades later seeking at least to abolish the unseemly slave trade in the nation's capital. Yes, such legislation by a slave-owning Southerner was another contradiction and placed him in agreement with many of his abolitionist-leaning, Northern congressional colleagues whom he castigated when they expressed such views. But again, those kinds of contradictions were necessary to Crapol's altering perceptions of Tyler as president.[25]

Tyler's biographer also addressed the story of Henry Clay's absolute animosity toward the idea of being passed over as the Whig Party's presidential candidate in 1840 in favor of Harrison. One of the men who most wanted to be president in American history but never was, Clay was frustrated by Harrison's selection to the point of "a drunken rampage." He was only placated when Tyler, one the Virginia delegates for Clay, received the vice presidential nomination. Although thought of as an odd choice at the time, Tyler's selection was entirely for Southern votes. However, it was still strange because of Tyler's background as a Democrat—an allegiance he maintained until his forebodings about President Jackson's abuse of power in the early 1830s and Van Buren's delaying tactics on Texas annexation later on.[26] Also, as an ongoing proponent of states' rights, he famously opposed Jackson's patronage actions during the Nullification Crisis, which contributed to his alliance with the Whigs as the 1840 election approached and more specifically with Clay. As a result, he was the Southerner deemed most appropriate to Whig hopes of undercutting Van Buren in the South and denying his re-election bid. "Brilliant! Virginian John Tyler has been put on the Whig ticket to wean the Jackson forces from the ranks of democracy," was one contemporary's example of the hopefulness with which Whigs chose to view their unexpected VP choice.[27]

Indeed, the Harrison-Tyler ticket proved very successful. Tippecanoe and Tyler too was not just the first presidential campaign slogan but remains probably the most famous in American history.[28] Crapol's first chapter even opened with the death of "Old Tippecanoe," who was also known as "Jefferson's Hammer" for his success in dealing with the Indian tribes west of the Appalachian Mountains, including his 1811 victory over the Shawnees at the Battle of Tippecanoe. Tyler appeared temporarily shocked by the news he received via messenger on April 4, 1841, at his Virginia home. Feigning surprise, in fact, may have been his way of approximating remorse, because Crapol reported he had been forewarned about the gravity of Harrison's pneumonia and was "not unprepared" for his 68-year-old predecessor's passing just a month into their administration.[29]

Tyler did not rush to Washington upon learning of Harrison's death, but he did get himself emotionally prepared before returning to the capital. He had obviously considered the constitutional consequences he would encounter upon the death of a sitting president for the first time in American history, and he was ready for the moment. The Constitution did not clearly specify the course to be followed upon a president's death in office. So by being the first vice president in that situation and immediately assuming full presidential power, Tyler created a legacy for the nation and himself, setting policy where only nebulous assumptions had existed. He established direct accidental ascension to the White House by taking control of an original circumstance, putting his stamp on it in a precedent-setting, history-making way. Crapol confirmed as much when he wrote:

> Although Tyler prided himself on being a strict constructionist, in this instance he opted for a loose interpretation of the language of the Constitution and decided that the vice president, in fact, became the president outright. By decisive action and adroit political maneuvering during his first weeks in office, Tyler forever made moot any future constitutional objections and established by usage the precedent for the vice president to become president on the death of an incumbent.[30]

After calmly informing his family of his succession plans, Tyler proceeded to Washington, completing the 230-mile journey in 21 hours. Once there, he executed what has been described as master strategy to win unqualified acceptance. While numerous members of Congress would have preferred an acting or interim presidential title for the assertive Virginian, Tyler was determined to assume all the powers and privileges of the presidency immediately.[31] Never once did he permit discussion of the idea of a special election to choose another president. He also rejected such possibilities as the Cabinet performing executive functions by a majority vote, holding firm to the premise that Cabinet members could never be co-equals to the president. They were welcome to remain in the Cabinet, but only with the understanding, according to Crapol, "that he alone bore responsibility for his [new] administration." Such unexpected decisiveness must have awed potential dissenters, because Harrison's entire Cabinet remained on board for the time being.[32]

Next in Tyler's well-orchestrated plan, he took the presidential oath of office even though he believed his VP swearing-in ceremony a month earlier had been constitutionally sufficient to ensure his lawful and automatic ascendance following a presidential death in office. He took his new oath April 6 with the Cabinet present and gave an inaugural address to further buttress his legitimacy. Crapol stated, "In a somber and forthright manner the new chief executive informed Congress and the American people that for the first time in the nation's history, an individual elected as vice president 'has had devolved upon him the presidential office.'" Leaving no doubt, Tyler "had assumed the mantle and accompanying powers" as the nation's founders intended.

After honoring the memory of Harrison, the Senate and House both passed resolutions acknowledging Tyler as president. His plan had worked to perfection. With a smooth transfer of power and no contested controversy, he had made history. "If for nothing else, John Tyler's place in history was secure as the author of the precedent that established vice presidential succession to the presidency," Crapol (and others) would maintain. He had been calm and collected, yet aggressive and unswerving in his approach to ensuring what would become known as the "Tyler Precedent"—a precedent that would be reaffirmed in less than a decade.[33]

As president, Tyler would move away from a purely Whig Party agenda, clashing repeatedly with Clay and ultimately severing ties with most of the Whig leadership.[34] Instead, with his Southern states' rights roots rising to the surface, he would consistently draw the ire of Northern Whigs who had only accepted his VP status to oust Van Buren and the Democrats.[35] He replaced their agenda with expansionist designs on Texas and the Pacific. In addition, he actively went against the grain of anti-slavery sentiment by attempting to defend the Southern institution abroad through the appointment of pro-slavery diplomats, while at the same time strengthening the U.S. Navy. Like many Southerners, he worried about the possibility of slave insurrection and allowed his bias of anything British to influence suspicions that the Brits might inspire slave uprisings. He also believed a stronger Navy could help limit the chances for such insurrection by making the nation's coasts more secure against foreign interventionists.[36]

On the other hand, the old bugaboo of rationalizing Black emancipation and racial equality as detrimental to all Whites, something commonplace among White Americans of that era (North and South), played a constant role in the policies and politics of John Tyler. No better illustration was the presence of the neighboring nations on a nearby Caribbean island, Haiti and the Dominican Republic, one Black and the other predominantly White. Both sought U.S. recognition while Tyler was president, but the mere existence of Haiti as an independent nation of Blacks was, in his mind, a threat to the South's slaveocracy. Not only did Southern-born leaders like Tyler and Calhoun prefer not to recognize Haiti, they even plotted its overthrow because of the perceived threat it posed to the Southern way of life. This diplomatic chicanery, which included withholding information from Congress, and his commitment to the defense of slavery would tarnish Tyler's image, but also expand presidential power. There can be no doubt, according to Crapol, that Tyler enlarged the power of the presidency on behalf of the slaveholding interests of his day.[37]

One such episode involved a diplomatic dispute between the United States and Great Britain, when a Canadian official who had helped British forces destroy an American ship on the Niagara River years earlier, an act of piracy (the 1837 *Caroline* affair) which led to the death of a U.S. citizen, was ultimately arrested in New York and was expected to be executed there—potentially precipitating yet another war with the British. To keep such talk from escalating, Tyler threatened to put the British ambassador under house arrest, denying his passport and detaining him in the United States, a strong-arm tactic to say the least. In so doing, Tyler was actually buying time until federal statutes could be put in place to supersede state statutes in the case. In what turned out to be a case of role reversal, President Tyler, normally a states' rights advocate, was pitted against New York Governor William Seward, normally a federalist. Luckily, when the New York court acquitted the alleged Canadian perpetrator, the confrontation was defused. As a result of Tyler's actions, however, Congress did enact the Remedial Justice Act of 1842, asserting federal authority over all such cases involving foreign nations in the future.[38]

At the same time, with Great Britain strengthening its naval bases in the Caribbean as well as Canada, and American provocateurs agitating Congress for a Canadian takeover, Secretary of State Daniel Webster (the only Cabinet member who remained with Tyler during his break with the Whigs) authorized some effective propaganda in the relatively new state of Maine, convincing early residents there to end a boundary dispute with Canada that was settled via the Webster-Ashburton Treaty of 1842. In all these dealings with the British Empire, the Tyler administration was what Crapol termed "gutsy and audacious," exhibiting attributes of "assertive" statesmanship and a willingness to take risks (including espionage) in the pursuit of diplomatic goals.[39]

While Tyler was known for his refined manners, he obviously had a behind-the-scenes persona historians missed—even when faced with one British provocation that challenged his Southern roots. It actually occurred before the signing of the Webster-Ashburton Treaty (named for Webster and Lord Baring Ashburton, Britain's primary negotiator), when a slave revolt aboard the *Creole*, a ship involved in interstate slave trade, took place on November 7, 1841. Nineteen of the 135 slaves on board mutinied and took control of the ship under the leadership of Madison Washington, a Virginia-born slave ironically named for two of the nation's "founding fathers."[40] Acting in what Crapol quipped was "the spirit of his namesakes," he ordered the ship's captain to set a course for the British colony at Nassau in the Bahamas, where slavery had been abolished in 1833 and where the *Creole* cargo was indeed set free.

Naturally, such liberation drew praise from abolitionists on both sides of the Atlantic, but stung the Southern-born U.S. president, especially with Southern outrage over the loss of property and two lives, including a slave owner who had been on board. Already in the midst of the treaty negotiations, relations between the two countries became strained for a time, and Tyler was awkwardly caught in the middle. Naturally, he came under intense pressure from fellow slaveholders to defend national honor, to return the *Creole* slaves to their rightful owners, and to imprison the 19 slaves guilty of mutiny and murder. Despite his concerted efforts to defuse the situation, including a strongly worded protest to the British government, complaints continued and frustrated the president.

Needless to say, it was a major dilemma for Tyler, who recognized the sweeping criticism and dissatisfaction caused by his apparent inability to uphold American honor. As a result, he was increasingly argumentative during the Webster-Ashburton negotiations. The

Creole incident exposed his Southern roots, and the British doubted ever getting the treaty done.

While the treaty negotiations went on during the long, hot summer of 1842, Tyler also had to face increasing animosity within his own party—or at least the party that had put him in the White House. John Minor Botts, a fellow Virginian, Whig, and Clay backer, was one of the legislators outraged by Tyler's vetoes and dismissal of Whig doctrines, including two national bank bills. In retaliation, he became the first member of the House of Representatives ever to broach the subject of presidential impeachment on the now-recognized constitutional grounds of "high crimes and misdemeanors." Although insulted by the charges, Tyler attributed them to "madcaps" and ignored the impeachment talk.[41] What he could not ignore, however, was the tension between the Whigs and himself over tariffs. Despite a career-long belief in free trade and minimal duties, and his previous vetoes, Tyler did compromise for the first and only time by signing a highly protective tariff in 1842, something historians have struggled to explain ever since.[42]

Regardless, Whig animosity, and specifically the charge that Tyler had withheld information from Congress related to the British treaty negotiations by claiming executive privilege, did not dissipate. Executive privilege, however, had never before been viewed as an impeachable offense despite its assertion numerous times by previous presidents, including Jefferson and Madison. Even more problematic for the president was his use of "executive agents"—undercover emissaries in Maine, whose work began shortly after Tyler became president in the spring of 1841. Apparently hatched by Francis O. J. Smith, a Maine politician, lawyer, newspaper publisher, and financier, it was a federally funded propaganda scheme designed to entice citizens of that state to accept compromise of the Canadian boundary dispute.

The trick was to get the Maine men to feel that the compromise had its origins among … the Maine men. Funded with Tyler's knowledge and blessing, Smith hired assistants, enlisted editors, lobbied civic, business, and government leaders, and generally converted the populace through a ten-month blitz of disinformation. Secretary of State Webster got involved as well, enlisting a well-known Harvard professor who had supposedly located an early, unknown map supporting the Canadian claims. Before the scam was finished, it had the complete support of Britain's Lord Ashburton, who conveniently feigned knowledge of the map and later admitted that without the border chicanery, the good citizens of Maine would have probably never agreed to the treaty.

Nevertheless, Crapol contended, "The Webster-Ashburton Treaty was a major diplomatic accomplishment and highlight of the Tyler presidency." It resolved and established a significant portion of the U.S. boundary with Canada. Also, eight years after Tyler left the White House, a settlement of the *Creole* controversy was finally reached with the Anglo-American Claims Commission awarding $110,330 to the Southern slave owners who lost slaves in the mutiny, vindicating American honor and the former president's restraint. Despite some opposition in the Senate, the treaty was ratified on August 20, 1842.[43]

Meanwhile, one other issue of interest to Americans and the British not included in the Webster-Ashburton Treaty was the Oregon question. It had been taken off the table until a later date, but with amicable feelings emerging from the successful treaty negotiations, the British almost immediately decided there would be no time like the present to revisit the issue of the Pacific Northwest. Tyler was at first receptive, but obviously had a change of heart when a short time later he threw the British a curveball, claiming that the entire Oregon region already belonged to the United States. By claiming Oregon in its totality, he seemed to undercut the existing Anglo-American joint occupation agreement, which had been in place since 1818.

Tyler, you see, was not ready to negotiate Oregon. Crapol suggested as much, indicating that the president actually stalled, going so far as to hatch a "tripartite scheme" that would have also involved Mexico and its unlikely relinquishing of Northern California (something he knew the Mexicans weren't willing to do) in order for America to gain sole dominion of the Oregon Country more easily at a later date. As anticipated, Tyler's proposed three-way negotiation was not something Great Britain was interested in, and the idea went nowhere—exactly where Tyler's biographer felt he wanted it to go.[44]

Texas annexation, however, became the focus and signature achievement of the Tyler administration despite starting out as a divisive point of contention between the president and his secretary of state. Although their combined efforts in securing the Webster-Ashburton Treaty had engendered mutual admiration between the two men, Webster had misgivings about Tyler and "his obsession with Texas." Tyler, on the other hand, believed the addition of Texas could earn him another term—party affiliation or not. As a result, he was not overly concerned when Webster resigned in May of 1843.[45] Despite Webster's disapproval of his Texas aspirations, Tyler's relationship with his former secretary would remain cordial. Theirs had been a working relationship of political expediency in foreign affairs, but Tyler felt much freer to pursue Texas once Webster was gone. The president, in fact, believed that his best hope of ensuring political success was to continue focusing on foreign affairs. Unlike domestic issues that more often than not required partisan support, diplomatic issues offered him freedom of action that might earn public acclaim. The opportunity for international diplomacy devoid of congressional oversight in pursuit of what he believed was the nation's westward destiny proved irresistible. Clay, his new-found political rival, hoped to render him isolated and irrelevant, but by betraying just a few of his normal policy beliefs, Tyler felt he could escape the political dead-end of party abandonment by the Whigs.[46]

Along with Texas, Oregon, and other expansionist ideas, Tyler was one of a select group of national leaders in the 1830s and 1840s who dreamed of far-flung American influence throughout the Pacific Rim. What made him and a few others different was their Southern heritage. Obviously, trade-conscious New Englanders and Northern manufacturers were always interested in opening new markets, but Southerners like the president and his secretary of the Navy, Abel Upshur, were equally interested in Asia, and particularly the Orient, when it came to global initiatives. For years, merchants and missionaries had been crossing the Pacific to places like Hawaii, the South Sea Islands, Japan, and China, and they returned with countless stories of opportunities on the other side of the world. Such continuous promotion inspired what Crapol characterized as "an enduring Pacific-mindedness."[47]

With an Opium War raging between imperialistic Great Britain and China, Secretary of State Webster, one of those trade-conscious New Englanders, got the idea of the United States serving as intermediary in the international economic conflict. Unlike Great Britain, the Chinese believed America was not interested in colonization and might deserve favored nation status. The United States, it was believed, ranked higher in Chinese confidence than any nation. Also, it was mistakenly assumed by China that U.S. merchants were not trafficking opium the way merchants from other countries were. We know that wasn't correct (for instance, Warren Delano, future President Franklin Delano Roosevelt's maternal grandfather, acquired a small fortune in the opium trade), but at the time, this belief gave America a leg up on gaining Chinese trust.

So despite other foreign priorities, including their treaty negotiations with Great Britain, Webster and Tyler both kept Pacific-based dreams in their diplomatic mix of possible pursuits. But while Tyler was as much responsible for economic aspirations in the Far East as his secretary of state, he was never given as much credit as "God-like Daniel," who along with Clay and Calhoun dominated American political thought for decades. Also, while involvement with China served as the ultimate goal of U.S. Pacific policy, it was the Hawaiian Islands that became the much more realistic goal of American policy makers. Making sure that European nations did not gain a foothold in Hawaii, as they had in so many other Pacific places, suddenly became a prerequisite of U.S. powerbrokers. That led to Hawaii becoming a U.S. territory and eventually our 50th state, but the story of how that all happened began with the Tyler administration, a little-known saga Crapol unveiled.[48]

With Tyler and Webster both promoting Americanization of Hawaii behind the scenes by what Crapol termed "a loosely-knit contingent of those same American missionaries and merchants," the U.S. began to gain influence over the Hawaiian ruling family. It started when American Protestant missionaries induced Hawaii's King Kamehameha III to issue an ordinance rejecting the Catholic Church throughout his kingdom. As a result, Catholic France reacted impulsively by sending one of its naval frigates to teach the insolent Hawaiian monarch and his intolerant contingent of anti–Catholic advisers a lesson. This the French did with a blockade of Honolulu's harbor and a threat to bombard the city. That forced the little island kingdom to back down by re-legitimizing all Catholics living there as well as granting special tariff concessions to France. Naturally, the Americans in residence took offense and interpreted the French aggression as preliminary to seeking outright possession of Hawaii.

Word of this perceived French threat was passed along through appropriate channels to the U.S. State Department, and when the more Pacific-friendly Tyler administration came on board, it was followed up by emissaries from the islands meeting with both the president and secretary of state. Making their argument on political and commercial grounds, these emissaries sold Tyler and Webster on the importance of recognizing Hawaiian independence in order to avoid further Europeanization of the Pacific. At the same time, King Kamehameha commenced his own initiative, lobbying the U.S. government for diplomatic recognition as the only global power that might be receptive to Hawaii's claim of national legitimacy.

Finally, after ignoring repeated entreaties for recognition of Hawaiian sovereignty, two American entrepreneurs, Henry A. Pierce and Peter Brinsmade, made a dent in the Tyler-Webster mindset, which had previously been to stay out of any entanglement with European powers, preaching instead the commercial necessity of a West Coast state—eventually California—and the equal need for a close, complementary Pacific trading partner like an independent Hawaii could be. With visions of Pacific Ocean ports dancing in his head, Tyler was at heart as much interested in a free California as a slave Texas.

As a result, upon receiving a proposed treaty of peace, trade, and recognition from the King, which had been developed not only by Hawaiians but also the American merchants and missionaries, the veneer of administration indifference finally began to crack. Reputedly, this change was due in part to the interest of a former president and New England mainstay, John Quincy Adams—by then a re-elected Massachusetts congressman. To some extent, the same racist sentiment that had motivated the anti–Haiti debate in the House was just as prevalent in discussions of Hawaiian recognition, especially with Hawaii having its own self-governing, dark-skinned people. Adams recognized as much, encouraging the King's diplomats not to give up in their persistence with the Tyler administration until they got the answer they were seeking.

Ultimately, it took the threat of Hawaii becoming a British protectorate to convince

Tyler to abandon his policy of procrastination. It was a stunning reversal, but it prevented British protection of the Hawaiian Islands and ensured the continuation of America's economic and political influence there, and it was issued despite the fact that a Southern-born, slave-owning president would be recognizing the government of a kingdom made up of people of color. As such, Tyler's very supportive biographer observed, "If securing the nation's political and strategic agenda in the Pacific Ocean demanded the unusual, the ever Pacific-minded president was happy to oblige." But as Crapol also confirmed, Tyler would never have extended Haiti the same recognition for obvious reasons—too close, too Black, and not as important.[49]

As a result, Hawaii got its letter of recognition from the U.S., but not a treaty. Webster indicated that it would have been asking too much all at once. Afterwards, Tyler sent a special message to Congress announcing his new Hawaiian policy, which has been termed the "Tyler Doctrine," and by extension, plans for the United States' first official diplomatic mission to China. It was all done in the best interests of the nation's commerce. In so doing, Tyler extended the 1823 Monroe Doctrine and its oversight of the Western Hemisphere all the way to the Central Pacific. It also set in motion events and precedents that led to the U.S. annexation of Hawaii half a century later and the creation of an open-door policy with China at the turn of the century.[50]

Along with the Webster-Ashburton Treaty, it would prove another diplomatic coup for our first accidental president. Even some of Tyler's most bitter political foes were forced to give him credit for his Pacific policy. At the same time, it aroused Great Britain, which questioned American intentions to the point that when a British seafaring captain sought restitution for his government from the Hawaiian monarchy, again threatening bombardment of Honolulu, Kamehameha kowtowed once more in the face of European threats by ceding his islands to the British in February 1843. As unpopular as it was, the Union Jack was hoisted up flagpoles throughout Hawaii, and further expansion of the British Empire threatened to become permanent. It was high-handed international aggression and portended a recurring American nightmare—one in which Britain always seemed to be involved.

Tyler, through his new acting secretary of state, South Carolinian Hugh Legare (Webster had resigned a week earlier), immediately sought to address this disturbing turn of events. The British had already occupied New Zealand in the Southern Pacific, so this aggressive action seemed yet another attempt to empire-build, with a string of oceanic bases circling the globe. The Charleston-born Legare was just as Pacific-minded as his new boss and predecessor. Shortly after sending a dispatch of protest to the U.S. ambassador in London, however, Legare unexpectedly died. Soon thereafter, Great Britain apparently thought better of its aggressive sea captain's actions and officially recognized Hawaiian independence, much to the relief of the Hawaiians ... and the Americans. Still suspicious of anything British and their actual intent, however, Tyler urged caution in assuming that the interlude was over. True to its word, however, Britain never again threatened Hawaiian sovereignty.[51] Unbelievably, Upshur, who followed Legare (who followed Webster) as secretary of state, was one of those tragically killed in the explosion aboard the *Princeton* that February of 1844. Upshur was replaced by Calhoun, giving Tyler four secretaries of state in four years (all of whom made significant contributions to his administration).[52]

Among the other fatalities on the *Princeton* was David Gardiner, the father of a young Washington woman who had captured the president's attention following the death of his first wife in 1842, just 17 months into his presidency. It was even reported that Ms. Gardiner fainted into his arms upon learning of the tragic demise of her father that day on the

Potomac River. Julia Gardiner, age 24 and exactly 30 years Tyler's junior, would, in fact, become his second wife two years later, marking the first time a sitting president wed while in office. Viewed rather scandalously at the time because of the age difference, at least one Pulitzer-winning historian of the 1950s took time to profile this late addition to the Tyler White House as follows:

> Among the gay young belles of the capital in the winter of 1844 was a girl named Julia Gardiner. She was tall with a full figure and the bearing of Greek statue. Grecian, too, were the classic lines of her nose and mouth, and the poise of her oval-shaped head crowned with a load of dark braids. But she was not a statue. She was radiantly alive although she certainly never dreamed that she herself would become the First Lady of the United States. Her preference for older men, however, was marked, her interest piqued by the incorrigible bachelor James Buchanan [a Pennsylvania senator and future president] and potent charms of the aging Henry Clay, but it was always the widower President Tyler himself, with his high-toned nature and graceful bearing, who won her warmest school-girl admiration.

They were married on June 26, 1844, and along with the seven surviving children of his first marriage, she would bear him seven more, making him (still) the president with the most children in U.S. history.[53]

Meanwhile, Tyler established his belief in America's need for more foreign markets at least two years before his second marriage. He recognized a U.S. surplus of grains, tobacco, and cotton goods—the kind of goods Asia would be interested in and in return would offer equally enticing goods to Americans. As a result, the president's call for a mission to China was greeted with optimism by still-developing American businesses, manufacturing, and even its agricultural communities. Caleb Cushing, a longtime Tyler political ally, agreed to be his envoy, and with Congress out of session, the president got to appoint him without congressional approval. The goals of Cushing's mission: to ensure American merchants' access to four Chinese ports-of-call and to convey to the Chinese people a goodwill message, hopefully establishing friendly relations between the two countries for the foreseeable future.

Following several banquets and dinners to kick off the mission, Cushing left with a fleet of four ships from Hampton Roads, Virginia. All along the way, Cushing sought input from other nations he visited, coming to the conclusion that the U.S. should ask for additional territorial rights for its citizens in China in compliance with prevailing norms. Once his flotilla arrived, however, Cushing had to wait several months before beginning negotiations, as the Chinese, who had been

Julia Gardiner, pictured here ca. 1846–1848, the second wife of President John Tyler, was 30 years his junior when she became in 1844 the first of only three women to marry a sitting U.S. president (Library of Congress Prints and Photographs Division—Reproduction Number USZ62-25781).

humiliated by Great Britain in the Opium War, counted on delay to avoid giving away too much to another Western power. Finally, Cushing's patience was rewarded with the Treaty of Wanghia, which gained trading privileges and extra territorial rights for Americans doing business with or residing in China.[54]

The Treaty of Wanghia arrived back in Washington to great fanfare and more foreign policy accolades for Tyler. It established favored nation status with a much-desired trading partner that only Great Britain had previously. The Senate gave speedy approval to the treaty, ratifying it unanimously in January 1845, just two months before Tyler would leave the White House, and from 1845 to 1860, American trade with China more than doubled. In other words, it proved to be visionary foreign policy that later presidents would endorse as a continuation of the Tyler Doctrine and an important development in U.S. global influence.[55]

It would not, however, be the most remembered accomplishment of Tyler's last year in office nor of his administration as a whole. That distinction will always remain Texas. According to Crapol, Tyler "had his eye on the prize of Texas from the moment he entered the White House" and indicated his hope to annex the independent Lone Star Republic just months after succeeding Harrison. Tyler was determined to add Texas' annexation to his legacy after years of American debate and incessant Texan entreaties for statehood.[56]

Previously, the 1819 Adams-Onix Treaty between the U.S. and Spain made Florida American property and denied potential American claims to Texas.[57] That long-ago detail, however, did not end America's expansionist aspirations or the pleas of Texas not to let such things stand in the way. After all, the territorial equation had changed. Mexico gained its independence from Spain in the 1820s, and Texas along with it. Mexico's claim to the province west of the Sabine River and north of the Rio Grande, in fact, went unchallenged and in place until the Texans themselves revolted in 1836, setting up their own, hard-won republic with the same, slaveholding economic system as the American South, where most of Texas' non–Hispanic settlers migrated from.[58]

Immediately after Sam Houston led the Texans to victory in the revolution's decisive victory over the Mexicans at the Battle of San Jacinto, the Lone Star leadership and people made it known that they desired U.S. statehood. But Houston's friend and fellow Tennessee native, Andrew Jackson, did not wish to create either trouble with Mexico or a campaign stumbling block for Martin Van Buren, his vice president and designated successor in the upcoming presidential election of 1836. As a result, President Jackson ignored Houston's repeated approaches, but did grant diplomatic recognition to Texas immediately after Van Buren's victory. As a New Yorker, however, Van Buren was also fearful of Northern, anti-slavery backlash should he consider annexation once installed in the White House, so he too put off the issue, causing Houston and his frustrated Texans to withdraw their request by October 1838.[59]

That's where Texas stood until Tyler entered the White House less than three years later. Unlike his predecessors, Tyler never viewed the slavery debate as a reason to squelch American expansion and its continental destiny. To the contrary, he felt that another slave state would merely continue the ongoing national balance of slave and free states, eventually working itself out naturally all the way to the Pacific. Tyler was determined to act where Jackson and Van Buren had dithered, despite obvious disagreement with some in his administration over the Texas question—notably Webster. He knew his annexation goal would not come easily.[60]

Indeed, the first controversy raised over Texas after Tyler became president was actually created by one of his allies in the House of Representatives, Henry Wise of Virginia, who let anti-slavery congressmen coax him into a defense of the president for sending a new minister to Mexico to better assess the Mexican government's view of the situation. To the anti-slavery coalition in Congress, this seemed an obvious ploy by the administration to induce Texas annexation. In so aggressively coming to Tyler's defense, Wise seemed to confirm that assumption. His response, in fact, necessitated damage control by the administration and suspension of any further Texas consideration until 1843. Instead, the previously discussed Canadian boundary dispute was given total diplomatic precedence.

Not wishing to arouse public opinion, Tyler chose discretion over valor when it came to Texas. He waited until January 1843 to initiate the next part of what Crapol judged a more "patented script," which outlined the national benefits that would result from annexation. Making his case through yet another Virginian, then–Congressman Thomas Gilmer, Tyler emphasized that Texas would provide an additional market for Northern manufacturers. Also, he challenged what he considered the misguided objections of non-slaveholders. He insisted that all citizens needed to focus on the added wealth and prosperity to be gained and the increased strength it would provide the nation as a whole.[61]

Gilmer also warned Americans of British imperialism, always lurking below the surface. In other words, to ignore the destiny of Texas annexation could lead to British incur-

ANTI-TEXAS MEETING

AT FANEUIL HALL!

Friends of Freedom!

A proposition has been made, and will soon come up for consideration in the United States Senate, to annex Texas to the Union. This territory has been wrested from Mexico by violence and fraud. Such is the character of the leaders in this enterprise that the country has been aptly termed "that valley of rascals." It is large enough to make *nine* or *ten* States as large as Massachusetts. It was, under Mexico, a free territory. The freebooters have made it a slave territory. The design is to annex it, with its load of infamy and oppression, to the Union. The immediate result may be a war with Mexico—the ultimate result *will be* some 18 or 20 more slaveholders in the Senate of the United States, a still larger number in the House of Representatives, and the balance of power in the hands of the South! And if, when in a minority in Congress, slaveholders browbeat the North, demand the passage of gag laws, trample on the Right of Petition, and threaten, in defiance of the General Government, to hang every man, caught at the South, who dares to speak against their "domestic institutions," what limits shall be set to their intolerant demands and high handed usurpations, when they are in the majority?

All opposed to this scheme, of whatever sect or party, are invited to attend the meeting at the Old Cradle of Liberty, to-morrow, (Thursday Jan. 25,)at 10 o'clock, A. M., at which time addresses are expected from several able speakers.

Bostonians! Friends of Freedom!! Let your voices be heard in loud remonstrance against this scheme, fraught with such ruin to yourselves and such infamy to your country.

January 24, 1838.

Anti-Texas meetings like the one advertised by this Boston posting were just one example of the predominantly Northern efforts used to counter President John Tyler as he strove to bring the Lone Star State into the Union (Library of Congress Prints and Photographs Division—Reproduction Number USZ62-57792).

sion back into North American affairs. It had obviously happened before and could happen again so long as political voids provided incentive for further empire expansion.[62]

Webster's resignation from the Cabinet aided Tyler's annexation desires by removing a source of contention. The Whig icon had served the administration well up to that point, but his usefulness was past. Tyler had essentially been cast out of the Whig Party, so his independent mindset on Texas was not surprising. Single-mindedly, in fact, Tyler bought into the Texas issue as the only means by which he might secure four more years. He was a president without a party, and he knew it.[63]

At the same time, his critics underestimated him constantly. According to Crapol, he surprised adversaries, proving to be a tough, strong-willed politician, with the use of patronage becoming one of his primary weapons as he sought to marshal support for his own re-election. After criticizing Jackson and Van Buren for doing the same thing, he began to replace officeholders for political gain—attempting to manufacture a third party. Unquestioning loyalty to the administration and support for Texas annexation were prerequisites for any new appointees, and over several months he purged and replaced more than 100 federal officeholders. But it was too late. As a lame duck Whig, he went too far in trying to fashion another constituency for himself, and his image suffered further as a result.[64]

After Legare's death and replacement by Upshur in late 1843, Texas annexation was fast-tracked. Not surprisingly, Upshur, a states' rights proponent like Tyler, immediately sought the advice of Calhoun, who followed him as secretary of state upon Upshur's tragic death. The threat of British intrusion on America's Texas ambitions was of paramount importance for Calhoun and other pro-slavery proponents, who anticipated an Anglo-American, anti-slavery conspiracy. To meet this perceived threat, Upshur initiated secret treaty negotiations in Washington with Republic of Texas Ambassador Isaac Van Zandt.[65]

Texans remained concerned they might be left-at-the-altar by the capricious Americans, so Sam Houston's government asked for U.S. guarantees, including protection from the possibility of a retaliatory Mexican attack. From a constitutional standpoint, granting such a thing had to give Tyler and Upshur pause, and despite reservations by many in the administration about the legalities of their quest, Upshur stuck doggedly to his goal of wooing a two-thirds majority in the Senate while at the same time convincing Houston of their sincerity to ensure his trust. The bottom line: finding enough Northern senators willing to put aside their anti-slavery reservations and cast their lot with the administration, which Upshur cleverly accomplished by linking settlement of the Oregon dispute with Texas annexation. It was a scheme later adopted by James K. Polk, the surprising Tennessean who emerged as the Democratic nominee for president in 1844 despite being twice defeated for governor of his home state.[66]

Before it ever got to that, however, Upshur had to become what Crapol labeled "the juggler, constantly seeking to maintain political balance," which included intrigue over British intentions and as much secrecy as possible, given the looming threat of war with Mexico. Even that threat, however, did not deter the Tyler-Upshur team. From the get-go, they treated Texas as a sovereign nation able to treat for itself.

Throughout his negotiations, Upshur walked a fine line of denial and evasiveness on the subject of Texas. For his part, Tyler did his best not to compromise the ongoing talks. Even in speeches, like his 1843 annual address to Congress, he intentionally maintained silence on the subject, making no mention of the ongoing talks. Together they understood that secrecy was the only way to keep the previously frustrated Texans at the negotiating table. They also refused to be intimidated by Mexican threats of impending war. The time had come for Mexico to let go of its former northern province, which had fought for and won its independence eight years earlier.[67]

Tyler was playing a high-stakes game. The strict constructionist from Tidewater Virginia was taking risks most Americans would never have anticipated. Out of public view, he was risking war with Mexico and not informing Congress of the military assurances he had made to Texas should the Mexicans attack. Keeping his eye on the ultimate prize, he remained focused as Upshur neared a final agreement with the Texans, and he seemed to have the necessary votes in the Senate. He obviously held to the belief that Texas would be the coup that re-established his re-election prospects, party or no party.

While Tyler believed that Texas would help make the entire South and its way of life secure, he was even more confident it would be an economic boon to all Americans and a landmark addition on the U.S. path to greatness. Opponents such as Clay were incredulous when they learned that Tyler apparently had a treaty and might have the votes to make it happen. Others with investments in Texas, North and South, began to take up the call for annexation. When concerns mounted that Texas would add too much land all at once, proponents reminded the country of the Louisiana Purchase in 1803 and how well that gigantic acquisition had worked out. When old complaints of slavery expansion and Black proliferation resurfaced, those same proponents argued that Texas would actually wean African American population away from the Upper South and in that way lessen the issue.[68]

On February 27, 1844, Secretary Upshur finally concluded his intricate negotiations for U.S. annexation of the Lone Star Republic as a U.S. territory. Citizens of Texas were to be granted full rights and privileges as Americans, including the right to own slaves, which was discreetly covered as "the preservation of property." To avoid controversy in the ratification process, slavery was not specifically mentioned. Texas public lands would become U.S. property, and the United States would assume Texas' public debt.

Unfortunately, on the day he got final approval of the agreement from Texas, Upshur also accepted an invitation to cruise the Potomac with the president and other special guests on the ill-fated *Princeton*. The secretary and six others (including the president's future father-in-law) were killed when the demonstration of the ship's latest armament went horribly wrong.[69] In the blink of an eye, Tyler was faced with the loss to himself and the country of the little-known public servant who had put his dreams of Texas within reach.

Although having declined two previous Tyler Cabinet offers, Calhoun, a former vice president and Cabinet member, seemed the natural choice to replace Upshur. At least that was the assumption of the impetuous Senator Wise, who again broached the subject with Calhoun before even checking with the president. The chance to finish the job of getting Texas into the Union, however, was a major motivation for the venerable South Carolinian (even at age 62), and he was quickly confirmed.[70]

Relieving Texan doubts resulting from Upshur's death and their sudden need to have assurances of U.S. military support in writing, Secretary Calhoun acted promptly and unequivocally to seal the deal. In April 1844, the formal treaty was officially signed. Almost immediately, a main body of the U.S. Army was moved to Fort Jessup on the Louisiana-Texas border, and a strong U.S. Navy presence was established in the Gulf of Mexico as a guard against possible Mexican retaliation. Also true to his word, Tyler sent both Houses of Congress a message recommending in the strongest terms that they act immediately to make Texas the 28th state in Union, utilizing the provision of the Constitution that gives Congress the authority to admit new states.[71]

Six months after the start of the secret negotiations, Tyler was thrilled finally to be on the verge of long-awaited rewards, and he framed the Texas question in a national way rather than the sectional one that had so often been used against it in the North. Upshur's death, however, threatened ratification. Hoping to placate recalcitrant senators, Tyler utilized the time-tested formula put forward by former president and constitutional framer James Madison—the idea that new states would always strengthen existing ones.

Nonetheless, in an obviously subversive move to damage the treaty's prospects, two abolitionist-leaning senators leaked its contents before ratification consideration and voting had occurred. The damage done, newspapers throughout the country fueled a national debate over whether the real objective of Texas was the preservation of slavery.[72] That was exactly the narrow, sectional view that Tyler had hoped to avoid, and treaty naysayers were further emboldened when a letter authored by new Secretary of State Calhoun, a man long recognized for his defense of the Southern way of life, was leaked. It had been sent to British Ambassador Sir Richard Pakenham. It included an audacious defense of the South's "peculiar institution." In no uncertain terms, Secretary of State Calhoun told Pakenham that Great Britain's intentions to abolish slavery throughout the world threatened the security of the United States. It also impugned British denials of reputed attempts they had made to aid the abolitionist cause. Calhoun asserted U.S. rights to annex Texas for defensive purposes as well as opposing the infiltration of abolitionism.[73]

Meanwhile, in what they obviously considered political expediency, the anticipated 1844 presidential candidates for the Whig and Democratic Parties, Henry Clay and Martin Van Buren, both came out against immediate annexation due to concerns it would provoke war with Mexico.[74] In the Senate, respected voices like Thomas Hart Benton of Missouri called the treaty a threat to the Union, all seeming to doom Tyler's carefully orchestrated crusade for Texas. According to Crapol, "Even members of the president's own Cabinet were split on the wisdom of his Texas machinations," and one Cabinet member resigned over what he considered Tyler's secret moves to align with and defend Texas before ratification had taken place.[75]

In response to all this negativity, Tyler again turned to his most loyal backers to sanction a different narrative. Many of the postmasters and other appointed officials throughout the country owed their jobs to the president. Instead of further illusions of a third-party re-election run, however, Tyler by this time hoped an organized political outcry would prompt Democrats to adopt a more expansionist platform than the one favored by Van Buren. Tyler wanted Texas, and once the Democrats rebuffed Van Buren in favor of James K. Polk, Tyler's wish came true. Indeed, while the Whigs settled on Clay for a third time and a platform that basically ignored Texas, the Democrats nominated an outspoken expansionist whose platform not only mirrored Tyler on Texas, but took expansion a step further, calling for immediate U.S. occupation of Oregon as well. It would be Kentucky's Clay versus Tennessee's Polk in the election of 1844, the "Old Coon" versus the "Young Hickory" (Polk entered the race with Jackson's blessing despite having ousted his previous Jacksonian standard bearer, Van Buren).[76]

Crapol contended that Polk's nomination was proof that Tyler's third-party ploy had worked. It caused the Democrats to realize their clearest path to regaining the White House, and another victory over Clay was with "a Texas man" who would pursue the Lone Star State regardless of what happened in the current ratification debate. Knowing his chances of re-election were by that time non-existent, Tyler orchestrated what he later claimed was "a great scheme" to ensure the continued consideration of Texas. He had anticipated initial rejection of the Texas treaty, which did occur on June 8. But unfazed, he also had a contingency plan up his sleeve—annexation by joint resolution, which he next pursued through the House of Representatives. His scheme accomplished and his objective realized with the candidacy of Polk, Tyler next officially withdrew from presidential consideration and threw his support behind the Democratic nominee, who, with his own desire for Texas, narrowly defeated Clay again.[77]

Polk's win was indeed cause for celebration at the White House. Tyler had effectively put Texas ahead of himself, and when Congress reconvened in December, America's outgoing chief executive made Polk's victory an electoral mandate for moving ahead on annexation. On February 28, 1845, exactly one year after Secretary Upshur's tragic death and just four days before Polk's inauguration, both houses of Congress passed a joint resolution by simple majority, which Tyler signed with Polk's blessing, setting the stage for Texas to enter the Union the following December. Tyler signed it just three days before he left office, March 1, 1845. The gold pen the president used to sign the Texas legislation into law he gave to his wife, and the second Mrs. Tyler would wear it triumphantly around her neck for the rest of her life. Such celebration ignored the fact that Tyler had perhaps compromised the Constitution to accomplish his preeminent presidential goal, and the constitutionality of the joint resolution has since always been questioned. Some historians still think Texas' entry into the Union should have occurred only via treaty. Despite recklessly courting war with Mexico, which did start the next year (1846), Tyler remained convinced he had done the right thing—and not just for the South ... for the nation.[78]

In retirement, Tyler would constantly seek reaffirmation of his Texas acquisition. As a more recognized Southern spokesman, Calhoun often claimed credit, much to Tyler's chagrin. In retaliation, the former president made known the entire scope of Secretary Upshur's efforts before his unfortunate death, thus negating and effectively silencing Calhoun. Tyler also waged another public relations war with Sam Houston, who did not like rumors left over from the annexation process that implicated Britain as a potential Texas partner during the negotiations so that the Texans might gain more advantageous terms. Tyler responded by taking even more credit for the entire process than ever before, further alienating Houston, who accused the former president of deceptive misdeeds throughout the negotiations, including constitutional ones—an unfortunate rebuttal by the iconic Texan that left them lasting adversaries in the high-stakes drama they had shared.[79]

At the same time, Tyler's place in history has been minimized by the fact that actual annexation did not take place until Polk was in the White House.[80] Apparently that was never an issue for Tyler, who saw his successor also pick up where he left off with Oregon. The two presidents remained on good terms even after the outbreak of hostilities with Mexico, the likelihood of which Tyler had dumped into his successor's lap. Almost certainly in full agreement, Polk would prove even more aggressive in his provocation of the Mexicans, including his stated intent to acquire California and New Mexico as well.[81]

While agreeing in principle with his successor's westward expansion goals, including Oregon, Tyler would always harbor the belief he could have done better and with less conflict if only granted a second term. He denounced the Wilmot Proviso four years later (1848), which was intended to stop the spread of slavery into any lands acquired during the Mexican War, as unnecessary considering slavery's natural, climate-driven limits. He considered it humiliating to slaveholders to exclude them from equal benefits of the expanding Union.[82]

For a time, Tyler remained a Southern voice for the importance of preserving the Union. By that, however, he meant a slave-holding Union—as it had been since its inception. An unrepentant slaveholder, he refused to contemplate universal emancipation—so much so, in fact, that by 1860, when Abraham Lincoln was elected on a platform of limiting slavery only to where it already existed and prohibiting it from the new territories, Tyler was ready to disavow his previous Unionist beliefs in support of Southern secession. This reversal by a former U.S. president earned him traitor status throughout the North. He never saw any moral inconsistency in believing the slave trade wrong but slavery okay.[83]

In retirement, he still owned between 60 and 90 slaves and was reputed to be a "benign master" who treated his African Americans "humanely." As Crapol admitted:

> Tyler took pride in his slaves and believed his treatment of them was compassionate and just. His conscience was clear. Tyler felt no obligation to manumit some or all of his slaves upon death, as his Virginia presidential predecessors Washington and Jefferson had done. Even his [White House] successor, James K. Polk, a hard-driving slave master and opportunistic proprietor of extensive cotton plantations, provided in his will for the emancipation of his slaves upon death.

Tyler's last will not only assigned the family's slaves to his 14 children, but undoubtedly assumed slavery would survive despite the ongoing buildup of sectional animosity and anti-slavery fervor. Less than a week after he signed that final will and testament, on October 10, 1859, John Brown raided Harpers Ferry, Virginia (now West Virginia), hoping to incite a slave rebellion, the eye-opening event that began a steady drumbeat to civil war less than two years later.[84]

That was also a turning point for Tyler in terms of his defense of the Union, one that he despaired over as he began to anticipate the breakup of the America he had led. Gradually he became committed to secession. To remain in the Union, he predicted, would necessitate eventually accepting African Americans as equal citizens, something Virginians (like most Southerners) were incapable of in 1861. On April 17, 1861, Virginia officially seceded. Nine months later, after also serving his state and new nation as head of the commission that negotiated Virginia's entrance into the Confederate States of America (as well as an elected representative to the first Confederate Congress), John Tyler, the tenth president of the United States, died as an enemy of the country he previously led.[85]

11

Fillmore and the Seeds
of Discontent

*"Mr. Fillmore was more amenable to the control of the leaders of Congress
and his party than the sturdy soldier whom he succeeded."*
—Woodrow Wilson, 1896

Paul Finkelman is a specialist in American legal history and constitutional law, so it was not surprising that his 2011 contribution to The American Presidents Series on Millard Fillmore lent a critical eye to our little-known 13th president, an accidental contributor to the final decade of discord before the Civil War. Although Fillmore is largely unknown today, with little attention paid to his role in America's sad drift to conflict in the 1850s, Finkelman unearthed evidence about Fillmore's 32 months as president to understand the treacherous course he put the country on at the start of that decade. At a time of mounting discord, this biographer revealed, Fillmore became a stubborn dis-unifier bent on short-sighted, immediate gains rather than the long-range vision needed from the White House in those years preliminary to war. His was the story of a nearly forgotten chief executive who missed the opportunity to be remembered much more.[1]

After all, Fillmore followed a very apolitical president who had risen to the nation's highest office purely by historic generalship. Zachary Taylor was another heroic military leader turned presidential nominee, much like George Washington, Andrew Jackson, and William Henry Harrison before him, and Ulysses Grant and Dwight Eisenhower later on. A battle-winning commander in the Mexican War who also had experience fighting the British and Indians, Taylor was the Whig Party's repeat formula for electoral success. Just as Harrison had won in 1840 primarily on the basis of his accomplishments against the Indians, so Taylor had triumphed over the Mexicans in places like Palo Alto, Resaca de la Palma, Monterey, and Buena Vista, earning an undefeated legend that prompted the Whig Party not to take no for an answer when his reluctant candidacy moved past the likes of Henry Clay and fellow general Winfield Scott in 1848. Ironically, again like Harrison, it was Taylor's vice president who would serve longer than he as chief executive after unexpected illness and death took his life just over a year into office. So the first two accidental presidents, John Tyler and Fillmore, would be inextricably linked in our nation's initial century before also leaving office as rejected incumbents.[2]

Gastroenteritis has remained the most accepted terminology for what brought on the death of the 65-year-old Taylor in July 1850. But regardless of the appropriate medical label, some kind of digestive malady thrust Fillmore, a little-known addition to the Whig ticket outside of New York despite three terms in his home state's assembly, four in Congress, and an unsuccessful run for governor (as well as a year as state controller), into the White House that July.[3]

Born on January 7, 1800, on a remote farm in Cayuga County, New York, near present-day Syracuse, Millard Fillmore was eventually apprenticed to learn the trade of cloth making and toiled in a textile mill for four years. At the age of 17, with only the most basic elementary school education, he became a rabid reader and enrolled in a local academy when the mill temporarily closed. While there, he met his future wife, a teacher at the school and two years his senior. Well-read and much more sophisticated, she inspired him to continue bettering himself, which he was fortunate enough to do as a law clerk for the local county judge. When the mill reopened, he used his law earnings to buy his way out of the apprenticeship and into his own freelance law practice. When that was deemed inappropriate because he was not a member of the New York Bar, he moved to Buffalo and taught school.[4]

A stylish dresser and highly intelligent, according to Finkelman, Fillmore usually made a good first impression. He was also able to resume his law preparation as a clerk when he impressed members of the local bar association so much that they helped him secure admission to their esteemed order at just 23 years of age. Rejecting offers to join existing law firms in Buffalo, however, he moved instead to the small, nearby village of East Aurora, where he became the only attorney in town—admitting years later that he initially lacked the self-confidence to practice in the more competitive big city. Possibly a reflection of his poor, rural youth and limited education, he would remain very deliberate and plagued by self-doubt, but against all odds he became a respected lawyer in Western New York.[5]

Finkelman pointed out how Fillmore's early life was similar to another future frontier president, Abraham Lincoln. Both were from poor, farm families and were largely self-educated before becoming successful attorneys in their respective parts of the country. But that's where the similarities ended, according to Finkelman, as Fillmore at least had supportive parents and a home he could always return to if need be, while Lincoln's mother died when he was very young, leaving him to struggle with an overbearing father who considered his desire for education a waste of time. Once Lincoln left home, he never looked back and turned into an aggressive self-starter, whereas Fillmore's approach was deemed more plodding and reactive. Also, while Lincoln jumped into the political arena even before he secured a steady income, Fillmore entered politics in unintended fashion. While Finkleman called Lincoln hungry for political advancement, he felt Fillmore could have easily remained happy as a lawyer and civic leader in his local area.[6]

Comparing them further, Fillmore's biographer noted that while Lincoln was a product of the frontier who never attempted to hide the backwoods from whence he came, Fillmore was constantly worried about appearances and whether his less-than-lofty beginnings might be held against him.[7] Unlike Lincoln, Fillmore also gravitated to what Finkelman labeled "oddball political movements, conspiracy theories, and ethnic hatred." One of those movements, in fact, launched his political career, the Anti-Masons of the 1820s. When that dissolved, he became a Whig, while also associating with anti–Catholic and anti-immigrant groups.[8]

Flashing back, Finkelman reconstructed Fillmore's professional life in East Aurora and the Buffalo area, where his fledgling law practice was initially propped up by his wife's teaching career. As noted, Fillmore entered politics for the first time with the emergence of the Anti-Masonic Party in 1827, a short-lived political movement designed to deny Andrew Jackson (one of our 14 chief executives who were Freemasons) the presidency. His involvement with that mostly Western New York cause would be the precursor of his later association with the anti-immigrant and anti–Catholic Know-Nothings of the 1850s. It seemed to his biographer that Fillmore always anticipated conspiracies, or at least hazards, to American society from what he considered outsiders—Catholics, immigrants, and even abolitionists—groups who jeopardized the status quo. A secret society like the Masons fit nicely into his perceived notions of a threat, obviously conflicting with his conservative, rural, and very Protestant roots. At the same time, he apparently was never outraged (or even overly concerned) by the existence of slavery.[9]

Attracted to the Anti-Masonic Movement, Fillmore rose rapidly in local political circles and was quickly designated a delegate to the 1828 National Republican Convention, the forerunner of the Whig Party. He found he enjoyed politics and soon ran for the State Assembly, being ushered into office in 1829 on the strength of a coalition ticket of National Republicans and Anti-Masons. It would be the first of three consecutive terms he would serve in Albany, the state capital and the place where he learned how legislatures work. He would put that knowledge to use by sponsoring legislation to abolish imprisonment for debt in New York. He even persuaded the state's Democratic majority to support his bill, convincing the Dems that putting people in jail eliminated their earning potential and ability to pay back creditors. According to Finkelman, Fillmore even withdrew his name from the bill's sponsorship, allowing Democrats to assume credit for its passage, a shrewd move and one of several he engineered to help spark the New York economy, earning him the reputation of a reform-minded business champion.[10]

By 1831, he had moved his residence back to Buffalo, having relinquished his chance for a fourth Assembly term in order to concentrate on his law practice as well as several civic and corporate boards. Buffalo, after all, was becoming a very prosperous city as the terminus of the Erie Canal with the Great Lakes, and the young lawyer was anxious to take advantage of the surging population and opportunities in one of the country's earliest commercial hubs.[11] By 1832, however, he had returned to politics and a seat in Congress, where he adopted the Whig Party as "a protégé" of Daniel Webster, the iconic senator and orator from Massachusetts, who sponsored Fillmore as a candidate for the bar of the Supreme Court. They even shared meals together as Webster took the fledgling congressman under his wing, a valuable connection for Fillmore that would last until just before Webster's death in 1852.[12]

Surprisingly, Fillmore did not seek re-election in 1834. He nonetheless stayed thoroughly engaged in New York Whig politics, even challenging rising star William Seward for ascendancy in the state party. In 1836, Seward lost in the race for governor before running again and winning in 1838 and 1840.[13] At the same time, Fillmore was returned to Congress in 1836, 1838, and 1840, where we was also runner-up for Speaker of the House while serving as chairman of the important Ways and Means Committee. In that role, he was able to halt a reduction of existing tariff rates and to guide them to increasingly protective levels before his congressional tenure was done, making him (once again) a hero to business and manufacturing interests, as well as to other Whigs.[14]

Taking another break, Fillmore decided not to run again in 1842, turning his attention instead to home state politics, where he clashed repeatedly with Seward.[15] According to Finkelman, "their differences were political, ideological, and personal." Seward was attempting to move New York into alignment with abolitionists, who were taking an increasingly aggressive stance against slavery. As governor, he refused to comply with fugitive slave restrictions, which occurred when Southern slave masters or their emissaries visited New York in search of runaways. By 1841, in fact, he went so far as to say that any slave brought across state lines into New York would be considered free, openly asserting that his state would not recognize any human beings as property.[16]

On the other hand, although Fillmore disliked slavery, he saw no reason to politicize the issue in a state without slaves, and he never displayed empathy for Southern slaves. Basically, he hoped the Whig Party could manage to avoid the slavery issue. If Southern slave-owners wished to travel to New York with a few slaves, he saw nothing wrong with that, especially if it maintained sectional harmony.[17] He also disagreed with Seward over Catholics and immigrants, objecting to the idea of parochial schools being entitled to state funds and steadfastly in favor of Protestant orthodoxy when it came to public education.[18]

It was during this off-and-on period of his political career that Fillmore surprisingly first sought the Whigs' vice presidential nomination in 1844. As an established defender of the tariff, he figured he could help the Whig ticket carry New York and neighboring Pennsylvania with all of their business and manufacturing interests. He also felt that his presence would balance a ticket again expected to feature Henry Clay of Kentucky for president, obviously hoping the seemingly ageless party spokesman's third nomination would prove his charm.[19]

Despite being a slaveholder, the 67-year-old Clay had been a key figure through three decades of legislative compromise on slavery and its potential expansion, including the Missouri Compromise of 1820, and he was definitely more moderate on the issue than his anticipated Democratic presidential opponent, James K. Polk of Tennessee. At the same time, Clay's character flaws had long been an issue, as his reputation for strong drink, gambling, and blasphemy was well known. Unlike Polk and most Southerners, Clay opposed the annexation of Texas, which was widely considered in the North as a Southern plot to increase the number of slave states.[20]

Plotting to become the Whigs' VP nominee in 1844, Fillmore based his hopes on "four prongs," according to his biographer. It was obvious that Clay would need to run with a well-positioned Northerner for ticket balance, and coming from the largest and most populous state in the Union, Fillmore was clearly that. Secondly, Fillmore had previously never taken a public position on slavery nor had anything to do with abolitionists, something he felt would work to his advantage when compared to Seward and other potential candidates. Also, he felt Southerners would accept him because he had never been openly anti-slavery. And finally, after three terms in the House as a party leader, supporter of the tariff, and someone committed to Whig programs, he believed most of his party rivals would ultimately accept him as well.[21] Unfortunately, his record and views were not well known outside of New York and the Northeast, and his belief that opponents would eventually rally around him was misguided. That was especially true of Seward, New York's governor at the time and a future presidential hopeful, who certainly did not wish to elevate a potential presidential rival from his own state.[22]

As a result, Finkelman confirmed, it was as much a mystery why Fillmore assumed he could be a vice presidential nominee in 1844 as it was when he actually became one four years later. All VPs prior to 1844 had held prominent offices before running for vice president, such as governor, senator, or Cabinet posts. Fillmore's career, by contrast, had been what his biographer described as "fundamentally insignificant," especially since he had never been elected to a statewide office.[23] At the Whig National Convention, he ran a distant third to Theodore Frelinghuysen, a former New Jersey senator dubbed the "Christian Statesman," who was acceptable to Southerners because he professed preserving the status quo on slavery. As a consolation prize, Fillmore did become the Whig candidate for governor of New York.[24]

The Whigs assumed Clay would crush Polk. They were wrong, having been ambushed by Texas annexation and the possibility of Oregon. Whereas Clay had been erratic on Manifest Destiny, Polk firmly believed and enunciated national expansion and the immense opportunities it could provide. Fifteen of the 26 states obviously agreed with the Tennessean, who was seen as a get-it-done protégé of Andrew Jackson.[25] As for slavery, most people saw no difference between the Democratic ticket (Polk) and the Whig ticket (Clay), with both being slaveholders. Ironically, Clay could have captured the election if he had only added New York to his electoral column, a fact that had to make him at least wonder what might have been if he had partnered with the Western New Yorker instead of the Christian Statesman.[26]

Meanwhile, Fillmore lost the governor's race to Democrat Silas Wright by just over 10,000 votes, as nothing made him attractive to anti-slavery voters, which most New Yorkers were. He opposed the annexation of Texas, but not because of the anti-slavery issue. Instead, he felt it would be unconstitutional and costly while leading to war with Mexico. Also, he opposed Catholics and held anti-immigrant views that did not play well with large voting blocks like Irish-Americans, who were already a force in New York City politics. To further exacerbate the problem, he supported mandatory Protestant bible readings in the public schools. As a result, even in Buffalo he failed to carry his own ward. Afterwards, he returned to his law practice and blamed his defeat on "foreign Catholics."[27]

Eventually proven right on his prediction about Texas annexation leading to war with Mexico, Fillmore argued that the conflict was all about adding slave territory and the result of a Congress and White House controlled by the South. While no longer a candidate himself, Fillmore helped his law partner become mayor of Buffalo and his former law partner earn his old seat in Congress. He even outmaneuvered the Seward faction to ensure that his preferred candidate received the next Whig gubernatorial nomination in New York (and the victory he had failed to achieve). He also accepted his party's nomination for state comptroller and was victorious with the largest margin of victory in New York history, prompting his temporary move back to Albany. Finkelman called it "the perfect position for him," given his interest in economics and finance, but his ambition and growing influence in state politics caused him to cut short what might have been a lasting statewide legacy to resume his pursuit of national office.[28]

Meanwhile, Polk's presidential victory over Clay in 1844 exposed the Whigs' lack of a clear national agenda, especially with the Democrats going all-in for expansion. That same inconsistency had hurt Fillmore in his New York governor's race. Polk's campaign slogan, "Fifty-Four Forty or Fight," highlighting Oregon's preferred border latitude, was a masterstroke in the looming debate over Great Britain's claims in the Pacific Northwest. By advocating expansion in that region as well as Texas, Polk placated Northerners with the promise of vast amounts of land—land presumably ill-suited for slavery and its warm-weather roots.[29]

As president, Andrew Jackson had resisted earlier pleas from his old friend Sam Houston related to Texas statehood as a matter of bad electoral timing.[30] Likewise, Jackson's designated successor, Martin Van Buren, saw no reason to antagonize Mexico or Northern voters by rushing to entertain Lone Star desires when he moved up from vice president to the White House in 1836.[31] It took the death in office of William Henry Harrison and the nonpartisan abandonment of Whig principles by his accidental successor, John Tyler, who concentrated instead on Texas statehood, to make that abandonment still impossible for Clay to overcome when he ran for the Whigs yet again.[32]

Obviously, the potential for starting a war with Mexico was not the deterrent that Whigs like Clay, Seward, and Fillmore had thought it would be. Since winning its independence from Mexico in 1836, Texas had struggled as an independent country and kept up its calls for U.S. annexation. At the same time, Mexico had patiently watched its former territory struggle as a separate republic without officially recognizing its independence. Only with Great Britain's threatened involvement as an intermediary did the lame-duck Tyler administration convince an equally lame-duck Congress to annex Texas. President-elect Polk, as equally committed to expansion as Tyler, was the willing beneficiary when he took office. Ultimately, the Whig Party was split on the issue along sectional lines, with Northern Whigs like a young "Abe" Lincoln in Illinois decrying the further expansion of slavery, while most Southern Whigs gave their approval for the same reason.[33]

To ensure that Mexico acknowledged and abided by America's absorption of its newest state, the new president also sent several thousand U.S. troops under General Zachary Taylor to Louisiana to monitor the situation before Texas had been officially accepted. "The Army of Observation," as it was called, was there to intimidate (if not arouse) the Mexicans. At the same time, President Polk claimed that Texas included land all the way to the Rio Grande River and not just the Nueces River, much further north. In other words, Texas covered a lot more territory than Mexico had reason to anticipate.[34]

But even as Polk sought to annex and extend Texas, he also demanded that Mexico sell the U.S. the huge amount of territory that would eventually become the states of New Mexico, Utah, Arizona, Nevada, and California. Finally realizing it was being treated with contempt and in danger of losing all of its northernmost possessions, Mexico sent troops across the Rio Grande in April 1846 to confront their American counterparts. Polk immediately went to Congress for a declaration of war, and two weeks later, on May 11, Democratic majorities in both Houses voted to declare war on Mexico, blaming the initiation of hostilities on the Mexicans.[35]

Most Northern Whigs had adamantly opposed such aggressive expansion, including Fillmore. Instead, he tried to focus attention on the tariff of 1842 and a program of federal river and harbor improvements, especially given his home region's doorstep on the Great Lakes, all things the Whigs could highlight as internal improvements and political talking points. With no elective office during the Mexican War, however, Fillmore was, for the most part, nothing more than a respected political bystander.[36]

As an influential lawyer and newly selected chancellor of the University of Buffalo, however, he remained a leader in the state party. In fact, he was a frequent critic of the Polk administration at a time when more and more Whigs and Northern Democrats were opposing slavery and its expansion.[37] More than partisan, the nation's divide was becoming sectional. Gradually the House of Representatives, where representation was based on population, voted to stop the spread, while in the Senate, where each state was equally represented, legislation to curb slavery's expansion was blocked by Southerners becoming increasingly paranoid over the North's growing consensus against it.[38]

So, after decades of compromise, kicking the can and the problem down the road, so to speak, the Mexican War dramatically changed the equation. According to Fillmore's biographer, where that left him and every other American politician in its aftermath would go a long way to deciding their individual futures.[39] Whig leaders like Clay and Webster were growing old. In their stead by 1848, Fillmore's party was again trending towards military celebrity in its haste to bounce back from Polk and westward expansion. Remarkably, one of the major generals who had been at the forefront of Mexican conquest, Zachary Taylor, emerged as a potential Whig nominee though he was a Kentucky slaveholder who had never been in favor of the war he had been called to lead. As a result, he was deemed acceptable for Americans who had been in favor of the Mexican War as well as those who opposed it. In other words, as Finkelman said, the "ideal candidate"—a popular choice that the outgoing president and his party couldn't diminish even though they tried.[40]

Finkelman also labeled Taylor a "curious" candidate, as he had never joined a political party; had never voted in a previous election; was raised on the frontier; and still owned slaves on Deep South plantations in two different states. Undoubtedly, Taylor was a non-partisan political novice. As a war hero, he was attractive to most voters. As a slaveowner, he was acceptable to the South. As someone with a "strong record of demanding fair treatment" for Native Americans, he was attractive to anti–Jackson elements, and as someone opposed to Texas annexation (even though he had helped pave the way for it to happen), he was even acceptable to Northerners still bemoaning the giant new state's slave-spreading potential. Taylor was, in other words, a self-effacing military figure—a celebrity candidate without political record whom the Whigs felt they could mold into a president.[41]

Still, there were partisan concerns among the Northern Whigs, who had been burned before by Tyler's independent leanings. As a result, support for Taylor at the 1848 Whig Convention was much stronger within the Southern branch of the party. Nonetheless, by the fourth ballot, he was nominated, ensuring that his running mate would be a Northerner and a party regular, as well as someone at least somewhat opposed to slavery expansion in order to better offset General Taylor's slaveholding past.[42]

Fourteen men were put forward as vice presidential possibilities, but only four were what Finkelman termed "serious candidates," including the New York rivals Seward and Fillmore. Seward, however, was never interested in the job. His only goal, in fact, was to keep Fillmore from getting it for fear it would further elevate his longtime rival. At the same time, Fillmore appeared the most agreeable of the candidates to Southern Whigs since he was a moderate on slavery, while most of the others (especially Seward) were not. Playing politics, Seward gambled that by withdrawing his name from consideration at the last possible minute, he might throw his support to someone other than Fillmore, but the ploy failed when support for "the other New Yorker" won out in order to ensure the Whigs carried the Empire State on election day. The fact that Fillmore's qualifications for vice president did not seem to measure up mattered little.[43] After all, what were the chances of another accidental presidency so close after Tyler? For the Whigs, with their contempt of Jackson, Van Buren, and Polk, it was worth the risk. For Fillmore, it was the moment of a lifetime.

Meanwhile, the perfect storm of circumstances that propelled Fillmore to his place on the Whig ticket was equally prevalent on the Democratic side in terms of helping ensure a Whig victory that fall. Michigan's Lewis Cass, a lackluster compromise candidate, emerged as the Democratic nominee, and some of their support also went to Van Buren, who decided to run again at age 66 as the choice of the recently formed Free Soil Party. As has happened so often in American political history, a third-party candidacy did nothing but keep victory from the major party from which it drew off the most support—in this case the Democrats. The three-way contest was still close, but Van Buren's 291,000 siphoned votes were enough to put Taylor in the White House.[44]

Ironically, Taylor and Fillmore had never met before being paired on the Whigs' national ticket. Unlike the top of the ticket, which was all about Taylor's celebrity, the relatively obscure bottom half had to do with Fillmore's lifelong party loyalty. Equally ironic was the little-known fact that the Southerner, Taylor, was politically opposed to the expansion of slavery, while his Northern running mate had never publicly opposed the South's distasteful institution and would even complain during the campaign about being rumored to be an abolitionist. Though slavery was evil, Fillmore considered it a state-endorsed evil and one the federal government had nothing to do with. Only at the moment of statehood, he asserted, should the question of whether a new state would be slave or free be decided.[45]

His failure to understand the increasing anti-slavery sentiment would "undermine his presidency" and "subsequent political career," Finkelman asserted. Because the Southern-born Taylor proved more closely aligned on the slavery issue with Whigs like Seward than his vice president, Fillmore witnessed his New York rival gaining the president's ear, something he never accomplished.[46]

Taylor's new administration was confronted by three main issues: the admission of California to statehood; the ongoing issue of slavery in the territories; and claims by Texas that much of the New Mexico Territory should actually be included within the Lone Star State's western boundary.[47] Fillmore was at odds with Taylor on all three. Taylor agreed with Seward on the immediate admission of California as a free state and resistance to Texas demands. He also saw no need for stronger fugitive slave legislation, something Fillmore vigorously endorsed in surprising agreement with the South.[48]

Shortly before Taylor's unexpected death, the vice president's most dramatic policy divergence occurred when Congress was debating the Compromise of 1850. Taylor opposed it and was prepared to veto it if passed. Meanwhile, with the Senate vote expected to be close, Fillmore, as VP and presiding officer, let it be known that he was prepared to break any deadlock with a deciding vote in the affirmative, much to Taylor's chagrin.[49] Magnifying the administration's divergence of opinion was the large number of patronage appointments the Whigs enjoyed once they finally regained the White House following Tyler's abandonment of the party and the Polk interlude of Democratic resurgence. Finkelman pronounced Fillmore too proud to approach Taylor to try to change his mind on the legislation, and the president too unskilled as a politician to woo his VP to his way of thinking. As a result, their relationship was strained.[50]

With the discovery of gold in California (December 1848), thousands of gold seekers began arriving on the West Coast, increasing demands for statehood, which by the summer of 1850 Taylor was striving to make happen immediately. He also felt New Mexico deserved statehood and was prepared to stand up to Texas border claims with Army presence should that become necessary. Under Taylor's plan, both California and New Mexico were to be admitted as free states.[51]

At the same time, the ongoing stain of an active slave trade in the District of Columbia, the federal seat of government, and the sore point this created for Northerners was tabled in Congress whenever it came up. Also, the fugitive slave issue was intensifying as better roads, riverboats, and railroads made it infinitely more possible for slaves to make their way north and escape their Southern masters. The first Fugitive Slave Act of 1793 had provided no due process protections for alleged fugitives, making it unconstitutional in the minds of many Northerners, especially since the Constitution had never authorized such a statute. In response, several Northern states passed so-called "liberty laws" to counteract the existing fugitive slave law and prevent what Finkelman described as "kidnapping" when it came to free African Americans who might be wrongfully accused of being escaped slaves. Several Northern governors even refused to recognize Southern demands for extradition of escaped slaves, deeming it a crime in their states for any person to be the property of another.[52]

It reached a boiling point on March 1, 1843, when the Supreme Court ruled that all Northern liberty laws were unconstitutional and that free states must comply with the 1793 mandate, undermining evolving African American freedoms in states like Pennsylvania, New York, and New Jersey, as well as all along the Ohio River. While prohibiting the free states from impeding the return of a fugitive slave, the Court ruling also held that a free state could not be made to enforce such a federal statute actively. Thus, when Taylor took office, Northerners were more and more opposed to slave catchers invading their states, and Southerners equally certain of their right to reclaim runaway property and expect Northern compliance with the law of the land.[53]

Taylor hoped to handle all those issues one by one, starting with the admission of California … and New Mexico.[54] As for the slave-related controversies, he sought compromise by relying on his military past. Having led men into battle from both the North and South, he understood the need to satisfy both sections. Unfortunately, the Whigs in Congress, and especially their longtime presidential wannabes, Clay and Webster, were in no hurry to follow his compromising lead.[55] They had both spent their careers contesting Democratic presidents and policies, and according to Finkelman, "they did not know how to work with a president of their own party," especially a political outsider. Instead, they plotted their own solutions for the nation's ills, which included siding with the new vice president conveniently presiding over their Senate. Working with the two Whig icons made political sense for Fillmore. "Moreover, supporting Clay and Webster was a vehicle for opposing Seward," Finkelman wrote, something Fillmore was always happy to do.[56]

This unusual alliance, with the vice president separated from his own administration, set the stage for what Finkelman termed "one of the great legislative debates in American history: the arguments over the Compromise of 1850." On a reportedly stormy night in

At a time of legendary legislators like Henry Clay, Daniel Webster, and John C. Calhoun, Millard Fillmore made an unlikely president. Here he is included with them and other national leaders in a historic lithograph. Fillmore is far right, supporting the American shield (Library of Congress Prints and Photographs Division—Reproduction Number DIG-pga-02601).

January 1850, Clay and Webster secretly agreed to work together on a compromise they thought could save the Union from what we now know was our nation's inevitable march to civil war. They aimed to circumvent the extreme dogma of their longstanding Southern rival, John C. Calhoun, who was by then seeking a separate "Southern Party" to encompass both Democrats and Whigs and bring about a reorganization of the American political system. They also sought to undermine Taylor's presidency.[57]

To accomplish both, Clay had devised eight resolutions in a single bill designed to appeal to legislators from both sections. Five benefited the South, and three were aimed at mollifying the North. They included a new and more stringent fugitive slave law; lack of restrictions on slavery in the new territories; federal assumption of the former Republic of Texas' outstanding debt; safeguarding of slavery in the District of Columbia; and guarantees against Congress interfering in the interstate slave trade. To offset these controversial concessions, Clay called for the immediate admission of California as a free state, the prohibition of the public sale of slaves in the District of Columbia, and settlement of the ongoing Texas boundary dispute in New Mexico's favor.[58]

Obviously, the North's greatest incentive for the bill was the immediate admission of California, where the population was expanding rapidly into verdant valleys and mineral-rich mountains. With only one percent of California's population African American in 1850, the bill confirmed what the new state desired—free state status. At the same time, the face-saving ban on slave sales in the nation's capital, when everyone knew the same sales would continue just across the Potomac River in neighboring Virginia, and the settlement of the New Mexico boundary dispute, which would keep that land away from Texas and slavery's spread, were viewed as minor repudiations in the North, and the legislation appeared one-sided in the South's favor. The reinforced Fugitive Slave Act of 1850 made the legislation seem especially so, and Finkelman exposed what Northerners believed "would be an enormous victory for the slave power" by creating "a national system of law enforcement" to keep alleged fugitive slaves, including possibly free African Americans, from their fundamental right of due process.[59]

Fillmore's biographer thus contended that California's admission, which would give the free states a majority in the Senate, was not the victory it was portrayed to be. Instead, he claimed "the wisdom of hindsight" and argued that with the status of territories like New Mexico and Utah yet to be determined, this legislative advantage at the time was viewed as possibly short-lived.[60]

The debates on the bill were legendary. In siding with Clay, something for which he was castigated as a sell-out by many of his Northern constituents, Webster's famous opening statement—"I wish to speak today, not as a Massachusetts man, nor as a Northern man, but as an American"—is just one of many platitudes remembered from congressional speeches of the time. Southern spokesmen like Calhoun and Mississippi's Jefferson Davis opposed the compromise, as did staunch Northern slavery opponents like Seward, who pointed to "a higher law than the Constitution" and concluded: "Slavery must give way, and will give way, to the salutary instructions of economy and the ripening influences of humanity."[61]

Like Seward, the president also believed Clay and Webster were giving away too much.[62] Fillmore presided over the contentious Senate debates that increasingly featured a lack of restraint (one senator even pulled a pistol on another). His biographer noted a few senators using "vituperative language," and in the absence of "decorum" ignored him repeatedly. Through it all, Clay continued to push his compromise towards the finish line, directly challenging Taylor's leadership while Fillmore sat back and watched it happen.[63]

Despite the intense disagreement and near-violence, Fillmore maintained his support for the bill and a determination to go against the president's wishes in the event of a tie. This would have forced Taylor's hand with a veto and embarrassed him. However, that never became necessary, as a week later President Taylor was dead and "the most obscure vice president ever [at least according to his biographer] was president."[64]

Like many vice presidents, Fillmore had not been included in Cabinet meetings and was never among Taylor's inner circle. He had been wounded by this omission—so wounded, in fact, that upon assuming the presidency, he fired the entire Cabinet, "an act that astounded the Whig Party." He was the only accidental president ever to do so.[65]

Thus, although still something of a novice on the national scene, Fillmore did not hesitate to rid himself of his predecessor's Cabinet on the very first day of his presidency. While leaning on the advice of longtime leaders like Webster, his old mentor, his nomination of a completely new Cabinet ten days later was an extraordinary example of intra-party hostility even in an age of rapidly changing political landscapes.[66] It "reflected a stubbornness" that Finkelman indicated "profoundly affected his presidency." This stubbornness prompted his complete support for the new Fugitive Slave Act and uncompromising enforcement of its policy dictates—dictates that did not jive with the majority of his Northern brethren.[67]

As a result, he seemed an anomaly in the White House from day one. While Webster came aboard as secretary of state, providing a measure of prestige to his fledgling administration, the Massachusetts mainstay had by then become a controversial voice thanks to his surprising, full-throated support of Clay's Compromise.[68] Finkelman even termed Webster "indeed a fallen angel" by the time Fillmore rescued him from constituent criticism and potential senatorial defeat by propping him back up as America's lead diplomat. It was an appointment, however, that further undermined Fillmore's standing in the North, where Webster was increasingly seen as a sell-out to the slaveocracy, a longtime presidential wannabe willing to appease the South for Southern votes.[69]

Fillmore further doubled down on the personal persona of his Cabinet appointments by choosing Thomas Corwin of Ohio for secretary of the treasury, a senator who had opposed the Mexican War and was openly "hostile" to the Abolitionist Movement; Kentucky Senator John Crittenden, a slaveholder, for attorney general; and his former law partner, Nathan Hall, an outspoken critic of Seward and his anti-slavery principles, as postmaster general.[70]

The new president also dealt with his first crisis in the form of renewed Texas demands for much of New Mexico, including the capital, Santa Fe. Absurd though most of these were, Fillmore failed to deal with them in a decisive manner. With the Texas governor arrogantly making claims that would have all but eliminated the integrity of the New Mexico Territory, Fillmore was less than decisive. He sent troops to confront Texas aspirations if necessary, but then gave into many Texas demands. Instead of a stern response, reminding the newly minted Texas state government that they were henceforth subject to federal jurisdiction and answerable to the commander-in-chief, he seemed "paralyzed by Texas saber-rattling"—Finkelman's words for his rejection of New Mexico's submission for statehood and lack of congressional guidance.

Instead of forcefully laying out a concrete proposal over the boundary dispute, a prerogative that would have been entirely within his presidential purview, he merely referred to the compromise bill as a path forward. Without presidential guidance, opposition Democrats took advantage of the political opening to formulate their own congressional commission and path forward, which they did in July 1850, a development that was termed "patently unfair" by Finkelman. As a result, the whole New Mexico issue was stripped from the Compromise bill.[71]

Clay's strategy to wrest control had failed. Instead of consolidating power under his congressional leadership, the Whigs were completely divided, with their former president dead and the new one providing little or no party leadership. Devastated by it all, the aging Clay left Washington before the amended Compromise was decided.[72] In his place, Democratic Senator Stephen A. Douglas of Illinois, the so-called "Little Giant," took up the challenge of putting Clay's Compromise back together. His efforts in that regard would raise him to prominence and reduce Fillmore's presidency to insignificance. By breaking Clay's Compromise into parts and with New Mexico statehood off the table, Douglas was able to guide the legislation through Congress as several unconnected laws. California statehood and the end of the public slave trade in the District of Columbia were the only positives the North achieved. Everything else went the South's way.[73]

In the end, appeasement got it all passed, thanks to a Northern Whig president working with a Northern Democratic senator. At the same time, Fillmore relinquished presidential oversight of boundaries, determining that Congress could pass judgment as to what New Mexico's territorial border should be. Finkelman used the word "bizarre" to describe the president's theory.

Fillmore apparently hoped to guide Congress towards a law that Texas would accept, and the final settlement gave the Texans 70,000 more square miles than Clay's original. It also opened the New Mexico Territory to slavery and granted Texas a huge debt bailout, all obviously popular in the Lone Star State. In so doing, Fillmore promoted the idea that anything else might have led to civil war between the U.S. and its newest state over nothing but desert. In his mind, it wasn't worth it. Webster managed to get several New England senators to join with the South in favoring the legislation, and four days later, the Senate passed California statehood. Legendary figures Sam Houston of Texas and Thomas Hart Benton of Missouri were among just five slave state voters in favor of the new West Coast state. Otherwise there was no compromise in the final Compromise. What passed instead was an uncompromising series of individual bills.[74]

Despite California's entry to the Union as a free state, Southerners were able to claim legislative victory, especially in September, when Fillmore signed the new Fugitive Slave Act. With Texas acquiring more land and money, and the status of New Mexico and even Utah still undecided, the South was ready for its peculiar institution to continue spreading west with the president's apparent blessing.[75] While everything else finally came off the table without a hitch, the new Fugitive Slave Act was doomed to dissention as soon as it was conceived. As indicated previously, Fillmore not only supported it, he aggressively enforced it. According to Finkelman, that support and efforts at enforcement would not only destroy his administration and re-nomination chances, but also what was left of the Whig Party.[76]

For the first time, a national system of authoritarian law enforcement was authorized, ensuring controversy. It replaced the Fugitive Slave Act of 1793, which Northern states had refused to enforce. Their judges were prohibited from hearing fugitive slave cases, and private slave catchers were prohibited from using state jails to incarcerate accused runaways. As a result, Southerners claimed that their constitutional right to recover escaped property was being infringed on, making it legally impossible to pursue fugitive slaves north of the Mason-Dixon Line. The 1850 law was designed to remedy that by the establishment of federal commissioners in Northern counties whose job it would be to hear fugitive slave claims and provide sufficient force to implement the law. Anyone who aided, harbored, or interfered in the reclamation of a fugitive slave was subject to fines and possible jail time.[77]

Northerners found the new provisions offensive, especially since African Americans could be detained just by being presumed to be fugitive slaves and possibly subject to legal jeopardy regardless of who they were or where they came from. Free Blacks living in the North were suddenly imperiled, and their White neighbors threatened by association. The hiring of persons of color in the North was greatly curtailed by suspicion, impersonation, and the threat of fugitive slave infiltration. The commissioners were charged with hearing and determining cases quickly and without a jury. Sufficient proof became very subjective and open to biased interpretations. The potential for fraud or mistaken identity loomed large and surfaced often.[78]

No wonder so many free Blacks were wrongfully accused of being fugitive slaves and so many Northerners despised the presence of outsiders coming into their states under the guise of law enforcement. Due process, that democratic concept supposedly ingrained in American jurisprudence, seemed trampled, as the differences between the sections were made obvious. The law was even written in a way that made it profitable for the commissioners to uncover more fugitives and a system that lent itself to potential bribes and often made finding the truth beside the point.

Early Fillmore biographers maintained that he delayed signing the new fugitive bill as long as possible because he found it repulsive to his conscience, but Finkelman would have none of that. Instead, he reported that Fillmore was "adamant about passing the fugitive slave measure," with no written evidence to the contrary. He wrote, "Nor is there the slightest evidence he hesitated or delayed signing the bill." Once the Senate and House both passed the Act, Fillmore signed it without comment.[79]

Over the next two years, Fillmore would constantly oversee enforcement of the new Fugitive Slave Act without regard to the 150,000 free African Americans it jeopardized in the North, without concern for the fraud it cultivated, and despite the hundreds of people it wrongfully ensnared without due process. "God knows I detest slavery," Fillmore is reported to have said to Webster, but according to Finkelman, his policies, speeches, and official acts all seemed to contradict that statement.[80]

Like most Whigs, policy for Fillmore had to do first and foremost with the economy. Unlike Democratic doctrine of the day, the concept of continental expansion was fine as long as it was done for economic reasons. To his way of thinking, internal improvements, tariffs, and trade opportunities were necessary offshoots of expansion.[81] He wanted to be considered a strict constitutionalist domestically and a non-interventionist when it came to foreign affairs. Congress did not initially react to Fillmore's appeal for internal improvements such as lighthouses and harbors, but he did get a $2 million waterways bill passed with most of that going to his home region—maybe the best thing he ever did for Buffalo and its sister Great Lakes cities. He also made postal rates more uniform, stimulated commerce and communication all the way to the West Coast, and was the first president to authorize plans for a transcontinental railroad, something that would come to pass three administrations later under Lincoln.[82]

At the same time, Fillmore allowed his nativist and anti–Semitic feelings to creep into his legislative leanings, creating problems for both himself and Secretary of State Webster in various foreign treaty discussions. His "most important" foreign policy achievement, according to Finkelman, was sending a four-ship, 560-man naval expedition under Commodore Matthew Perry in November 1852, to open relations and trade with Japan, hoping to end 250 years of isolation by that Asian nation and make the U.S. the first Western power to gain favored nation status with the so-called "Chrysanthemum Kingdom."[83] By the middle of the 19th century, America had heavily invested in Pacific whaling and desperately needed Japanese ports to replenish coal and provisions for its whaling ships.

Fillmore sent a letter by Perry to the Japanese emperor, proposing, "The United States and Japan should live in friendship and have commercial intercourse with each other." Unfortunately, it would be months before the reclusive Japanese would trust the Americans enough to let them anchor and come ashore. During that stalemate, Perry's flotilla wintered at Hong Kong and didn't return to the Japanese islands until spring 1853. By then they were prepared to return fire if attacked. Previous Western expeditions had been fired upon and forced to leave, so Perry took no chances until negotiations were confirmed. Interestingly, the first signs of improving relations came when a boatload of Japanese artists approached the American ships and began sketching them and the men aboard. Later, a more official emissary arrived, and once Perry's intention to deliver President Fillmore's letter to the emperor in person was understood, the threat of conflict dissipated, and diplomacy was finally allowed to happen. Eventually, Perry did earn the concessions he was seeking for the U.S., which were confirmed in the Treaty of Kanagawa, but not until 1854 and the administration of Fillmore's successor.[84]

A Japanese depiction of U.S. Commodore Matthew Perry, this rendering was done when President Millard Fillmore sent Perry's naval squadron to Asia, hoping to open trade with that previously isolated island nation (Library of Congress Prints and Photographs Division—Reproduction Number USZC2-6516 [Ikoku Ochibe Kago, Artist]).

At the beginning of his presidency, Fillmore had inherited rumors of other expansionist designs not of his choosing. For the most part, they were the extended and illegal visions of Southern statesmen, entrepreneurs, and adventurers, all seeking to take economic advantage of another, much closer island nation—Cuba. Naturally, he opposed and condemned evil schemes that threatened private invasions of that nearby Caribbean isle. Such unlawful expeditions were to be subject to stiff penalties, including fines and three-year imprisonment. Despite his warnings, however, an actual invasion force of 400 men set out from New Orleans in May of 1850 with the goal of liberating Cuba from Spain. Instead, they were killed, captured, and some even executed by alerted Spanish troops, inciting riots back in their hometown, New Orleans. It was left to Fillmore to negotiate the release of the remaining American captives, but once returned to U.S. soil, the survivors were never prosecuted and the rioters never held accountable, a "lackadaisical" response, according to Finkelman, that contrasted sharply with his very aggressive approach to the fugitive slave issue.[85]

That's as good an example as any of why his presidency was compromised. In his support for the Compromise of 1850 and his confidence in its potential to quell the growing drumbeat of sectionalism, he failed to adequately judge the national mood that would prove so costly a decade later. Perhaps a more perceptive president would have seen how inflammatory, rigid enforcement of the Fugitive Slave Act could become in the North and how that policy alone might undermine the spirit of any further compromise moving forward.

Whole communities became galvanized against the law, leading to protest and violence, and several high-profile cases involving falsely accused free Blacks actually undermined the justice it was instituted to ensure. Nonetheless, Fillmore stubbornly held to the premise that as president, it was his job to see that the law was enforced. While he was obsessed with enforcement during his two-year tenure, fugitives, abolitionists, and free African Americans banded together and became equally intent on ensuring individual liberty for anyone in question.

In response, Fillmore authorized federal troops to uphold the law and confront opposition, and stubbornly refused any modification to make the law more palatable for the Northern majority. Instead, he consistently defended the Compromise while calling for sectional harmony. According to Finkelman, he told the nation the Compromise was "necessary to allay asperities and animosities that were rapidly alienating one section of the country from another and destroying those fraternal sentiments which are the strongest supports of the Constitution." Basically, his literal interpretation and enforcement exposed his lack of compassion and concern for African Americans, free or slave, and his hatred of abolitionists. Fillmore feared offending the South for political reasons much more than any abolitionist inspired dissention in the North. His hope of winning another presidential term was based on winning a number of Southern states, something every previous Northern-born elected president had managed to do and something he misguidedly put too much stock in. Thus, he did not seriously challenge the Texas border claims; he did not follow through on prosecution of the Cuban invaders; and he did not pay attention to the fugitive slave law's many detractors. To win in 1852, Millard Fillmore was convinced he needed the support of Southern Whigs.[86]

The Compromise threatened the goals of Southern extremists, but most of the South's leadership recognized it as a win for their section. While Unionists would remain ascendant in the South for the time being, including the 1852 elections, Fillmore's fugitive slave policy hurt him more in the North than it helped him in the South. This was especially true after his administration aggressively prosecuted four high-profile fugitive slave cases in 1851, three of which it lost at enormous cost in the court of public opinion.

Despite previous biographies to the contrary, Finkelman was reluctant to accept the notion that Fillmore never wanted another term. He based that on the number of partisan newspapers that came out for Fillmore in 1852 and the fact that Fillmore's former law partner turned postmaster general had actually done a good job of assuring his patronage power come election time. At the same time, Webster announced his surprising intention to throw his proverbial hat in the ring, which was highly unusual for a Cabinet member of a sitting president. To this rather shocking development, Fillmore had little or no response. Finkelman believed this could have been a calculated gamble on the president's part, knowing his aging secretary of state was in no shape to win the office, but figuring he might serve as an effective placeholder until the Whigs returned to their senses and renominated their incumbent. This final gambit failed, however, when he made the mistake of also courting support from a new anti–Catholic movement as well as Deep South Whigs. The South had never before had a Northern-born president who actively defended the rights of slaveholders, but by connecting these two divisive groups, the Whigs decided it would be far safer to nominate yet another general, Winfield Scott, their winning formula two times before.

Scott eventually lost to little-known Democratic Senator Franklin Pierce of New Hampshire. Both 1852 political conventions were dysfunctional affairs, requiring more than 40 ballots each to decide their presidential nominees. Fillmore finished second among the Whig candidates after not declaring his candidacy until early 1852 and only after becoming convinced that Scott's nomination would hand the White House back to the Democrats. Ultimately, the delegates Webster did siphon off cost Fillmore renomination, a circumstance Finkelman held him personally accountable for as an indecisive, insecure incumbent who should have nixed Webster's candidacy from the get-go. Not only was Webster's candidacy and role in denying Fillmore the Whig nomination what Finkelman termed "one of the great humiliations in American political history," it also created an irreconcilable divide between the aging mentor and his former political protégé before the convention ended.[87]

His administration a "tragedy," according to his biographer, Fillmore's life after the White House did not fare any better. His wife died suddenly from a cold contracted at Pierce's inauguration just a month after he left office, and his 22-year-old daughter died, just as tragically, a year later.

Two years later, Fillmore left on a grand tour of Europe, meeting with Queen Victoria and Pope Pius IX (as ironic as that seems). Upon returning home, he also re-entered presidential politics as a third-party candidate in 1856, representing an agenda that prohibited Catholics from holding public office and required immigrants to have 21 years of continuous U.S. residence before they could obtain citizenship. Known as the Know-Nothing Party, it was made up of conservatives who detested abolitionists, feared foreigners, and wished slavery would just go away. The Democrats won again in 1856 with our only bachelor president, James Buchanan of Pennsylvania. He had most recently served as minister to Great Britain and would win the general election over Western explorer John C. Fremont, the first presidential nominee of the newly formed Republican Party, which by that time had succeeded the Whig Party, which Fillmore's accidental presidency had helped to destroy.[88]

12

The First Johnson Struggles
to Measure Up

*"No man has a right to judge Andrew Johnson in any respect who has not
suffered as much and done as much as he for the nation's sake."*
—Abraham Lincoln, 1864

Before Bill Clinton in the 1990s became our only other president to face impeachment, Andrew Johnson was merely an afterthought. All we tended to remember about him was that he succeeded Abraham Lincoln, our most revered president. In the aftermath of the Civil War and Lincoln's martyrdom at the hands of our first presidential assassin, John Wilkes Booth, no man, no matter how equipped to manage the affairs of state, could have measured up to the man who held the country together during its darkest hour, and Johnson, a simple tailor from Tennessee, certainly did not. One historian of the Reconstruction era even commented:

> Given that the country was emerging from the trauma of a devastating civil war, the ascent of a man like Johnson after a genial intellect like Lincoln struck Radicals [congressional Republicans] as tragically unfortunate, for in personal style the new chief executive was a stubborn loner never adept at conciliatory politics. When the need for national healing and inspired leadership could not have been more acute, America was bequeathed not a Washington or Jefferson, but a man who was not supposed to be president.[1]

Nevertheless, according to a 1989 biography by Hans Trefousse, Johnson's failure to do so was not so much ineptitude as the cards he was dealt in a suddenly reunited, but still very much divided country. While his reputation has remained suspect, our 17th and extremely accidental president was most of all a product of his turbulent times, an energetic politician who remained in the Union when no other Southerner would, yet disavowed Union aspirations once presidential leadership was thrust upon him.[2]

Trefousse enunciated this crucial part of the Johnson story in his preface when he wrote: "What was it that made Andrew Johnson in 1861 first defy Southern opinion by staying loyal to the Union, and then in 1865 challenge a Northern majority in Congress to break with the party that had elected him vice president?"[3] That, in fact, was the question that mystified congressional leadership and others in his administration at the time and gradually intensified opposition to Lincoln's successor, leaving him no future in national politics. No other American political figure ever travelled a more controversial course in the face of constant opposition and bitter attacks from both below and later above the Mason-Dixon Line. Confirming as much, Civil War general and postwar departmental commander William Tecumseh Sherman once said, "Johnson attempts to govern after he has lost the means to govern. He is like a general fighting without an army." Such a political dilemma alone was worthy of a book.[4]

Before going there, however, Trefousse first established the humble beginnings of this president, who he claimed was our only chief executive never to attend a single day of school. Born in Raleigh, North Carolina, on December 29, 1808, Johnson was the third child of a working-class family whose ancestors migrated south from Virginia. Although landless and illiterate, his father worked in a variety of jobs and reportedly "enjoyed the respect of the community." His mother was a seamstress.

When Andrew was three, his father died, the result of a boating accident in which he saved the lives of several people. Left to fend for two young sons as a single parent, his mother struggled to make a living and eventually remarried. His older brother was soon apprenticed to a local tailor shop, but the younger Johnson's initial options were not as promising. Nonetheless, his biographer noted, although poor, the future president realized early on that he was not at the bottom of the Southern social scale, thanks to the presence of African Americans, who made up one-third of Colonial Raleigh's population. Although his playmates often included Black children, there's no doubt he was exposed to slavery and racism at an early age, and indoctrinated with Southern attitudes. Like other White children, even poor ones, he undoubtedly grew up looking down on African Americans. At the same time, his namesake, Andrew Jackson, was a hero on everyone's mind after his army defeated the British at New Orleans in the War of 1812, so it's also easy to understand how youngsters throughout the Carolinas would come to idolize Jackson, as Johnson did, especially those from similar, humble beginnings.[5]

Despite no formal schooling, Johnson was anxious for knowledge and, after following in his brother's footsteps at age 13 to an apprenticeship in the same tailor shop, he learned the alphabet and how to read, and began to come in contact with men of means who offered him books. Johnson, however, remained restless, and when he got into trouble with the tailor, he and his brother ran away and hid in the small towns and villages of the Appalachian Mountains, where they honed their skills as itinerant tailors. Later, he briefly returned to Raleigh to try to make amends and to obtain his release from the apprenticeship, but when that entreaty failed, Johnson balked at any remaining commitment and left North Carolina for good, permanently crossing the mountains into Tennessee.

He would settle in Greeneville, the county seat of Greene County and home to several colleges.[6] Johnson liked the peaceful setting of the Scotch-Irish village with the Great Smokies section of the Appalachians looming on its eastern horizon. His choice was made easier by the fact that the town's tailor was growing old and was on the verge of retirement. And, so the story goes, it wasn't long before the town's new tailor fell in love with a well-educated shoemaker's daughter, resulting in their marriage.[7]

Some account books from Johnson's Greeneville tailor shop have survived and reveal a flourishing business. In addition, with his family growing (four children) and Johnson concentrating on his educational betterment by reading every book he could get his hands on, he began to take an interest in local affairs and express his opinions in public, becoming a persuasive speaker and member of two debating societies.[8]

At the same time, with Tennessee's Jackson rising to the presidency by 1829, government and politics were becoming subjects of everyday life throughout the Volunteer State, and Greeneville was no exception. Among those seeking local office, in fact, would be the town's increasingly influential tailor, who was elected city alderman in his first attempt and was re-elected the very next year. Five years later, as one of Greeneville's most esteemed citizens, he was chosen mayor.[9]

Always impeccably dressed, as might be expected of a tailor, and impressive with his dark, swarthy complexion and piercing eyes, Johnson was a formidable figure in Upper East Tennessee politics by the time he began to get involved at the state level. His first opportunity came as the state convened a convention to write a new constitution in 1834. The ratification process was "tailor-made" for an upstart like Johnson trying to make a name for himself, and the experience whetted his appetite for the state legislature. Soon thereafter, he entered a three-man race for the seat representing Greene and neighboring Washington Counties, and in his first debate surprised everyone by totally bettering his opponents. One of the two dropped out, and when the ballots were tallied a few weeks later, the 27-year-old tailor turned politician had won with approximately two-thirds of the votes. He was on his way to the state legislature in Nashville.[10]

Between legislative sessions, Johnson expanded his tailoring business and staff to meet the growing needs of his family, but he remained far too ambitious not to seek re-election in 1837. A reluctance to support railroads, however, was used against him, and he suffered his first and only defeat at the polls before the Civil War. To fashion a comeback in 1839, he converted to the Democrats. Riding the Jacksonian coattails of Martin Van Buren, the new president after serving as Jackson's vice president, and Tennessee Governor James K. Polk, he recaptured the Greene-Washington seat and built a solid party organization, one in which he was the star. With his acquired oratorical skills, he would be constantly pitted against the best the Whig Party had to offer in that part of the state, including the redoubtable William G. "Parson" Brownlow, the caustic East Tennessee newspaper editor with whom Johnson would form a lasting rivalry. But despite his best efforts to extend Democratic influence beyond his two county's borders, most of the Upper East section of the state leaned to the Whigs and inhibited his designs on higher office.

The national election of 1840, the one of Tippecanoe and Tyler too, offered Johnson his first chance to make a true statewide name for himself. Both U.S. Senate seats were available in Tennessee, and with the Democrats holding a slight majority in the State Senate and the Whigs in control of the House, a bitter feud ensued in the legislature over the selection of new senators, whom state legislatures selected in those days. It got so bad, in fact, that when the next Congress convened in Washington, Tennessee remained unrepresented in the U.S. Senate. Although Democrats at the state level received most of the blame for this unconscionable situation, it did afford Johnson an opportunity to advance his status as the primary spokesman for his party during the deadlock, which lasted until 1843.[11]

At the same time, the permanent location of Tennessee's capital was being challenged, with Knoxville in East Tennessee seeking to replace Nashville and the Midstate. Taking the debate even further, Johnson argued for the creation of a new state to be carved out of the mountainous counties of East Tennessee, Western North Carolina, Southwest Virginia, and Northern Georgia. Such a radical idea seemed certain to fail, but it illustrated his growing concern for the slaveholding power in the South and the political discrimination it inflicted on the sections of those states where slaves were not the primary labor force and the plantation-based Southern aristocracy was irrelevant. That, along with his attack on redistricting and the three-fifths provision regarding how slaves were to be counted when determining representation, caused his opponents to label him an abolitionist. Trefousse indicated that such accusations were ridiculous, as Johnson merely sought more political leverage for his section of the state, and the attacks served to solidify his position as the recognized leader of East Tennessee Democrats.[12]

By 1843, this improved regional influence enabled Johnson to focus on a congressional career. The U.S. House of Representatives was the natural next step for an ascending politician, who had served in both houses of the state legislature. While his efforts on districting had not hurt the Whigs locally, they had benefited the Democrats statewide, and he was the first to take advantage by becoming the representative of Tennessee's First Congressional District for the next ten years. Called the "last Jacksonian" in the U.S. House, he defended slavery while also remaining a proponent of the frontier, agrarian lifestyle. He also began exhibiting a pronounced steak of stubbornness that Trefousse emphasized would become "his calling card," both in politics and public relations.[13]

Entering Congress at a time when men of lasting significance dotted its roster, he supported the annexation of Texas, the constitutionally guaranteed rights of slaveholders, and the intellectual inferiority of the Black race. His biographer noted, "That Johnson was a Southerner was never much in doubt." At the same time, he was independent in his voting patterns when it came to party, something that did not endear him to strict Democrats, and he was surprised when Polk, a fellow Tennessean, was elected president in 1844.

Johnson's second congressional term solidified his standing as a political maverick, as he voted in opposition to a number of Democratic initiatives and introduced the controversial 1846 Homestead Bill, which would have made every poor White male in the U.S. who was head of a household eligible to receive 160 acres of the public domain without cost. That concept, plus his support for the annexation of faraway Oregon, angered Southerners. He also broke with Polk on various party initiatives, casting Johnson as an outsider in many Democratic circles. Regardless, he shrewdly managed to keep his support at home and achieved re-election even when his margin of victory shrank to 300 votes.[14]

Stressing economy in government, his Homestead Bill, and constitutional reform over all other issues, Johnson's remaining terms in Congress were remarkable in the distance he managed to keep from the sectional divide that had begun sweeping the country. By his fourth term in the House, he was becoming known throughout the nation. He still considered slavery unalterably linked with the country's other institutions and any attack on its existence unpatriotic, but he also believed firmly in preserving the Union. By tying those two issues together, he was in sharp contrast with more extreme Southerners, and when the Compromise of 1850 finally passed, Johnson supported all of its provisions except one—the ending of the slave trade in the District of Columbia.[15]

That was typical of some of his more radical stances on issues of the day. At the same time, he continued to concentrate on his Homestead Bill, enlisting the assistance of Massachusetts' great orator, Daniel Webster, and making it a key component of his next re-election campaign versus Landon Haynes, a lawyer and former minister who claimed that homesteading was an abolitionist plot and disadvantageous to the South. Both candidates were guilty of mud-slinging and name-calling, but once again Johnson emerged victorious in his fiercest and final House election.[16]

Soon thereafter, he realized the dream of seeing his Homestead legislation get through the House, and as another presidential election neared in 1852, Johnson favored almost anyone over New Hampshire's Franklin Pierce, a handsome, well-bred Northerner who nonetheless got the Democratic nod. Pierce went on to defeat General Winfield Scott, an aging hero of the Mexican War who had replaced incumbent Millard Fillmore on the Whig ticket.[17]

By the time his fifth consecutive term in the House drew to a close, Johnson's ambition moved him to seek another political challenge—Tennessee's governorship. Actually, he became the consensus choice of the state nominating committee not because he was so well-liked, but because he offered the Democrats their best chance to win. That didn't stop Brownlow from unloading on his old East State rival over his longstanding opposition to government-financed internal improvements. Nonetheless, Johnson's populist appeal continued, and he emerged victorious in his first statewide election, becoming Tennessee's 15th governor in October 1853.[18]

In those days, Tennessee's chief executive officer faced lots of limitations, but the position remained a potential pathway to bigger and better things, as Polk had demonstrated. As such, Johnson set out to do all he could within the state's legal parameters to make his mark. For one thing, he brought attention to Tennessee's public-school system, calling it the second-worst in the country and suggesting state and/or county taxes be added to correct it. He also advocated a coherent plan of public works that would ensure that the three divisions of the long state (East, Middle, West) were interwoven together, a concept Tennesseans have promoted and adhered to ever since. As governor, Johnson also rarely missed an opportunity to advertise himself or his ideas. When the question of his re-nomination arose in 1855, the Democrats were only too happy to stick with what Trefousse called "the strongest vote-getter in the state." Indeed, the Greeneville tailor defied the odds and won yet again, continuing an 18-year political run worthy of approbation.[19]

As a result, when the Democrats met to select a presidential nominee in 1856, Johnson was hopeful they might turn to a pro–Union, pro-slavery governor like himself, especially with Pierce's re-nomination unlikely. Instead, they chose James Buchanan of Pennsylvania, a former secretary of state and someone Johnson considered "the slowest" of all possible nominees, but a surprise presidential winner nonetheless. At about the same time, he decided that with chances for a Democratic majority in the state legislature improving, his opportunity for a U.S. Senate seat might never be better. It would mean giving up the position he already held, but it was a high office on the national stage, and for him a gamble worth taking.

Johnson campaigned vigorously for Democrats in the state elections, knowing their success would aid his own senatorial chances. His efforts were rewarded when another Democrat, Isham G. Harris, succeeded him as governor by carrying the state in record fashion. The party also achieved a clear majority in the legislature. As a result, Trefousse said, Johnson "reaped his reward" on October 8, 1957, when that same majority elected him to the U.S. Senate.[20]

Taking his populist, agrarian ideology back to Washington, Johnson moved into the Senate at a time when the old guard was changing. Gone were the larger-than-life personalities of the Jacksonian era, senatorial giants like Clay, Webster, Calhoun, and Benton. In their place were fervent anti-slavery men like Seward, Charles Sumner of Massachusetts, and Ben Wade of Ohio, and equally zealous slavery defenders like South Carolina's James Hammond and Mississippi's Jefferson Davis (future president of the Confederacy).[21] Upon entering this contentious mix, Johnson immediately pressed for his Homestead Bill, which he had nurtured through the House, only to see it never pass the Senate because it remained unpopular in the South. Intense sectionalism filtered into everything, and although supported by most Northerners, Johnson's pet bill scared his fellow Southerners, most of whom considered 160 acres not enough land to support slavery. Johnson strove to temper Southern reluctance by arguing that the agricultural middle class was key to American society, and with the proliferation of homesteads westward, the North would finally recognize the usefulness of slavery as free labor. It was a doomed argument, however, and his bill again failed.[22]

Upon returning from the 1859 congressional recess, Johnson took advantage of the buzz surrounding John Brown's attempted slave insurrection at Harpers Ferry to try to put himself right with his Southern colleagues. He still needed their support for his Homestead

Bill if it was ever to pass the Senate, and, Trefousse believed, he was also currying support for a possible run at the presidency. To entice them, he delivered a strongly worded address based on the Declaration of Independence that, according to Trefousse, proclaimed, "all men created equal could not apply to Negroes." Continuing, he stressed his belief that God had created racial differences for a reason, and he took issue with Northern attempts to do away with an institution of such importance to the South's economic well-being.[23]

In the end, his Homestead legislation became increasingly politicized to the point that other versions were introduced. Although ultimately gaining enough support to see it pass the Senate, the House by this time had introduced a series of new provisions to reconcile Southerners. Compromise became essential if it was to pass both Houses and land on the president's desk. Even last-minute compromise, however, was not enough to sell Buchanan, and he vetoed the measure, yet another death knell to Johnson's longstanding legislation. Trefousse stated, "For the Southern father of the Homestead Bill, it was once and for all embarrassing."[24]

Nevertheless, he continued to believe he still had a shot at the presidential nomination if he could find enough common ground between his Northern and Southern sources of support. He was, after all, a Southern moderate, firm on slavery, but known for his homestead advocacy, which remained popular in the North. Undoubtedly, the 1860 Democratic frontrunner was Stephen Douglas, who was openly contesting the anti-slavery Lincoln in their home state (Illinois), but whose extreme popular-sovereignty stand rendered him unpopular in the South and seemed to make Johnson the second contender in line, especially once Tennessee made him its favorite-son candidate.[25] Johnson's hopes were dashed, however, as the Democrats, who were holding their convention in Charleston, South Carolina, the hotbed of secessionist sentiment, began to pull apart. Unable to make a choice in Charleston, they adjourned and reconvened in more moderate Baltimore, Maryland, a month later. Many thought a Douglas-Johnson ticket was the only pairing that could threaten the candidacy of Lincoln, who had been nominated by the Republican Party a few weeks earlier, but the divisions of Charleston had not healed, and the Democrats split, with Douglas the candidate of the moderates and John Breckinridge of Kentucky, a states' rights advocate and Buchanan's vice president, the choice of secession advocates.[26]

The 1860 presidential election would prove a disaster for Southern Unionists like Johnson. It was ominous in that in ten Southern states, the Republican ticket of Abraham Lincoln of Illinois and Hannibal Hamlin of Maine did not receive a single vote. Like other states in the Upper South, Tennessee still favored Union, but with the election of Lincoln, that loyalty became tenuous.[27]

Shortly thereafter, Johnson returned to Congress, which had appointed two committees of compromise to try to appease the so-called "Ultras" of the Deep South. While attending a Southern caucus on December 8, he was appalled to learn that many of his congressional colleagues were already charting a course of separation for their southernmost states. South Carolina was famously taking the lead. Furiously, Johnson and others sought constitutional amendments to stem the secessionist tide, but it soon became apparent that the die had already been cast, and nothing they could come up with would compromise anything anymore. Despite an impassioned speech in which he defended the Union and called on a nation of patriots to stand together and preserve it, an address that drew tremendous accolades throughout the North and Border States, most of the Deep South condemned his sentiments as playing to the abolitionists.[28]

Tennessee, meanwhile, was divided, but along unusual lines. Most of Johnson's Democratic supporters came out against him after his speech, while traditional foes like Brownlow voiced surprising support. In the slave-centric community of Memphis on the banks of the Mississippi River, his image was hung in effigy and burned. The state legislature and governor even initiated a movement to oust him from his Senate seat.[29]

Realizing the significance of his precarious public stand and doubting its political future, Johnson nonetheless doubled down on his earlier address with another in which he pleaded for national unity despite the totally sectional, just completed election results. Once again, Republicans applauded his efforts while Southerners were outraged with his seemingly Northern stand. Trefousse acknowledged: "The senator from Tennessee was rapidly becoming a hero in the free states." Despite Deep South outrage, his words did help in his own state against the rush to secession, as voters temporarily defeated the call for a secessionist convention. Some even credited Johnson for the temporary victory.[30]

With similar impoverished backgrounds and overachieving careers, the new president had to appreciate Johnson's repeated Unionist stands. Along with Kentucky Senator John Crittenden, Johnson even co-authored several resolutions just days before the Civil War's first major battle at Manassas, Virginia, hoping to retain the loyalty of Unionists in the seceded states.[31] With no Republicans in Tennessee, the new administration automatically turned to Johnson regarding the Volunteer State. His increasing popularity in Washington, in fact, began manifesting itself in more nuanced ways, with locals cheering his comings and goings, as he sought to convince people that Tennesseans would remain loyal. Unfortunately, that was proven incorrect when Lincoln reacted to the Deep South's ordinances of secession and firing on the federal fort in Charleston Harbor (Fort Sumter) by calling for troops from each remaining state to put down the rebellion, something that was bound not to go over well in the Upper South.[32]

It didn't, especially in Tennessee, where Governor Harris refused Lincoln's call, and the secessionists quickly assumed command. Johnson returned home after Sumter to again try to rally Union sentiment. Twice en route he was threatened by mobs alongside his train. Only the intervention of by-then Confederate President Davis, who did not want a Union martyr on his hands before Tennessee officially seceded, ensured his safe travel back to East Tennessee. However, it didn't get better once he was home. Despite the best efforts of Johnson and other East Tennessee political leaders, Harris and the rest of the state, both the middle and western sections, were firmly in the Confederate column and bent on joining their sister Southern states. Johnson ultimately had to escape Tennessee via back roads through Cumberland Gap and neutral Kentucky. He would not see his home again for eight years.[33]

By contrast, upon reaching Washington, he was back in his Senate seat immediately and hailed as a hero wherever he went. Northern Democrats spoke of him as a future president, and Republicans even vied for his support. Accordingly, his biographer noted, "As the only senator from a seceding state to have remained loyal, he enjoyed a unique position." He was someone "Lincoln listened to attentively."[34]

As the war began with surprising Southern successes and Washington nearly cut off from the rest of the North, Johnson lost none of his zeal for eventual reunification. The South should retain its rights once reunited, he maintained, while at the same time advocating extraordinary war powers to the president. Daily he grew more popular north of the Mason-Dixon Line, while both a "fugitive and refugee," in Trefousse's words, from his own state. Meanwhile, the East Tennessee Unionists he had left behind expected help. But as much as Lincoln wished to provide military succor to East Tennessee's loyalists, wartime strategy prohibited it until more critical targets had been addressed. Many of Johnson's friends and family were jailed, went into hiding, or joined guerrilla bands operating against the Confederate government. His property was sequestered.

Truly an exile, he continued to advocate in Congress and with the military for a march on East Tennessee and the liberation of his home region, all for naught.[35] Fortunately, his frustrations were relieved somewhat when Union victories at Forts Henry and Donelson opened the western and middle sections of his state to invasion and capture.[36] That's when Lincoln approached him about becoming Tennessee's military governor, a logical choice that put him in position to make a difference in the conflict moving forward and the reunification to follow. He departed his lone Southern Senate seat in early February 1862.[37]

Heroic though he may have been in the minds of Northerners, however, he was anathema to most in the South, and his appointment was a gamble given the built-in animosity of most Tennesseans. It was feared by many that attempts on his life could be in the offing as a natural expression of secessionist revenge. But with no state legislature to re-elect him to the next U.S. Congress, Johnson had little recourse but to accept Lincoln's assignment and do the best he could to govern Tennessee as the first Confederate state to be largely subdued. Needless to say, he was not enthusiastically received upon reaching Nashville and remained under constant threat of assassination.[38]

Although at least partially under Union control, Tennessee would remain in the crosshairs of major battles like Shiloh, Stones River, and Chattanooga, and of Confederate raiders like Nathan Bedford Forest and John Hunt Morgan.[39] Throughout the chaos of it all, Johnson remained entrenched and under constant personal threat amid the still rebellious majority, but more committed than ever to renewing Union loyalty in his native state. To do so, he remained committed to reconciliation while at the same time ensuring that the subjugated population under his jurisdiction understood the mistake and futility of further resistance.[40]

Johnson also continued to administer the civilian government as best he could and to deliver animated speeches about what he deemed the Southern aristocracy, their hostility towards popular government, and the ascendancy of the Union guaranteed through the Constitution. At the same time, he continued to face the question of slavery and his defense of it in the guise of the Constitution. In his mind, at least, everything the founders had allowed should remain unchallenged, especially given its importance in the South's agrarian culture and economy. As an appointee of the Lincoln administration, it was the single most important issue he had to face. With congressional radicals and foreign governments echoing each other in their revulsion of the peculiar institution, and Lincoln himself leaning towards emancipation, Johnson had to walk the tightrope of Unionist commitment with the retention of slavery. Although conquered, Tennessee's majority expected as much.[41]

It was at this point in his story that Trefousse revealed how clever Johnson could be as a politician. With Lincoln on the verge of a preliminary emancipation proclamation, liberating all slaves held in areas still in rebellion, Johnson moved to ensure that Lincoln did not include Tennessee among the areas still in rebellion, a reprieve the president was willing to grant his military governor to avoid local backlash.[42] Nevertheless, as his biographer stated, "Johnson had now reached a dividing line in his military governorship." Ultimately, he came to the realization that emancipation had to become part of his future. He had often said he was for Union first and Southern slavery second, and it was apparent that his acceptance of the dissolution of the latter would be imperative to any political hopes he might have moving forward. By agreeing to unconditional emancipation, he could earn the gratitude of both Lincoln and the Republican Party, so he opted for the course of common sense. The handwriting was all over the wall when it came to what would surely be the post-war nation when the Union prevailed or, if by some stretch of the imagination, it didn't and the Union was indeed split. Either way, his political future, at least in his home state, seemed resoundingly over.[43]

Instead, a higher calling would be the vice presidency. In the words of one Lincoln biographer, Johnson's addition to the 1864 ballot cleverly provided "a bold voice for Lincoln's more conservative option," while another Pulitzer-winning Lincoln scholar pointed to Johnson's Border State influence as the reason for his addition to the national ticket.[44]

According to Trefousse, Johnson had harbored presidential hopes since 1852, and in 1864 he emerged as a strong contender for higher office. In fact, as a lifelong Democrat, many had him penciled in as a likely presidential candidate to oppose Lincoln in 1864.[45] But in all actuality, did anyone really have a chance of displacing Lincoln after the fall of Atlanta, the capture of Mobile Bay, and Grant's steady march on Richmond, which heralded victory and the end of the Civil War?[46] While a Democrat might have had a chance earlier in the war when expectations had crashed and burned during a series of Confederate victories, the tide had turned at Vicksburg and Gettysburg, and the North's overwhelming advantage in resources and manpower wasn't about to let it turn back.[47] Fact was, only Lincoln's vice president was really in jeopardy by the time the 1864 election drew near. Hamlin, his incumbent VP from Maine, seemed to lend nothing to the ticket the second time around, and Lincoln was interested in adding appeal with a War Democrat like Johnson.[48]

At the same time, the constitutionality of naming a Southerner (even a loyal one) was questioned, but such concerns did not faze Johnson. He took special pride in being Lincoln's vice presidential choice from a "rebellious state" and the symbolism that implied, as if Tennessee had never officially left the Union. To his way of thinking, he had defended the government "to which he had always been devoted, but slavery had gotten in the way and must disappear." By firing on Fort Sumter, he maintained that the secessionists (not Lincoln) had actually taken the first step towards freeing the slaves, and the Radical Republicans in Congress loved it.[49] When the election was finally held, Lincoln and Johnson won a majority of both the popular and electoral vote, carrying every eligible state except New Jersey, Kentucky, and Delaware. Naturally, none of the 11 Confederate states took part.[50]

Meanwhile, Southern forces ceased to exist in East Tennessee, and Confederate General John Bell Hood, with one final and desperate thrust into Middle Tennessee, was so thoroughly defeated that his army literally disintegrated at the Battle of Nashville. Observing this final act of the Civil War in his state, Johnson dissolved his military governorship and began the process of a new, duly elected state government and his own transition to higher office in Washington.[51]

Many influential voices in Washington were calling on Lincoln to give more responsibility to his new vice president in the re-elected administration, hoping the Southern War Democrat could be a mediating voice for the returning, reconstructed states. Unfortunately for the new VP, however, his first impression turned out not so good. Illness set in during his return trip for the inauguration activities, and in an already weakened state, he misguidedly allowed himself three glasses of whiskey before taking his oath of office in the Senate Chamber. During his acceptance speech, his remarks became slurred and quickly sank to a political "harangue" unworthy of the occasion. Trefousse admitted, "the audience was horrified," and the president couldn't have been happy.

Naturally, the opposition press gloried in the new vice president's undignified failure upon assuming office, and it only got worse when his illness persisted and he had to miss several days overseeing the Senate, his primary role. Despite the embarrassment of the moment and public scorn, Lincoln remained convinced his new vice president was not an alcoholic and would bounce back. He even said, "I have known Andy Johnson for many

ABRAHAM LINCOLN,
OF ILLINOIS.

ANDREW JOHNSON,
OF TENNESSEE.

This Republican campaign poster is a historic reminder of the larger-than-life legacy Andrew Johnson was faced with living up to once he replaced the assassinated Abraham Lincoln, still America's most revered president (Library of Congress Prints and Photographs Division—Reproduction Number DIG-ppmsea-19255).

years; he had a bad slip, but you need not be scared; Andy ain't a drunkard."[52] And he retained his trust in Johnson at war's end, even when his VP sounded a less lenient tone than his own regarding the defeated rebellion leaders. Lincoln and Johnson were last together at the White House on April 14, 1865—Good Friday. John Wilkes Booth, an accomplished actor, shot Lincoln later that same night while he and Mrs. Lincoln were attending a play at Ford's Theater.[53]

The first assassination of a president in American history came at the end of one of the longest and bloodiest civil wars in world history, so although it shocked and reviled the war-torn country, no one should have been surprised in an era before sufficient presidential security and precaution. An evening at the theater in the midst of post-war celebration ended in extreme alarm because of an angry Southern sympathizer's unwillingness to accept defeat. Along with a contingent of co-conspirators, he attempted to take national reconciliation into his own hands. In addition to the president, a serious and near-successful attempt was made on the life of Secretary of State Seward, and Vice President Johnson was also in the conspiracy crosshairs until his would-be assailant got cold feet. Trefousse wrote:

> Johnson had gone to bed early that night. Shortly after 10:15 he was awakened by a loud knock at [his] door. [A] fellow boarder at Kirkwood House called in a loud voice, "Governor Johnson, if you are in this room I must see you." The door opened and Johnson was excitedly told the news. The president had been shot. The vice president, stunned [held] on [to his informant] for support. Soon there were guards outside to prevent any attempt to murder Johnson. No one knew how widespread the assassination plot was.

Lincoln was dead by the following morning. Johnson had briefly gone to the dying president's bedside, but did not stay long. He was officially notified of his death by the Cabinet and sworn in at his hotel between 10 and 11 a.m. Chief Justice Salmon Chase administered the oath, and the new president issued a brief and this time "dignified" address.[54]

At his first Cabinet meeting the next afternoon, Johnson asked them all to remain in their posts. With Mrs. Lincoln as distraught as humanly possible, he delayed moving into the White House. In the meantime, all kinds of rumors made their way through Washington and the country, as paranoia set in over the fact Booth had concocted an elaborate plot to eliminate the entire Union leadership.[55]

Johnson immediately set the stage for what would be the new administration's troubles with the Radical Republican Congress it had been dealt. Gone and anointed with both martyrdom and sainthood was Lincoln, and in his place was a man without a party or section to call his own. Johnson had burned a lot of bridges by the time he ascended to the White House. His revised stance on slavery while moving from the Senate to the military governorship and joining a Republican administration after rising through Democratic ranks put him on precarious ground even before dealing with congressional radicals bent on imposing their will and the pragmatic Lincoln no longer around.[56] According to Trefousse, Johnson took his time before declaring any of his own policies, but his Jacksonian belief in the power of the chief executive was well established. Despite early efforts at diplomacy with the Radicals, who did their best to pick his brain, Johnson was noncommittal. While speaking of stiff retribution for Confederate leaders, something the Radical Republicans loved to hear, Johnson merely bought himself time with such tough talk.[57]

His main goal in those earliest days after the assassination was reassuring the nation. Following the somber yet impressive days of the Lincoln funeral, the high point of his opening weeks as president was a huge victory parade on back-to-back days in May down Pennsylvania Avenue. The new commander-in-chief basked in the spotlight of Union heroes Ulysses Grant and Sherman, as well as an enlisted cast of thousands. In that moment, he could sense he had the support of the country as he began to determine policy. It was a feeling of acceptance, however, that had to be tempered with knowledge of what the nation faced. With the Southern states re-entering the Union, how (exactly) was that to be accomplished, and what could be done about the freedmen, the vast majority of African Americans in the South who suddenly had rights and freedom? A speedy restoration of Southern states' rights had the potential to elevate the Democratic Party as the result of that section's aptly-named Solid South mentality, a unity of purpose the Republican majority in Congress obviously deemed contrary to what the war had been fought to rectify.[58] Trefousse wrote, "From the very first Johnson was disinclined to interfere with voting requirements. The Constitution clearly left voting qualifications to the states and convinced the seceded commonwealths were still part of the Union, he considered interference a violation of his firmly held belief in states' rights."[59]

Such inclinations and beliefs clearly ran counter to congressional imperatives of the time. The Radical Republicans in the House and Senate began to grow uneasy, and their anxiety only intensified when the new president decided to restore Southern statehood as quickly as possible. The Cabinet was split, with half supporting Johnson's accelerated pace and states' rights objectives, and the other half lining up with the Radicals when it came to voting rights and suffrage for the "freedmen." By summer, Radicals were beseeching Johnson to call Congress into special session to establish policy for what would be "their Reconstruction," more specifically, a policy to their liking without the states' rights allowances the president was making. They sought his cooperation, but they were rebuffed repeatedly, and Senator Sumner even commented that Johnson wished to surrender Reconstruction "to the tender mercies of the rebels."[60]

Meanwhile, the president's friends in the Upper South applauded his rapid moves toward reinstatement of states after certain prerequisites had been met, and one by one the Confederate states were invited back into the Union with provisional governors hand-picked by Johnson. Unfortunately for him and those in the South who universally praised his benevolent attitude towards re-admission along with most Northern Democrats, the more extreme congressional majority offered just as much criticism.[61] Trefousse wrote, "According to Johnson's theories, the end of the war required as speedy a normalization and as near a return to pre-war conditions as possible," and while he embraced emancipation as a necessary step in the national reunification process, he never changed his conviction of the inherent inferiority of the freedmen.[62]

The provisional governors Johnson put in place rapidly initiated his Reconstruction desires, calling for state conventions to officially abolish slavery within their borders, nullifying or repealing secession ordinances, and repudiating Confederate debts. But despite those desired objectives, Johnson failed to apply pressure for their acceptance. Perhaps his ultimate belief in state sovereignty restricted him from doing so, but whatever the reason, his reluctance to do so proved disastrous as Southern voters again turned to staunch conservatives consumed by the South's "Lost Cause," who passed Black Codes so rigid they all but renewed slavery. In view of these developments and resistance to Southern change, the Radical Republicans naturally became more and more alarmed.[63]

Between December 1865 and July 1866, those Republican fears worsened as the president took an obstinate course. Johnson simply had no interest in compromising his personal goals for Reconstruction. With all his political experience, Trefousse maintained, it's hard to believe he did not realize the stormy road he was taking. He obviously hoped to rally conservatives from both parties, a bipartisan course fraught with pitfalls. A lifelong Democrat before the war, he had never embraced Republicanism despite working for the Lincoln administration during the conflict, and he was not about to embrace it afterwards. Trefousse even headed a chapter "Pugnacious President," and it would not be a stretch to identify the reason for that title being the predominant factor in Johnson's historic legacy. What has come down to us from his term in office is the resulting controversy that has trailed his name ever since. The fact is that the man put himself in an untenable position politically. Maybe he should be viewed differently for being principled even if his principles were flawed, but regardless, his choices in the midst of tragedy (the Lincoln assassination), acute enmity (post-war America), and social upheaval (how to deal with the freed slaves) seemed to justify debate and compromise on almost every issue facing the deeply divided country. Johnson simply wasn't interested in any of that, to his political detriment.[64]

Although favorably received and given the benefit of the doubt, at least initially, due to the catastrophic way he came to office, he failed to cultivate allies in the congressional ranks even on the most basic post-war issues (like expansion of the Freedman's Bureau), and he vetoed bills designed to get the reunified country started again in a more enlightened, progressive spirit. He simply wasn't willing to concede anything when it came to the constitutional prerogatives of the individual states. Republicans believed he had severed ties with their party and re-united with their adversaries. His stance and vetoes created the kind of furor he had been used to on a lesser scale in Tennessee politics, but unlike his home state, he found it was not easy to make direct appeals from the White House, especially when he went off the rails with personal attacks on individual congressmen and senators who opposed him. Some sort of civil rights legislation was needed, but when the chance to reach compromise was afforded him, Johnson cast it aside and did not sign legislation because Southern states were not yet represented, and because a complete break with Congress might realize his hope of a new political alignment.[65]

He was treading on thin ice. His repeated vetoes seemed to indicate he would not approve any protections for the newly freed slaves, leaving that instead to the returning and formerly mutinous Southern states. Ultimately one of his vetoes was overridden, and any congressional support he enjoyed at the start of his accidental presidency eroded. Undaunted, he maintained, "Sir, I am right. I know I am right and I am damned if I do not adhere to it," but his views began to undermine what all Republicans and most Northern voters felt the war had been fought to ensure, and public sentiment, except in the South, began to turn against him. Indeed, his positions left him stranded between various constituencies, each of which he attempted to cater to through patronage, creating a muddled mix of support that offered little help. Always he assumed that the people would back his middle ground, but without a strict party path to call his own he was vulnerable.

Southerners may have appreciated his avoidance of hardline Reconstruction measures, but they did little to reinforce his generous treatment. Instead, avowed rebels were returned to local seats of power, and acts of racial intimidation became commonplace, all of which the Radical Republicans would pin on the president. Outrages against African Americans and Southern White Unionists were aired before a Joint Committee on Reconstruction in January 1866. Something had to be done in the way of acceptance and protection for the powerless new Southern citizens, the result being the Fourteenth Amendment. Johnson, however, remained opposed to anything that amended the Constitution until all new Southern senators and congressmen had been elected and seated. Until that happened, he chose to use the influence of the presidency to stop ratification.[66]

Serious consequences were the result. Johnson considered the Fourteenth Amendment "an expression of congressional opposition to his program," even though a little give and take on his part would have lent itself to "a much less dramatic course," according to his biographer. However, "the president would not yield," and the history of Reconstruction took a most contentious course as a result. To Johnson, as long as Congress was "in the hands of the Radicals," bringing the Southern states back in and returning all the states to their proper relationship would be impossible.

Meanwhile, the new amendment had received the necessary two-thirds vote in both Houses by mid–June 1866, but since the 11 Southern states were not represented in that vote and since the joint resolution had not been forwarded to the president as was customary, Johnson took it upon himself to go to the Capitol and confront Congress about what he deemed an inappropriate act. "Nobody wanted him, nobody expected him, nobody felt he had any business [being] there," the *New York Tribune* reported, and Trefousse added, "His opinions were becoming irrelevant and unless he was careful, he would be left without any support." Seriously weakened, his vetoes from then on would all be overridden, and his views on Southern reinstatement and constraints on federal protections of the newly freed African Americans were dismissed.[67]

"Beleaguered" is the word his biographer used next to illustrate the political corner Johnson had backed himself into, and "defiant" is the one he chose to acknowledge how Johnson would handle his remaining two years in office. To extricate himself from his party-less position by the summer of 1866, he hoped a new party would arise and embrace his formula for restoring the Union. His hopes for the new political organization received sustenance from political moderates such as Seward and Thurlow Weed, and Democrats, who valued the traditions of Presidents Jefferson and Jackson as much as he did. Any real possibilities of a new party developing, however, were dealt an unsustainable blow when his Cabinet began to fall apart.[68]

Seward could be counted upon and did remain as secretary of state, but Secretary of War Edwin Stanton, a Lincoln mainstay, was never a Johnson fan and was allowed to remain at his Cabinet post too long. As a result, he became an ally of the Radical Republicans and especially their leaders, Sumner and Congressman Thaddeus Stevens of Pennsylvania, a committed abolitionist who was labeled "churlish," "sarcastic," and even "intimidating" by three different recent historians and "a political brigand [and] rude legislative jouster" by contemporaries. He moved awkwardly, the result of a birth defect, wore imposing wigs, the result of a chronic scalp condition, and was certainly the most vindictive and punishment-prone of the Radicals when it came to perceptions of an unrepentant "White South."

Three other Cabinet members also resigned over Johnson's opposition to the Fourteenth Amendment and aspirations for a new party. Further damaging his hopes were riots and deaths in Memphis and New Orleans, where Southern conservatives and police clashed with freedmen and Unionists over immediate African American suffrage, a situation he and his strict constitutional stance were blamed for throughout the North.[69]

Johnson heard the attacks and responded the only way he knew how—through stump speeches and campaigning for his principals in the face of mounting congressional disapproval. It was what he had always done when attacked politically in Tennessee, and although warned that such things were not becoming of a sitting president, he nevertheless continued his parade of impromptu speeches whenever and wherever the opportunity arose, even when his comments were in response to hecklers. "The result," Trefousse stated, "was a series of confrontations that greatly hurt the president's cause."[70]

To most people, it was Congress versus the president, and the more he defensively responded to attacks, the more the Northern public seemed to take Congress' side. Fear of renewed Southern political power was a far greater factor in the North after the war than any racial undertones that might be aroused by former slaves actually getting to vote. Without an established party to call his own, Johnson faced an uphill battle. Only through more and more patronage could he count on Democratic support, and only through a severe prosecution of Southern re-entry could he court Republicans. He was not prepared to do either, and talk of impeachment began to surface as the Rad-

Leader of the so-called "Radical Republicans" in Congress, Thaddeus Stevens of Pennsylvania was an unyielding opponent of President Andrew Johnson and his Reconstruction policies after the Civil War (Library of Congress Prints and Photographs Division—Reproduction Number USZ62-63460).

ical Republicans swept Northern state elections. While Seward remained loyal, Stanton increasingly identified with Congress, and Johnson's closest friends pushed him to replace the secretary of war. For self-preservation, they also urged him to give in and accept the Fourteenth Amendment, something he was not prepared to do.[71]

Stubborn to a fault, he refused to mandate racial equality or military jurisdiction over his returning Southern brethren by endorsing the Fourteenth Amendment, causing his congressional opponents to become determined to oust him once the 1866 midterm elections revealed just how much the country sided with them. With the threat of reducing Southern states to territories, Congress introduced legislation requiring universal male suffrage as a prerequisite for state constitutions before readmission. With the president still opposed, Southern legislatures, considering the amendment as written, beginning with Alabama, took their lead from his continued opposition and rejected it.[72]

Then it became Congress' turn to become inflexible. Led by the irascible Stevens in the House, many congressmen and senators were suddenly aiming for a fight. Moving forward without consulting Johnson, Congress passed a bill limiting the president's pardoning power. In addition, the Radical Republicans moved to construct a Tenure of Office Act, essentially to take away his power to remove officials appointed with the Senate's consent until a successor had been approved. There was even incorporated into military appropriations a measure requiring the president to issue orders through the ranking general of the Army (Grant). Angrily, Johnson viewed it all as congressional interference with his prerogatives as commander-in-chief.[73]

And finally, there was the Reconstruction Act of 1867, undoing completely Johnson's earlier reconciliation efforts, which Congress passed in exasperation over Southern refusals to ratify the Fourteenth Amendment. It defined the existing Southern state governments as provisional in addition to providing for military jurisdiction in the South, with the prerequisites of ratification and impartial suffrage before restoration of the affected states could take place. In response, the president asked his Cabinet for unified opposition to provisional status, something every Cabinet member agreed to except Stanton. When it passed anyway, Johnson refused to sign it into law, leaving Congress to override his veto again, and the president depressed. Whenever impeachment came up, he swore violently, complained he was not going to be threatened, and pledged to move forward with or without congressional sanction.[74]

The initial advocate for impeachment was Ben Butler, a controversial former Union general and military governor of Louisiana turned Massachusetts politician. Butler was joined in pursuit of Johnson's ouster by an influential group of House leaders that included Zachariah Chandler of Michigan, James Ashley of Ohio, Benjamin Loan of Missouri, and, of course, Stevens, who was convinced no rational Reconstruction plan would work until Johnson was removed. In early January 1867, Ashley officially introduced the "impeachment of Andrew Johnson for high crimes and misdemeanors against the government of the United States." Among the charges was "usurpation of power and violation of law by corrupt use of his appointment, pardoning, and veto powers; the corrupt disposition of property belonging to the U.S.; and direct interference in [state] elections." Ashley's resolution was promptly referred to the House Judiciary Committee.[75]

At the same time, there were numerous Republican doubts that anything of the sort was possible, given that presidential removal would require not only a majority in the House, but also two-thirds of the Senate.[76] Conducted in private, the committee's inquiries looked for supporting evidence—such things as possible correspondence between Johnson and Confederate leaders, illegal appointments of military governors in the South, and any wrongful disposal of railroads seized by the federal government during the war. When these avenues of investigation proved insufficient, Johnson's bank records and the motives behind his vetoes were explored, as well as fake connections he was maliciously rumored to have had with Lincoln's assassin—in other words, what modern-day political theorists might label "a witch hunt."[77]

Despite the animosity between Congress and the president, one accomplishment of the period that was initially criticized but later proved visionary was the U.S. purchase of Alaska from Russia. Orchestrated by Seward, who had stayed on in the Cabinet and who, unlike Stanton, retained Johnson's trust, the treaty, acquiring what was mocked as "Seward's Folly" and Johnson's "Polar Bear Garden," was completed and ratified by the end of March 1867. Also, Nebraska became a state in 1867 due to another of those congressional overrides of a Johnson veto. Both now seem surprising given the hostility that engulfed everyone.[78]

For example, the relations of Johnson and Stanton continued to deteriorate. The secretary of war was by then guilty of undermining his new commander-in-chief, but for some reason (perhaps Stanton's support when he was military governor), Johnson refused to dismiss him. Finally, Stanton's disagreement with the president's more relaxed approach to Southern reinstatement came to a head in the summer of 1867, when Johnson was compelled to plan his removal. Only the Tenure of Office Act stood in his way, but with Stanton's decision to empower his generals to supersede the decisions of local officials in the South whenever they ran counter to congressional dictates, there was no turning back.[79]

Johnson decided to rid his administration of Stanton no matter the roadblocks. To do so, he needed to confer with the ever-popular commander of the Army, Grant, and he made his move during a congressional recess in order to make an interim appointment that would not violate the Tenure Act. Actually, he implored Grant to take over as secretary of war once Stanton was removed, but Trefousse confirmed that Grant was hesitant. He "professed to be unfamiliar with many of the administrative duties" and even put his objections in writing. Predictably, Johnson took the matter up with the rest of his Cabinet while Stanton was absent, but received only mixed support. Most thought that to relieve Stanton while Congress was away would risk driving the president's remaining supporters into the Radicals' camp. Johnson, however, was undeterred and issued a letter of dismissal to Stanton, who promptly replied that "public considerations of a high character" constrained him not to resign before the next meeting of Congress, obviously banking on the Tenure Act and the Radical majority to sustain his service at the head of the War Department.[80]

Johnson was unsurprised. A few days later, on August 12, 1867, he sent a suspension order to Stanton, making sure it was in conformity with the Tenure of Office Act. It read: "By virtue of the power and authority vested in me as president by the Constitution and laws of the United States, you are hereby suspended from the office of secretary of war and will cease to exercise any and all functions of the same." Stanton was to transfer his duties at once to Grant, who would act as interim secretary. Grant's reluctant acceptance of the president's wishes was the only reason Stanton was willing to comply, denying Johnson's authority without congressional approval, but willing to yield his office if Grant was put in charge.[81]

Not so trusting were the Radical Republicans. Johnson's dismissal of Stanton was a prelude to him also getting rid of the Army's ranking commander in the South, Phillip Sheridan, who had jurisdiction over Texas and Louisiana. That did not sit well with Grant, and again he protested in writing, which Johnson took as insubordination. Both Sheridan and Daniel Sickles, another former Union general presiding over the Carolinas, were dismissed, to the delight of Southerners, and Johnson's relations with Grant became strained.[82]

Johnson actually considered replacing Grant, according to Trefousse, after previous Democratic gains in the 1866 midterm elections buoyed him into believing Northerners would understand if he had to do so to speed reconciliation with the Southern states. According to his biographer, one of Johnson's goals was "rescuing the South from Negro rule," which he was convinced would happen if the Radical Republicans had their way. The election results had seemed to confirm his belief in the necessity of White supremacy throughout the country. Although free, African Americans in his mind would always be inferior.[83]

But those same election results had also alarmed the Radicals, who rekindled impeachment proceedings. They had become convinced that Johnson's defiant removal of Stanton and the generals was the abuse of power and obstruction that would have to be addressed if the reconstructed nation (with their goals) was to move forward. Despite less evidence than they had hoped for, the House Judiciary Committee moved for impeachment. Its majority report was what Trefousse termed "a hodge-podge of charges centering on Johnson's Reconstruction policies." Included was his pardoning of the leading Southern traitors; his alleged profiting from illegal disposal of railroads while military governor of Tennessee; his supposed responsibility for the New Orleans riot the previous year; and his defiance of Congress by his series of vetoes designed to deny its right to reconstruct the South and prevent ratification of the Fourteenth Amendment.

Johnson learned of the report on November 21 and aggressively asserted its lack of legal or constitutional basis. As expected, this first effort at impeachment by the House failed, prompting the exultant president to arouse his accusers further by immediately moving for additional protections for the reconstituted South, his way. He fired more generals over the military districts and continued to impede congressional initiatives. Southerners rejoiced at the president's actions, as they sought to return their states with as close to their pre-war social and political fabric as possible.[84]

At the same time, Johnson acted upon the provisions of the Tenure Act by communicating Stanton's suspension to the Senate, which rejected his reasoning, prompting an emboldened Stanton to defiantly return to the War Department in early January 1868. Trefousse confirmed that these events created controversy for Grant, who was still overseeing the War Department. Worried by implications of military penalties attached to the Tenure Act, Grant officially returned the office to Stanton on January 14 despite Johnson's consternation.

With the national press exposing embarrassing details of this ongoing administration soap opera and Johnson's rift with Grant growing more obvious by the day, battle lines were further etched in stone. Johnson, in fact, knew his ties to the Republican Party had been irrevocably shredded, and he was angling for a possible 1868 Democratic nomination with his forgiving stance towards the South and that party's repudiation of Grant, the Republicans' presumptive presidential nominee.[85]

Convinced he was in the right and that either Stanton had to go or he probably would, the president pressed what he perceived as political advantages the very next month. Knowing the Republicans were coming off setbacks in the last elections; gambling that they would be opposed to working with the caustic president pro tempore of the Senate, Ohio's Wade, who was in line to succeed Johnson by virtue of no vice president if he was impeached, almost as much as they were opposed to him; and realizing that Grant's backers wished to make the general's nomination a foregone conclusion before the Republican Convention, Johnson decided upon Adjutant General Lorenzo Thomas to succeed Stanton as secretary of war and to appoint him under the guise of the Constitution, while at the same time confirming Stanton's removal on February 21.[86] But instead of yielding to the president and his replacement, Stanton, who detested Thomas, resisted, barricading himself in his office and touting the Tenure Act with congressional support of the Republican majority. The Senate wasted no time going into executive session, crafting a resolution to deny Johnson's power to remove Stanton, and the House took it a step further, reconsidering impeachment by an overwhelming vote.[87]

So, while Johnson hoped to have the Tenure of Office Act thrown into the courts as a way of testing its constitutionality, the trial everyone was actually getting ready for was his own. On a rare, leap-year 29 of February, the House committee reported nine articles of impeachment, with all but the last two focusing on the president's dismissal of Stanton and appointment of Thomas. Supreme Court Justice Salmon Chase swore in the court of senators five days later, but the trial did not begin until March 30.[88]

In what Trefousse described as a tense, dramatic atmosphere, Johnson maintained that he had been impeached over "a violation of the Constitution and the laws." In reality, he argued, he was the one maintaining the Constitution, which Congress was "trampling under foot." As politically astute as ever, Johnson picked a distinguished panel of both Democrats and Republicans for his defense team, and he did not attend the proceedings. Meanwhile, Ben Butler presented the case against him, seeking to prove that Stanton had been illegally expelled under the Tenure Act and Thomas illegally appointed as a result. He "thundered" that "murder most foul" had led to Johnson's succession to the presidency and not "the people," marking a renewed supposition that the death of a sitting president, and particularly one assassinated, should not necessarily be followed by the automatic ascension of the vice president, but thanks to John Tyler that supposition went against established precedent and was viewed as "undignified."[89]

Actually, that would be the trial's most intense moment. In a display of legal mastery, the president's defense team illustrated that the fact that Stanton had been appointed by Lincoln and not by Johnson actually gave him the right to test the Tenure Act, and successfully argued that the rest of the House charges were nothing more than a challenge to free speech.[90] When final arguments were made, "excitement in the city rose to fever pitch with political pressure mounting on Republicans to vote for conviction," according to Trefousse. The Senate vote wasn't taken until mid–May, with every senator present. One by one, the roll call of senators went forward alphabetically, with each responding to the charges against the president as "guilty" or "not guilty." Every Democrat voted not guilty, while all but seven Republicans voted to convict. The final vote was one shy of the two-thirds needed for conviction.[91]

President Johnson was delighted—his congressional opponents were distraught. Rumors surfaced that one dissenting Republican had accepted a bribe. Democrats lauded the result even as they regretted being saddled with the incumbent. Meanwhile, as expected, the ensuing 1868 Republican Convention nominated Grant unanimously and basically unopposed on the first ballot.[92]

Trefousse admitted that the short time Johnson had left in the White House may have contributed to his acquittal. Voting for impeachment may not have seemed essential with the next presidential election just months away. Most in the House and Senate had tired of the process and were ready to see it end, but in the estimation of the fiercest Radicals, the wait on their Reconstruction goals had been long enough and the rightful destiny of the freedmen delayed by what they considered Johnson's "imperious presence." On the other hand, Johnson was convinced he had done what he had to do to preserve the Constitution and in so doing had assured future presidents of never having to face impeachment for purely political reasons.[93]

Except for Southern Unionists, his acquittal was cause for jubilation in the South, the kind not experienced since the last Confederate victory. Trefousse expressed the sentiment that Johnson's adamant opposition to the Radicals' much sterner approach "laid the foundation" for "Jim Crow" segregation in the South, which remained unrepentant "White man's country" for nine more decades.[94]

Vindicated (though the lamest of all lame duck presidents), Johnson spent his final months in office still coveting the 1868 Democratic nomination and Southern support, having gone from wartime traitor to Reconstruction savior in the eyes of his home region. He also had considerable support among Northern Democrats. What he didn't have, however, was forgiveness from that party's regulars for becoming Lincoln's running mate in the previous election or his initial patronage policies as president when he appointed Republicans. As a result, he never actually had a chance for the Democratic nomination, which went to Horatio Seymour, the wartime governor of New York and inevitable loser to the ultimate Union hero, Grant.[95]

In his remaining time in office, Johnson would issue a multitude of presidential pardons, including one for Jefferson Davis. He also continued to veto bills with impunity, though most would be overridden.[96] Stubborn and contentious to the end, he even had parting shots for his political enemies in his farewell address, before concluding: "The Constitution and the Union, one and inseparable."[97] Still in his early 60s at the time, he would seek a return to political office in Tennessee and amazingly accomplish that feat six years later—being sent back to the U.S. Senate in 1875, the only former president with that distinction. It was vindication for one of the most polarizing politicians in American history, but just five months into his Senate return at age 65, he died at his East Tennessee home after suffering strokes on consecutive days.[98]

13

The Surprising Story
of Chester Alan Arthur

*"On the civil service question he has no faith in reform, but in deference
to public sentiment, he yields to recommend an appropriation to carry it
out."*—Rutherford B. Hayes, 1881

In The American Presidents Series, Zachary Karabell took on the seemingly unenviable task of writing about Chester Alan Arthur, our 21st and largely unknown president. Accidental in the way he ascended to the presidency (as with three others through assassination), Arthur was even more accidental in the way he was positioned to ascend. Possibly nowhere in American history is the modern word "fluke" more apropos than as a description for how this lawyer turned "party hack," with little or no other office-seeking aspirations, found himself in position to assume the highest office in the land.[1] Early in his first chapter, Karabell wrote:

> Arthur is one of the forgotten presidents. Mention him to the proverbial man-on-the-street and
> blankness is a likely response. Even among those who consider themselves well educated, Chester
> Alan Arthur remains a cipher, one of those late-nineteenth century inhabitants of the White House
> whose echo has been muffled by more memorable individuals and whose footprint has been tram-
> pled and all but erased.[2]

In accepting his man and the moment, however, Karabell also set a surprising course of vindication for what Arthur accomplished in the three and a half years he occupied 1600 Pennsylvania Avenue. As illogical as it seems, Karabell contended that Arthur should be remembered (if not revered) for seeking to cure the very patronage-dominated system that produced his own ascendance. Arthur was perhaps the living embodiment of absurdity in a political process that had somehow cast a man of limited governing experience, one without the essential ambition to lead, into a position of extreme responsibility. This overwhelming realization settled upon "Chet" Arthur once he embraced the fact that he really was president. It had to be a realization that made little or no sense. But regardless, the fact that he would become the first American chief executive to significantly change the way civil service was viewed and handled in this country was significant and worthy of lasting admiration.[3]

"Not well known to the general public before 1880," Arthur was the product of a time after the near-removal of Andrew Johnson, when Congress dominated the federal government, but not because of any lasting individual leaders, as was commonplace before the Civil War.[4] Devoid of any charismatic orators like Daniel Webster, compromisers like Henry Clay, or radical thinkers like John C. Calhoun, Thaddeus Stevens, or Jefferson Davis, the Capitol was nonetheless the home of often corrupt partners, as industry and big business took over domination of the home front in the decades between Johnson and Theodore Roosevelt. Although important to the expanding goals of partisan politics, the White House after Lincoln became home to mostly rubber-stampers and yes men, as the nation seemed too busy to care much about who was in charge and Congress determined direction based primarily on the motivation of big business.

Generally speaking, it was government for the few, with everyone else striving to elevate their personal stock in order to earn a larger slice of the economic pie, including the thousands of immigrants flooding America's shores.[5] Historian Henry Adams, whom Karabell termed "the disillusioned sage of [that] era," stated, "The government does not govern. Congress is inefficient and shows itself more and more incompetent to wield the enormous powers forced upon it, while the president is practically devoid of necessary strengths due to the jealously of the legislature."[6] Amidst such a get-rich and me-first ideology, and the mingling of private-public leadership, the American way of handing out government jobs became little better than medieval fiefdoms. Who was on top, whom you got to know, and their connections up the legislative food chain were much more important than experience, education, or background in the selection process.[7]

According to Karabell, "State and local politics were controlled by party machines that prized loyalty" above all else. Although the public good and public service were talked about, those in government did not seem especially interested in things like "freedom, democracy, and equality," concentrating instead on "order, stability, and prosperity." Political machines ruled the cities. They were close-knit organizations that rounded up votes, collected a percentage of the profits, and kept the peace. Politics nationally rested on a "pyramid" of patronage at the lower levels of government. To the victors of elections, perhaps more than any other time in American history, "went the spoils," literally—jobs were doled out to supporters in return for getting out the vote. Government appointees were expected to give back monetarily via contributions—what Karabell termed "assessments" in a "self-perpetuating cycle."[8]

This was the Spoils System of which Arthur was both a product and a part as much as any man in America.[9] As established earlier in this book, he was a lawyer by trade who had gotten behind the idea of limiting the expansion of slavery, so much so, in fact, that he had briefly moved to Kansas, where the legalities of that idea were severely tested before the Civil War. But "Bleeding Kansas," as it became known, was not a place where the Eastern-born Arthur ever felt comfortable, and he soon returned to New York to resume his practice there in 1856. At the same time, his brief foray on the front lines of the slavery question led him to become a member of the Republican Party, which championed the cause of free soil under the leadership of New Yorkers Seward and Weed, Illinois' Lincoln, Ohio's Salmon Chase, and other former Whigs from the northern tier of states.[10]

Back in New York City, Arthur built a successful law career. He also cultivated connections with powerful Republicans, including New York Governor Edwin Morgan, who appointed him chief engineer and quartermaster for the state as hostilities with the South became increasingly anticipated, especially after Lincoln's victory in the presidential election of 1860. In what would be a non-combatant role, Arthur was responsible for the supply and feeding of several hundred thousand New York troops during 1861 and 1862, while also solidifying a place in New York's patronage network. When the Democrats returned to power during the Union's most dire moments of 1862, however, the same statewide patronage system that had given him a job left him out of one.[11]

Regardless, he was able to use his former position and connections to further his law career by litigating lucrative government contract disputes and becoming one of the best-paid lawyers of his time.[12] He was also able to further his standing in the state's Republican ranks by becoming affiliated with the more conservative wing, including party founders Seward and Weed, and a rising star, Roscoe Conkling. Senator Conkling would, in fact, provide the relationship by which Arthur would rise to patronage heights. Taking his political cues from the so-called "Apollo of the Senate" amidst Conkling's intense intra-party rivalry with Maine's James G. Blaine (just as elegantly nicknamed "The Plumed Knight"), Arthur emerged with one of the nation's top federal jobs in 1871—collector of the New York Customhouse under President Ulysses Grant. Also, by partnering with the ambitious Conkling, Arthur became an important player in the state party.[13] Nevertheless, when the financial panic of 1873 brought on depression and wide-spread unemployment, a reformist movement ended what Karabell called the "moiety process" by which customs officials like Arthur could (and did) double and triple their salaries, earning a percentage of the value seized and the fines levied from illegal shipments snared when brought into their ports. As a result, Arthur's annual salary dropped almost 80 percent, from more than $50,000 to about $12,000. "He was still a rich man" for that era, Karabell emphasized, "but no longer an embarrassingly overpaid one."[14]

Added to this financial setback was a political one, when the ever-popular Grant decided not to seek what would have been a precedent-setting third presidential term in 1876. As a result, the Blaine-Conkling rivalry re-surfaced, causing the Republican Convention to turn to a compromise candidate, Rutherford B. Hayes of Ohio, who, unlike Blaine or Conkling, was untainted by a Spoils System under increasing scrutiny.[15] Famously, it would become the second of five instances in American history when the Democratic candidate for president, Samuel Tilden of New York, outpolled his political foe in the popular vote but lost the election via the Electoral College (the others: Andrew Jackson vs. John Quincy Adams in 1824, Grover Cleveland vs. Benjamin Harrison in 1886, Al Gore vs. George W. Bush in 2000, and Hillary Clinton vs. Donald Trump in 2016).[16] The election of 1876 was so close, in fact, that three Southern states chose two sets of electors, and only after months of squabbling and negotiation (with no constitutional solution) did a specially created congressional committee award Hayes and Republicans the victory.[17]

For much of the electorate, the election was deemed fraudulent, and Karabell referred to it as still "the most controversial outcome in American [presidential] history." To ease the potential for nationwide unrest as a result, a deal was reached by the two parties—the Republicans got their president, and the Democrats got the removal of federal troops from the South, effectively ending Reconstruction and setting back African American gains for nearly a century. In addition, Hayes called for civil service reform, including the elimination of political activities by federal employees, an agenda that was not good for either Blaine or Conkling and their respective wings of the Republican Party, both of which had been built on political spoils. Suddenly, patronage was a dirty word and office-seeking a recognized evil. As such, the election made Arthur a target. Suddenly, by virtue of his lofty appointment at the Port of New York, he was under scrutiny and vulnerable.[18]

Karabell recorded: "Chester Arthur had never been the target of an investigation and had maintained a benign reputation. At worst, he was seen as a party hack, but no one had seriously challenged his probity" until the election of 1876. Along with his benefactor, Conkling, he was cast as "part of a corrupt system." True, he had received kickbacks, but only those allowed. Previous reformers had portrayed him as an honorable public servant, and he had been rewarded with a previously unprecedented second term as collector. With the new administration, however, that all changed.[19]

Needing examples, Treasury Secretary John Sherman, the younger brother of legendary Union Civil War General William Tecumseh Sherman, launched an investigation of the major customhouses. The largest, Arthur's shop in New York, was found to be out of order, and despite his good reputation, Sherman's charges proved severe. Although not personally implicated, Arthur was charged "with looking the other way" and excessive tardiness when it came to his job. Ultimately the victim of a Spoils System built on political loyalty, Arthur was removed by Hayes from his post.[20]

Stern protests over his removal ensued from Conkling, Morgan, and others, but to no avail. In response, Karabell indicated, the Stalwart branch of the Republican Party "declared war." They challenged the president's right to remove Arthur on the same grounds that had been used to try to impeach Johnson ten years earlier, the Tenure of Office Act. They also defended Arthur as someone "above rebuke." With the tradition of "senatorial courtesy" suddenly ignored by the Hayes administration when applied to federal appointees from a senator's own state, the Senate even rejected the man nominated to replace Arthur, Theodore Roosevelt, Sr., ironically the father of a future accidental president.[21]

Trapped in the middle of his reform initiative and the backlash he was experiencing from his own party, Hayes reacted even more willfully when Arthur finally spoke out, defending his record and rebuking his critics. Karabell indicated that Hayes "was not listening" and rendered Arthur's expulsion irrevocable. Rather than ruining Arthur's reputation, however, the president's resolve thrust him into the national spotlight. Instead of a tainted civil servant, Arthur was viewed as a scapegoat for an administration bent on legitimizing itself after what had been widely viewed as a counterfeit election. As a means of avoiding further controversy, the Senate elected to forgo overturning Hayes' decision.[22]

Once again returned to private law practice, Arthur was buoyed by Conkling setting him up to be New York's Republican party chairman, a fund-raising post and lifestyle that was right up his alley, and one he thoroughly enjoyed for three years. Karabell noted, "There were few things Arthur enjoyed more that wining and dining in the company of like-minded men." So despite his controversial firing, life remained good for the tall, genial man about town until his devoted wife suddenly and tragically died of pneumonia at only 42 years of age on New Year's Day, 1880.[23]

Devastated, Arthur eventually managed to overcome his grief by concentrating on the upcoming presidential election of 1880 and his hope, along with Conkling, that former President Grant would return to the political wars and seek a third term, thus denying Hayes re-election.[24] At the same time, Blaine plotted to put his own name atop the Republican ticket. Ultimately, Hayes realized he had alienated too many people to seek re-election, and when the Republican Convention became deadlocked over Grant and Blaine, with neither able to achieve the necessary two-thirds of delegate votes, a compromise candidate was in the offing. Once again, a political party turned to a lesser-known, dark-horse candidate as a means of moving on in a unified way. In this case, the compromise choice was James Garfield, another Union Civil War general and 18-year Ohio congressman, who was well-liked and agreeable to both wings of the party.[25]

Karabell confirmed that Conkling and the other Stalwarts were upset that Grant had not won, but equally pleased that Blaine had been blocked. The biographer next related the saga of how Arthur (of all people) came to be nominated for vice president. He credited a reporter named William Hudson with the story, but not until 30 years after the fact. Hudson's account of the VP choice went as follows:

Garfield's partisans settled on Arthur as an unobjectionable sop to the Stalwarts. Garfield could not win New York without them and he would [have been] hard-pressed to win the election if he lost

New York. Arthur was identified with the Stalwarts and universally liked. Conkling, however, was in no mood to see his [longtime] lieutenant vaulted ahead of him. While no one really coveted the vice presidency, what most annoyed Conkling was the blow to his pride. Arthur was approached directly by the Garfield camp. Conkling was not asked first and didn't learn about it until Arthur informed him. "Ohio men have offered me the vice presidency," Arthur told Conkling. "Well sir," Conkling was said to have replied, "you should drop it as you would a red hot [horse] shoe from the forge." But to Conkling's astonishment [and obvious consternation], Arthur did not.[26]

Arthur considered the offer a great honor and more than he had ever dreamed of, and even though Conkling tried to convince him that Garfield was going to lose and that he should "contemptuously decline," Arthur saw even "a barren nomination" as a great honor and one he was not willing to turn down with or without Conkling's blessing. "Senator Conkling, I shall accept the nomination and carry with me a majority of the delegates," he is said to have uncharacteristically asserted, much to Conkling's disbelief and everlasting chagrin. It was role reversal. As soon as Arthur elected to ignore (and surpass) his political mentor, Conkling's "star began to wane." On the other hand, as strange as it still seems, in just over a year from their convention exchange, Arthur would be president of the United States.[27]

In the summer of 1880, no one would have predicted a Garfield-Arthur victory that fall. While Garfield's nomination was well received by most Republicans, Arthur was viewed purely as a throw-in to placate the party's minority wing. Influential members of the party, in fact, were overheard using phrases like "a ridiculous burlesque" and "a miserable farce" to describe Arthur's selection. After being castigated and fired from the best-paid appointment in the federal system, Arthur had been elevated back to a vice presidential nominee less than two years later. It didn't make sense.[28]

Running against yet another, even better-known Union Civil War general, Democrat Winfield Scott Hancock, a hero of Gettysburg (but with no political experience), Garfield benefited from the better-run organization and more party loyalty, as the patronage system, although under attack, nonetheless continued to manifest itself on Election Day. Also of help was the Democratic Party's ongoing link to the South both before and after the Civil War, as Republicans continued to "wave the bloody shirt" in national campaigns the rest of the century.[29] Garfield and Arthur took advantage of such things and made enough pledges to overcome Conkling's lack of support until very late in the campaign, when a handshake in Garfield's hometown was dubbed the "Treaty of Mentor." The result was a narrow victory in November in which the Garfield-Arthur ticket received 4,454,416 votes to the Democrats' 4,444,952, a margin of less than one-tenth of one percent. Not a single state south of the Mason-Dixon Line went Republican, and no state north of that line went to the Democrats. The election was decided by California, Colorado, and Oregon, all of which finished in the Republican column.[30]

The new president and his VP celebrated separately. After all, they barely knew each other, but that didn't stop Arthur from trying to get as many Stalwarts as possible into the Cabinet. Garfield, meanwhile, sought intra-party balance. He named Blaine secretary of state, but left Conkling out, another perceived slap. While Conkling was clearly in decline, Arthur stood by his old friend when he resigned from the Senate along with Thomas Platt over Garfield's nomination of Blaine backer William Robertson for the collector's position in New York. As a result, both the vice president and former senator were not without suspicion when Garfield was shot in the back by a disgruntled (and totally deranged) Stalwart office seeker, who acknowledged upon his arrest that he wanted Chester A. Arthur to be president. Garfield would die three weeks later.[31]

Karabell termed it "not the best way to become president." To the contrary, it was the worst possible.[32] Due to his past political connection to the suddenly discarded Conkling, the vice president seemed implicated by association. Suddenly with suspicions rampant throughout the country and the killer claiming he did it for the Stalwarts, Arthur was in an unenviable position as the illogical, ascendant president, someone who had been devoid of individual political ambitions until destiny came calling with a totally unexpected vice presidential bid.[33]

Upon learning of Garfield's death on September 19, 1881, Arthur was found "sobbing alone" in his library. Karabell indicated that the rest of the nation was not as "grief stricken," however, as following the Lincoln assassination at the Civil War's conclusion six years earlier, or even when President McKinley was shot and killed by a professed anarchist 20 years later. Unlike both of those cases, "there was little hand-wringing about the fate of the nation," he wrote. "Garfield had not touched a chord yet. His personality was too moderate, and

A late–1800s magazine of political satire, this issue of *Puck* featured a cover cartoon of Charles Guiteau, the disgruntled office seeker who assassinated President James Garfield, putting Chester Alan Arthur in the White House (Library of Congress Prints and Photographs Division—Reproduction Number DIG-pga-09026).

his assassin turned out to be less than initially supposed."[34] His killer, Charles Guiteau, came across as more crazy than anything else once more was learned of his psychopathic, lone-wolf stalking of the president after being repeatedly denied positions he was not qualified for in the Republican administration. Guiteau believed killing Garfield would solve that omission by putting Arthur and the Stalwarts in charge. Delusional to the end, he actually believed Arthur would free him from his prison cell once he learned of his motivation.[35]

On the other hand, Arthur remained disconsolate. He had tried to avoid any thoughts of becoming president, forcing himself to believe Garfield would recover. After all, there was no way someone as unassuming and unambitious as he was should have to assume such enormous responsibility. At the same time, once conspiracy theories dissipated, more and more people decided to give the new president the benefit of the doubt. The *New York Times* even ran a lengthy story in which Arthur was praised as "a hard-money man in favor of the protection of American industry, a friend of the working class—able, upright, honorable, and efficient." Allaying the public's fear that he had previously been too beholden to Conkling and machine politics, the same article stated, "The new president is a much better and broader man than the majority of those with whom his recent career has been identified."[36]

After initially taking the oath of office in his New York City living room in the wee hours of September 20 and accompanying Garfield's funeral train from Elberton, New Jersey (the deceased president's summer home, where he had been taken for convalescence) back to Washington and eventually burial in Cleveland, Ohio, Arthur took the oath a second time and delivered an inaugural address. In it he said, "Men may die, but the fabric of our free institutions remain unshaken. No higher, more assuring proof could exist of our popular government than the fact that though the chosen of the people be struck down, his constitutional successor is peacefully installed without shock or strain."[37]

Karabell emphasized, "No one knew what direction the Arthur administration would take—not even Arthur himself." Garfield had only been in office for four months with his agenda far from being in place, giving Arthur ample room to determine and set his own. "Unlike most vice presidents who abruptly become president, Arthur could steer just about any course he chose," his biographer asserted.

But Karabell also admitted, "there was something odd and unsettling about Arthur becoming chief executive." Even in a time of declining presidential prestige, "Americans wanted to believe that the president, at worst, was first among equals." This was true even though there had been previous disappointments (with Karabell pointing to Andrew Johnson as his example). Nevertheless, he confirmed that Arthur was not like any other president, having never been an elected office holder before becoming vice president and, as a result, unproven as a leader.[38]

Regardless, he surprised all observers, emerging as a thoughtful and independent chief executive. True, he had not been ambitious, but it went without saying that lofty ambitions did not always produce the best leaders. The new president also had fewer political enemies than most of his contemporaries. Although having never attracted passionate allegiance or support, he had avoided passionate animosity and was well-versed in the political game.[39] Again according to Karabell, "The qualities he did possess allowed him to rise farther than many others who were more intelligent, dynamic, or driven." His bottom line: the abilities and attributes he did possess allowed him "to govern more successfully" than most Americans of his era expected.[40]

Obviously a product of partisan politics, Arthur would prove surprisingly nonpartisan and equitable in his approach. Without an inflated ego, Karabell contended, he set out to have an "inclusive administration" in the interest of "national unity."[41] Conkling was shocked when he was still not offered a Cabinet post, but Arthur recognized that his presidential credibility would take a hit with such an appointment. Instead of playing the game by the old partisan patronage rules, Arthur decided to take up the cause of civil service reform, which had been pushed to the forefront by the Garfield assassination.[42]

At his first message to Congress less than three months after assuming office on December 6, 1881, Arthur surprised everyone again with his demonstrated understanding of international and domestic affairs. Along with checking off issues of the day like Indian affairs, tariff laws, maintenance of the Army, and the need for better relations with the nations of South and Central America, he saved the best for last when he wholeheartedly endorsed civil service reform. Using the British system as his model, he advocated a required civil service exam, pension guarantees, and job tenure, all with the promise of the most qualified applicants being attracted in order to frame civil service as a worthy career with job security.[43]

His was a dramatic departure from the deadlock that had previously hindered civil service reform, but reformers cautiously applauded his conversion. They had been burned before. Nevertheless, his consideration and unexpected knowledge of the issue was appreciated, and he was able to finish the year accomplishing more than his critics had expected. The country, meanwhile, anticipated the bar being raised with the new year of 1882, when his words would be put to the test in Congress.[44]

With Blaine having resigned as secretary of state after the assassination and a host of other vacancies to fill, Arthur continued to distance himself from the Stalwarts and the potential appearance of unfair patronage. He made few bad moves in his first six months as president. After establishing what Karabell termed "grudging respect," however, he confronted Congress about a popular but very controversial bill.[45]

Like so many other times in our nation's history, our nation of immigrants was not without its immigrant controversy in the 1880s. This one involved the Chinese, about 250,000 of whom were living on the West Coast but not as citizens, since the Naturalization Act of 1870 had made it impossible for them or any other immigrant who wasn't Caucasian or of African descent to obtain citizenship. Following their initial surge as a result of the California Gold Rush (1849–1855), most were laborers or "coolies" brought to the U.S. to build railroads, harvest crops, or serve as domestics in the California cities. While admired for their stamina, discipline, and work ethic, they were also feared and reviled because of their willingness to work longer hours for lesser pay. As such, Karabell emphasized, "racism alone wasn't the cause of the backlash" against their presence—economics also made it easy for local politicians to assign blame, fanning the flame of anti–Chinese sentiment.[46]

Finally, a bill calling for the expulsion of all Chinese immigrants for 20 years reached Arthur's desk, and to the astonishment and outrage of many in Congress and throughout the country, he vetoed it because of an earlier U.S. treaty with China's emperor, which made the bill, in his mind, an act of bad faith. As the chief executive, he felt it was his duty to temper Congress' rush to judgment by preserving his nation's diplomatic credibility.[47] The traditionally more liberal press applauded his decision in the face of what Karabell called "popular demagoguery." Lauding the role Chinese labor had played in the development of the country, Arthur warned that the bill would have actually backfired, hurting the American economy by abusing trade with the Orient and limiting the labor force in still-underdeveloped areas of the country. Congress did not overturn his veto. Nonetheless, his hard-won and already tenuous popularity plummeted. He was burned in effigy in many cities and towns of the West, and was confronted by another, revised bill delivered by his own Republican Party. This time he acquiesced. Karabell phrased it, "Rather than be a martyr to principle, he submitted and pragmatically signed a [reduced] ten-year Exclusion Act."[48]

Unfortunately, the Chinese Exclusion Act would usher in decades of racial violence on the West Coast by severely marginalizing Chinese laborers already in the U.S., much like what was still happening to African Americans in the South. Many Chinese were driven from their homes, and some were even murdered by small-town gangs (as in Eureka, California) and bigger-city mobs (as in Los Angeles, California, and Tacoma, Washington). Renewed by Congress in ten-year increments for over five decades, the legislation was not repealed until 1943. Some local ordinances prohibiting Chinese inclusion even remained in place into the 1950s—again, much like Jim Crow segregation in the South.[49]

In addition to the Chinese Exclusion Act, the trial of the assassin Guiteau took center stage during the Arthur administration. His attorneys used the only defense they really had—insanity. In those days, it was a novel and largely untested defense, especially in so high-profile a case, and the defendant had only made it seem more plausible by his actions in jail, including his delusional planning of a lecture series "once President Arthur decided to pardon and release him." In his mind, it made perfect sense, and his frequent interviews on the subject and bizarre optimism captivated the country. His trial, though seemingly cut and dried, lasted for the better part of two months. In the end, however, Guiteau's own self-assurance and bashing of his legal team's insanity plea rendered him too believable for his own good.[50] On January 23, 1882, he was sentenced to die, and six months later he was executed, bringing to a close one of the most bizarre episodes in American history and presidential lore. After finally coming to grips with the fact that the president would not be coming to his rescue, even in his final hours, Guiteau declared, "Arthur has sealed his doom and the doom of this nation."[51]

While not paying much attention to the legal proceedings of the man who put him in the White House, Arthur paid lots of attention to another 1882 bill. This one would authorize a capital outlay of over $40 billion for river and harbor improvements, mostly along the Mississippi River. He considered it "legislative pork," according to Karabell, the creation of a financial windfall for certain legislators and their powerful constituents. Meanwhile, those congressmen backing his reform initiatives viewed the Rivers and Harbors Bill as outrageous, and with their support (but against the wishes of his own party), he used his veto power once again to block what he considered bad government and unethical expenditure. In so doing, he acknowledged that while many of the issues it proposed to fix would have been to the public good, many others were not designed for national welfare, benefiting only individual localities, and were beyond the purview of federal authority.[52]

He called on Congress to return to the drawing board to narrow its target only to improvements that were truly national in scope, leaving the others to the more appropriate auspices of the individual states, but his veto was overturned. As a result, Arthur found himself in the same place as two of his previous accidental brethren, Tyler and Andrew Johnson—in jeopardy of losing the support of the party that "brung" him to the White House. Twice his vetoes had been used against the wishes of the Republican majority, just as Tyler's had been used in opposition to the Whigs in the 1840s and Johnson repeatedly against the Radical Republicans in the 1860s. Like them, he too became a president without a party, something that did not bode well for him or the Republicans.[53]

The year 1882 also represented the beginning of health issues for the president. He was diagnosed with Bright's disease, a kidney ailment that resulted in headaches, swelling, chronic fevers, and fatigue, as well as the gradual poisoning of his entire system due to his body's inability to rid itself of toxins. The way Karabell put it, "The once ebullient bon vivant found himself tired and cranky much of the time. His blood and body were slowly being poisoned by his own digestion."[54]

So, with his health declining and his party in disagreement, time was of the essence for Arthur by the time he began his second year in office in the fall of 1882. Given the toxic political climate, Arthur's political honeymoon was definitely over, while his appetite for civil service reform grew stronger every day. Luckily, there was a bill stuck in committee, the Pendleton Bill, that actually dealt with civil service reform. It had been proposed in 1880 and offered major revisions along the lines of the British system, including exams and a screening process based on merit. It had the support of state reform leagues and other associations across the country, but it still languished in committee, only increasing public discontent.[55]

As a result of westward expansion, the largest group of federal employees had become the Post Office Department, opening it to potential malfeasance and a post-Civil War scandal known as the "Star Route Frauds." That entailed the awarding of mail routes in the underdeveloped West, where regular mail service did not previously exist, and the lucrative government contracts that went with those routes to friends and family of local, state, and even national officials. What resulted was graft, conspiracy, and kickbacks throughout the emerging system. Indeed, fraud was so extensive that it was constantly being exposed. It continued because leadership looked the other way until Arthur's administration decided to pursue the conviction of one of the leading perpetrators, Senator Stephen Dorsey of Indiana, along with eight other officials in the Star Route trials.

In September 1882, with many of the defendants on the verge of acquittal, the jury foreman alleged that he had been offered bribes, resulting in a mistrial. It was a verdict that fueled discontent, but the party in power, the Republicans, failed to recognize the shifting sentiment. They felt the mounting calls for reform could still be ignored and critics would, as Karabell said, "run out of steam." No amount of national development and internal improvements, however, could hide the spread of greed, fraud, and scandal. As a result, the election of 1882 shocked the Republicans, shifting leadership to the Democrats for the first time since the Civil War.[56]

Along with a suddenly more assertive press, blame for the Republicans' poor showing reached all the way to Arthur, but the president had recognized the electorate's changing mood much sooner than his party. Within weeks of their election debacle, Republicans were jumping on the bandwagon he had been professing since ascending to office. For many, at least a decade of opposition to civil service reform fell by the wayside—even more so for Democrats who had also failed to take full advantage by embracing reform. Instead, they were mistakenly hoping to finally enjoy the spoils of a Spoils System they had long been denied.

The lame duck Republican Congress, which was headed for replacement in just a few months, saw an opportunity to reassert leadership temporarily and take advantage of the national mood. Seizing the initiative while they still could, Republicans suddenly embraced the Pendleton Bill (even though it had been authored by a Democrat), which they had previously kicked to the curb for the better part of two years. It proposed creation of a civil service commission with a board to set exam standards and test the suitability of applicants for every federal position.

As perhaps the best living example of how patronage and the Spoils System lent itself to less than qualified office holders, Arthur also understood better than most the need for change. Needless to say, he embraced the opportunity. Congressional debate was remarkably short, and with the advent of a new Democratic Congress looming, the Pendleton Bill was passed with no Republican voting against it and was quickly signed into law by the original reform convert, Chester A. Arthur, in mid–January 1883.[57]

Karabell pointed to how history has tried ever since to account for the change in attitude that came over Republican leaders with their sudden shift back towards the president they had all but disowned. With their hold on the patronage power suddenly gone, however, the chance to deny Democrats the same influence moving forward had to be as good a reason as any to embrace civil service standards at that particular time. As a result, much credit should have never been their due. On the other hand, the president who verbalized the need for civil service reform, despite what the Spoils System had meant to him and his career, should be worthy of acclaim. That, after all, was Karabell's point all along. To ensure that thought, he wrote:

> Symbolically it marked a before and after moment in American politics. Before, the political system had been controlled by a professional class that treated elections as contests over patronage. After the Pendleton Act, it no longer was. The bill articulated a new standard. Civil servants were to be appointed because of their capacity to do the job, not because of whom they new or what they could pay. Their performance was to be assessed by objective standards.[58]

Nothing in Arthur's final two years on the job would equal the lasting effects of the Pendleton Act. After all, the way he came to office and his earlier ideological separation from not only his Stalwart base, but also the entire Republican Party, rendered him a lame duck. Much like Tyler and Johnson (again), Arthur had to know early on that there was no way he would be re-nominated by his party with a chance to win in his own right. With the government operating with an immense financial surplus, reformers temporarily satisfied, and labor unrest contained, the domestic scene was remarkably quiet. According to Karabell, Arthur took advantage of the "relative calm" to travel the country, to bring added attention to foreign affairs, and to strengthen the U.S. military.[59]

Undoubtedly, he had never sought the presidency and derived no personal pleasure from it. He never felt at home in the White House and had no particular issue to address after civil service reform, leading his biographer to consider him "bored." With his party deserting him and Bright's disease taking its toll, depression seemed the natural by-product for his state of mind.[60]

He did support a tariff commission, but his moderate stance did nothing to bring the two competing sides (industrialists and business versus farmers and workers) any closer. He also worked to rebuild the military, which had eroded since the end of the Civil War, especially the Navy. His years as collector in New York had educated him to the influence and benefits a strong and visible U.S. Navy could have on the world maritime stage. He set that stage for further naval development in years to come under Presidents William McKinley and Theodore Roosevelt.

Arthur "also devoted considerable energy to bilateral tariff negotiations," his biographer noted. "Trade had to increase for American influence to increase." His administration worked behind the scenes to establish "reciprocity agreements with individual countries and governments," allowing circumvention of some U.S. tariff laws and improved international business relations.[61]

Domestically, Arthur also worked for more westward expansion by encouraging avoidance of further Indian wars in the West. He ordered the U.S. Army to improve negotiations with the Native Americans in order to absorb their communities by sharing American rights. He helped establish Indian schools to teach U.S. laws and customs, and he urged Congress to pass legislation that would limit the hazardous state of relations with the various tribes. His time in Kansas had exposed him to the vast potential of underdeveloped acreage stretching to the horizon, and he was anxious to see for himself what lay beyond the Mississippi River before his term ended.[62]

Prior to leaving on a Western junket, however, he visited Florida, still in its infancy in terms of commercial development, on a health-seeking excursion. Unfortunately, the swampy heat and humidity did the opposite, aggravating his illness and causing him to conceal just how sick he really was.[63] He recovered in time to return to New York City and participate in the opening of the Brooklyn Bridge, one of the innovative "technical wonder[s] of the world" and, Karabell added, "a symbol of the emerging power, creativity, and industriousness of the American people."[64]

Along with the mayors of Brooklyn and New York City and New York Governor Grover Cleveland (soon to be Arthur's successor as president), he inaugurated the magnificent new suspension bridge that connected the neighboring cities on May 24, 1883, in one of the most-hyped American events ever. Thousands of residents and visitors literally flooded the East River shoreline for the daylong celebration that began with Arthur and Cleveland walking across the span for the first time and ended with perhaps the biggest U.S. pyrotechnic display up to that time later that evening.

It was the biggest event in New York since the opening of the Erie Canal in 1825. Schools and businesses closed; invited guests and favored customers perched in windows

This Currier & Ives lithograph of the Brooklyn Bridge was published the same year President Chester Arthur led a huge celebration to mark the grand opening of the famous span over New York's East River (Library of Congress Prints and Photographs Division—Reproduction Number DIG-pga-09026).

and atop buildings as far as the eye could see; an impressive contingent of U.S. warships was in the harbor with their canons booming throughout the day; and enterprising steam ship companies ran charter excursions up and down the river, giving those willing to pay the fare a close-up view of the massive structure that electricity would later illuminate from shore to shore once darkness settled in and the fireworks started.[65]

Two months later, Arthur embarked on his trip west to Yellowstone, the nation's first national park (1872), accompanied by General Phil Sheridan and Secretary of War Robert Lincoln, the oldest and only surviving son of the late, great president. An avid fisherman who had often fished the lakes of Upstate New York, Arthur enjoyed the opportunity to catch trout on the Western rivers, and the cool mountain air and low humidity did wonders for his illness. However, even before his trip was over, the journey was being derisively described as the "Presidential Sporting Excursion of 1883." Although protected by Sheridan's troops in what was still a wild section of the country, at least one titillating news story also surfaced during his sojourn, when a plot was hatched to kidnap the president and hold him for ransom. Although uncovered, the perpetrators were never caught, adding to the reputation of the lawless West.[66]

He returned to Washington in September in seemingly better health. His renewed outlook took a turn for the worse, however, when the Supreme Court struck down an 1875 Civil Rights Act as unconstitutional, setting back the cause of racial equality in the country for another 70 years, something Karabell called "one of the worst [American] travesties." Although argued by the U.S. solicitor general, the case never really had a chance, as the end of Reconstruction six years earlier (1877) had set the stage for a return to government dominated by the individual states and eight decades of Jim Crow segregation below the Mason-Dixon Line.

Arthur was one of the few who recognized what the decision would mean. An ardent opponent of slavery before the Civil War, he said, "It was the special purpose of the [Fourteenth] Amendment to insure to members of the Colored race the full enjoyment of civil and political rights," and the Court had betrayed that principle. In fact, he called on Congress to overturn with legislation what the Court had undone, but as a largely ignored and party-less chief executive, his request fell on deaf ears, an omission that, had it been acted upon, might have elevated Arthur's legacy by confronting the tide of segregation that was being renewed in the South.[67]

With his influence obviously receding and the Republican Party in search of a new direction, Arthur still believed he warranted a second term. At the same time, the irrepressible Blaine had emerged as the party frontrunner. Blaine had overcome the Stalwarts, resigned from Arthur's Cabinet, and begun to circulate a plan that would return federal surplus dollars to the states, an idea sure to attract votes. But The Plumed Knight remained polarizing and a major reason for the rise of a Republican splinter group called the "Mugwumps." Even though Arthur still enjoyed support, he had no base. He had governed more effectively than most imagined possible after becoming president in such unexpected, accidental fashion, but that was not enough to sway party leaders looking for a more exciting alternative to oppose the surging candidacy of the popular, pro-business Governor Cleveland, a Democrat already enticing Mugwumps to cross party lines.[68]

The resulting 1884 campaign between Blaine and Cleveland was one of the nastiest in American history, and despite doing what he could to help the party, Arthur was forced to watch as Blaine's tainted candidacy, which linked him back to a scandal during the Grant administration when he was Speaker of the House, proved too much to overcome in a close election.[69] Arthur's biographer noted that his only vindication was Cleveland carrying New

York, where the incumbent's supposed drop in approval had been cited as reason enough to deny his re-nomination.[70]

Still in his mid-50s when he left the White House, Arthur eventually looked forward to returning to private life and private law practice, but his health continued to worsen. Once the *New York Times* revealed his Bright's disease in 1886, he was confined to bed and would die a few months later after a paralyzing stroke at age 57. Known later as "The Gentleman President," the title of Karabell's epilogue, Arthur's reputation did not rise or fall in all the years since, "it disappeared," something at least one biographer did a convincing job of trying to amend in The American Presidents Series.[71]

14

America's Change Agent—
Theodore Roosevelt

"Well, the mad Roosevelt has a new achievement to his credit. He succeeded in defeating the party that furnished him a job for nearly all of his manhood days."—Warren G. Harding, 1912

Edmund Morris authored a Pulitzer Prize-winning book in 1979 entitled *The Rise of Theodore Roosevelt*, a biography of the early life and career of the man who became our nation's youngest president. It was a lasting precursor to another biographical narrative Morris would write 22 years later, *Theodore Rex*. That one would pick up where the first left off—the moment then Vice President Roosevelt, who would become known to the world as TR (or Teddy), was notified that President William McKinley, who had been shot by an anarchist at the Pan-American Expedition in Buffalo, New York, nine days earlier, had contracted gangrene and was near death.

It was Saturday, September 14, 1901, and of all places to learn that he was about to become the nation's fifth accidental president, the remote recesses of Upstate New York's Adirondack Mountains would seem a little strange. But not really for this scion of upper-crust New York society, who long before had adopted the strenuous outdoor life while also rising rapidly in Republican political ranks by challenging corruption and the status quo.[1]

As he hurried down Mount Marcy on foot and horse-drawn buckboard, and raced on aboard a specially provided train towards his rendezvous with destiny in Western New York, Roosevelt confronted the idea of taking over for a president whose 19th-century ideals he had never embraced. He knew he needed to assume control in a compassionate yet purposeful way by immediately assuming the national leadership he had always envisioned for himself. It was not the route to the White House he would have preferred, but given the country's fragile state following its third presidential assassination and the threat of further anarchy, he was not about to step back from the precipice of responsibility that had suddenly been thrust upon him. No, not this Roosevelt, who had already lived through tremendous personal loss, multiple real-life adventures, the rough and tumble of partisan politics, and even his own "crowded hour" while leading famous charges in Cuba during the Spanish-American War. He would do so without benefit of an election, at least at the start, and he would do so in a way that Morris convinces you was as if he had been doing the job for years.[2]

Unlike at least a couple of his accidental predecessors, TR could count much more than vice presidential experience on his governmental resume. Coming up through the ranks, he already knew the ropes of Washington from six years on the U.S. Civil Service

Commission and nearly a year as assistant secretary of the Navy, and he understood where most of the political bodies were buried as the youngest New York assemblyman ever; as a New York City police commissioner; and as governor of that same state, the nation's most populous.[3] In other words, while political opponents were already his in droves, he had mastered the art of public opinion and possessed the kind of charisma and intelligence necessary to get things done no matter the obstacles. Esteemed American writer Mark Twain termed him "the most popular human being that has ever existed in the United States."[4]

Morris' second Roosevelt biography was a day-to-day, chronological account of this ever-popular president during the seven and a half years he occupied the White House, "years in which he entertain[ed], infuriate[d], amuse[d], strong-arm[ed], and seduce[d] the body politic into a state of almost total subservience to his will," according to the book jacket's promotional description. He was a nationwide sensation, "a personality without parallel," who enlivened the White House the way few, if any, have done before or since.[5]

A British writer born in Kenya, Morris provided us the perspective of a non–American writing about one of our most famous Americans, one of just four on that most American of monuments, Mount Rushmore. His was a very objective recounting of the TR White House years, 1901–1909—years of progressive change, award-winning diplomacy, imperialistic acquisition, industrial control and progress, the introduction of conservation, and yes, even controversy. Another more recent historian labeled him a constitutional "renegade" and "the progenitor of prerogatives presidents now use to justify their actions." Morris addressed all of it, the good, the bad, and the ugly of the TR presidency.[6]

Upon his arrival in Buffalo and after being sworn into office as the 26th president in the front parlor of a friend, Ansley Wilcox, TR spent almost a week amidst the trappings of an official state funeral, as would be expected, including the train ride back to Washington with the deceased president's body and the requisite stops for "respects" all along the way.[7] On his first active day in office, September 20, Roosevelt met with McKinley's Cabinet and asked them to remain in their posts, at least for the time being (some would eventually be reassigned or let go), and he also met with the Washington press corps to establish their confidence in him and, equally as important, his confidence in them.[8]

Thus, by the time McKinley's widow had vacated the White House and one of the largest First Families had moved in (Morris termed it "the Roosevelt menagerie of six mostly young children and their animals"), the first of the controversies was about to take place. In fact, Morris went to great lengths in his opening chapters to set the stage and report the residue of the famous White House visit of Booker T. Washington, the most influential African American of the early twentieth century. During his first month in office, TR had "consoled and inspired a stricken nation, steadied the stock market, established standards of patronage, and tempered the mutual hatreds of race and party," but as Morris quoted a British correspondent, "Trouble [was] bound to come."[9]

Having already established a line of communication with the Roosevelt White House during the ongoing era of Jim Crow segregation, and with the awful specter of racially motivated mob lynchings occurring all too often in the turn-of-the-century South, the impressive Mr. Washington was in the capital on business less than a month after McKinley was interred. Hearing of his visit and hoping to address whatever could conceivably be broached on race relations, the new president issued an invitation to the "Negro leader" to dine with him at the White House and, in fact, Washington did join the Roosevelt family for dinner. Innocent though the dinner was, the fact that a brief *Associated Press* report chronicled that day's White House guest list set off a firestorm of Southern indignation that underscored the intense bigotry still prevalent below the Mason-Dixon Line 36 years after the Civil War. Although Morris cited numerous examples of Northern support for the president's dinner and initiative in trying to address the lasting racial divide, the fact remained that his naiveté as a new president had contributed to a rare (for him) public relations nightmare in his first month in office.[10]

Later that fall, TR faced his first confrontation with the titans of big business. Railroads, still the most get-rich-quick vehicle of that era, were the subject of a meeting of financial giants on November 11, when James J. Hill, E. H. Harriman, and a hand-picked representative for J. Pierpont Morgan got together for the purpose of expanding their respective empires in the Western half of the country. For months, Hill's Great Northern line and Harriman's Union Pacific had vied for control of Morgan's Northern Pacific. "Also at stake was the Burlington & Quincy road, connecting the three systems with Chicago," according to Morris. As a result of Hill's and Harriman's competition and the overall economic influence and involvement of Morgan, the idea of a trust so immense it would encompass the stock of all three railroads in a single holding company was proposed. It would be worth about $400 million and be called the Northern Securities Company.[11]

As Morris pointed out, "the flaw" in this financial scheme was that the Great Northern and Northern Pacific were direct competitors, chasing the same consumer and shipping dollars. Their bargain implied restraint of interstate trade, prohibited by the 1890 Sherman Antitrust Act. But with the best legal minds in the country under their employ, the tycoons were confident their agreement could pass the test of the courts, based on other legal decisions up to that time. Their confidence, however, had failed to take into consideration the new force in the White House.

When revealed 24 hours after their secret pact had been signed, Roosevelt immediately called for his able attorney general, Philander C. Knox, who along with Secretary of War Elihu Root would remain TR's Cabinet favorites. Already, newspapers like the *New York Journal* had called the pact "another step towards universal monopoly," the very thing Roosevelt was most concerned about when it came to big business. Although committed to the free enterprise system that had elevated America to major nation status ever since the Civil War, he was determined to take advantage of laws designed to control the overreach of men like Morgan, laws often ignored or arbitrated around in order to give labor a vested interest and legitimate seat at the table of industrial development—something workingmen had rarely had in the past.[12]

It was the earliest of the progressive tendencies he would increasingly espouse during his years as president, even more so when he ran as a third-party candidate in 1912. Despite being labeled "that damned cowboy" by legislative powerbrokers like Senator Mark Hanna of Ohio, Roosevelt emerged undeterred in his reformist aspirations, a lesson New York bosses had learned the hard way before he joined the Republican national ticket in 1900. On September 20, 1901, congressional leaders got the same lesson when morning papers brandished headlines about the federal government bringing a suit against Northern Securities. It would supersede a suit already brought by Minnesota Governor Samuel Van Sant on the same Sherman Antitrust basis and ensure the young president much favorable publicity. Morris wrote, "Henceforth he and not the governor would be seen as David battling the Wall Street Goliath."[13]

The financial establishment reacted in horror. Morgan and his legal entourage descended on Washington in the face of TR's unyielding acceptance of strict adherence to existing antitrust law. When Morgan famously said, "If we have done anything wrong, just send your man to deal with my man and they can fix it up," Roosevelt replied, "That can't be done," and Knox added, "We don't want to fix it up, we want to stop it." There was no way a private magnate, even one with the financial power of Morgan, could be allowed to negotiate on equal terms with the president of the United States. The message was clear: established law would be adhered to with TR at the helm.[14] At the same time, it was the start of some rocky moments with entrenched Republicans, most of whom wanted to stay on McKinley's course by maintaining the status quo. "Old Guard" congressional leaders like Hanna, Nelson Aldrich of Rhode Island, Orville Platt of Connecticut, John Spooner of Wisconsin, and William Allison of Iowa were suddenly on notice that a new president was in town with a new way of doing things.[15]

TR's next major test and challenge to the existing order would come the following August (1902), as thousands of coal miners in Pennsylvania threatened to go on strike unless management increased their wages and recognized the United Mine Workers (UMW) as their bargaining representative. Morris confirmed, "The mine operators refused to consider either demand," and with fall and then winter just ahead, the greatest labor stoppage in history threatened the ability of Americans to heat their homes. A national crisis of unfortunate dimensions would unfold unless it could be averted by mediation, and TR felt that with "the public interest threatened," he, as president, had to get involved.[16]

As a group, the financiers who owned and operated the mines and coal-bearing railroads made up what Morris termed "the greatest industrial monopoly in the United States," and they declined even to talk. No matter how long the strike lasted and how much coal it tied up, their spokesman emphasized, "We will not surrender."[17]

The arrogance of management was further exposed when that same spokesman issued a statement reading, "The rights and interests of the laboring man will be protected and cared for—not by labor agitators, but by the Christian men to whom God in his infinite wisdom has given control of the property interests of the country." Such pious condescension was more than TR could stomach. On August 23, 1902, while speaking to a crowd of 20,000 people in Providence, Rhode Island, he threw down his first gauntlet for government control of big business "whenever need of such control is shown."[18] Reviews of his speech were mixed, but by the end of September, with temperatures already descending in the North and his administration being blamed for the coal strike and rising prices, the traditional rebuttal that it was a state issue was losing adherents throughout the country. With the coal strike five months old and violence on the verge of breaking out in coal country, Roosevelt (despite nursing injuries from a freak trolley car accident in Pittsfield, Massachusetts) reached out to the mine owners and union leaders, inviting them both to meet with him in Washington.[19]

The meeting started in the morning of October 3 at 22 Jackson Place, the temporary executive residence while the White House was undergoing extensive renovations. UMW chief John Mitchell and two of his district leaders represented the miners, and George Baer of the Philadelphia and Reading Railroad, Eben Thomas of the Erie Railroad, and William Truesdale of the Delaware and Hudson represented the owners. Still recovering from the accident the previous month, TR was confined to a wheelchair, but "dee-lighted" that they had graciously accepted his invitation. To expedite things, he had committed his opening statement to writing with a reminder that three parties were actually involved in their ongoing dilemma, "the operators, the miners, and the general public." He noted that his involvement, while not on legal grounds, was a desire to use what influence he could to end what had become an "intolerable" situation. In Morris' words, "a coal famine" was upon them, and it had become imperative that they come to some agreement to resume operations in the mines in order to "meet the crying needs of the people." Mitchell immediately indicated the miners' willingness to submit the deadlock to a tribunal of the president's choosing and abide by its decision even if it went against their claims. Before Baer could offer his response, TR called for a recess of several hours for all to further consider his opening statement. They were to re-gather at 3 p.m. that afternoon.[20]

At the appointed hour, Baer returned with a political lecture for the president on the U.S. Constitution and the violence that had been brought by strikers against non-union men seeking to take their place in the mines. It was no secret that he expected Roosevelt to intervene on both accounts. Aware that the anthracite coal industry did indeed face a significant threat from the more plentiful bituminous veins unless operations were resumed, Roosevelt was somewhat sympathetic. At the same time, his sympathy was short-lived once the operators arrogantly refused any consideration of arbitration and stormed out. The next morning, newspaper reports were filled with praise for the president's attempt at mediation and the union's composure in the face of accusations and intransigence, and blame for management's "insolvent, audacious, sordid behavior."[21]

With input from former President Grover Cleveland, Roosevelt continued to search for an avenue to reconciliation amidst mounting unrest in coal country. Public pressure built, and Morris referenced "the mayors of more than one hundred of America's largest cities" calling for "the nationalization of anthracite coal." But just when the impasse seemed too great to overcome, the specter of J. P. Morgan was suggested as perhaps the key to any solution. After all, didn't Morgan sit on a number of the coal industry boards, and wasn't TR's only other alternative the Army and a forced re-opening of the mines? So with the added threat of a general strike in favor of the miners beginning to sweep the country,

Known for his willingness to take on big business, President Roosevelt had some major run-ins with the likes of J. P. Morgan, the most powerful financier of that era, a tycoon used to having his way, as illustrated by this obviously confrontational photograph of him from the early 1900s (Library of Congress Prints and Photographs Division—Reproduction Number DIG-ds-11626).

Roosevelt was under siege and faced with defying the Constitution by seizing private property without due process. Approaching wits end, he famously said, "The Constitution was made for the people and not the people for the Constitution," while also insisting that the Constitution's authors had no way in 1789 of anticipating the issues of industrialized society.[22]

It was the evening of October 13 when Morgan himself appeared at Roosevelt's door. By doing so, did "The House of Morgan" finally acknowledge the supremacy of the federal government? A case can be made that it did, but the document he brought with him still leaned defiantly towards management with its suggestion of a five-man commission to consider and resolve the coal dispute. Nevertheless, it unintentionally opened another door for TR. Realizing that the problem was not arbitration per se, but rather recognition of the UMW, a factor Mitchell could be convinced to concede as long as mediation occurred in good faith, Roosevelt jumped into the breech. Morgan, too, seemed sure the operators would entertain negotiation as long as it came without the UMW.

Named for Morgan's yacht, the *Corsair*, reputedly the most opulent American pleasure craft of that era, the "Corsair Agreement" that came out of that meeting did eventually end the coal strike with its selection of a seven-man commission put forward by the president and tasked with achieving an equitable settlement. According to Morris, Roosevelt's mediation between capital and labor earned worldwide attention. He was "the first head of state to confront the largest problem of the twentieth century," and TR "basked" in the public adulation, an outpouring that boded well for his 1904 re-election campaign.[23]

Another topic and potential campaign issue that worked well for him was his steadfast defense of the Monroe Doctrine, America's mentorship and near "landlordial" maintenance of the Western Hemisphere, especially in the face of continued European interest in the underdeveloped nations of South and Central America—what became known as the "Roosevelt Corollary." Even when confronted with colonial or expansionist designs by the militarized likes of Germany, TR brandished his Big Stick theory ("speaking softly but carrying a…") while maintaining a sizable presence in the emergence and ensured independence of Latin American nation states.[24]

At the same time, when faced with the opportunity to better all mankind and improve America's ability to defend itself on both of its bordering oceans, he would not be deterred in his pursuit of the long talked about canal through the Isthmus of Panama. When one of those emerging Latin American states, in fact, could not be reasonably influenced (paid) to go along, he was not above resorting to other, more controversial means to achieve what many leaders would certainly have abandoned. Indeed, deadlocked ideas and negotiations with Colombia in regard to what Morris termed its "fetid little province" of Panama—the narrow landmass connecting South and Central America—had been under way for years, ever since the French gave up on the project in 1889. By the time TR became president, the McKinley administration and Congress had already renewed the idea of an inter-ocean canal that would greatly reduce the time it took the U.S. Navy, as well as all the world's trading ships, to go from one side of the globe to the other by not having to circumnavigate South America. Along with Panama, a canal across Nicaragua utilizing a giant lake of the same name had been considered, but the six-mile-wide strip through the Panamanian jungle that the French had started and worked on for nearly a decade remained the focus of any legitimate plans. Stepping into this proposition as president after previously serving as assistant secretary of the Navy, TR knew well the potential of the project and dreamed large. He was not about to take no for an answer from a country interested only in holding his and the world's vision hostage in order to pad its coffers unreasonably. As a result,

Colombia's annual rent request of $500,000 was more than the U.S. was willing to pay, but not the deal-breaker for TR that it might have been for most U.S. presidents. "I took the Isthmus," in fact, was a claim later attributed to him by more than one historian.[25]

The original U.S. lease offer had been $100,000 annually, and TR had maxed that to $250,000 by January 1903. Morris confirmed that the Colombian government "had everything to gain" by accepting such an arrangement, what would have been a profit of over $7 million in the original 30-year proposal.[26]

Meanwhile, around the same time, TR's mind shifted briefly to conservation initiatives while visiting some of our great Western vistas on a two-month-long train and speaking tour aboard his specially adapted rail car, the *Elysian*. One of several such cross-country or regional railway excursions he would undertake as president, it took him through Nebraska, South Dakota, Wyoming (including Yellowstone National Park), New Mexico Territory, Arizona (with its Grand Canyon), California (and its Yosemite National Park), Oregon, Washington State, Idaho, Montana, Utah, and Colorado's highest Rockies before re-crossing the more easterly prairies and former Border States en route back to the nation's capital. Only then did his mind revert to Panama and what could be done to hasten his dreams of a canal.[27]

The treaty with Colombia, although signed by both countries, was challenged in the Colombian Congress following angry protests in the capital of Bogotá over any perceived surrender of sovereignty to American interests. Revered Secretary of State John Hay, the same John Hay who had been one of Abraham Lincoln's personal secretaries as a much younger man, had kept the deterioration in Colombian-American relations a secret from TR during his Western tour, but with the diplomatic breakdown finally disclosed, TR moved quickly to squelch local dissent by having Hay send an unusually forceful

One of the most popular U.S. presidents ever, Theodore Roosevelt was a great campaigner, using "whistle-stop" railroad appearances throughout the country, including this one in Eugene, Oregon (Library of Congress Prints and Photographs Division—Reproduction Number DIG-ppmsca-36612).

telegram. Considered by TR an all-important communication for America's future, Hay's message was reprinted verbatim by Morris, all caps, just as it would have appeared when received by American Ambassador Arthur M. Beaupre in Bogotá. Conveyed by him to the Colombian minister for foreign affairs, it "mystified" the Colombian leaders as it threatened "action" if the "friendly understanding" previously initiated by Colombia and agreed to by the U.S. Congress was "compromised" by any "undue delay" in its ratification.[28]

Later that same day, a news leak occurred, resulting in a story in the *New York World* that blared the headline: "The State of Panama Ready to Secede if Treaty is Rejected by Colombian Congress." Indeed, just such a political upheaval had been rumored in Latin American diplomatic circles for years, so coming as it did in the wake of apparent treaty disagreement, the story seemed to have validity, especially if the Colombians were seeking additional compensation or wanted to get out of the deal entirely. The state and people of Panama obviously wanted the canal and were willing to secede from Colombia and make their own deal to get it. Morris further noted that the article indicated support by the Roosevelt cabinet and congressional leaders should the Panamanian secession occur. His biographer also identified the likely leaker as none other than the president himself.[29]

Five months later, on November 4, 1903, a day later than had been speculated by that same *New York World,* a brief but successful revolution took place in Panama despite the presence of over 400 Colombian troops. At the time, two U.S. warships full of Marines just happened to be in harbors on both sides of the Isthmus. The go-between with Panama's revolutionary forces and the president had been a little-known, self-made Frenchman with ties to the original canal company. He had the opportunity to reap the rewards of being one of the few remaining stockholders in the construction assets the French had been forced to leave behind if TR and the U.S. did assume the massive, unfinished project. His name was Philippe Bunau-Varilla, and behind the scenes he would coordinate an unspoken alliance with Roosevelt that led to one of mankind's greatest achievements.[30]

In keeping with his chronological format, Morris separated his canal narrative into individual entries, including a blow-by-blow account of the days and hours just before and after the fateful steps of the Panamanian secession and revolution that November. In that series of entries, the calm, quiet determination of TR in the face of intrigue and later intense criticism is made obvious. Rarely has proactive presidential assertiveness been more apparent. For instance, with knowledge that a Colombian troop ship was indeed en route to Colon, Panama, by late October, at the same time the U.S. was deploying ships to the same objective, Morris wrote, "Roosevelt's last tactical move of the day was to approve a secret and confidential cable that addressed two uncertainties—would an American gunboat arrive before the Colombian troop ship, and could it be relied on to control events?" It stated: "Prevent landing of any armed force, either government or insurgent. Prevent their landing if in your judgment this would precipitate conflict."[31]

With the new agreement formerly rejected by the Colombians, TR loosely based such daring (if not unscrupulous) behavior on an old treaty, the 1846 Treaty of New Granada, in which Colombia guaranteed the United States free transit across the Isthmus during the presidency of James K. Polk. The Panama Railroad that connected the two coasts, in fact, had been built by Americans and operated ever since to the financial benefit of both the United States and Colombia.[32]

Later, amidst mounting criticism over the aggressive support TR had provided the Panamanian uprising, Morris noted, "Roosevelt did not feel the world as a whole would long deplore what had taken place. All his readings in history and geography, all his thrusting of Americanism, every consideration of international morality and expediency told him that after four hundred years of dreams and twenty years of planning, the Panama Canal's time had come" and Colombia had been "clearly guilty of fatal insolence." In TR's mind, it had been a "most just and proper revolution."[33] The rest, as they say, is history, and it would be hard ever to argue against the 48-mile Panama Canal once it was finally opened in 1914 (five years before TR's death) as the kind of lasting achievement that elevates one's individual legacy to the immortal realm. By ultimately overcoming the diseases, manpower shortages, and engineering miscalculations that had undone the French, the much more disciplined and organized U.S. effort justified TR's visionary commitment for the ages.[34]

As Morris continued to illustrate, however, his presidential vision was just getting started when construction on the Panama Canal began in 1904. As important as that was, it would be followed by such milestones as a bevy of bills under his watch that regulated and structured American life, including the Pure Food and Drug Act, Meat Inspection Act, and Hepburn Act, which established much-needed rate controls on interstate commerce; his nurturing of a national conservation movement that would become the envy of the world, including the Antiquities Act, giving presidents the power to protect federal lands as national monuments; and his mediation of a major international conflict, the Russo-Japanese War, which made him America's first Nobel Peace Prize recipient.[35] All of those presidential highlights would take place in what amounted to his second term, his first having basically filled out McKinley's second term (all but six and a half months) following his assassination. All except his war settlement, in fact, occurred in 1906, the middle year of his final term, a term that in all likelihood would not have been his last if not for an ill-conceived comment he made after being re-elected by a landslide in 1904.[36]

Along with others, Morris confirmed that unforeseen comment in just two paragraphs. In them, he indicated that TR was being "reverential to the memory of George Washington," who famously declined to accept a third presidential term after serving as the country's chief executive its first eight years, thus establishing something of a precedent that more than two four-year terms was too much. TR's statement that day concluded, "The wise custom which limits the president to two terms regards substance and not form. Under no circumstances will I be a candidate or accept another nomination." It was a shocking declaration that took his family by surprise and one he lived to regret, a spur-of-the-moment commitment that might have rendered a lesser leader a lame duck.[37]

The Russo-Japanese settlement he negotiated in 1905, in fact, further established his already burgeoning international reputation, as he inserted himself into negotiations to end one of the bloodiest conflicts up to that time, a war for domination of the Asian Pacific that had started when Czarist Russia attempted to control Manchuria, the most northern and eastern of China's far-flung provinces and one Japan also had its eyes on after its conquest of the Korean Peninsula.[38] On February 8, 1904, Japan unleashed a devastating naval attack on the Russian Oriental Fleet at Port Arthur, a surprise initiation of hostilities much like the one it would unleash on the U.S. at Pearl Harbor 37 years later. Roosevelt announced that the U.S. would remain neutral.[39]

It was a war TR had long anticipated as he observed the transformation of Japan from a very closed and isolated island society to a much more industrialized, aggressive, modern state anxious to expand its influence throughout the Far East. Although still a force in world politics, Russia was not a military match for the more modernized forces of Japan, and the war was taking on an imbalance that might lead to Japanese domination when Roosevelt decided to get involved. Although an admirer of how the Japanese had altered their nation and their future, he foresaw trouble ahead if they prosecuted the war to the fullest extent, potentially bringing Russia to its knees. TR realized that Asian stability hung in the balance. By March 4, 1905, his inauguration day, Roosevelt was ready to test his expanding cachet on the worsening Asian conflict. "Any settlement of the Russo-Japanese War was going to need younger, stronger hands," according to Morris, and in assuming responsibility on the world stage, TR concluded, "Much has been given us and much will rightfully be expected of us."[40]

A week later, he made Japan's government aware that should it so desire, he would be glad to be of use in any effort to arrive at a negotiated settlement. His willingness and availability were conveyed as a leak so as not to give the appearance of a one-sided proposition, even though the Japanese were clearly taking control of a situation that became even more dire for the Czar's forces after a crushing Japanese naval victory that May. It was a defeat the already reeling, riot-cursed government of the Czar would not recover from, and TR believed something should be done to try to stave off what would become the Russian Revolution by the end of World War I.[41] While in awe of how decisively Japan had established itself, TR was unsympathetic to Russian instability and unable to understand how the Russians could lie so easily. To reinforce that point, Morris quoted Secretary of State Hay as saying, "It has been impossible to trust any promise [Russia] made. On the other hand, Japan's diplomatic statements [had] proved good."[42]

Despite this Czarist flight from reality, a renewed sense of urgency to save Russia from collapse prompted TR to wait no longer to take the initiative of inviting the belligerents to meet for the purpose of direct negotiation. It was mid–June before both Japan and Russia accepted Roosevelt's invitation and the international press got wind of what he was doing. To Russia, his message was one of failure and losses no matter how long it kept fighting. To Japan, TR emphasized the costs involved and the need to consolidate gains and appear magnanimous. Although both were determined to save as much face as possible before consenting to negotiate, those approaches apparently hit home when the leadership of both countries agreed to come to the table by early August. This they did at the East Coast town of Portsmouth, New Hampshire, where TR tried to make sure Japan didn't ask for too much and to provide Russia room to negotiate. Nevertheless, for nearly a month the losers (Russia) felt that the winners (Japan) were asking for too much. Only through TR's stubborn resolve and realism was the conflict ended and the president's acclaim magnified, both at home and abroad. Morris wrote:

> The peace [Roosevelt] had made possible at Portsmouth was the result of an inexplicable ability to impose his singular charge upon plural power. By sheer force of moral purpose, by clarity of perception, by mastery of detail, and benign manipulation of men, he had become, as historian Henry Adams admiringly wrote at the time, "The best herder of emperors since Napoleon."[43]

As his settlement of the coal strike had done domestically, the 1905 Treaty of Portsmouth served to validate TR on the international stage. It would be the year 1906, however, that would highlight his powers of legislation and executive order. It's not a stretch to say that the series of bills enacted during TR's second term, mostly in 1906, would rewrite American life, beginning with the Hepburn Act, a bill to regulate railroad rates. Previously, minimum rates were simply the domain of the individual railroads, with complete backing of the Republican-dominated Senate. After all, as Morris pointed out, "Was [it] not free enterprise's right to set its own prices in a competitive marketplace?" Instead, TR believed such growth had to be regulated when it became destructive, and the federal government was the only entity big enough to do that.[44] He also wanted to impress on the Republican leadership that unless it listened a little more to its progressive wing, a third, spinoff party might result.[45] Faced with the fact TR had risen from accidental to previously unseen heights of presidential popularity primarily through constant cultivation and active partnership with the press, even the most domineering Senators had to acknowledge Roosevelt's manipulative power when it came to public opinion.[46]

In TR's mind, there had to be "a surrender of capital ... of its high percentage of profit," and with a pro-regulatory House of Representatives taking his lead, the Senate was the bastion of corporate dominance that he had to overcome. Trying to appease TR and the pro-regulation press, the Senate's Committee on Interstate and Foreign Commerce offered up a bill of its own, but one that called for private rather than public monitoring.[47] TR instead remained committed to a bill Jonathon Doliver of Iowa, a junior senator, had drafted for him and one that got buy-in from the committee's co-chair, William Hepburn, also of Iowa. Although everyone knew it had come from the president, the bill became known as the Hepburn Act. The House approved it quickly, but the Senate's Old Guard of corporate interests went into delay mode. *Cosmopolitan* magazine even headed a series of articles "The Treason of the Senate" to bring attention to the congressional collusion that was occurring in the upper chamber, and eventually, after inclusion of an amendment for "national review," everyone got a compromise they could live with, and the Hepburn Act finally passed.[48]

This much-needed railroad regulation, under the auspices of the Interstate Commerce Commission that TR had previously strengthened, would become law and lead to other regulatory legislation dictated by the president and his progressive-leaning partners in the press. The next domino to fall would be food processors and the meat-packing industry. The activist Upton Sinclair authored his legendary novel *The Jungle*, which first exposed unsanitary practices being practiced on a daily basis by the major packers, Armor, Morris, and Swift.[49] A report instigated by Roosevelt in lieu of Sinclair's book was so defaming and inflammatory that TR decided not to release it to the public, but he did release it to Congress with the rare result that it inspired immediate regulatory legislation. The Meat Inspection and Pure Food and Drug Acts, in fact, became law just one day after the Hepburn Act.[50]

Roosevelt's progressive agenda also included signing an act for the preservation of American antiquities that had been championed by Iowa Congressman John Lacey, resulting from concerns over the protection of prehistoric Native American ruins and artifacts in the American Southwest. TR, however, took advantage of that empowerment to go to extraordinary lengths in his conservation and preservation efforts, turning over 200 million acres into government monuments and preserves by the end of his administration. As a result, he would become the founding force in the national park movement and what became the National Park Service, exhibiting the same commitment to nature that had led him to found the U.S. Forest Service a year earlier.[51]

TR's last two years in the White House were years of some financial disruption, as happened in October 1907, when two failed Wall Street speculators set off a brief panic that required Morgan and other great financiers to restore what Morris termed "confidence and calm." TR even congratulated "those conservative and substantial businessmen who have acted with wisdom and public spirit." Such response became part of his ongoing campaign against men of privilege like John D. Rockefeller of Standard Oil and E. H. Harriman of the Santa Fe Railroad, whenever their financial investment in politicians initiated corruption.[52] He also became a purveyor of unabashed national self-promotion, as when he exhibited America's newly built naval might by sending America's "Great White Fleet" around the world. This earthly circumference by such an impressive U.S. flotilla generated great global reviews and concluded just ten days before he exited the White House.

He was even vindicated by the Senate Committee on Military Affairs for the dishonorable discharge of 15 African American soldiers stationed at Fort Brown in Brownsville, Texas, after local citizenry accused them of disturbing the peace, destroying private property, and the murder of one White citizen during a wild shooting spree on the night of August 13, 1907, charges the accused soldiers decried as false and based on racial hatred. The controversy came after they broke curfew to enjoy a night on the town. Although never actually proven, their apparent complicity in obstruction of justice during the investigation led Roosevelt to uphold the findings of a military tribunal, which included dishonorable discharges for the entire company. It marked a hardening of his previous stance in racial matters, a change that played well with the South but not with African American voters, who had previously always sided with the Republicans, the so-called "Party of Lincoln." At the same time, two dissenting senators indicated "the weight of the testimony showed the soldiers to be innocent," and it became a subject TR would avoid for the rest of his life, including in his autobiography."[53]

Whether or not his avoidance was evidence of guilty feelings, especially after his old friend and advisor, Booker T. Washington, lobbied him strenuously for their pardon, it was a rare discrepancy in the proactive policy of perhaps our most confident chief executive ever. Morris labeled it "the major mistake of his presidency," another esteemed historian deemed it "a lasting scar on his legacy," and a third pointed to the episode as a mitigating factor in suddenly festering "estrangement between the president and Congress."[54]

To recap the decade between the end of his presidency and the end of his life, TR would lead a big game safari to "Darkest Africa"; visit the crown heads of Europe; stage a political re-emergence so impactful in the presidential race of 1912 that he would split the Republican Party, handing the election to the Democrats; survive an assassin's bullet while campaigning in Milwaukee, Wisconsin; explore South America's infamous "River of Doubt" for the American Museum of Natural History (which nearly cost him his life and left his health compromised); and engage in endless opposition to President Woodrow Wilson's administration, especially its initial avoidance of World War I, which all four of his sons would serve in with military distinction and during which one would die.[55] Although personally crushed by his youngest son's tragic fate as one of the earliest U.S. casualties in the new age of airplane warfare, he still felt somewhat cheated by having not had the opportunity to preside over a war during his years in the White House, something he believed elevated presidents like Washington and Lincoln to greatness.[56]

Upon TR's sudden death at age 60 on January 6, 1919, (while asleep) due to a coronary embolism, one of his sons informed the others, "The old lion is dead." He went to his grave still believing the country might turn to him as a presidential candidate in 1920. Whether such a belief had any basis in political reality is doubtful, especially given how much the nation had changed following its participation in its first global conflict (World War I), but it does speak to the sheer tenacity of Roosevelt's personality and self-esteem to the bitter end, an accidental president that biographers like Morris, H.W. Brands, and others have unendingly portrayed as arriving at just the right moment in the American story.[57]

15

Reinventing "Silent Cal" Coolidge

"He [Calvin Coolidge] is very self-contained, very simple, very direct, and very shrewd in his observations."—William Howard Taft, 1923

It's ironic that an American decade best remembered for its excess and frivolity was also the era of a president best remembered for his thrift and sensibility. That was the theme, in fact, chosen by one of his most recent biographers as a means of elevating our most conservative president and, it could be argued, the most successful conservative ever to reside at 1600 Pennsylvania Avenue.[1]

Although accidental in his ascendance to the presidency as a somewhat shy, soft-spoken politician of few, well-chosen words, Calvin Coolidge was reinvented by biographer Amity Shlaes to be a much more important part of the 1920s than previously understood. Fulfilling the fiscally conservative mantra of reducing the federal budget during a time of economic growth, increased wages, lower taxes, and low unemployment, Coolidge had previously been remembered as a beneficiary of the good times enjoyed by the nation as a whole while he was in the White House rather than as a significant contributor. But Shlaes disagreed and authored a book to prove it.

In her introduction, she laid the groundwork for "Silent Cal's" legendary frugality and how that contributed to her overhaul of his legacy by writing:

> In his personal life, Coolidge brought saving to a high art. Coolidge was so parsimonious that he didn't buy a house even after he was governor of Massachusetts; so careful that he didn't own a car until he achieved the presidency; [and] so strict about money that his son never [got over] it. Thrifty to the point of harshness, Coolidge rarely relented when it came to money.[2]

Furthering that premise, Shlaes maintained that he "hacked away" at the federal budget with a discipline tragically missing from his equally well-intentioned predecessor, Warren G. Harding, a popular but scandal-riddled chief executive who shockingly died with over a year left in his term. But despite pressure to expand programs and increase spending, political pressure as unyielding as it is today, his "vigilance was steadfast," she maintained, even casting him as a throwback to an earlier time when spending and excess were not as much a part of the American scene. She recorded Coolidge's 67 months in office (the remainder of Harding's term plus his own re-elected four years) as a time "when government was kept out of the way of commerce," leaving it smaller than when he moved into the White House in a way no one has been able to do since. Using similar parlance, another recent historian added: "As the faithful steward of limited government, Coolidge used the office the way the founding generation intended. He protected the balance between federal and state governments and did not allow Congress to run roughshod over the Constitution by safeguarding the proper separation of powers."[3]

To Shlaes, the magnitude and "extent" of that achievement has been lost in American history. She "puzzled" over the relative obscurity of this president, "this placeholder between Roosevelts," and she wished to call attention to the unfortunate void the lack of Coolidge attention has had in subsequent studies of intervening presidents. "Without seeing Coolidge in the [upper] ranks," she emphasized, "[one] cannot entirely appreciate the office." She even equated ignorance of Coolidge with a misunderstanding of the era.

At the same time, she readily admitted his shortcomings as president—such things as an irrational trust of world leaders like Italy's Benito Mussolini and countries like Germany and Japan; a lack of anticipation of the extent to which succeeding presidents would diverge on economic issues; and his lack of anticipation of the national economic meltdown to come just a few years hence. In so doing, however, she deemed his inaction a positive, referring to him as "our great refrainer" when compared to presidents who have since felt compelled to make an individual difference either out of necessity or some preconceived, elected agenda. She said Coolidge was willing to be "unpopular" and called him "among the most selfless of our presidents," serving the law and ranking individual rights above political constituency. Shlaes also cast doubt on blame long affixed to Coolidge for his place on the timeline just ahead of economic downturn and the Great Depression, calling that reputation "a stretch." Instead, her defense of Coolidge was well-established from the start, leaving her readers to judge whether she succeeded or failed in revising the legacy of our sixth accidental president.[4]

But what has always been known for sure: Coolidge did achieve national hero status as Massachusetts governor, the result of his strong, unyielding support of Boston's local authorities during its police strike of 1919. Capitalizing on that notoriety, he also became a popular pick for vice president at the 1920 Republican Convention, a much more consensus choice, in fact, than Harding, whose presidential bid was born in the backrooms of "Grand Old Party" stalemate and double-dealings. As such, the rural Vermont native was a steady addition to the Ohio senator's campaign after eight years of rare Democratic governance under President Woodrow Wilson. Not quite sure what they were getting from the boss-driven selection of Harding other than his call for normalcy, the voting public was buoyed by the sensible Governor Coolidge's addition to the Republican ticket.[5] Shlaes brought this out when she wrote, "The enthusiasm that had been lacking for Harding was there for Coolidge." Unlike their presidential choice, the delegates picked Coolidge for vice president without any behind-the-scenes activities.[6] And like many another convention presidential runner-up, the initially reluctant Coolidge was soon compelled to accept the number two role.[7]

Thus was born the unusual political pairing of what another historian termed the "soft, easy-going Ohioan" (Harding) with the "hard-bitten New England Yankee" (Coolidge), a "hedonist" and a "Puritan."[8] Running against an uninspiring Democrat in newspaper publisher James Cox and his more inspiring but still young vice-presidential running mate, Franklin Roosevelt, the outgoing assistant secretary of the Navy, the Harding-Coolidge victory was considered a sure thing from the start, which it proved to be with over 60 percent of the vote.[9] Coolidge identified with most of the policies Harding professed. Only their lifestyles differed significantly. But in terms of a reduction of progressive goals and progressivism, Coolidge could agree with Harding's intention to move away from the "New Freedom" of Wilson or even the professed "Square Deal" of Theodore Roosevelt to what he termed the "Old Deal" and the assurance to be gained by "an efficient administration of our proven system."[10]

In other words, Harding was seeking to turn back the clock to the pro-business days of Republican domination at the turn of the twentieth century. With the international adventures of World War I in the rear view mirror and Wilson's League of Nations defeated in his own country, Harding looked to restrict the expansion of government and to control the federal budget in ways that war had not allowed and the Democrats had sought to continue once it was over.[11] He did so, however, surrounded by a Cabinet and staff comprised largely of his Ohio associates, many of whom were ill-equipped, not qualified, or looking to take advantage of the system if opportunities presented themselves. Collectively, they were known as his "Golf Cabinet," "Poker Cabinet," or even the "Ohio Gang," and their presence in and around the White House opened a Pandora's box of problems for Harding. Scandals surfaced in Veterans Affairs, the Justice Department, and Department of the Interior, where Naval petroleum reserves left over from the war years and later transferred from the Navy were released without government-required bids, a miscarriage of justice we remember as Teapot Dome that would take its rightful place among the most notorious political scandals in American history.[12]

Amidst this two-year hemorrhaging of ethics and propriety, Coolidge was assigned to be a conscientious spokesman for the Harding administration, and he remained a loyal player in administration efforts to initiate a reduction in the overall size of government, the legacy that had made up his mind when the vice-presidential bid was offered. Unfortunately, things like Teapot Dome kept getting in the way, and Progressive Party diehards like Senator Robert La Follette of Wisconsin kept demanding investigations. Increasing unions and strikes also limited recovery and upward economic trends, and as the 1922 midterm elections approached, Republican prospects did not look good.[13]

As resulting administration shakeups began to occur, including Cabinet resignations, Harding's political capital began to wane, and Coolidge started to have trouble reconciling his attachment.[14] To rescue his sagging approval ratings, Harding scheduled an ill-fated, 15,000-mile Western tour that would ultimately end with his illness and death.[15] On August 2, 1922, while the vice president was visiting his family home in Vermont, the shocking call came from across the country—the president was dead—and the new president, Calvin Coolidge, was sworn in by his aging father, a justice of the peace, in the leafy hamlet of his birth, Plymouth Notch.[16]

Reaction throughout the country was mixed. Perhaps the most remembered was that of powerful Massachusetts Senator and instate rival Henry Cabot Lodge, who famously stated, "My God, that means Coolidge is president." Another sudden and unexpected chief executive, Coolidge did what most of our other accidentals had done or would do before and since: he determined to finish what his predecessor and running mate had started; he would take the country back to a time of smaller government. According to Shlaes, "the presidency was a job for which his whole life had prepared him. That was the message he needed to convey to a sorrowing country." "I am taking stock," he surmised, "and I believe I can swing it."[17]

Such confidence moving forward was a direct response and remembrance of what he had observed in his own lifetime, when Roosevelt assumed the presidency in the wake of the McKinley assassination. Coolidge had been impressed with the irrepressible TR, especially during his earliest days in office when he reinforced McKinley's goals while also protecting the office through flawless management of the transition process. True to his always fiscally responsible position, Coolidge knew he needed to prevent crisis and keep the country calm; avoid disruption within the stock market; and navigate his way through any major strikes, including another one already threatened by the coal industry for later that fall.[18]

Again, as with most of the other accidental Presidents, Coolidge decided to retain his

The quaint village of Plymouth Notch, Vermont, the birthplace of Calvin Coolidge, is also the place where he was sworn in as president following the death of Warren G. Harding. The darker building at left is the one in which he was born (photograph property of the author).

predecessor's Cabinet—even though a clean sweep had to be tempting given the Harding administration's scandalous past. But in the end, the need for "continuity" won out, according to Shlaes, and the ten-for-ten Cabinet members returning to work under the new president was both impressive and somewhat surprising. Back were Secretary of State Charles Evans Hughes, Secretary of the Treasury Andrew Mellon, Secretary of War John Weeks, Postmaster General Harry New, Secretary of the Interior Hubert Work (the replacement for disgraced Albert Fall, guilty of conspiracy and bribery in Teapot Dome), Secretary of Agriculture Henry C. Wallace, Secretary of Commerce Herbert Hoover, Secretary of Labor James Davis, and even Attorney General Harry Daugherty and Secretary of the Navy Edwin Denby, both of whom had already been implicated in improper activities and would soon be gone, the eventual subjects of investigation and resignation. Coolidge would also see fit to replace several others once he entered his own, elected term in 1925.[19]

Nevertheless, continuity with restraint would remain Coolidge's guiding principle in the earliest days of his administration, along with always prioritizing economy in government. Tax cuts had been front-and-center on Harding's professed agenda, and Coolidge would continue that philosophy, but take it to another level. Working well with Mellon, they presented a plan of "scientific taxation," what Shlaes termed a "shared moral outrage at expenditure." By their prognosis, the money that flowed into the economy when they cut taxes would pay off the federal debt faster than the larger tax dollars brought in. Theirs was the founding trickle-down principal that has become so much a part of modern Repub-

Pictured at the head of this table (*left*) with his Cabinet, Calvin Coolidge was the first president to champion "trickle down economics," the concept of cutting taxes and limiting government services to spur commercial growth (Library of Congress Prints and Photographs Division—Reproduction Number DIG-ds-09331).

lican dogma. Soon after assuming the Presidency in 1923, Coolidge announced his tax-cutting intentions this way:

> For years the people have borne with uncomplaining courage the tremendous burden of national and local taxation. These must both be reduced. The taxes of the nation must be reduced now as much as prudence will permit, and expenditures must be reduced accordingly. High taxes reach everywhere and burden everybody. They wear most heavily upon the poor. They diminish industry and commerce. They make agriculture unprofitable. They increase the rates on transportation. They are a charge on every necessity of life. The country wants this measure [to take precedence] over all others.[20]

At the same time, he had to get the country past the Harding scandals. At his first address to Congress after Harding's death in December 1923, Coolidge stated, "Our main problems are domestic problems." To him, "the federal household" would matter most. The budget system was working and he planned to maintain it, while also prioritizing what his biographer labeled "new tax law." The speech exceeded expectations. Shlaes said he spoke "artillery style" and easily transitioned his no-wasted words approach from the Halls of Congress to the new medium of radio, which was just taking hold around the country.[21]

Within months of reaching the White House, he was actively running for re-election despite the Harding scandals still resonating. To combat ongoing Democratic charges of corruption, Coolidge focused on taxes and showed "wonderful composure," according to new Chief Justice of the Supreme Court and former President William Howard Taft, who had since been appointed to the Court by Harding.[22] Faced with a Bonus Bill that would basically provide pensions to World War I veterans and immigration legislation that would exclude Japanese, Coolidge hired external investigators and a special prosecutor to separate himself from the scandals, compromised on the immigration issue in order to further his tax plan, and vetoed the Bonus Bill that, if passed, would have essentially ended those same tax initiatives.[23]

In the end, his first, 1924 Revenue Act had to be compromised in the hope that a temporary 25 percent credit would earn enough votes to ensure his re-election and another chance at more lasting tax reform, the kind he and Mellon had actually been plotting. A few days later, he vetoed a Post Office Department salary increase, another early example of his determination to make the federal government smaller.[24]

Later that year at the Republican Convention, the incumbent accidental president was the easy choice. His running mate in 1924 would be Charles Dawes of Illinois, Harding's director of the Budget Bureau.[25] At the same time, the Democrats were divided. When their top two candidates repeatedly could not get the required delegate count to claim victory, John Davis, a little-known Wall Street lawyer, was their compromise choice. But regardless of whom he was running against, Coolidge was determined to make tax reform his signature issue. To get his new law, the president sustained his campaign against governmental waste by focusing on savings. Despite having to deal with the tragic death of his oldest son due to a freak injury, Coolidge waged a determined campaign based on policy to offset the equally conservative Davis and a formidable third party progressive, La Follette. Sticking to "brass tacks and common sense" was the Republican theme amidst overall prosperity and surplus. Sustaining the budget by remaining faithful to their promotion of savings, Coolidge and Mellon returned to their theory of lowering tax rates as a means of creating more business and thus more revenue. Even the hard-to-help farmers, who were being pinched in what was otherwise an era of plenty, were considered in play for Coolidge if food prices went up before the election.[26]

La Follette went after Coolidge over corruption, charging that Republican-backed tariffs were actually paybacks for certain industries. The fear was that La Follette's Progressives might unite with the Democrats to oust Coolidge and undo the savings and reduction of government he had already initiated, but with the economy humming and the incumbent president exhibiting a thick skin, he was able to avoid being drawn into a war of words with his challengers. As a result, he carried 35 of the 48 states and looked forward to a much easier road for his tax overhaul following Republican gains in the House and Senate.[27]

Although compromised somewhat by how little he knew during the previous administration, especially after being left out of Harding's Cabinet meetings, Coolidge was able to re-launch tax reform while continuing to cut the federal budget. Putting it into words, he proclaimed, "Economy reaches everywhere. It carries a blessing for everybody." The budget surplus surged to over $100 million, employment was high, and with the aviation industry just starting to scratch the surface of its enormous potential, Coolidge argued to keep it in private hands rather than controlled by the military.[28]

In October of 1925, he and Mellon were finally able to launch their expanded Revenue Act. It was passed in early 1926. Skewed to the wealthy, it freed up money for private investment.[29] Shlaes gave special emphasis to the milestone legislation by noting, "The president and his Cabinet secretary laid it out: income tax cuts, including a reduction of surtaxes worth $193.5 million." The federal deficit was already down to $20 billion, thanks to what Shlaes termed, "a refinancing skill worthy of [Alexander] Hamilton [our nation's first Treasury secretary]."[30]

At the same time, with his father in failing health (he would die of a stroke with his son still in the White House in March 1926) and the demands of office starting to encroach on his physical and mental state, Coolidge temporarily sank to a new low of depression when he said, "I am the most powerful man in the world, but great power does not mean much except great limitations. I cannot have any freedom.... Thousands are waiting to shake my hand."[31] Nevertheless, scientific taxation did prevail. Estate taxes came down, and one in every three who paid taxes before was not subject to them going forward. The famous actor, humorist, and columnist Will Rogers joked, "We have paid back more money than we ever paid in," and on the morning of February 26, 1926, President Calvin Coolidge finally signed the tax legislation he had been seeking all along. On paper it cost the government $388 million, but the great experiment to reduce federal revenue in order to spur U.S. business had begun.[32]

Having been electorally confirmed in his own right by 1926, and the proud new "father of American tax reform," Coolidge embarked on the last years of his presidency anxious for the surge of progress that such things as aviation might inspire; bracing for new rounds of credit to farmers in order to avoid systematic price management; and standing on the cusp of the highest standard of living in American history. A tax refund that redistributed millions of the national surplus went a long way towards making the president's tax plan popular, but Coolidge remained eager for more obvious evidence that the experiment was working. Talk of another term for "Silent Cal" was in the wind, a testament to his popularity but something he never truly considered.[33]

Continuing his budget austerity, he denied federal pensions even for the few remaining widows of Union Civil War veterans because of the bad precedent such a concession would create.[34] Coolidge insisted it took courage to continue the conservative frugality his administration had been following, and he wasn't about to loosen any purse strings if he could avoid it despite an expanding congressional wish list.[35] At the same time, long-standing Republican tariffs continued to anger American farmers and foreign trade partners. Politically, it was a toxic situation that risked losing the Western side of the country. In addition, Commerce Secretary Herbert Hoover, a rising star in the Republican Party, along with Nebraska Senator George Norris, a rare, bi-partisan facilitator, were leaders of a growing contingent hoping to construct huge hydroelectric dams on the Western and Southern rivers for much-needed electricity in those regions.[36]

With these and other spending pressures gradually mounting for the inherently reluctant president, the economic dam literally did break in the spring of 1927, when the worst flooding in memory spread misery throughout the center of the country on a scale that devastated thousands. The Mississippi, by far the nation's largest river, rose to unseen levels and began overflowing its banks and levees. Half a million people were forced to flee their homes, and Southern governors and mayors began calling for federal assistance to deal with the mounting crisis. Almost overnight, Coolidge was confronted by a great national disaster applying pressure to the national coffers he had worked so hard to build up.[37]

Shlaes succinctly illustrated his dilemma when she wrote, "This was the sort of test George Washington had warned of, a test of federalism. A commander-in-chief might lead a nation to war. He might order destroyers across the Atlantic or dispatch troops. But Coolidge did not deem it appropriate for a president to march south like a general into governors' territory to manage a flood rescue." In his opinion, a president's job in such situations was to coordinate, offer supplies, and provide encouragement. It went no further. It was wrong to intrude on governors. The work of rescue and reconstruction was for the individual state governments. It was an opinion shared by a few state chief executives, but it was an opinion that cost Coolidge much of the hard-won approval he could previously claim. He didn't even visit any of the disaster sites, something presidents today would be "raked over the coals of indifference" if they failed to do. Instead, Shlaes referenced how he sent "his best emissary," his relief engineer, Hoover, who assumed the role of "flood chief" and began accumulating accolades that might otherwise have gone to the president. Hoover headed a Red Cross drive that raised more than $8 million for the flood victims and set up refugee camps for several hundred thousand people. He also had each of the affected states name a "director of resources" that he could work with and through. Given the scale, Shlaes called Hoover's feat "amazing."[38]

Coolidge, meanwhile, worked hard to stimulate additional charity. In a matter of weeks, he had driven his appeal for monetary assistance to $10 million. He also set a policy for the federal government of "rescue yes, but reconstruction no." Hoover backed him by maintaining that the affected states must take the lead in disaster reconstruction, but secretly he hoped for "a greater role by Washington." At the same time, Democrats like Franklin Roosevelt called for immediate congressional action. With pressure mounting, it became apparent that flood management would become the largest peacetime infrastructure project in the years just ahead. Hoover had upstaged Coolidge, something that cooled their relationship, but Coolidge would never relent to a special session of Congress to consider federal aid.[39]

Internationally, a Five-Power Agreement on certain naval limitations that Coolidge sought to extend disintegrated due to disagreements, lack of interest, and even hostility among Japan, Great Britain, Italy, and France, leaving the United States something of a lone voice for consensus. That disappointment, however, was offset by the astounding achievement of an American pilot, Charles Lindbergh, the first person to fly across the Atlantic Ocean. Shlaes placed as much emphasis on "the flier" as "the flood," illuminating Coolidge's enthusiasm and excitement over the private aviation achievement and the potential it implied for the future. Amid much pomp and circumstance, the president (along with the flier) "presided over a weekend of congratulations and celebration in the nation's capital" that was broadcast nationwide on radio.[40]

Another celebration for the president and Mrs. Coolidge followed shortly in the Black Hills of South Dakota. That's where the renowned sculptor Gutzon Borglum was set to promote his monumental Mount Rushmore project for the first time, in hopes of renewed federal support. Many within the Republican Party, still hoping to coax Coolidge into running again, also viewed the First Family's Western sojourn as important. With the economy still expanding and his visit hopefully placating Western farmers (still about the only large group of voters he couldn't count on), there was growing momentum to keep Cal in the White House after 1928. The old saying, "if it ain't broke, don't fix it," seemed an increasingly Republican refrain as the summer of 1927 continued. Additional importance of the president's visit could be measured in the auto-driven tourism it inspired. Along with improving vehicles, improved roads were starting to appear in the West, and automobile traffic was starting to become a major force in the economies of many Western states, including South Dakota. "Within weeks of his arrival, thousands of Americans were heading to the Black Hills," Shlaes noted.[41] Staying beyond their originally planned three weeks, the Coolidges made South Dakota their adopted state. Indeed, the Western White House lasted long enough for Coolidge literally to spell out that he did "not choose to run again for president in 1928." He made his surprise announcement at a hastily called press conference on August 3, 1927, in dramatic fashion, with his decision written out on small, folded slips of paper that were handed to each of the 20 or so reporters in attendance.[42]

Predictably (with what may have been the first press release), it didn't take long for the reporters to stampede to telephones or the telegraph office, and within hours, Republicans across the country were astonished to read of their incumbent's decision. Many thought he was bluffing. Others believed he could still be talked into running again if nominated. Regardless, near the end of a summer-long stay, Coolidge let it be known that nothing had changed, and there would be no additional presidential term in his future (even though, like TR before him, another successful run would have been almost a certainty given his popularity).[43]

Coolidge and the First Lady did not return to Washington until September. They missed a major Vermont event honoring the sesquicentennial of the Revolutionary War and the Battle of Bennington. They did so in order to remain longer in their adopted Dakota Country, a fact that did not sit well with many of their fellow New Englanders. But Coolidge was already turning away from such infringements on his personal time as he approached his last year in office. Instead, he wanted to focus on defending and preserving his already established policies. In Shlaes words, "a consistent legacy would be a stronger legacy."

Besides, Congress was quickly treating him like a lame duck. Rather than rewarding him, they soon pressed him to give ground on issues where he previously would not budge. Along with extra naval appropriations, they still wanted more money for waterways. Behind the scenes, Hoover was already laying the groundwork for a giant flood control system and much more.[44]

To Coolidge, the federal government should always spend less on internal projects than the states, a philosophy that began to be questioned by the formally friendly press and congressional critics, who increasingly wanted a special session to fund federal relief. Past war debts dating from the Spanish-American War also frustrated the president as his fifth year in office drew to a close. There seemed no way to reach his $3 billion goal, with veterans' care and other military commitments constantly requiring funds.[45]

Again according to Shlaes, he also foresaw trouble ahead in the financial markets. He believed in principle that it would be wrong to intervene with the Federal Reserve, Treasury, or the markets, but he also saw the potential for economic disaster. Shlaes requoted his lead Secret Service aide, Edmund Starling, who had heard Coolidge state, "Well, they're going to replace me with Hoover and he's going to have some trouble. He's going to have to spend money, but he won't spend enough. Then the Democrats will come in and they'll spend money like water." It would prove a pretty accurate pre-Depression premonition.[46]

As for his emerging dislike for Hoover, water power would provide their ultimate falling out. As the presumptive Republican nominee in 1928, the commerce secretary needed a public relations coup that winter to ensure ascendance and ammunition to campaign on the following fall. Unlike the progressive party, he never advocated complete government ownership of hydroelectric dams and power plants, but his moderate approach would also require federal buy-in. As fate would have it, another major flood, this one inundating much of New England, occurred right before the first major snowstorm, leaving icy floodwaters throughout the region, especially in Vermont.

Shlaes called it "retribution of biblical proportions." The nation watched to see if the president would offer more to his "native land" than he had to states along the Mississippi.

Sticking to his principles, however, he believed there was nothing he could do about flood control in his home state or region. All he could do was dispatch Hoover again, who had won acclaim for his earlier efforts in the South. Although Hoover never gained the notoriety and applause he received from earlier flood relief, his boss, President Coolidge, would remain the target of disdain in Vermont, as the state legislature was forced to go it alone with an $8-plus million repair bill, roughly half the little state's annual budget, that Shlaes referenced as "enslavement" in the minds of many Vermonters.[47]

Hoover, meanwhile, returned his attention to the South, publishing his Commerce Department's economic report ahead of Coolidge's last annual "State of the Union" address to Congress. In it, he touted the nation's overall prosperity. He also assured Southerners that funding for spillways and other flood control measures was on the way, regardless of what the outgoing president might say. When Coolidge did address the subject without offering further federal assistance, the South voiced its fury, calling his lack of relief for the states "an impossibility" in the Lower Mississippi Valley, where poor states were without the means for "substantial contributions" to flood control. And because Hoover hinted at more, the anger directed at Coolidge intensified.[48]

As he entered his final year in office, in fact, Coolidge turned from domestic issues to foreign affairs. Hoping to accomplish the legacy Woodrow Wilson had famously been denied, when his League of Nations as a worldwide peace-keeping organization after World War I was famously rejected by Congress. Coolidge instead sought a treaty that would maintain U.S. independence and avoid European entanglements, while at the same time ensuring peaceful international negotiations. Orchestrated by his hard-working new secretary of state, Frank Kellogg, one of the few Republicans who had earlier backed Wilson's League while a Minnesota senator, along with outspoken Senator William Borah of Idaho, the 47-nation Kellogg-Briand Treaty was an unexpected highlight near the end of the Coolidge presidency, what Shlaes termed his "final political victory." Just as he had teamed with Mellon so well on taxes early in his administration, he combined with Kellogg to demonstrate his understanding of the legislative process in accomplishing a foreign peace treaty that was overwhelmingly ratified by the Senate. "Coolidge had succeeded where Wilson had failed," Shlaes proudly claimed, creating a "multilateral treaty" designed to make future worldwide aggression against the law. With so much of his focus having always been on domestic affairs and what, in his mind, should be the proper performance of the federal government, it was ironic that his final presidential plunge was international. What did make it true to form was his attempt at law and order on the world stage.[49]

But was his Kellogg-Briand Treaty truly a victory on the world stage? As with his hands-off financial policies that encouraged 1920s speculation before the Great Depression, some historians have questioned the "shortsightedness" or "naiveté" of a treaty that did not address the brooding "mess" left over from the First World War that would lead to the rise of totalitarian governments and World War II less than 20 years later.[50]

Upon leaving the White House, Coolidge deemed himself lucky to have survived. Even in retirement, however, Silent Cal could not fade away. The townspeople of Northampton, Massachusetts, the home he returned to after Washington, simply would not allow it, with his comings and goings reported at every turn. One involvement he did assiduously avoid was Wall Street, further evidence he may have known a crash was coming and hoped to distance himself from its aftermath. Indeed, as the first stock market crash was about to happen in September 1929, the 30th president busied himself with a brief autobiography and additional writing opportunities for *McClure's* magazine, authoring a short daily syndicated column that earned him $3,000 a week and a comfortable New England lifestyle.[51]

In his columns, he cautioned the American people about expecting too much from their federal government as the economy began to spiral downward. Outside influences and opposition writers like Will Rogers and Sinclair Lewis were reaping awards and casting doubts on the fiscally restrained policies of the Coolidge years, something he felt personally compelled to defend. Shlaes wrote, "To see his accomplishments so challenged by events and government policy under Hoover was hard." The Republican Party was adrift and could not "elude responsibility for the country's growing financial trouble." Steadily, the popularity of New York Governor Franklin D. Roosevelt, a "big government" Democrat, was gaining momentum, and when the old soldiers of World War I finally congregated in Washington during the summer of 1932, demanding bonuses for the military service they had rendered in Europe over a decade before, the Hoover administration may have ensured FDR's initial presidential victory by sending troops to contain (and ultimately remove) the veterans from the nation's capital in one of the worst public relations (and political) decisions ever.[52]

With his Republican successor struggling to keep his head above water as the tide of public opinion turned irrevocably towards the Democrats, Coolidge refused to enter the political quagmire brought on by the worst economic collapse in American history, the Great Depression. Along with what he wrote in his columns, he briefly tried to defend Hoover in a speech at Madison Square Garden, where he warned against "switching horses in the middle of a race," and again in a nationwide radio address just before the election. Neither, however, had any last-minute effect on the election's rather obvious direction, as Roosevelt surged past Hoover to victory and into the cauldron of a bankrupt economy. Shlaes referenced Coolidge's use of the term "experimentation" to predict what the new Democratic administration would surely do. Gone for good would be the normalcy that Coolidge had believed in when he joined the 1920 Republican ticket. In its place, he knew FDR would probably accelerate what Hoover had already started—government spending to spur economic activity.[53]

Soon after FDR's election but before he took office and instigated the New Deal policies Coolidge had predicted, the former president from tiny Plymouth Notch collapsed at his Massachusetts home and died of a massive heart attack on January 5, 1933. Like Theodore Roosevelt before him, he was only 60 years old.[54]

16

Overachieving with "Give 'em Hell Harry"

"President Truman is beloved by the American people because of his candor, honesty, frankness, and principle."—Hubert Humphrey, 1952

Ten years in the writing and nearly 1,000 pages long, David McCullough's magisterial biography of Harry Truman was published in 1992 and remains the recognized authority on the life and times of our 33rd president. Titled simply *Truman*, it's a single volume without preface, prologue, or introduction, written in the easily read narrative that is a McCullough trademark in all his books, including stories of the Brooklyn Bridge, Johnstown Flood, and Panama Canal, to name just a few. Like his other acclaimed biography of another American president published almost a decade later, *John Adams*, it won a Pulitzer Prize, and probably ranks as the most memorable achievement of a most memorable American historian.

While biographies of the president Truman replaced, Franklin Delano Roosevelt, have been numerous and continue to be written every few years, McCullough's recounting of the common man from Independence, Missouri, who had to fill FDR's sizable shoes, is probably more enduring. Called the "first full scale biography of Truman," it's still regarded as the best and should remain the most remembered. From it, the lasting takeaway will always be the simple, plain, everyman quality of the guy suddenly thrust onto the world stage in 1945 by circumstances beyond his control, a guy who never wanted to be president and certainly not the one to succeed FDR, our longest-serving and most recognized modern chief executive.[1]

Without a college degree and considered a failure at everything he had tried before the Army (World War I) and politics, Truman came from a low-income, farming family of Middle America. As previously established in this book, only as a compromise, best-available replacement for FDR's fourth and final presidential ticket did this product of Missouri machine politics end up as leader of the free world less than four months after being sworn in as an ill-prepared number two man, a stunning circumstance in the midst of World War II.

McCullough illustrated that moment midway through his book, when he wrote:

To the country, the Congress, the Washington bureaucracy, to hundreds of veteran New Dealers besides those gathered in the Cabinet Room [for Truman's swearing in], to much of the military high command, to millions of American men and women overseas, the news of Franklin Roosevelt's death followed by the realization that Harry Truman was president struck like massive earth tremors in quick succession, the thought of Truman in the White House coming with the force of a shock wave. To many it was not just that the greatest of men had fallen, but that the least of men—or at any rate the least likely of men—had assumed his place.

Even Truman, during his first day on the job, seemed to echo McCullough's sentiments by stating, "There have been few men in all of history the equal of the man into whose shoes I am stepping. I pray God I can measure up to the task."[2]

In the immediate aftermath of FDR's death, Truman went back to the Capitol the very next day, seeking support and understanding from colleagues in the Senate he had been presiding over for less than three weeks. The experience gap Truman faced was immense. He had not been kept abreast of the ongoing war effort and the constantly changing international landscape. Treated instead as an administration outsider, he was in desperate need of extensive briefings once he suddenly became the most powerful man on earth.[3]

While struggling to come to terms with his own suddenly ascendant status, Truman took part in the three days of solemn events that began with the arrival of FDR's casket in Washington, the slow funeral procession and service in the East Room of the White House, and finally the presidential train to FDR's home in Hyde Park, New York, for burial in the family rose garden. Only after the iconic Roosevelt was laid to rest on April 15, 1945, did Truman feel comfortable moving forward with his own presidency.[4]

First on his new agenda was an address to Congress on Monday the 16th, a 15-minute speech that earned 17 standing ovations and universal prayer. According to McCullough, "People everywhere felt relief, even hope, as they listened. He seemed a good man, so straight forward, so determined to do his job." By the end of his speech, people everywhere, American citizens who had grown accustomed to FDR, all wanted the "new man" to succeed. "He's one of us," reporters heard over and over—from both leaders and constituents in all manner of places. He talked like them—sounded like them without the high-minded syntax or accent of the elite, "Easternly-bred" Roosevelt and his inner circle.[5]

As a product of rural America, Harry Truman seemed unqualified to stand up to the Soviet Union in what was shaping up to be a so-called "Cold War" between potential superpowers following World War II. With the world war entering its final stages, one of the first things the unknowing new chief executive was confronted with was immediate knowledge of the massive but amazingly secret military mission FDR had put in motion three years earlier, a mission to develop and build an atomic bomb.

The Manhattan Project by name, it had started as a result of Nazi Germany's pursuit of such a weapon, and it had already cost billions of dollars and involved 200,000 people when FDR died without briefing his vice president and potential successor about its existence. Imagine being the new guy faced with such world-altering power. Imagine being Truman, knowing that there would soon be a devastating weapon that could end the war and save American lives, but also change forever the potential of international conflict and possibly even human existence. Needless to say, it was a lot of responsibility, especially for someone who never wanted the job in the first place. McCullough did a good job of bringing readers along slowly from here on, gradually examining the project's continued progress with Truman's approval, all leading to ultimate deployment of the weapon at Hiroshima and Nagasaki.[6]

It was one of the many issues facing the new president that McCullough blended throughout his narrative of Truman's first three-plus years on the job. Another rather obvious one was the recalcitrant Soviet Union, an ally in name only as World War II wound to a close. At the Potsdam Conference (a German suburb of Berlin), filling for the first time the Big Three role that FDR had previously played with Great Britain's Winston Churchill and the Soviet Union's Joseph Stalin, Truman felt out of his element. At the same time, he was confident in his ability to prepare and engage world leaders, and after three weeks at sea on the voyage to Europe, he emerged well-rested and determined to get along with both the British prime minister and the Soviet dictator.[7]

On July 16, 1945, Truman met Churchill for the first time, the British champion who had faced Adolf Hitler alone during World War II's earliest stages and had developed a famous partnership with his American counterpart, FDR, during the previous four years. Afterwards, Churchill expressed confidence that he could work with the new American president. After touring the bombed devastation of Berlin following German surrender, Truman finally got his first face-to-face with Stalin, who had purposely arrived late "to accentuate his own importance."[8]

To Truman, the Russian dictator seemed old beyond his years as a lifelong chain smoker with "squinty eyes" and "pockmarked" complexion, but the new president sought to engage him as a friend and to assure him he was not someone to "beat around the bush," something that seemed to please Stalin.[9] Meanwhile, Truman was equally pleased to learn that the Soviets would soon honor their pledge to Roosevelt at the previous Yalta Conference by declaring war on Japan and by recognizing Manchuria as officially part of China.[10]

The conference's first negotiations were held that same afternoon, and according to the *New York Times*, "Never in history had such an aggregation of victorious military forces been represented." Also, never had there been a meeting with graver, more complex issues for all mankind. Under the strictest security, the conference careened off-track over several issues, with Truman seeking decisions and not just discussion, while Churchill, whose government was nearly bankrupt and devoid of its previous influence on the world stage, struggled to delay the proceedings if possible via long-winded speeches. Stalin, meanwhile, focused on only a few "tangible topics" such as how to divide the German Navy or how the defeated German state would be regarded and administered moving forward. Such world-shaping topics as the fate of Eastern Europe and particularly Poland, the invaded ally that brought Churchill's England into the war, were also discussed without Stalin revealing his true intentions when it came to the other Slavic states his armies had overrun while pursuing retreating Germans.[11] The Russians, by the end of World War II, truly hated Germany with a vengeance both deserved and distressing. What Hitler had overrun on Europe's Eastern Front, resulting in the deaths of millions of Russians, Stalin was determined to both avenge and dominate.[12]

Needless to say, not much was accomplished at Potsdam. From the American perspective, the most exciting moment at the last of the major Allied conferences had to be when Truman received confirmation that the atomic bomb had been successfully tested in the New Mexico desert and would be ready for use against Japan in a matter of days. Germany was defeated, and suddenly the prospects of defeating Japan without invasion appeared much better. Truman's second week at Potsdam was filled with anxious anticipation—the anticipation that this new super-weapon offered ultimate, overall victory. Like Germany, Japan's aggression and transgressions were about to be repaid in full.[13]

McCullough makes obvious, in fact, that Truman was going to use the bomb as soon as it was available no matter what. No matter the obvious concerns a nuclear weapon might create for the future, the immediate issue of ending a war that America had been waging for four years against a foe that initiated the conflict with an unprovoked, surprise attack was uppermost in Truman's mind. According to McCullough, "With the start of his second week at Potsdam, Truman knew that decisions on the bomb could wait no longer." Targets were discussed, and it was decided that Hiroshima, the southern headquarters and depot for Japan's homeland army, would be first. Truman's principal biographer also wrote of a consensus at Potsdam among his secretary of state, secretary of war, chairman of the Joint Chiefs, and commander of the Army Air Corps (which would, of course, deliver the bomb) that the weapon should be used to ensure not just Japan's defeat, but also Japan's unconditional surrender.[14]

Despite Japan's defeat seeming inevitable by the time Truman went to Potsdam, Americans continued to die in the Pacific theater, thanks to the Japanese ninja-samurai warrior ethos of never giving up, even if it meant the complete isolation of their island nation. A quarter of a million American troops was the conservative estimate that could be lost in any war-ending invasion of the Japanese homeland, so use of the bomb and the annihilation it could bring to several Japanese cities had to be the far lesser of evils in the mind of Harry Truman. At Potsdam, "the spirit of mercy was not throbbing in the breast of any Allied official," McCullough quoted one of them saying. What would have been the reaction of the American people if an invasion had been launched with a resulting massive loss of U.S. lives and then knowledge of the bomb's availability been exposed? How would Truman (or any president) have explained that?[15]

Although no one knows for sure when President Truman signed off on the bomb, it was during their second week at Potsdam that he made the weapon known to Churchill and Stalin. Although not officially recorded, McCullough noted that Truman remembered, "I casually mentioned to Stalin that we had a new weapon of unusual destructive force and all he said in response was 'glad to hear it' and 'hope you will make good use of it against the Japanese' (begging the question, did the Soviets already know about our A-bomb?)." At the same time, Churchill noted in his voluminous memoirs of the Second World War that he concurred in the president's decision to drop the bomb as a means of affecting "Japanese will to continue the war."[16]

The Potsdam Declaration, which was issued on July 26, 1945, was an ultimatum to Japan demanding unconditional surrender. To not comply would initiate "prompt and utter destruction." At the same time, word was received that the first bomb and the operation to deliver it would be ready and possible by August 1. By July 31, Truman's official go-ahead had been delivered. It read, "Suggestion approved. Release when ready, but no sooner than August 2." McCullough makes clear that by this response, the president wanted to be on his way home and away from the Russians when the bomb was dropped. The conference had gone as well as could have been expected given Stalin's intransigence.[17]

On August 3, aboard the cruiser USS *Augusta*, Truman shared with the press accompanying the American delegation news of the bomb on condition of their silence (a story for the ages that they all had to sit on). Three days later, as the president was finishing lunch with several sailors in the ship's mess just after noon, the message he had been anxiously awaiting finally came. The world's first atomic bomb had been dropped on Hiroshima, Japan, at 7:15 p.m. Washington time the day before, August 5, 1945. It was an overwhelming success. Within minutes of the initial euphoria and on-board announcement, the ship's radio carried news bulletins out of Washington about the bomb, along with a message from the president.[18]

Faced with what Truman called "a rain of ruin from the air the likes of which have never been seen on earth," everyone anticipated Japan's acceptance of surrender terms. Over 80,000 people died instantly, and as many as 60,000 more as a result. By August 8, Truman was back at work in Washington with still no word from the Japanese. A day later, word came that a second atomic bomb had been dropped on Nagasaki, a Japanese seaport, with 70,000 dead. The "whirlwind" had been "sowed" and finally, less than 24 hours after

Perhaps no U.S. president faced more momentous decisions in the opening months of his presidency than Harry Truman, including his decision to use atomic bombs against Japan to force a quicker end to World War II (Library of Congress Prints and Photographs Division—Reproduction Number DIG-ds-05458 [U.S. Army Air Force photographer]).

the second atomic bomb was dropped, Japanese Emperor Hirohito bore "the unbearable" and asked for surrender terms. Although allowed to continue on his throne, he was to be subject to the supreme commander of the Allied Powers, as close to unconditional as possible without bringing additional shame to Japan's masses. On August 14, shortly after 6 p.m., Truman received word of Japan's capitulation, and World War II was finally, officially over.[19]

The end had not come on Franklin Roosevelt's watch. McCullough stated, "In just three months, Harry Truman had been faced with a greater degree of history, with larger, more far-reaching decisions than any president before him." To illustrate, his biographer pointed out that neither Lincoln after taking office (and faced with impending civil war) nor FDR (amidst economic depression) in his famous first hundred days had had to contend "with issues of such magnitude and all coming at once ... if ever a man had been caught in a whirlwind not of his own making, it was he." Included had been the launching of the United Nations, the Soviet Army's ongoing presence in Eastern Europe, Britain's bankruptcy, the unbelievable realization of the Jewish "Holocaust," the advent of the nuclear age, and the end of a global war. Such was the strain that many now believe had killed FDR.[20] But in his place, Truman measured up.

Thus ended the swirl of history that engulfed an accidental president in 1945. From then on his presidential pace would lessen, but the pitfalls of life in the White House would only grow—to the point of potentially conspiring to deny him his own, elected second term. While flush with wartime victory and praise in 1945, Truman would soon run head-long into a populace anxious to make up for four years of war and limitations with victorious excess; another super power in the Soviet Union hell-bent on spreading its communist influences around the world; a labor force unwilling to wait on better pay and benefits now that war and depression were in the rear view mirror; and a Congress dominated by Republicans for the first time in over a decade, a party determined to reverse many of the progressive programs FDR had put in place.[21]

With Truman a suddenly minority president by 1946, McCullough posed the following questions: "Was Harry Truman an ordinary, provincial American sadly miscast in the presidency? Or was he a man of above average, even exceptional qualities and character who had the makings of greatness?" One reporter of the time called it "a test of democracy," and influential columnist Walter Lippmann spoke for many when he voiced his conviction that the ongoing Truman administration, after initial approbation on the coattails of the transcendent FDR, was now destined for failure.[22] From the lofty affirmation of his initial months in the presidency and the molding of public opinion in support of the common man in the White House, Truman entered the reality of division once the common cause of war was over and our boys came home. Labor and labor unions began demanding a bigger slice of the American pie. Over the remainder of FDR's fourth term, with Truman as his "stand-in," the tide of public perception began to turn against him despite a revitalized economy and all-time highs in food production. Prices went up, but wages did not. Over one million workers took part in nearly 5,000 strikes nationwide, including a crippling railroad strike that wasn't resolved until the president threatened to draft striking employees of the railroad into the Army, an act that if carried out would have undoubtedly been among the most unconstitutional executive orders ever. Thankfully, his threat to Congress ended the strike.[23]

Meanwhile, with revered former Army Chief of Staff George C. Marshall universally applauded as his new secretary of state, Truman began to focus more on foreign affairs, including Europe's postwar devastation. With Soviet troops and influence dominating Eastern Europe, peripheral nations such as Greece and Turkey were in need of "bucking up" lest they too fall victim to communist expansion. Great Britain, for so many decades the primary economic and political overseer of the Eastern Mediterranean, was gradually scaling back under the weight of huge wartime debts.[24] Speaking to the American people in early 1945, Truman stated, "It is the policy of the United States to support free peoples who are resisting attempted subjugation by armed minorities or outside pressures." That would be the Truman Doctrine, both politically and militarily. Economically, it would become the Marshall Plan. Despite the program's $400 million price tag, both Truman and Marshall would garner favorable public opinion as the suddenly prosperous United States began to flex its superpower muscles in hopes of containing the latest, expansion-motivated, totalitarian power—the Soviet Union. In the aftermath of World War II, Americans seemed to accept global leadership, fearful for the first time that if Europe went down, America could follow. That's also why they accepted the European Recovery Program and costs that eventually totaled $13 billion.[25]

McCullough indicated that "the loyalty of those around Truman was total," but the Republican-controlled Congress still made his life hard. The Democrats suffered severe losses in the 1946 midterms, and Truman knew that the progressive gains of the previous 16 years would be under siege and could be undone totally if a Republican made it into the White House. So it was that at some point in mid-1947, the president who never wanted the job suddenly became the president who wanted to retain it against all odds. "To Truman, Woodrow Wilson and Franklin Roosevelt were the giants of the century, and he had no choice, he felt, but to fight for the Democratic heritage that had been passed on to him," his biographer emphasized. In his thinking at the time, what he wanted to do personally was "not important." Like it or not, what he had to do for "the welfare of the country" was run for re-election.[26]

With racist atrocities multiplying in the South, Truman's homegrown Southern sympathies began to shift morally, much to the chagrin of 52 congressional, Southern Democrats, who were suddenly voting with Republicans on anything that had to do with civil rights.[27] There was also the dilemma of thousands of Jewish refugees returning to their "Promised Land," Palestine, from all over Nazi-torn Europe. Despite wavering, the president eventually assured Jewish leaders (and by extension Jewish-American voters) that he would support their idea of a Jewish homeland, in stark contrast to Secretary of State Marshall, Assistant Secretary of State Loy Henderson, and his secretary of defense, James Forrestal, who all advised against angering the oil-rich, Muslim nations of the Middle East.[28]

These and other contentious issues caused an increasingly stand-pat electorate to concentrate on the home front and their own pocketbooks, and caused Truman, the stand-in president, to make a campaign directly to the people via a "Presidential Special" train trip that covered 9,505 miles through 18 states with 73 speeches reaching about 3,000,000 people in June of 1948. Later that fall, he would follow that up with an even longer, 33-day, 21,928-mile "Whistle-Stop Tour" that completely rebuffed old notions of sitting presidents not taking full advantage of their exalted position to try to get re-elected. That's when the "Give 'em Hell, Harry" moniker first surfaced, and his "if you can't stand the heat, get out of the kitchen" comment seemed to portray the never-say-die tenacity with which he approached what most pundits still considered his political swansong.[29]

As a result, his shocking victory in 1948 inspired an inaugural that was the biggest, most costly on record up to that time. Like one of his heroes, Andrew Jackson, Truman's upset of New York Governor Thomas Dewey was seen as a victory for the American common man, and more than a million of them showed up for his inauguration in Washington. In addition, it was the first inauguration to be televised, adding at least 10,000,000 viewers in 14 cities, as more Americans saw Harry Truman sworn in on January 20, 1949, than all previous presidents combined.[30]

Following the arduous, come-from-behind campaign and a two-month retreat to his "Little White House" in Key West, Florida, Truman enjoyed every minute of inauguration day on January 20, 1949—what his daughter termed "his day of days." With the White House undergoing major renovations, the First Family was quartered across the street at the Blair House, and the president endorsed everything that could possibly be done to bring the historic executive mansion up to speed. Still professing that there "were probably a million men in the country who could make a better president," he accepted the job for another four years, intent on doing it to the best of his ability. He hit the ground running, calling for a Fair Deal on domestic issues and the largest peacetime budget ever. At age

64, he was already older than most of his recent presidential predecessors had been when they died (Wilson, Harding, Coolidge, and both Roosevelts), and he was determined to make the most of the extended term he had been granted by the American people. McCullough observed, "No president in [American] history had ever taken office at a time of such prosperity and power."[31]

Meanwhile, the Berlin Airlift, which had begun the previous summer in response to a Soviet land blockade of the western, Allied-controlled portion of the subjugated German capital, succeeded as a providential lifeline combating Russian ill-will and as an early symbol of American resolve in the budding Cold War. While the Soviet Union's "Iron Curtain" (according to Churchill) had descended over Eastern Europe at the end of World War II, Greece and Turkey had resisted takeover, and Italy and France had also withstood communist intentions via reconstituted democracies. Only in China, where a Nationalist regime vied with a growing communist movement in the wake of Japanese defeat, did the surge of communism seem inevitable. All would lead to the creation of the North Atlantic Treaty Organization (NATO), a unified approach to protecting free people and democracies in the future. "For the United States," McCullough wrote, "It marked a radical departure— the first peacetime military alliance since the signing of the Constitution."[32]

By midsummer 1949, however, things had taken a dramatic turn for the worse. Along with malicious and politically motivated rumors of communist plots within the federal government, Truman entered a time of international peril as events in China and the Soviet Union rocked the Western world. First the communist forces of Mao Zedong engineered the complete takeover of China, forcing the Truman administration to issue an extensive report on U.S. relations with the Chinese from 1944–1949, including an admission that due to "internal decay, rampant corruption, lack of leadership, and indifference to its people," the Nationalist Chinese regime had failed, and the United States had never had the wherewithal to truly influence that country's outcome. It was an admission with a $2 billion price tag, making it doubly hard to swallow. Then, just a few weeks after release of this "China White Paper," another event even more troubling came to pass—knowledge that the United States was no longer the world's only nuclear power. It had been confirmed: the Soviet Union, America's Cold War rival, had successfully tested its own atomic weapon. On September 23, Truman released a "mimeographed statement" to that effect. It read:

> I believe the American people, to the fullest extent consistent with national security, are entitled to be informed of all developments in the field of atomic energy. That is my reason for making public the following information. We have evidence that within recent weeks, an atomic explosion occurred in the U.S.S.R. [Union of Soviet Socialist Republics].[33]

This news came three to five years ahead of expectations. Following as it did on the heels of China's communist takeover, the world suddenly seemed a much more threatening place than it had just four years earlier in the wake of World War II victory and America's singular superpower status. To contend with foreign diplomacy amidst this new American worldview, Truman turned to a new, Harvard-educated secretary of state, Dean Acheson, who seemed the exact opposite of the largely uneducated, rank-and-file politician Harry Truman. For health reasons, Acheson had replaced Marshall, who had seamlessly moved from command of the American military apparatus in World War II to overseeing the State Department after retirement from the Army. Truman would call Acheson his "top brain man," and it would take brains and extreme loyalty to his boss to navigate the Cold War landscape they both encountered during Truman's second term.[34] A "super bomb," or hydrogen version, was by then on American drawing boards, and although initially rejected by the Atomic Energy Commission as a devastating deterrent gone too far, it was still open to debate as to who was for it and who was against it in Washington policy circles. "The 'H-bomb' became a Washington obsession," McCullough admitted, and renowned physicists like Albert Einstein, who had brought the massive destructive potential of atomic energy to FDR's attention, now attempted to rein in further development of American atomic power with talk of the danger of worldwide radioactive fallout. In light of Acheson's endorsement and the Soviets' new threat, however, Truman agreed to let the H-bomb project proceed.[35]

At the same time, California Congressman and future President Richard Nixon and his Republican colleague, Wisconsin Senator Joseph McCarthy, began witch-hunts for suspected communist sympathizers in the Truman administration. Nixon's came first, famously implicating Alger Hiss, a State Department official, of espionage, a charge eventually turned into a perjury conviction, but McCarthy took such political ploys to new heights by alleging all manner of communist cover-ups, particularly when it came to the rest of Acheson's State Department staff.[36] Of the times, McCullough wrote: "With the on-rush of so much sensational, inexplicable, bad news—China lost, the Russian bomb, Alger Hiss, and potential treason—breaking with such clamor, all in less than six months, the country was in a terrible state of uncertainty."[37]

"Casting about for an issue that might lift him from obscurity" to the national spotlight, McCarthy found the mother lode, but almost immediately began to overplay his hand to the point of demagoguery and obsession. Eventually, Truman and the media struck back and McCarthy would, indeed, "destroy himself," as the president predicted. His false claims of communist sympathizers would eventually dissolve amid new alarms.[38]

One year into his second term, Truman also drafted a statement to be made public two years hence, in which he indicated his determination not to seek another term, what McCullough saw as "a rebuke to the memory of Franklin Roosevelt," who had been re-elected three times. Reinforcing the two-term doctrine that all previous presidents except FDR had previously adhered to, Truman made it official that he would not seek a third term in 1952.[39]

Amidst such future considerations also came shattering news on a Sunday morning, June 25, 1950. Truman, in fact, was enjoying a rare weekend at home in Missouri when a call from Acheson shattered his tranquility. Acheson's message: "Mr. President, I have very serious news. The North Koreans have invaded South Korea." Thus was Truman advised of the start of the Korean War, the defining issue of his second term. Divided by a central borderline and home to a communist North and democratic South, the Korean Peninsula had become a hotly contested land of competing ideologies when World War II ended and the Japanese were finally expelled. Hurriedly, his trip cut short by the shocking news, Truman returned to Washington that same day to begin dealing with America's second chapter of Asiatic aggression in less than a decade.[40]

Like the Japanese assault at Pearl Harbor (which, of course, brought America into World War II), "the attack by North Korea had come as a total surprise," according to Truman's biographer. The border along the 38th parallel that divides the two Koreas was not viewed with as much apprehension as other, East-West places of more obvious contention in 1950—until 75,000 soldiers of the North Korean People's Army came pouring into South Korea bent on the reunification of their homeland under one, communist regime. It had been five years since the United States first occupied South Korea near the end of World War II, and American stewardship there was ongoing as a result of the nearby communist presence. After the war, U.S. Chairman of the Joint Chiefs Omar Bradley reportedly said,

"We must draw the line somewhere," to which McCullough added, "Korea was as good a place as any." Taken together, these statements convey the pervading sentiment of the time and the need for an ongoing American military presence in that corner of the world. Truman wholeheartedly agreed despite his fear of possible Soviet intervention.[41]

Thus began the Korean conflict, what amounted to a three-year, American-led United Nations military response to ensure the post–World War II status quo on the Korean Peninsula. Early on, it seemed doomed to defeat as North Korea's surprise invasion of the South reached all the way to its largest southern port city before finally being halted along a hastily constituted defensive line known as the "Pusan Perimeter." Composed mostly of American troops, the UN forces that retreated to Pusan bought time for General Douglas MacArthur, the supreme U.S. commander in the Pacific theater after World War II, to orchestrate a dramatic landing behind North Korean lines at Inchon in September of 1950—a landing that forced the communist invaders to withdraw back across the 38th parallel. Taking full advantage, MacArthur pursued the retreating enemy all the way to the Yalu River, which marks North Korea's border with Chinese Manchuria, despite warnings that the Communist Chinese might enter the conflict if the U.S. advanced too far. MacArthur deemed such warnings fabricated and ridiculous, but by November, Chinese troops had crossed the Yalu, escalating the situation to third world war potential.[42]

To the concerns this escalation caused Truman was added an attempt on his life. It occurred while the First Family was residing at Blair House, with the White House still undergoing renovations. On an unusually warm November 1 in the nation's capital, two Puerto Rican nationalists, hoping to bring attention to their cause, attempted to assassinate Truman by storming the Blair House entrance and its contingent of Secret Service agents and White House police. One of the would-be assassins carried a German Walther P-38, the other a German Luger. Between them they had 69 rounds of ammunition. In a frenzy of gunfire that lasted about three minutes, one member of the guard detail was killed and two others seriously wounded. One of the assailants was also killed, and the other would spend 29 years in Leavenworth Penitentiary.[43]

Such was the start of what McCullough termed "the darkest, most difficult period of Truman's presidency," what amounted to the holiday season of 1950. With McCarthy's accusations in full swing, the president lost allies in the Senate and lamented to his wife how sad it was that "McCarthyism" had such effect on midterm elections. At the same time, the midterms were "a minor worry" compared to Korea, where MacArthur was increasingly going rogue, making decisions without input from American leadership at the Pentagon or White House.[44]

That November, MacArthur unleashed an attack up both sides of the Peninsula, well beyond the 38th parallel. By month's end, however, the Chinese had responded with overwhelming force, approximately 260,000 strong, forcing the American/UN forces to return to the defensive for the first time since Pusan.[45] As a result, the weight of the world rested firmly on Truman, who had previously allowed MacArthur plenty of rope while taking the fight into North Korea. At a National Security Council meeting with Truman presiding, the decision was made not to let this escalate into a world war. To do anything else, McCullough expressed, would have been to fall into "a carefully laid Russian trap." To continue the UN effort of stalemate and exit with honor became the only objective moving forward, despite MacArthur's repeated calls for more troops and for use of atomic weapons against the Chinese. If the general had been allowed to overextend at that moment, the fear was that Russia would further arm the Chinese, whose manpower advantage seemed endless. America could have been plunged into another global conflict even more devastating than the one a decade earlier—not a prospect Truman was even remotely willing to consider.[46]

At the same time, resolve had to be shown. Just as he had with the Berlin Airlift, Truman took a stand. According to McCullough, he "was resolved to stay in Korea." In a statement released on November 30, he emphasized, "We may suffer reverses as we have suffered them before, but the forces of the United Nations have no intention of abandoning Korea. We shall continue to work to halt aggression [and] we shall intensify our efforts to help other free nations strengthen their defenses in order to meet the threat of aggression elsewhere."[47]

With those words, the die was cast, and the world knew that the American industrial complex that had so recently been the determining factor in World War II was ready to be turned against the growing "Russo-Communist" pattern of confrontation. In a follow-up press conference, Truman had to defend MacArthur for exceeding directives and intensifying the conflict. McCullough let us know that to do otherwise would have risked the resolve and morale of the entire military establishment. The president also let it be known that regardless of what military steps might ensue, every possible alternative, including atomic bombs, would be considered. Truman's biographer portrayed the drama of that moment thusly: "The room was still. The topic that had never been considered appropriate for a press conference had suddenly become the focal point."

Whether or not Truman would have resorted to the use of another of America's atomic weapons, after his earlier use killed over 150,000 Japanese in a matter of days and brought that aggressor nation to its knees, will never be known, but McCullough did make sure his readers knew Truman had said too much. The resulting fallout was worldwide in scope. Media reports trumpeted the U.S. threat of atomic retaliation.[48]

Still, the threat remained as long as the president empowered his supreme military commander in the field with every weapon in the U.S. arsenal. It did not take long for Truman's advisers, both civilian and military, to realize that with the atomic threat in play, a change of commanders would be necessary. MacArthur had deliberately disobeyed orders, failed to consider new strategies, and even cast doubt on leadership back home for his battlefield woes. His was the pompous self-esteem of a lifelong soldier and five-star, 78-year-old, conservative icon, who had grown contemptuous of civilian authority and set in his belief that no one knew better than he when it came to dealing with communists.[49] Finally, one of MacArthur's subordinates, General Matthew Ridgeway, provided the opening the administration needed to reverse course and try something new. MacArthur had not been obeying orders, and once a ranking fellow officer confirmed that fact, the State Department proposed that he be relieved of command.[50] Truman, however, was leery of removing the legendary commander and having it appear that he was being fired for failure. With talk of even evacuating American troops from the Peninsula, the times were indeed bleak if new leadership and strategies were not put in place. The entire Far East seemed up for grabs if the Americans pulled out.

"The goal of uniting Korea by force had been abandoned"—the best hope remained an armistice at the same 38th parallel the North Koreans had initially attacked, a return to the previous, Cold War status quo. At the same time, MacArthur continued to urge a widening of the conflict to respond to the level of war already imposed by the Chinese. Again according to McCullough, the old general was ready "to drop thirty to fifty atomic bombs on Manchuria and the mainland cities of China."[51]

After refusing to reprimand MacArthur and treating him with "infinite patience," Truman finally got good news about the situation on the ground from Ridgeway. Rather than attacking with atomic bombs or evacuating immediately, here was a secondary commander providing a different scenario—one that had been stabilized through proper defensive warfare and one that could negate and punish any further mass attack. Applying common sense and concentrated artillery principles for great victories in intense winter battles, Ridgeway had managed to work around his recalcitrant, ego-driven commanding officer, and soon offensive maneuvers were resumed. On January 25, 1951, the twice-retreating UN forces began "rolling forward" for "Operation Killer." Again quoting General Omar Bradley in Washington, McCullough wrote, "MacArthur had become 'mainly a prima donna figurehead being tolerated.'"[52]

But Truman would not tolerate him much longer, and when MacArthur's need for personal acclaim began to get in the way of Ridgeway's renewed offensive, the president finally acted, and not a minute too soon. The realization that his ultimate war with Communist China and/or Soviet Russia was not going to happen drove MacArthur to begin issuing his own communiqués to the press, the enemy, and even his Republican confidants in Congress, undercutting at least one cease-fire attempt and totally undermining the president. Reflecting, Truman would write, "MacArthur thought he was proconsul for the government of the United States and could do as he damned well pleased."[53]

Still, realizing the immense prestige of the old general and how it would look if MacArthur were promising victory while he was merely striving for status quo, Truman refused to act impulsively, utilizing what McCullough termed "political guile." Despite the lowest presidential approval ratings in history (26 percent), Truman drew on the experience of Abraham Lincoln, who had relieved an equally popular Union general, George McClellan, at the height of the Civil War. Lincoln too had been patient, but Truman resolved that his final course must be the same.[54] Finally on April 9, with the backing of the Joint Chiefs, Truman announced that he would fire Douglas MacArthur, touching off the worst firestorm of his second term. MacArthur returned stateside to a stupendous hero's welcome. Congressional Republicans en masse took the general's side and threatened impeachment proceedings. At the same time, a freshman Senate Democrat from Oklahoma, Robert Kerr, rose to remind his colleagues that if MacArthur's ideas were what they wanted over the president's, then a "declaration of war against Red China" would need to be their next policy decision.[55]

With thousands of longshoremen walking off their jobs in protest; with plans for a women's march on Washington; with hundreds of petitions, telegrams, and letters objecting to MacArthur's removal cascading into the nation's capital; and with the president even burned in effigy at least once, partisan politics had rarely been more heated. Meanwhile, both internationally and domestically, the press sided with Truman, and the national rancor began to subside once MacArthur was afforded his moments in the sun—his famous "old soldiers never die" farewell speech before Congress and the largest tickertape parade in American history through the "canyons of New York."[56] Truman had anticipated that the tumult would diminish by summer, and he was proven right after an investigation by the Senate Foreign Relations Committee and testimony by the Joint Chiefs revealed the necessity of MacArthur's removal, completely vindicating the president. That investigation also introduced a new concept to military operations, what MacArthur labeled "appeasement"—something that has since become more and more acceptable to an America that before Korea had always fought wars to win. Nonetheless, by June 25, 1951, in a speech opening a new Air Force testing facility in Tullahoma, Tennessee, Truman announced plans to seek a negotiated settlement ending the Korean War at the 38th parallel, where it had started.[57]

The Korean War, remembered now via this multi-statue memorial in the nation's capital, began with North Korea's invasion of South Korea, an act of aggression that led to U.S. confrontation with Communist China and a stalemate on the Korean Peninsula, narrowly averting another world war (Library of Congress Prints and Photographs Division—Reproduction Number DIG-highsm-04257 [Carol M. Highsmith, photographer]).

At age 67 and still in excellent health entering his seventh and final year in office, Harry Truman would live with the Korean stalemate for the remainder of his White House days (the war would not officially end until 1953), and Senator McCarthy would continue to exploit the American public's fear of communism by constantly implicating officials in the Truman administration. But whenever asked about Joe McCarthy and all his rumors and claims, Truman would always offer "no comment," consistently preferring not to descend to below-the-belt politics.[58]

Weathering these storms, Truman took pride in reopening a greatly renovated White House that had been accomplished on his watch while also seeking a Democratic successor for 1952. Supposedly he even scouted out the political inclinations of General Dwight Eisenhower, the overall Allied commander in Europe during World War II and the nation's No. 1 hero. Both denied any such vetting had taken place, and Eisenhower would eventually run as a Republican, while Truman and the Democrats turned to Adlai Stevenson, the progressive governor of Illinois. An "urbane" graduate of Princeton University, Stevenson was totally unlike the man he was trying to succeed. McCullough indicated that Truman wanted Stevenson to "save the world from Eisenhower," who was inexperienced politically and was sure, he felt, to become the captive of Republican powerbrokers. In addition, he wanted Stevenson to hold off Senator Estes Kefauver of Tennessee, a Truman naysayer four years earlier who was also seeking the Democratic nomination. Needless to say, Truman's endorsement went to Stevenson.[59]

Truman's final months in office were haunted by labor unrest and strikes. Public utilities came first and then a nationwide steel strike that resulted in him seizing the mills and keeping them open, what McCullough termed "one of the boldest and most controversial decisions of his presidency." He was convinced that in a state of national emergency, he had the habeas corpus right to do so, and "to prevent a paralysis of the national economy," he did. "The president has the power to keep the country from going to hell," he assured his staff, and Supreme Court Chief Justice Fred Vinson, a Truman appointee, agreed.[60]

Truman witnessed the steelworkers agree to a smaller pay increase than their original request after not receiving one for several years, while at the same time the steel companies rejected the compromise, "recklessly forcing a shutdown." As a result, he sided with the workers and, in his last major act as president, he averted a shutdown by instigating a constitutional crisis. The *Washington Post* called it "one of the most high handed acts ever by an American president," and to his amazement, when the case went before the entire Supreme Court, it ruled against him and in favor of the steel companies, with Vinson in the minority. For Truman the defeat was humiliating, since either he or FDR had appointed all nine justices. With his government seizure of the mills thus rejected, the steel strike dragged on for seven weeks, becoming one of the longest and most costly work stoppages in U.S. history. Ironically, with the strike continuing and Congress doing nothing, his demand for a settlement was what finally ended it after all, just one day before the start of the 1952 Democratic Convention.[61]

With Eisenhower already nominated and the Republican bandwagon picking up speed, Truman had a much greater effect on the Democratic choice than anyone could have imagined. Once he threw his full-throated support to Stevenson, the other candidates, including Kefauver, never had a chance. But as Truman commented privately and history revealed, no one could have beaten Eisenhower that year, as he carried all but nine of the 48 states.[62]

Upon returning to Independence to a hero's homecoming, Truman began to work on his memoirs and to raise money towards his presidential library. He and his wife resided in the same house she had grown up in and the two of them had lived in with her mother (by then deceased) since their marriage 33 years before. By early 1955, he turned in a 500,000-word manuscript for which he received a first check of $110,000, with the promise of $600,000 more in installments by January 1960. For a couple without the independent wealth of most former presidents, it was welcome compensation.[63]

The next spring (April of 1956), with his *Memoirs* at the publisher and his daughter (and only child) recently married, "Give 'em Hell Harry" did what many of his presidential predecessors had done before him—tour Europe, including visits with various heads of state and his old friend Winston Churchill. By the next year, the Truman Presidential Library was finished and he had become a grandfather. His final political involvement came in 1960, when he campaigned for Democrat John F. Kennedy after eight years of Eisenhower.[64] For almost 20 years after he left Washington, he could be seen having a daily morning walk on the streets of Independence. Harry Truman lived to be 88. He died in December of 1972 and was buried behind his library. Upon her death ten years later (1982), his wife bequeathed their home and many of its contents to the federal government for preservation as a National Historic Site ... and so it remains today, just as she left it.[65]

17

The Second Johnson
Weaves a Powerful Web

*"Millions of Americans will always remember a bitter day in November
1963. Lyndon Johnson rose above the doubt and fear to hold this nation on
course."*—Richard Nixon, 1973

Following his ascendance to easily the most accomplished Senate majority leader of
the 20th century, Texan Lyndon Baines Johnson's two years-plus as vice president, January
1961 through November 1963, can only be described as a humbling experience full of 26
foreign visits "just to give him something to do."[1] He had gone into the VP job fearing the
label of failure after being shut out of his lifetime objective, the White House, by the younger,
less experienced John Fitzgerald Kennedy of Massachusetts, while also realizing that his
new role might be his last, best path to presidential power. The sheer fact that ten previous
vice presidents had ascended to the presidency, and seven of those had been elevated to
the nation's highest office by death rather than the ballot box, made the chances of it happening again somewhere between 21 and 30 percent, odds he had to consider at a time
when other potential paths appeared negligible.[2]

After all, LBJ was a Southerner, tainted nationally by the legacy of racial segregation,
and even though his acceptance of the second spot on the Kennedy ticket enhanced JFK's
chances of keeping the South in the Democratic column, his own chances for future presidential ascendance could only be achieved if he absolved his Southern roots and legislative
past by connecting with the more liberal forces in his party. To a seasoned political pro
like LBJ, it must have seemed the only path forward, even for the most powerful senator
in Washington. Johnson knew that not accepting the VP offer if it were extended would
sentence the Democrats to almost certain defeat in the conservative-leaning South, so
much so, in fact, that blame for that loss would probably be laid at his feet. The Kennedys
and their Eastern elite, whom he deeply distrusted, would no doubt see to that, making it
impossible for him to be considered nationally again. And should Kennedy pull off an
upset of the sitting vice president in what had the makings of a very close presidential race,
the new president was sure to establish his own legislative agenda and expect total cooperation by his suddenly subordinate Senate majority leader.[3] It was a scenario that held the
prospects of a very different dynamic from the personal mastery and deference LBJ had
accrued and had become accustomed to in Congress during the Republican administration
of Dwight Eisenhower, a popular president he often led Democrats across party lines to
support.[4]

"By accepting [Kennedy's offer], Johnson ran far less [political] risk." So stated biographer Robert Caro as he described what went through Johnson's mind after Kennedy's nomination in 1960 as he contemplated the suddenly very real possibility that JFK would come calling, looking for a powerful Southern running mate. After eight years as Senate leader, Johnson's confidant and legislative troubleshooter, Bobby Baker, stated, "[he] didn't have a thing to lose by running with Kennedy." John Connolly, his longtime Texas campaign advisor and future governor of that state, indicated that he really had no choice. Connolly even stated, "Suppose you take it and he's [JFK] defeated—you'll still be a senator and majority leader." In other words, "you can't really be hurt" either way. Both Baker and Connolly reputedly used the term "only a heartbeat away" to convince LBJ to take the vice presidential bid if offered.[5]

It was a bitter pill for Johnson to swallow after believing for most of the previous four years that he was in line to be the next Democratic nominee, only to see Kennedy, the son of one of the wealthiest men in America, riding a charismatic wave of approval and organizational momentum to the top of the polls and primaries by the time the convention rolled around in July of 1960. While LBJ, who had delayed his official entry into the presidential race for months, fearing the stigma of failure, was forced to hope for some kind of first ballot intervention that might derail JFK's victory at the convention, the well-oiled and well-financed Kennedy campaign was so on top of any threat to ultimate success that Johnson could only watch and wonder what might have been.[6] Once he was offered the number two spot on the Democratic ticket (over liberal opposition) and accepted, he was thrust into a nearly three-year purgatory from political power that included regular interaction with Attorney General Robert F. Kennedy, JFK's brother and the person on whom Johnson placed blame for most of his problems in dealing with what he perceived as the "better educated" and, as a result, "lofty" inner circle of the Kennedy administration.[7]

"Bobby" (or RFK) never wanted his brother to consider LBJ as a running mate and tried repeatedly to have him expunged from the ticket, even though he made sense for JFK's chances. Separated by only 46,000 votes, the case can be made that Kennedy actually won the presidency by carrying the Southern states of Texas, Arkansas, Louisiana, Georgia, and the two Carolinas, which he almost certainly would never have done without Johnson on the ticket. However, that seemed the extent of Johnson's usefulness to the new administration, and despite the fact that he was given domestic appointments and foreign assignments to go with his primary role of presiding over the Senate, LBJ became the object of derision among the Kennedy team and the subject of replacement rumors as 1964 Democratic re-election efforts began.[8]

With this devalued status hanging over his head, Johnson was among the principal players taking part in one of JFK's earliest re-election endeavors, his tragic fund-raising trip in November of 1963 to Texas, a conservative state where the president was not very popular and where LBJ no longer provided the same political capital as three years earlier. In fact, an ongoing, intra-party and in-state feud between Governor Connolly and influential Texas Senator Ralph Yarborough threatened to upset the president's Texas visit before it even started, when the more liberal senator refused to ride with Connolly's long-standing ally, LBJ, during a preliminary stopover in San Antonio.[9] Once more rational temperaments returned to the proceedings, it was on to Fort Worth and eventually Dallas and the ill-conceived parade of open cars (convertible limos) through downtown that led to the shots heard round the world in Dealey Plaza, the fourth presidential assassination in U.S. history. No living American would ever forget that day: November 22, 1963.[10]

Caro's 2012 book, *The Passage of Power*, recounts Johnson's days, months, and years just before and immediately after that unforgettable day in American history, beginning with a five-year lead-up to the transformational, 1960 presidential election. From a submissive and devalued vice president, who had relinquished political power three years earlier when he chose to give up Senate leadership, to the new leader of the free world, LBJ's persona in the moments after the national tragedy in Dallas did a complete 180. It was almost as if he had been prepping in his own mind for just such a happening before it became reality.[11]

Impressively, it was Caro's fourth biographical narrative on the life of Lyndon Johnson. The others have included *The Path to Power* in 1982, *Means of Ascent* in 1990, and *Master of the Senate* in 2002, and a fifth and final edition of his masterwork was still in progress when this book was being written. Encompassing Johnson's White House years, the finale of the series was to include extensive research by Caro in Vietnam, an actual, on-site accounting that does seem essential when considering the drastic effect that Southeast Asian nation would have on the legacy of our 36th president.[12] Obviously exhaustive in the way he approached LBJ, Caro owns a Pulitzer Prize (*Master of the Senate*) and National Book Critics Circle Award (*The Passage of Power*) for those efforts, as well as a National Humanities Medal presented by President Barack Obama in 2010.[13]

While never forgetting the milestone that made Johnson president, most Americans would never know the complete change that came over him in the moments after President Kennedy was pronounced dead, moments Caro dramatically described.[14] Unlike Chester Arthur or Harry Truman, who reacted with unashamed tears and unabashed shock, respectively, when their predecessors died, Johnson more closely resembled Theodore Roosevelt in the way he expressed grief and sympathy while at the same time grasping the reins of national leadership immediately.[15] Even while being sped under cover from the scene at Parkland Hospital, where Kennedy was confirmed dead almost on arrival, to Air Force One at Love Field (see dedication page photograph), where he would make sure to take the oath of office before taking off for Washington, LBJ would exude a take-charge attitude, confidence in what he was doing, and a determination to exhibit the kind of governmental continuation so important to a democracy.[16]

According to Caro: "[His] hangdog look was gone," replaced with an expression that Texas Congressman Jack Brooks, who was there that fateful day, would describe as "set."

> Johnson's aides and allies, the men who had known him the longest, knew that expression: the big jaw jutting out; the lips above it pulled into a tight, grim line; the corners turned down in a hint of a snarl; the eyes under those long, black eyebrows narrowed and piercing. It was an expression of determination and fierce concentration, and when Lyndon Johnson wore that expression, a problem was being thought through and decisions made.[17]

Accepting the fact that the assassination could have been part of a much larger conspiracy, Johnson exhibited what Caro termed "coolness" and "decisiveness" under supreme pressure. He asserted control of what can only be described as a crisis immediately and much more obviously than his predecessors in the same circumstance—Andrew Johnson, Chester Arthur, and Teddy Roosevelt—each of whom faced the crushing burden of rising to the democratic necessity of succeeding a murdered president.[18] Only the hyper-energetic and assertive TR could remotely be perceived as acting as decisively as LBJ when McKinley died, and that ascension came several days after the assassin's bullet struck its mark, providing hope for the president's recovery without the instant inevitability of Kennedy's demise.[19]

So LBJ's assumption of power, while carefully observing the proper respect and attention to the suddenly martyred legacy of his fallen predecessor, actually utilized intense public uncertainty and dismay to galvanize the Democratic agenda already in place. Like John Tyler before him, he left no doubt of his ascension to the office that he had dreamed of ever since 1937, when, as a junior congressman from Texas he had first met his political hero and model, President Franklin Delano Roosevelt. Although assuming office as an unelected, illegitimate president in his own mind, LBJ was obviously determined to put the kind of positive, domestic stamp on his presidential opportunity that FDR had established during the Great Depression, no matter how unexpected his new status was to the American people. According to Caro, he set about laying the groundwork for that from the beginning.[20]

First and foremost, following the immediate days of intense mourning and the burial that followed Kennedy's assassination, a national spectacle that was covered like no other before via the relatively new medium of network television,[21] Johnson's initial approach was built around ensuring his standing as the new standard-bearer of the Democratic Party in the looming 1964 election less than 12 months away. To do that, he knew he needed immediate help from Kennedy's team and their collective commitment to furthering the dead president's previously established goals. LBJ got that ball rolling by seeking immediate retention of Kennedy's Cabinet and most of his White House staff, making no bones about the fact that he and the country needed them more than ever. It was the kind of political sales job that Lyndon Johnson could do like few others in American history, and he succeeded, giving early renewal to public confidence and the perception that the new president was someone to be trusted and followed.[22]

One of the first things Lyndon Johnson did upon becoming president was seek to retain the Cabinet of his popular predecessor, John F. Kennedy, including Secretary of State Dean Rusk (left) and Secretary of Defense Robert McNamara, seen here on either side of the new president (Library of Congress Prints and Photographs Division—Reproduction Number DIG-ds-07431 [Warren K. Leffler, photographer]).

Perhaps the best example of his astute political perception came upon learning that 35 of the nation's governors had journeyed to Washington for JFK's funeral, a situation he quickly turned to his advantage by summoning those individual state leaders to an impromptu meeting before they dispersed and returned home. In it he said:

> I want to appeal to you … to get your state delegations to help break through congressional impasse. I not only need your hands, I need your voice. If there is anything you can do to help us get action, we need you. Yesterday I sat here with our great former president who led our forces to victory [Eisenhower]. He came in to offer his help. We did not discuss party or politics. We just discussed what needed to be done in this country to save it. We have hate abroad in the world, hate internationally, hate domestically, where a president was assassinated one day and the law taken into someone's hands the next with the killing of his alleged assassin [Oswald], who was brazenly shot and killed while being moved from the Dallas Police Department. That is not our system. We have to do something about that. We have to do something about hate. You have to get to the roots of hate, which are poverty and disease and illiteracy. We don't really recognize how fortunate we are until something tragic like this happens to us. We have to do something to stop hate and the way to do it is to meet the problem of injustice that exists in this land, meet the problem of inequality, the problem of poverty, and the unemployment that exists in this land. The best way is to pass tax [relief] and get more jobs, investments, and revenue, and pass the civil rights bill so that we can say to the Mexican in California or the Negro in Mississippi or the Oriental on the West Coast, or [even] the Johnsons in Johnson City, Texas, we are going to treat you all equally and fairly, and you are going to be judged on merit and not ancestry or how you spell your name.

When he was finished, the gathered governors gave him a standing ovation.[23] It was a prime example of take-charge leadership and one more example of his political instincts. Once again, few men, if any, ever knew more about getting things done in Washington than Lyndon Johnson. Indeed, in the aftermath of acute national tragedy, his new administration seemed off to a good start. LBJ's timely meeting with the assembled governors, in fact, prefaced his quick turnaround of the legislative agenda that had been languishing on Kennedy's watch, establishing the too-often unrecognized credit LBJ deserves, at least during his earliest presidential years, for legislation JFK would have taken much longer (if ever) to achieve.[24]

The most obvious of these initiatives was civil rights. With the country in the late 1950s and early 1960s torn by a suddenly more assertive African American community and leadership now recalled as the "Civil Rights Movement," Johnson came into the presidency having warned his predecessor that new civil rights legislation should wait (by necessity) on the rest of his legislative agenda to avoid the long-standing, contentious nature of any such racially charged law, especially with old-line, filibustering Southerners still in control of the Senate. To not do so, he advised, would undoubtedly delay everything else. When his forecast came true between 1960 and 1963, racial tensions and confrontation mounted to a never-before-seen extent that was captured daily by network television, exhibiting in vivid detail the racism and segregation that had been a Southern (and to a lesser extent urban) way of life in America for almost 100 years—basically ever since the ill-fated, seven-year run of Reconstruction following the Civil War.[25]

Although a leading advocate for two lesser civil rights bills that had attempted to tamp down the growing intensity and national outcry over racial discrimination in the 1950s, LBJ as president accepted the premise that once and for all, something had to be done for equality in a democratic nation that had farcically prided itself on a legacy of unalienable rights. He also accepted the fact that as a Southern-born president who had risen in the Senate as a protégé of Southern stalwarts like Georgia's Richard Russell, South Carolina's Strom Thurmond, and Mississippi's John Stennis, veteran senators who had long postponed

America's racial reckoning, it was best for an end to the South's segregated bastions to come under his watch. Like his political hero, FDR, who administered hope with his New Deal in the midst of the Great Depression, LBJ immediately set about establishing his own domestic legacy, termed The Great Society, by addressing racial inequality and poverty while the country was rebounding from tragedy. Taking advantage of the moment to ensure the martyred Kennedy's legacy, his initiatives had an overdue, cleansing quality that resonated with most of the country and truly spoke to his sixth sense in terms of political prowess.[26]

So it was that Lyndon Baines Johnson and not John Fitzgerald Kennedy would seize the moment, navigate the immediate legislative impasse that existed over taxes and the budget, and avoid the tricks the Senate's legendary Southern segregationists had always used to maintain status quo when it came to such essential stopgaps as racially separate facilities, accommodations, and voting rights in their respective states. Without such basic rights, nothing would ever change. LBJ knew it—knew the lasting legacy whoever changed it would achieve, and assuming the mantel and motive of his murdered predecessor, acted upon his political instincts to ensure it finally happened … with a Southerner in the White House. Forget the fact that the Democratic coalition—the one that had controlled Congress since FDR's first term in 1932, the Solid South along with labor in the Midwest's so-called "Rust Belt," the far more progressive Far West, and the liberal Eastern elite—would have to be sacrificed. Even though it would mean the conservative South voting Republican ever since—LBJ charged ahead and got it done.[27]

In his much-anticipated first address to Congress four days after the assassination, Johnson surprised most of the country, and especially leaders of the Civil Rights Movement, by not only eloquently eulogizing the fallen president, but also by prioritizing Kennedy's entire legislative agenda, including, first and foremost, the cause of racial equality. Before anything else, he said, "No memorial could more honor President Kennedy's memory more than the earliest possible passage of a civil rights bill for which he fought so long. We have talked long enough in this country about equal rights. We have talked for one hundred years or more. It is time now to write the next chapter and to write it in the books of law." While those words were met with thunderous applause from almost every corner of the House Chamber, Caro made sure to note that the approval was not unanimous. One group not applauding was the Senate's Southern Caucus, "the men who had raised Johnson to power in the Senate, supported him for president in 1960, and swallowed the weak 1957 and 1960 civil rights legislation he passed" primarily because of his presidential aspirations. At that moment, those men and others were rather obviously not applauding their new Southern-born president.[28]

Praised by newspapers throughout the country, Johnson's first presidential address, which also called for passage of Kennedy's pending tax bill, education bills, foreign aid legislation, and appropriations bill, was viewed as a huge success. Although he was sometimes awkward and "bullying" in previous orations during his decades in public office, none of that was part of his inspiring 27-minute address to Congress on November 27, 1963. First impressions being everything, LBJ made a great first impression as president—except in the South, where the word "traitor" was suddenly on the lips of many White, Democratic voters. Richard Russell, in fact, when confronted by LBJ about running over him if he stood in his way, famously warned, "You may do that, but it's going to cost you the South."[29]

Half a year of political wrangling later (as only LBJ could do), following passage of his Civil Rights Act of 1964 and even more racial violence, including two murders, "Bloody Sunday" happened in Selma, Alabama, in March of 1965. That's where and when network

TV cameras were fixed on Civil Rights Movement marchers as they crossed the Edmund Pettus Bridge en route to the state capitol in Montgomery to call for assurance of voting rights, which were creatively still being denied African Americans in the Deep South. Suddenly, the marchers were viciously attacked and beaten back by local, White law enforcement officers on horseback, and those cameras brought it all home to a horrified nation. Eventually, the march would go forward without further incident, thanks to the president posting FBI agents, federal marshals, and National Guard troops all along the way. But more importantly, Johnson introduced voting rights legislation with the presidential backing that had previously been missing. In another milestone speech designed once and for all to signal the end of voter suppression by individual states, he demanded, "This time, on this issue, there must be no delay, no hesitation, and no compromise. Their cause must be our cause, because it's not just Negroes but all of us who must overcome our crippling legacy of bigotry and injustice. And—'we shall overcome.'" This adoption of the Civil Rights Movement's own rallying cry left no doubt of his determination to eliminate the last vestige of Southern segregation. As a result, Caro philosophized in his *Means of Ascent* that although Lincoln "struck off the chains of Black Americans," it was LBJ "who led them into the voting booths."[30]

Unfortunately, along with the historic Voting Rights Act of 1965, what LBJ himself called his "greatest accomplishment," and his passage of Medicare and Medicaid, that same year marked his escalation of the Vietnam War. All followed his re-election in a history-making landslide over Republican firebrand Barry Goldwater in 1964.[31] When Johnson suddenly become president in late 1963, 16,000 U.S. troops were in South Vietnam, serving as military advisors, and there was talk within the Kennedy administration of bringing them home. "By the time Johnson left office at the start of 1969, 549,000 American forces were mired in a hopeless jungle war and more had died than total participants when it started." Add to that the fact that much of this escalation had come under less than honest pretenses, beginning with his Gulf of Tonkin Resolution in August 1964, and you have Caro's assessment that LBJ escalated the war while keeping the total escalation out of the news through "duplicities," "misstatements," and lies. And the protestors ... by the time network TV images of the obviously escalating war were being beamed into American living rooms in 1965 and 1966, young people had begun taking to the streets in increasing numbers with chants like "Hey! Hey! LBJ! How many kids did you kill today?" The protests got so bad, in fact, that military bases were the only places the president would appear in public.[32]

By emphasizing this discontent, Caro illustrated how LBJ's secrecy marked the beginning of U.S. distrust and cynicism (now rampant) when it comes to America's chief executive. His point: no longer would the public view our presidents as unassailable moral leaders, always honest and seeking the best course for the country. Over forever would be the days of presidential icons like the two Roosevelts, General Eisenhower, and idealistic "Jack" Kennedy, presidents whose popularity put them on pedestals. "After Lyndon Johnson, trust in the president [meaning any president] was tarnished forever," to quote a White House correspondent of the time. His biographer took that a step further when he stated, "It is difficult for most Americans today to remember or to understand reverence for the institution of the presidency, so lasting has been the damage inflicted on it. While much of the damage was inflicted by Richard Nixon, Johnson's successor, it was under Johnson the damage began."[33]

He further contended that the presidency of LBJ was a "watershed presidency ... one of the great divides in American history in the evolution of not only its policies, but also its image." Caro added, "His was not the triumphant presidency" it had begun as. Instead

Despite all he did for civil rights and the well-being of America's senior citizens through Medicare, Lyndon Baines Johnson's legacy as president will forever be tainted by his escalation of the Vietnam War and the many protests it inspired, such as this one right outside the White House (Library of Congress Prints and Photographs Division—Reproduction Number DIG-ppmsca24360).

it became "a tangled course" compromised by "a thread much darker," a thread that would compel Johnson to surprise everyone by not seeking re-election in 1968, leading to the even more cynical and compromised presidency of "Tricky Dick" Nixon.[34]

En masse, Caro's voluminous works on Johnson are among the most thorough ever written on any American president. Anything and everything pertaining to our 36th chief executive was covered in thought-provoking detail by a master biographer. To second-guess Caro when it comes to LBJ would be like questioning whether race has played a part in our national story. Intimately acquainted by his research, his understanding of Johnson is beyond reproof. His *Means of Ascent* opened with a return to Johnson's roots in the Texas Hill Country west of Austin, one of the poorest sections of the country during his formative years. By age 13, in fact, Johnson had been witness to the financial failure of his father, Sam Johnson, who went from being one of the most respected men in the community, a state legislator and civil servant, to one of the most ridiculed after he invested heavily in a rambling parcel of land along the Perdernales River that he sought to bring back as the Johnson Ranch. Instead, he incurred tremendous debt and "owed everyone in town." One of his local political opponents of the time was heard to say, "Sam Johnson is a mighty smart man, but he's got no sense," and "penniless" was the word Caro used to describe LBJ's adolescent years.[35]

At the same time, the younger Johnson was the spitting image of his father, a fact that subjected him to derision from neighbors, many of whom professed that he, like his father, would never amount to anything. Both father and son, in fact, were forced to work on county road crews to keep the family afloat, and Caro termed "his youth a poverty so severe that often he and his brother and three sisters would have gone hungry were it not for food given as charity by relatives and friends—food seasoned with small-town sneers."[36]

From such downtrodden beginnings emerged an LBJ who wished to be seen as not just smart, but "shrewd, wily, and [even] sly." At an early age, he learned to cultivate older men of influence or power of one kind or another who might advance his ambitions. Contemporaries would label him a "professional son" in the way he used flattery to ingratiate himself into the good graces of political and financial powerbrokers. Also obvious on his early career path was his willingness to apply what Caro called "pragmatism" to politics, in other words, an ability to steal elections (if necessary), as he did for himself and others in campus elections at Southwest State Teachers College in San Marcos, where he earned his undergraduate degree, and later as an aide in the office of Texas Congressman Richard Kleberg. It was in that role that he knowingly "stuffed" the ballot box for himself and allies in elections of the so-called Little Congress, an organization of congressional assistants on Capitol Hill. Upon learning of such chicanery years later, another former U.S. president remarked, "My God, who would cheat to win the presidency of something like the Little Congress?"[37]

LBJ would continue those kinds of behind-the-scenes machinations as he progressed up the political ladder. Following his appointment as director of the National Youth Administration in Texas in 1935, he captured a surprising congressional seat two years later, representing Austin and its environs in a special election by running on a straight New Deal platform at just 28 years of age. Perhaps that one was too easy, because four years later in 1941, he would learn the hard lesson of Texas state politics when he allowed former Texas Governor W. Lee "Pappy" O'Daniel "to steal one" from him in another special election, this one for a suddenly vacant U.S. Senate seat. That's when a big early lead inspired overconfidence within the Johnson campaign and Texas' notorious habit of "late" returns from slow-reporting counties spoiled what hours before seemed certain victory. In losing, LBJ recognized he had not held true to his belief to do whatever it took to win until the last hour, and it cost him. It was a career setback for the still young congressman, but one he would not repeat when given another senatorial chance seven years later.[38]

In the interim, he also had the patriotic/political good sense to go from lieutenant commander in the Naval Reserve to becoming the first enlisted, active duty congressman following Pearl Harbor and America's entry into World War II (December 1941). His tour of duty in the regular Navy included one ten-week stretch inspecting training sites along the West Coast and just over a month as a combat observer in the South Pacific (during which he earned a Silver Star). Back in Washington by July 1942, he resigned his commission in accordance with President Roosevelt's order requiring all congressmen in uniform to resume their legislative duties.

LBJ's whatever-it-takes way of thinking would re-emerge six years later (1947–1948) when O'Daniel's popularity waned, causing him not to seek re-election. Johnson, a six-term congressman, was by then ready to make another run at the U.S. Senate. Ironically, it would come against another former governor and legendary Texas vote getter, Coke Stevenson.[39]

"By far" the most popular governor in Texas history, according to Caro, Stevenson was, in fact, known as "Mr. Texas" by the time he decided to run for the Senate in 1947. "Who could possibly beat him?" That was the question being asked as the primary neared. To have a chance against the most popular politician in Texas, Johnson knew he would need money "on an unprecedented scale." He took advantage of the powerbrokers he had previously cultivated, particularly George and Herman Brown of Brown & Root, a Texas contracting firm to which Congressman Johnson had steered dam building contracts in an era of constantly expanding public utility construction. The Brown brothers had "lavishly" financed his first Senate campaign in 1941, and they were prepared to do the same in 1948.[40]

Also, even though Stevenson was "immensely popular" in Texas, Caro elaborated on how in the "cactus and mesquite"-covered country from San Antonio south, the largely Hispanic population living in the Rio Grande River Valley, that popularity did not hold the political sway it did elsewhere in the huge state. Instead, those Texans were inclined to vote the way their local officials told them to vote and, as a result, always seemed to have a bigger impact on Texas elections than they should have. Among their leadership, one name also seemed to stand above all others—George Parr—the so-called "Duke of Duval" County. Actually, "Boss Parr" was probably a more appropriate label for the man who had followed in his father's footsteps to officially become the county judge and unofficially "a replacement for the patrones," to whom Hispanic citizens south of the border in Mexico had always owed allegiance. To illustrate the influence Parr had in the region, Caro re-quoted a Corpus Christi, Texas, reporter of the time, who wrote, "It is not easy for the average person to imagine what it was like to oppose Boss Parr. A word from him was sufficient to get a man fired or denied welfare payments. Merchants who opposed him faced the sudden loss of their trade. [Both] farmers and ranchers were intimidated."

At the same time, what motivated the Duke was money—kickbacks from his own interests, which included a beer distributorship, oil rights, and land leases, but also money from his county for such things as road projects and oil and gas leases. "Seemingly no amount of money was enough," Caro wrote. Such was "the Duchy of Duval" that Parr's outreach extended into at least six other counties, where alliances with other judges and townspeople assured him additional dominance and deference, especially when it came to statewide elections. So it was that in 1948 an aspiring young congressman with plenty of money at his disposal was able to upset a Texas legend for a coveted United States Senate seat in one of the closest races in Lone Star history. Asked sometime later about an investigation into the election that had been halted and what it would have shown if allowed to continue, a federally appointed court official reportedly said, "Lyndon was put in the United States Senate with a stolen election."

Unbeknownst to Coke Stevenson, the Johnson campaign had left nothing to chance and actually entered the race with a 25,000-vote "head start," courtesy of Parr. To read Caro's account of this story is to get up-close and personal with one of the best tales of political intrigue in American history, setting the stage for the supreme political genius LBJ would display as Senate majority leader and later in his earliest days as president.[41]

Caro's massive *Master of the Senate*, in fact, would illuminate Johnson becoming "the youngest and greatest" majority leader, a role that would have been enough for most American politicians, but not for LBJ. No, for him the presidency, accidental or otherwise, was all that would satisfy the extreme ambitions he had developed as a downtrodden Hill Country youth. Johnson never forgot those lean, demeaning times, never tired of the political infighting and intrigue so necessary to get to and stay on top; and left the top of the political mountain he had ascended by whatever means necessary only when the weight of public opinion became unbearable for a man who wanted to be loved and could not stand losing. Upon deciding there was absolutely no way he could run again in 1968 and retiring to his ranch on the Pedernales, LBJ became a disconsolate chain smoker who grew his hair long and rarely set foot in public. Plagued by arteriosclerosis since his days in the Senate, he lived for five more uneventful years, dying in 1973 following his third heart attack at age 65, having never fully accepted the political mountain he had scaled or the public opinion cliff he had ultimately fallen off.[42]

18

Gerald Ford—Right Man
for a Time Gone Wrong

*"Under Ford this nation has become number two in military power in a
world where it is dangerous—if not fatal—to be second best."*
—Ronald Reagan, 1976

One of our nation's most recognized contemporary historians, Douglas Brinkley, has authored biographies of Henry Ford, Jimmy Carter, Dean Acheson, James Forrestal, John Kerry, Rosa Parks, and more recently Presidents Theodore and Franklin Roosevelt. In 2007 he also contributed to The American Presidents Series with a concise read on Gerald R. Ford (entitled the same). Only 160 pages long in obvious compliance with the series format, the book opens with what can only be taken as the author's statement of admiration. Speaking of Ford, Brinkley wrote: "His decency was palpable. Following the traumas of the Vietnam War and Watergate scandal, he was tonic to the consciousness of his times, a Middle American at ease with himself and the enduring values of our Constitution." That, Brinkley said, "was the genius of Gerald Ford."

Portraying him as a very competent leader of "independent thought and conscience," who "never placed party loyalty ahead of right and wrong," rather than the clumsy fill-in without much chance of presidential success so often portrayed by the media of that time, Brinkley sought to elevate Ford's legacy. While largely ignored by scholars of the late-20th century intent on turning the page from the disgrace of Richard Nixon to the decency of Jimmy Carter and, even more so, the clarity of Ronald Reagan, the presidency of Gerald Ford has been treated as a transition or calming interlude following the Nixon storm, a necessary but uneventful two and a half years of accidental mediocrity.[1]

Contrary to that pre-conception, Brinkley calls attention to his decorated academic and athletic background at the University of Michigan, where he starred in football; a stellar congressional career for his state and party (Republican); and a surprising ability to rise to the White House despite his total lack of any preconceived presidential ambitions. The product of a broken Nebraska home who owed much to a stepfather who adopted him, raised him as his own, and formally conferred upon him his own name (Gerald Rudolph Ford, Jr.), the young Ford grew up in Grand Rapids, Michigan, a prosperous community where values and deeds mattered and where, as a teenager, he once told a classmate, "If you accentuate the good things in dealing with a person, you can like them even though he or she had some bad qualities. If you have that attitude, you never hate anybody."[2]

Applying that approach to Ford's career, Brinkley revealed a simple litmus test that candidate and Congressman Ford would rely on over the next three decades while charting

157

a legislative course that his constituents could believe in and rely on. So much so, in fact, that after playing for an undefeated, Big Ten Conference champion University of Michigan team as a senior and turning down professional football offers from both the Green Bay Packers and Detroit Lions; after trying to get into Yale University Law School while also flirting with a modeling career, including an advertising appearance in *Life* magazine; and after earning ten World War II battle stars as a carrier-based Navy seaman, he returned from the South Pacific determined to take on the boss politics still prevalent in mid-20th century America. In doing so, he announced his first candidacy for Congress in Michigan's Fifth District on June 17, 1948, taking on the Michigan political machine of Frank D. McKay, a pre-war isolationist. Few gave him much chance in the Republican primary that year, but with a consistent message and diligent campaigning, he surprised the McKay-backed incumbent, 23,632 votes to 14,341. It was the start of 13 straight congressional elections in which the soft-spoken, square-jawed, straight-shooting Ford would garner at least 60 percent of the vote and never again face a primary opponent.[3]

According to Brinkley, "complacency was not in his character," and he would prove "deceptively ambitious." From the beginning, his goal was always congressional change and his party's place in that change, and he set out to accomplish that "vote by vote."[4]

Among his best and earliest congressional friends were fellow newcomers Nixon of California and John Kennedy of Massachusetts, the former with whom he shared party affiliation and the latter with whom he shared neighboring offices in the House Office Building. While both of them and others of his boldest congressional colleagues would aspire to the presidency during the largely American-dominated 1950s, Ford kept his sights always on "the Speaker's chair," as in Speaker of the House of Representatives, and early on looked for the best (or surest) route to that goal. Catching a break for a congressman so young, he earned appointment to the prestigious House Appropriations Committee by cozying up to the ranking Republican, who then added him to the committee when another Michigan congressman on Appropriations decided to run for the Senate. Making the most of that assignment, he developed a reputation as a tight-fisted, "ideologically dodgy nice guy, the epitome of an 'Eisenhower Republican,'" who echoed the largely non-partisan course set by the popular president and former general during that halcyon, middle class-inspired decade. He fit perfectly into the moderate political approach of the times before the turbulent 1960s and transitional 1970s, even though his party remained the minority in Congress, to the detriment of his ongoing Speaker ambitions.[5]

In fact, Brinkley made sure to differentiate between the continuous, extreme right wing politics of Barry Goldwater, the Republican presidential candidate versus Lyndon Baines Johnson in 1964, and Ford's advocacy of recapturing the political middle ground. Portraying him as innovative and public relations-oriented, his biographer also illustrated the ways Ford reached out to constituents and the countless speeches he made on behalf of Republican colleagues. That same nice-guy approach helped bring those same colleagues in line with his way of thinking on contentious votes. He truly seemed less concerned with his own image than with the politics and perception of the Republican Party, as well as with avoiding what Brinkley termed "intraparty schisms."[6]

Not the bullying, cajoling, or arm-twisting congressional leadership so associated with 1950s Senate Majority Leader Lyndon Johnson, Ford never coerced or punished Republicans who occasionally voted against him or didn't see eye-to-eye on a particular party-line issue. Although "plodding" at times, as Brinkley confirmed, his easy-going legislative style produced results.[7]

At the same time, when his old Republican friend, Nixon, followed LBJ into the White

House in 1968, he seemed unwilling to work with Ford or Congress, taking instead "a solo course," again according to Brinkley. Over the next four years, that led to President Nixon having very few true allies on Capitol Hill.[8]

As a result, when Nixon's initial hand-picked (but surprising) vice president, Spiro Agnew, came under investigation for bribery and tax evasion while an executive in Baltimore County, Maryland, and later as governor of that state, there were few party regulars shedding a tear over his resignation and his face-saving plea deal arranged by the administration. Under terms of the twenty-fifth amendment, which had only recently been ratified (1967), Nixon needed to name a replacement, and Ford became the best available man during the onset of what became the Watergate scandal (the Republican-orchestrated break-in of the Democratic National Committee headquarters) and resulting cover-up. For a variety of reasons, including their past congressional friendship, Ford was the logical choice of an increasingly embattled Nixon.[9] Brinkley termed his selection "the most acceptable for an administration on the verge of collapse," which prompted Democrat Alan Cranston of California to remark at the time, "I doubt if there has ever been a time when integrity has so surpassed ideology in the judging of a man for so high an office."[10]

That was high praise but praise well earned, as it turned out, for the new vice president soon became the trusted "front man," used (and abused) to proclaim his old friend's innocence when making the administration's case as the investigation began to overwhelm the Nixon White House. Ford just couldn't conceive of anyone in Nixon's inner circle being involved in the Watergate break-in and unwittingly took on the role of the president's chief apologist. Brinkley also maintained that no other U.S. vice president was ever put in such a politically sensitive position.[11]

To many onlookers, Ford appeared "an outright fool for continuing to proclaim Nixon's innocence," but he refused to appear disloyal to his new boss and old friend, and as the newly appointed VP, he certainly did not want to come across as wanting Nixon's job. Bottom line, he supported Nixon when practically no one else did, and upon Nixon's resignation on August 9, 1974, the ex-president's own words attested to Ford's loyalty and support, when Nixon wrote, "This is just a note to tell you how much I appreciated your superb and courageous support over these past difficult months. It's tough going now, but history will, I am sure, record you as one of the most capable, courageous, and honorable vice presidents we have ever had."[12]

Of course, once he became president, Ford would be demonized by the press for his history-making, September pardon of Nixon, who would have undoubtedly faced impeachment for what he knew about the break-in and cover-up (proven eventually by secret White House recordings) had he not resigned. In anticipation of that happening, Ford seized on the concept of a presidential pardon as admission of guilt without the needless trauma of a demeaning trial, something he hoped would make his actions more palatable to the general public. As a new president moving into the White House with less than two years to go before the next election, however, his pardon never had a chance in the court of public opinion.[13] Neither did his 1974 "Whip Inflation Now" (WIN) campaign, which had to be abandoned as "too gimmicky" in the midst of a deepening recession, and his 1975 Helsinki Agreement, since all it really accomplished was the promise of non-interference in the affairs of the "Communist Bloc" nations of Eastern Europe as a means of easing tensions with the Soviet Union.[14]

So, despite the national inexperience of a largely unknown 1976 Democratic opponent, former Georgia Governor Jimmy Carter, Ford found himself at an immediate disadvantage in the polls, facing an untainted, born-again Christian from outside the Washington mainstream preaching the need for a fresh start after the Republicans' Watergate mess. In response, Ford would argue the country's need to move past the Watergate nightmare as quickly as possible as the reason for his decision to pardon his disgraced predecessor, and he would make 1976 a much closer bi-centennial presidential race than initially anticipated. Nonetheless, it would prove a hill too steep to climb.[15]

Part of that climb resulted from a rare campaign challenge to the incumbent president from within his own party by former California Governor Ronald Reagan, who had catapulted to fame among conservative Republicans by absorbing the mantle of Barry Goldwater, the Grand Old Party's outspoken landslide loser in 1964. Reagan considered Ford merely "a care-taker" in the job, and he would return to assume the Republican nomination in 1980 and deny Carter re-election at a time of high inflation and "a crisis of confidence," the start of three straight Republican terms in the White House (two by Reagan and one by his vice president, George H. W. Bush).[16]

Ford would never forgive Reagan for mounting his challenge in 1976, something he was certain undermined his chances for re-election—and it did seem a direct repudiation of Reagan's own "Eleventh Commandment," which was, as Brinkley asserted: "A Republican should never criticize another Republican." On the other hand, Ford would develop an ironically great friendship with Carter that lasted long after the two of them were president. As early as his inauguration, in fact, on January 20, 1976, Carter famously opened his inaugural address with the words, "I want to thank my predecessor for all he has done to heal our land," a shocking testament to the historic burden and thankless task Ford had faced on behalf of his country as Nixon's replacement. On his last day after 28 straight years as

No U.S. president, accidental or otherwise, ever faced the unique challenge Gerald Ford had to deal with when he replaced Richard Nixon. Shown here addressing Congress, Ford elected to pardon his disgraced predecessor, but that decision injured his own re-election chances (Library of Congress Prints and Photographs Division—Reproduction Number DIG-ppmsca-08445).

a steadfast congressional public servant in our nation's capital, it was a fitting gesture that Ford would never forget.[17]

On the outside back cover of Brinkley's book, the biographer mentioned that not only did Ford leave the presidency "in far better shape than he had found it," but "perhaps even healthier that it had been in decades." For such a longstanding chronicler of the American past, that was a bold and thought-provoking statement.[18] Consideration of at least the previous three decades, however, might prove his point. Not only would that include the Nixon-Watergate debacle at the end of those 30 years, but before that Lyndon Johnson's Vietnam deceit, John Kennedy's apparent support of schemes to topple Cuban dictator Fidel Castro (the Bay of Pigs and "Operation Mongoose"), and the little-known, espionage-induced Cold War maneuvers of Dwight Eisenhower's administration (particularly the unscrupulous, espionage-prone Dulles brothers, John Foster and Allen, as heads of the State Department and CIA, respectively) to understand the depths to which the American presidency had arguably sunk following Harry Truman's "the buck stops here" approach.[19] Rather than a return to normalcy that had been the stated case of Warren Harding and Calvin Coolidge much earlier in the century, the need for reconciliation in government became an unofficial rallying cry for both Ford and Carter in the 1970s.[20] Amazing how both of those concepts now seem lost completely in one of our most tribal, untruthful, and contentious eras ever ... one totally lacking in historical context.[21]

Ford, in fact, would have a hard time today recognizing the democracy he so bravely attempted to put back on track before exiting the White House in 1977 and dying 29 years later as our oldest surviving president up to that time, age 93 in 2006 (a record since eclipsed when both Carter and Bush turned 94 in 2018, and now held solely by Carter, who would turn 95 in October 2019).[22] Ford's retirement from political life lasted nearly three decades, but thankfully he was gone before witnessing another decline of American governance and values to the level of Watergate (although he and Carter did urge censure by the Senate instead of impeachment during the congressional trial of President Bill Clinton in 1998). Yet as Brinkley pointed out, while Ford's friendship with Carter in their presidential afterlives has been frequently discussed, "the odd role Nixon continued to play in his pardoner's life has been neglected." In essence, whenever Ford was criticized in the aftermath of his brief White House stay, Nixon would be among those coming to his defense, a debt of history Tricky Dick obviously sought to repay.[23]

Ford did consider running again in 1980 when Carter was struggling and the chance for payback (on Reagan) for what he still considered party disloyalty and the seeds of division in 1976 were unearthed, but thinking better of the life he had since made for himself and his family, he refrained from any such vengeful urge. "Always the loyal Republican," as Brinkley emphasized, he eventually even campaigned for Reagan, openly criticizing Carter for his handling of the ongoing Iranian hostage crisis despite their budding friendship ... and Reagan's previous stab in the back.[24]

Following Reagan's ultimate victory, Ford contented himself with raising money for his presidential library in Ann Arbor, Michigan, and presidential museum in Grand Rapids, Michigan, the only president since Hoover to have two such separate facilities. When Egyptian President Anwar Sadat was assassinated in October 1981, both he and Carter were asked by the Reagan administration to represent the U.S. at the funeral of a man they had both worked with and admired. Traveling together, this pilgrimage to the Middle East only "deepened" the ties of the former rivals, and they would continue to work together for various causes and projects.[25]

Throughout his remaining years, Ford would remain an easy target for anyone wishing to second-guess the Nixon pardon. Vindication for him would come in the form of a Presidential Medal of Freedom, presented by President Clinton in 1999, and the John F. Kennedy Profile in Courage Award in 2001. Revisionist reporters also eventually reversed their previous attacks on Ford's pardon decision by admitting he had been right about sparing the country further turmoil and embarrassment. Brinkley concluded that Ford's stubborn insistence that the Nixon pardon was a national imperative eventually won converts in both parties and throughout the nation. At his death on December 26, 2006, Ford was remembered as a "healer" and as someone with no hidden agendas or secret life. Brinkley also summed up Ford's recent rise in the presidential ranks with the thought he "had transcended being merely an accidental or pardon president."[26]

PART III

Their Burden:
Rankings, Similarities
and Contrasts

19

Where They Rank

"No one has a right to grade a president who has not sat in his chair, exam-ined the information that came across his desk, and learned why he made his decisions."—John Kennedy, 1962

Begun by *Time* magazine in 1948, presidential rankings and grades in recent years have become commonplace. Now that 45 chief executives (actually 44 since Grover Cleve-land served non-consecutive terms) have guided our nation, comparisons, contrasts, and evaluations occur more often and with increasing evidence. Like any other special group, the growing sample size of White House residents makes drawing conclusions more exact and based on a lot more facts. Faced with the same or similar trials, tribulations, stresses, and awesome responsibility, American presidents have exemplified surprising similarities and differences to allow historians to categorize them and their administrations in a variety of ways, including the nine who have ascended accidentally.[1]

In 2018, one such poll of the American Political Science Association (APSA) rated the U.S. presidents, with the best possible score of 100 representing greatness, 50 being average, and 0 total failure. C-SPAN, the Cable Satellite Public Affairs Network, conducted three similar surveys of U.S. historians over the past two decades and released the results for not only the most recent (2017), but also the previous two polls in 2009 and 2000, illustrating variations in the way some of our presidents have come to be viewed over time. While most of the individual rankings remained fairly consistent, some fluctuated, either rising or falling in the estimation of qualified evaluators, as well as some being further diminished or elevated as more presidents were added to the list.[2]

Based on an overall, perfect score of 1,000, Abraham Lincoln (as to be expected) remained the consistent, runaway leader in the C-SPAN polling, ranking No. 1 all three times, with a most recent score of 906 points. At the same time, George Washington (867) and Franklin Delano Roosevelt (854) remained second and third in the C-SPAN rankings. More recently, the APSA agreed on Lincoln being number one with 95 of a possible 100 points, Washington second at 90, and FDR third with 89. It's fairly safe, in fact, to conclude that Lincoln, Washington, and FDR have been the top three-rated presidents in virtually all presidential surveys of the last 60 years.[3]

Coming in at number four in both the C-SPAN rankings and the APSA survey was one of our accidental presidents, the larger-than-life change agent Theodore Roosevelt. He was truly the president who introduced America to the modern age. Different from his predecessors in so many ways, the indomitable TR received an 807 score in the 2017 C-SPAN poll and 81 in the 2018 APSA rankings, which was 63 points higher than fifth-rated Dwight D. Eisenhower in the historians' poll and, more recently, one better than number five, Thomas Jefferson, among the political scientists. Either way, TR appears indisputably our top-rated president among those who have been elevated to our nation's highest office in accidental fashion.[4]

Harry Truman was the next-highest accidental president in both polls, coming in sixth for both C-SPAN and APSA with 737 points and 75, respectively, while Lyndon Johnson, the ultimate politico, was tenth in both with 686 points in C-SPAN and 69 in APSA. The next-highest-ranked accidental was Gerald Ford, much further down both lists at number 25 with 509 and 47 points, respectively. Indeed, the nine accidental presidents seemed to fit into three distinct groups in the rankings, with TR, Truman, and LBJ in the top tier; Ford joined by Calvin Coolidge and Chester Arthur among the mid-range presidents; and John Tyler, Millard Fillmore, and Andrew Johnson all ranked near the bottom. Coolidge and Arthur were 28th and 31st in the APSA survey, and 27th and 35th overall in the C-SPAN rankings. Meanwhile, only James Buchanan, the bachelor president right before Lincoln and the Civil War, was ranked worse than Andrew Johnson by C-SPAN. At the same time, APSA had Tyler ranked 37th, Fillmore 38th, and Johnson 40th, each with less than one-third of the 100 points possible.[5]

As for the combined C-SPAN polls, which began in 2000, Ford, Arthur, Fillmore, Tyler, and Andrew Johnson all declined in the rankings. Ford went down three spots from a high of 23rd in 2009. More gradually, Arthur declined three spots since 2000, while Fillmore and Johnson dropped two spots each. Tyler endured the most precipitous drop, going down four spots from 2009 to 2017. A similar APSA poll from 2014 had both Johnsons and Arthur moving up one or two spots each, while Ford, Tyler, and Fillmore all declined.[6]

Suffice it to say, the nine accidental presidents display as wide a range in their overall rankings as any other select group of chief executives in our nation's history. Despite coming into office in the same way, their ability to achieve success and approval revealed more disparity than most presidential groupings— for instance the eight Virginia-born presidents, all but one of whom served during the country's first century, or the seven major generals who became president, three of whom had no previous political experience. In other words, there

Like Andrew Johnson (see Prologue), Millard Fillmore is remembered with a statue prominently displayed in his hometown, Buffalo, New York. Although still a favorite son in terms of local heritage, Fillmore, again like Johnson, has not been viewed so favorably by history overall. Both are among our lowest-rated presidents (photograph courtesy of Aaron Fallon, city of Buffalo).

can be no consensus drawn from their backgrounds or the way they each did the job by virtue of the common burden that was suddenly thrust upon them. While all faced the same awesome responsibility with similar objectives in the earliest stages of their administrations, they approached their presidencies differently, with differing values and expectations, and ultimately succeeded or failed due to a variety of factors—many beyond their control. No matter the power of the presidency, each came to office faced with unique issues and circumstances that would require random solutions and means of addressing whatever problems graced the national landscape in their particular era. For some it was an overwhelming challenge—for others, an opportunity to put their stamp on the nation's future.[7]

As recently as 2016, traditional historical rankings were questioned for five of the accidentals among 13 presidents overall in a book by Brion McClanahan. In it, he challenged the mostly positive reputations of assertive presidents like Andrew Jackson, Abraham Lincoln, and Franklin Roosevelt as actually being unconstitutional in their approach. Also in his mix of nine who "screwed up America" were Theodore Roosevelt, Harry Truman, and Lyndon Johnson, our three top-rated accidental presidents, each of whom broadened presidential prerogative—of that there is no argument. On the other end of McClanahan's political spectrum, among four other presidents "who tried to save" America constitutionally, were two other accidentals, John Tyler and Calvin Coolidge. In his surprising estimation, Tyler "was arguably the best president in American history" and Coolidge "was more principled than popular," and as a result the best of our twentieth and post–twentieth century presidential allotment. Emphasizing Tyler's staunch defense of states' rights over constitutional overreach by the federal government and Coolidge's stewardship of limited government overall, he makes an ideologically elevating case for both that their historical proponents, including biographers Crapol and Shlaes, have also made, but one done in the context of how they should stack up alongside (in his estimation) more obvious presidential "over-reachers."[8]

In the end, however, no better gauge of presidential success or failure can probably be found than the ballot box. Of our nine accidental presidents, four were elected to an additional term while five were not, including four not given the opportunity to run as incumbents. While Teddy Roosevelt, Coolidge, Truman, and Lyndon Johnson all won twentieth century elections in their own right, Tyler, Fillmore, Andrew Johnson, and Arthur were all summarily rejected as incumbents in the 19th century by the party through which they had ascended. Meanwhile, it can be argued that Ford failed to win re-election due to his party's failure to get behind his incumbency in a wholehearted manner. In Ford's case, future President Ronald Reagan's controversial entrance into the 1976 race probably had as much to do with his defeat as his general election opponent, Democrat Jimmy Carter.[9]

While the ballot box has been the best judge of all presidencies, accidental or otherwise, and a guide to presidential rankings, individual grades have also been handed out from time to time, offering an even more telling conclusion as to just how effective each of our chief executives has been. One such grading occurred in the previously referenced book by Kenneth Davis, *Don't Know Much About the American Presidents*. Those letter grades for the nine accidental presidents were as follows: Theodore Roosevelt A+, Harry Truman A, Lyndon Johnson B, Chester Arthur C, Calvin Coolidge C, Gerald Ford C, Millard Fillmore F, and Andrew Johnson F—historic judgment rendered academically.[10]

20

Humble Beginnings;
Absence of Ambition

"This office seeking is a disease. Men get it and they lose the proper balance of their minds."—Grover Cleveland, 1885

For at least six of our nine accidental presidents, humble would be as good a way as any to describe their collective start in life. While Theodore Roosevelt and John Tyler were members of affluent families in New York and Virginia, respectively, the social status Andrew Johnson, Harry Truman, Calvin Coolidge, Millard Fillmore, Lyndon Johnson, and even Gerald Ford were born into was somewhere between the poverty level and low-income status. Both of the Johnsons experienced poverty in their early lives. Fillmore's birth came in a log cabin, and his early family life on a hardscrabble farm in upstate New York was much like the Trumans' in Missouri and even the more stable Coolidges of Vermont. Meanwhile, Ford entered the world to a Nebraska family tormented by spousal abuse—a young family split and relocated to the much-needed security of his maternal grandparents' home in Michigan.[1]

For those latter six, early life was not easy for them or their families. The first Johnson lost his father at age three and had to be apprenticed along with his older brother at age 10 in return for food, clothing, and a trade. The second Johnson had to earn spare cash as a childhood hired hand, printer's devil, and shoeshine boy for his cash-strapped family, the result of his father's poor decisions and financial setbacks in the rocky Texas Hill Country. Similarly, Fillmore was born into what one historian termed "squalid poverty" before he too had to be apprenticed for his family's financial sake at age 14.[2]

Truman's rural boyhood included an admittedly "sissy" reputation among boys his own age that stemmed from wearing thick eyeglasses, avoiding contact sports, taking piano lessons, and a bout with diphtheria that temporarily cost him the use of his arms and legs. When his father, who had also suffered financial losses from speculation in commodities, was irreparably injured in an accident, Truman was compelled to spend much of his young adulthood just keeping the family farm afloat. Likewise, Coolidge followed a similar childhood, plowing, planting, stacking wood, picking fruit, and taking part in that most common of rural Vermont practices, tapping and processing maple sugar.[3]

As for Ford, although he did not grow up on a farm, his formative years were in "modest circumstances" after his mother remarried a Michigan man who would become his stepfather and namesake, Gerald Rudolph Ford, Sr. Always athletic and industrious, he grew up tending the family's coal-fired furnace, mowing neighborhood lawns, and doing other regular chores.[4]

Such was the work ethic and lower economic bracket shared by the families of six young men who would grow up to be accidental presidents. As already noted with two of the other three, Roosevelt and Tyler had the natural advantages of well-to-do fathers, assuring their access to social elites and the best education at schools like Harvard (Roosevelt) and William & Mary (Tyler), and Arthur was just a notch below that on the social ladder as the son of a Baptist minister, who ensured his son would have access to a local academy before going on to Union College.[5]

This division of the accidental presidents into two distinct sub-sets in terms of their upbringings and formative years can also be seen in their respective ambitions for the highest office in the land. While all were thrust into the White House by circumstances beyond their control, no less than four clearly had no ambition for the office before their ascension. Only after they were in the presidential role and surprising even themselves with their acumen for the job did Truman, Ford, Coolidge, and even Arthur truly warm to the task of leading the nation. Truman and Coolidge relished it so much that they determinedly won second terms—Truman in a stunning upset and Coolidge by a surprising majority—and Ford to the point of running again despite dissatisfaction and a serious challenge from within his own party.[6]

After assuming the policies of his deceased running mate, but without the accompanying scandal that plagued Warren Harding's personal life and administration, Coolidge justified the faith of Republicans who had originally made him a favorite-son candidate and later a vice presidential nominee by fulfilling many of the conservative, tax-cutting measures Harding had merely hinted at before his death in 1923.[7] Both Coolidge and Truman had to have some arm-twisting before they would acquiesce to vice-presidential bids at presidential conventions in 1920 and 1944, respectively.[8]

Also, it has long been accepted how well Truman did in continuing the progressive spirit of Franklin Roosevelt's New Deal approach and World War II aims during the first three years of his seven in the White House. Even before his surprise re-election in 1948, he was putting his own stamp firmly on presidential leadership through such things as the Truman Doctrine, North Atlantic Treaty Organization, Marshall Plan, and Korean War.[9]

Similarly, Arthur shocked supporters and foes alike when he became a leading proponent of civil service reform after personally prospering in Republican ranks as a beneficiary of the Spoils System. His nurturing of the Pendleton Act in 1883 angered old political friends and delighted former reformist foes, etching him a foothold among presidential overachievers. Unfortunately, by alienating his only base of conservative backers, Arthur as reformer never really had a chance for election in his own right in 1884. He was denied the Republican nomination that eventually went to the controversial James G. Blaine, who proceeded to become the first GOP presidential loser since the Civil War. Blaine fell to Democrat Grover Cleveland by just one percent of the popular vote and 219–182 in the Electoral College vote.[10]

Unlike Arthur, Ford would get to run as an incumbent in 1976, but his alienation of ultra-conservatives among Republicans, his connection to Nixon, and the taint of his pardon were all too fresh in the nation's psyche to provide him much of a chance, no matter who he was running against. Thus, a little-known former governor like Jimmy Carter was able to take advantage of the national backlash and hold off a surprising charge by Ford in the campaign's final days. That would cut Carter's final margin of victory to just two percentage points (297–240 in the deciding Electoral College) in a presidential election with the lowest voter turnout in 60 years. Apathy and timing were everything for Carter, and in the years to come the public perception of Ford would soften, and his presidency would be given more credence by pundits, historians, and political leaders alike. Chances are no Republican could have emerged victorious in 1976. "Jerry" Ford was no exception.[11]

Although much like Arthur and Truman in that he had never in his wildest dreams wanted to be president (but Speaker of the House instead), Ford had similarly responded to the call of duty when his party looked to him to replace the suddenly discredited Spiro Agnew (tax evasion) as Nixon's replacement vice president. Obviously, that was before the even more debilitating scandal of Watergate rocked the Republican Party to its core. Although among the last to accept the idea of an administration cover-up, once Ford did, there can be no denying he charted his own course and moved forward in the best way he deemed possible. Award-winning historian Jon Meacham attested to as much in his recent biography of President George H. W. Bush when he quoted Ford saying to Richard Nixon in the last days of his presidency: "No one regrets more than I do this whole tragic episode. I have deep personal sympathy for you, Mr. President, and your fine family. But I wish to emphasize that had I known what has been disclosed in reference to Watergate in the last twenty-four hours, I would not have made a number of the statements I made either as minority leader or as vice president."[12]

On the other end of the presidential spectrum, our five other accidentals all very much wanted the office. As already illustrated, no one ever enjoyed being president more than Theodore Roosevelt, and no one craved presidential power more than Lyndon Johnson. Both ascended to the White House via assassin's bullets, and both hit the ground running, embracing the reins of national leadership in respectful yet proactive ways that left little doubt who was in charge.[13]

Certainly, theirs was the fulfillment of John Tyler, the original ascender and the man prepared to establish precedent as soon as William Henry Harrison died just one month into office. Just like Tyler in 1841, the first Roosevelt in 1901 and the second Johnson in 1963 were ready when only a heartbeat away from their date with tragic destiny, and it's easy to imagine they would have both reacted exactly like Tyler, setting the same, emphatic standard if they had been first. After all, as their biographers so clearly illustrated, both entertained presidential aspirations long before assassins made them reality.[14]

In the same way, while not to the dominant, out-front level of a New York governor (Roosevelt) or a Senate majority leader (Johnson), both Andrew Johnson and Millard Fillmore displayed tendencies designed to elevate their political stock in their most aspirational moments, better positioning themselves to become national candidates before presidential deaths in office unexpectedly did the trick. Both left office believing they deserved a much better fate than being relegated to also-ran incumbents in the eyes of the political rank-and-file of those days.[15] Amazingly rehabilitated in his own state, Johnson would represent Tennessee again in the Senate in 1875, and Fillmore would actually allow his name to be put in nomination again as a third party presidential candidate of the anti–Catholic Know-Nothings in 1856, an election in which the former president actually carried one state, Maryland—the only state originally founded as a colony of religious tolerance for England's Roman Catholic minority. How's that for accidental irony?[16]

21

Accidental Similarities

"If you are as happy entering the White House as I shall feel exiting it, you are a happy man indeed."—James Buchanan, 1861

Whether ranked, graded, or grouped, the nine presidents who rose to the nation's highest office in unelected fashion had a number of similarities other than their non-traditional route to the White House. For instance, four of the nine survived assassination attempts themselves. Ford, in fact, survived two in California, both by women. The first occurred in early September 1975, when Lynette "Squeaky" Fromme tried to shoot him in Sacramento. Later that same month, a second woman, Sarah Jane Moore, attempted to do the same thing in San Francisco. Ever since, most U.S. presidents have donned bulletproof vests under their clothing whenever attending outdoor events.[1]

The irony that the only two would-be women presidential assassins in U.S. history would both make attempts on the life of Gerald Ford, one of the best-liked chief executives ever on both sides of the political aisle, and less than a month apart, is one of those hard-to-believe historical facts—what one recent writer termed "strange indeed." Thankfully, neither was able to add her name to the likes of John Wilkes Booth, Charles Guiteau, Leon Czolgosz, and Lee Harvey Oswald, and both were released from prison following Ford's death at age 93 in 2006.

Thankfully, despite being targets of at least four assassination attempts or plots, none of our accidental presidents have been victims so far of the kind of national tragedies that brought four to office. In recounting the other two attempts, we have already detailed Truman's 1950 brush with assassination. The two Puerto Rican Nationalists who made that attempt (with one dying and the other going to prison for three decades) were obviously ill-advised, considering Truman, probably more than any other president, advocated Puerto Rico's right to determine its own, official relationship with the mainland U.S. Unlike Theodore Roosevelt, for instance, who wielded a Big Stick when it came to Latin American and Caribbean diplomacy, including support for the annexation of Puerto Rico, Truman authorized Free Associate State status for the island with autonomy in 1952. That was later confirmed by a vote of the islanders and remains the relationship Puerto Rico has enjoyed with the U.S. ever since—a statehood movement having never materialized.[2]

Theodore Roosevelt's encounter with assassination actually occurred after he had been president, while running again as a third party candidate in 1912. A German immigrant brandishing a Colt revolver, John Schrank, fired the shot that struck TR in the chest while en route to a speaking engagement in Milwaukee, Wisconsin. Exhibiting the machismo he was known for, Roosevelt famously went ahead and delivered his speech anyway—actually waiting an hour before seeking a doctor's care. Luckily, the bullet had to pass through his

Although the target of assassination attempts and the subject of ridicule for pardoning Richard Nixon, Gerald Ford did enjoy a few moments of adulation as president, including this Alabama campaign stop with controversial Governor George Wallace and legendary football coach Paul "Bear" Bryant (Library of Congress Prints and Photographs Division—Reproduction Number DIG-ppmsca-08527).

metal glasses case and the folded pages of his prepared speech before striking a rib, thus limiting its potential harm and allowing him to recover. Meanwhile, his would-be assassin recounted to authorities that the ghost of President William McKinley had appeared to him in a dream and ordered him to avenge McKinley's assassination by shooting his successor. Schrank was judged insane and spent the rest of his life in an institution.[3]

As for "Andy" Johnson, you are reminded that the assassination attempt on his life never materialized because his would-be assailant got cold feet. Remember the night Abraham Lincoln was shot and killed while attending Ford's Theater and Secretary of State William Seward was assaulted in his sick-bed at home; Vice President Johnson was also a target at his hotel before the co-conspirator assigned to the VP, George Atzerodt, lost his nerve. Only later were his identity and intentions revealed, and he was hanged along with three others as a result of the conspiracy organized by Booth (Lincoln's assassin), who was killed during the massive manhunt that followed.[4]

Meanwhile, the flipside of presidential assassinations might be surmised in the suspicions that surrounded Arthur and Lyndon Johnson following their own ascension due to assassinations. In Arthur's case, the fact that he was the product of a different faction in the Republican Party (the so-called Stalwarts) than his predecessor and running mate, James Garfield, briefly opened him to rumors of subversion as we have seen, especially when Garfield's assassin expressed a delusional desire to make Arthur president. Needless to say, Arthur condemned, denied, and distanced himself from such radical notions.[5]

More than eight decades later, Lyndon Johnson faced the same kind of behind-the-scenes scrutiny and conspiracy theories when John F. Kennedy was shot and killed in Dallas.

The new president immediately recognized the possibility of threats, not only to his own life, but also from rampant public suspicion. Conspiracy theories abounded—such as Russian infiltrators a year after the U.S. confronted the Soviets over putting nuclear missiles in Cuba; or assassins working for Cuban dictator Fidel Castro, whom the CIA (with JFK's supposed blessing) had reputedly conspired to eliminate first; as well as organized crime (aka "the mob") feeling the pinch of investigations brought by the Kennedy administration and supposedly taking advantage of JFK's trip to politically hostile Texas as a good time to carry out his murder. As vice president, even Johnson (like Arthur) came under suspicion. After all, there was his well-known frustration over Kennedy knocking him out of the 1960 Democratic presidential nomination and his contempt for the entire Kennedy clan and the Eastern intelligentsia from whence they came. The now-famous Warren Commission, however, found nothing to implicate anyone other than the sniper Oswald in Kennedy's assassination, a subject that still arouses conspiracy theorists and Johnson detractors.[6]

Interestingly, the first four accidental presidents all failed to gain re-election bids from the major parties, while the next four all did and were successfully re-elected. It changed with the ascendance of Theodore Roosevelt, who is now credited with changing the nature and influence of the U.S. presidency itself. After the presidencies of Tyler, Fillmore, Andrew Johnson, and Arthur, the first four accidentals, all of whom were compromised to a great extent by assertive, opposition congressional leadership, TR offered a different kind of presidency, one in which the chief executive aggressively took the reins of power in ways not seen since the days of Andrew Jackson. TR's stamp on the office relegated Congress to a more secondary existence in the federal hierarchy than had been the case throughout much of the 19th century and especially since the Civil War, and made it easier for the remaining accidental presidents to assert themselves in the future, including the cost-cutting Coolidge, the Cold War-fighting Truman, and the socially conscious LBJ.[7] Only with Ford's pardoning of his tarnished predecessor, an act deemed too blatant to overcome, was the run of re-elected accidentals stopped in 1976.[8]

Another similarity of note among the nine included the way Chester Arthur and Calvin Coolidge became Western enthusiasts, never to the level of Theodore Roosevelt, the recognized leader of America conservation and Western parks, but important advocates nonetheless. This became especially true after Arthur vacationed in Yellowstone, the nation's first national park, and Coolidge established his Western White House in the Black Hills of South Dakota during the summer of 1927, the getaway where he announced his intention not to seek re-election a second time in 1928.[9]

Three of the accidental presidents also toured Europe after leaving office. Fillmore, Roosevelt, and Truman all enjoyed the pomp of touring with their wives as recognized former heads of state. In Fillmore's case, he even had an improbable audience with the Pope, despite his anti–Catholic leanings, and a shared visit with fellow former President Martin Van Buren to the British House of Commons. Meanwhile, the crown heads of Europe treated TR like royalty just a few years before they would go to war with each other in World War I. While in Europe, former President Roosevelt would conveniently even represent the U.S. government at a royal funeral following the death of England's King Edward VII.[10]

Ironically, two of the accidental presidents were also the only U.S. chief executives ever to have the term "traitor" attached to their legacies. For John Tyler, of course, this occurred 17 years after his leaving the White House, when he endorsed Virginia's leaving the Union to join the Confederate States of America. At about that same time, Andrew Johnson was judged a traitor by his home state and region when he chose to remain a sitting U.S. senator, the only one from the South when Tennessee seceded from the Union along with the other Confederate states. For 50 years after his death in 1862, Congress refused to erect any kind of presidential memorial at Tyler's grave and, as previously reported, Johnson was hung in effigy by Tennesseans when he chose to remain in Washington at the start of the Civil War.[11]

Three accidentals were faced with trying to bring the country back from legendary governmental corruption when they ascended from the vice presidency. Republicans Coolidge and Ford had to stabilize their administrations after the two worst political scandals in American history—Teapot Dome and Watergate, respectively—misconduct so damning that the legacies of Presidents Harding and Nixon will forever be stained regardless of any good they accomplished. Add to that decades of abuse via the corrupt patronage of the Spoils System that accompanied Arthur to the White House, including by his own New York Republicans, and you have a sense of why his transformation to reform was so surprising once he moved away from his past via the Pendleton Act.[12]

As established, at least two of the accidental presidents owe their emergence to the impact of dramatic, nationally exposed events. Coolidge was little-known outside of New England before he backed Boston's mayor and embattled police commissioner as Massachusetts governor during the city's famous police strike of 1919. By adopting the precedent that "there is no right to strike against public safety," he captured the country's attention and admiration. In no less dramatic fashion, Andrew Johnson's already acknowledged choice to remain at his senatorial post in Washington when every other Southern legislator headed home in 1861, established the East Tennessean as a hero in the Northern states and an obvious candidate for future laurels within the Lincoln administration.[13]

To a lesser extent, Harry Truman's heading of a 1940 Senate committee charged with policing malfeasance in the defense industry during the pre-war lead-up to World War II also brought the previously little-known Missouri senator to the nation's attention. Before that, congressional colleagues had ridiculed him for his association with machine politics and Kansas City's infamous big city boss, Tom Pendergast, a relationship that got Truman into local politics, for which he was indebted, but one he made sure he was never beholden to for corrupt purposes.[14]

Indeed, Truman's connection to a political machine closely resembled that of Arthur, the beneficiary of Roscoe Conkling's Stalwart machine in New York. Arthur unashamedly rode Conkling's coattails to probably the best unelected political job in the country in the 1870s, the collectorship for the Port of New York, a powerful, seven-year position that made the future president a player in state and national politics without benefit of any elected office. Ironically, a controversy brought on by another president, Rutherford B. Hayes, made an example of Arthur amid reports of out-of-control patronage at the Port. However, removing Conkling's protégé from his lucrative position only increased Arthur's Republican visibility and prominence.[15]

No less than three of our pre–1900 accidental presidents also had to face intense congressional pressure while in office—and equally ironically, all from the political parties that brought them to presidential power. Tyler, Andrew Johnson, and Arthur, in fact, all became lame duck incumbents as the result of views and policies that differed dramatically from their party majority in the House and Senate—Tyler in conflict with the Whigs and both Johnson and Arthur with Republicans. Although an avowed Democrat, our first Johnson president briefly switched his partisan allegiance at the start of the Civil War to prolong his political life, a transition he would be ill-suited to preserve once Lincoln was gone, leading to impeachment proceedings.[16]

Tyler and Roosevelt also exhibited a similar willingness to take international matters into their own hands when faced with recalcitrant political powers or processes. That was evident in the corners Tyler cut in the last days of his administration to push Texas annexation, and in TR's behind-the-scenes intrigue to ensure Panamanian resistance to Columbia when he was dead set on building the Panama Canal. Undoubtedly, other presidents (especially modern ones) and their administrations have resorted to covert action to suit undercover purposes—see Dwight Eisenhower/Shah of Iran, John Kennedy/Bay of Pigs, Ronald Reagan/Iran-Contra—but there's no doubt that our Virginia squire and New York Knickerbocker, about four generations apart, conspired in regard to Texas and Panama, and were both mighty glad they did, reaping historical credit ever since.[17]

In addition, Tyler was similar to the first Roosevelt in the way they survived tragic accidents while residents of the White House. You will recall Tyler's brush with death came aboard the warship *Princeton*, when a new cannon on display for a contingent of assembled dignitaries exploded on its third firing, killing the secretaries of State and Navy as well as Tyler's future father-in-law.[18]

Meanwhile, Roosevelt survived a bad carriage accident in Pittsfield, Massachusetts, while president in which a Secret Service agent was killed. Although thrown onto the pavement when an onrushing trolley struck the carriage in which he was riding, TR's legendary toughness enabled him to keep a Midwestern speaking tour just a few days later. Eventually, however, his trip had to be interrupted by his need for emergency surgery in Indianapolis, Indiana, the result of an abscess that had formed on the president's leg due to the accident.[19]

One of those uncommon people who reshaped the politics of his time, TR also ushered in the progressive era at the expense of the boss-driven leadership that had become commonplace in America in the latter stages of the 19th century. But his dramatic efforts to influence the Republican Party also led to its breakup and departure from national leadership for almost a decade—just one of several examples of political change wrought by this group of accidental presidents. Along with the first Roosevelt's politics-altering career, the second Johnson effectively brought an end to what had been the Democratic Party's Solid South ever since the Civil War with his equally well-documented efforts on behalf of African American civil rights in the 1960s. LBJ even said so when he admitted his Civil Rights Act of 1964 and Voting Rights Act of 1965 would sacrifice traditionally Democratic Southern states to the Republican Party for the foreseeable future, which it did and has continued to do ever since.[20]

Lesser known but in much the same way, Fillmore's personal intolerance of immigrants and Catholics, and his Southern-leaning, Southern voter-aimed stance supporting a tougher Fugitive Slave Law as part of the Compromise of 1850 would diminish the Whig Party in Northern eyes and lead to its replacement by the Republican Party less than a decade later. Likewise, Andrew Johnson's rapid reconciliation efforts on behalf of the defeated Southern states were in such conflict with the radical (and even moderate) objectives of the Republican majority then in Congress as to actually limit (or stall) Reconstruction following the long and bitter Civil War. The resulting political chasm that led to our nation's first presidential impeachment proceedings reflected the ongoing sectional divide that would last a century, maintaining the social animosity of racism and Jim Crow segregation in the South, as well as a rise in partisan identification that has become increasingly detrimental to our democratic system (even as the major parties flipped ideologically).[21]

Two accidental presidents never attended college—Fillmore and Andrew Johnson, who actually never attended a single day of school at any level.[22] Tyler, Fillmore, and Arthur all succeeded generals—Harrison, Taylor, and Garfield, respectively—and Theodore Roosevelt, Coolidge, and Arthur remain the only three presidents to take the oath of office in private homes—TR, the youngest president at 42, in the front parlor of a personal friend in Buffalo, New York (the city where President McKinley had been shot and eventually died); Coolidge while visiting his family home place in Plymouth Notch, Vermont, with his father, a local notary and justice of the peace, presiding; and Arthur at his own home in New York City.[23]

In an age when blue-collar, indentured apprenticeships at an early age were common, especially among families with limited means, both the first Johnson and Fillmore would be tasked with similar starts in life when they were consigned to the tailoring and cloth-making trades, respectively.[24] In addition, at least two of our accidental presidents were related, if the later of those is to be believed, as Truman always claimed great-great-great nephew-hood with the original, precedent-setting Tyler of over a century before—a claim, however, later disputed by Truman's primary biographer.[25]

Another interesting, family-based common bond among our accidentals would be three of the five White House weddings involving presidential daughters that have taken place in the Washington mansion's East Room. Those were Elizabeth Tyler's 1842 wedding to William Walker, Alice Roosevelt's much-publicized wedding to Congressman Nicholas Longworth in 1906, and Lynda Bird Johnson's wedding to Charles Rabb in 1967. While White House Rose Garden weddings have happened frequently among families of sitting presidents, the only other East Room weddings involving presidential daughters were those of Nellie Grant in 1874 and Jessie Wilson in 1913—daughters of Ulysses Grant and Woodrow Wilson.[26]

Deaths among family members of the accidental presidents also tragically happened to Coolidge (son), Tyler (wife), and Arthur (wife) either right before or during their presidential terms. Along with Woodrow Wilson, Tyler remains the only president not only to suffer through the death of his first wife in office, but also to wed a second while still in the White House.[27]

Arthur, though plagued by Bright's disease, would be one of five of the nine accidental presidents to die after a stroke—the others being Tyler, Fillmore, Johnson, and Ford. Also, six of the accidentals would share in the most famous presidential curse—the "Curse of Tippecanoe," which apparently had its origins in Native-American lore—the result of General William Henry Harrison pillaging and setting fire to the large Indian village of Prophetstown following his 1811 victory at the Battle of Tippecanoe in disputed territory (now West Central Indiana). First reported in Ripley's "Believe It or Not," the Shawnee Chieftain The Prophet supposedly put a deadly curse on Harrison that day for his devastating orders, which in turn was apparently passed on to all future U.S. presidents elected in years ending in zero. If we are to believe such things, seven of our first eight accidentals all became president as a result, beginning with Tyler, who obviously succeeded the suddenly deceased Harrison (1840) just a month into his presidency; and joining him would be Andrew Johnson, who succeeded Lincoln (1860); Arthur, who succeeded James Garfield (1880); Theodore Roosevelt, who succeeded McKinley (1900); Coolidge, who succeeded Harding (1920); Truman, who succeeded Franklin Roosevelt (1940); and Lyndon Johnson, who succeeded Kennedy (1960). Legend has it the curse, after lasting over 100 years, was finally put to rest following the election of Ronald Reagan (1980), who did survive the last serious presidential assassination attempt in our nation's history in 1981.[28]

22

Party Abandonment
or Abdication

"We have called by different names brethren of the same principle. We are all Republicans, we are all Federalists."—Thomas Jefferson, 1801

Instances of party affiliations gone bad were fairly commonplace among our accidental presidents. At least three—John Tyler, Andrew Johnson, and Theodore Roosevelt—abandoned or even abdicated lifelong party credentials in the face of intra-party opposition or outright conflict once in the White House.[1]

Tyler's case came about as a result of him souring on the autocratic tendencies of President Andrew Jackson in the 1830s. This caused him to align with the Whigs, a move that made him conveniently available as a Southern complement to General William Henry Harrison on the surprising Whig ticket of 1840. It was a choice that would to be second-guessed repeatedly by Whig leaders in the months and years ahead, especially once Harrison contracted pneumonia at his inaugural and died a month later. No shrinking violet when it came to his surprising succession opportunity and precedent-setting assumption of presidential power, Tyler would also prove an uncontrollable chief executive and states' rights advocate, much to the chagrin of Henry Clay and other congressional Whigs. After all, the new president had never actually changed his political spots, only his party. Instead of the more malleable Harrison, who had been nominated for president over Clay because of anti–Mason elements at the Whig Convention who refused to countenance Clay's Masonic membership, the party regulars were left to work with a wolf in sheep's clothing, an anti-bank, anti-tariff Southerner who had recently ingratiated himself into their midst because of his own, personal falling out with Jacksonian overreach.[2]

At 68, Harrison was the oldest nominee (and president) before Ronald Reagan in 1980, but despite his age and tumultuous personal history of battles and dealings with the Indian tribes of the old Northwest, the former general, territorial governor (Indiana), and senator (Ohio) enjoyed the confidence of the newer Western states—Ohio, Indiana, Michigan, and Illinois—as well as the Whig brain trust, which looked to guide his presidency once 12 years of Democratic, Jacksonian control had finally been stopped. Imagine the consternation of those same Whig congressional leaders, who had waited so long to be in charge, when Tyler, Harrison's stand-in, proved a less than willing legislative partner. To quote a young Whig of the time, Abraham Lincoln:

> It is true the victory of 1840 did not produce the happy results anticipated; but it is equally true the unfortunate death of General Harrison was the cause of the failure. It was not the election of General Harrison that was expected to produce happy effects but the measures to be adopted by his

administration. By means of his death and the unexpected course of his successor, those measures were never adopted.[3]

Instead of going along with the party line and resurrecting the national bank that Jackson had taken great pride in doing away with, Tyler stayed true to his Democratic roots by refusing to accept his new party's agenda. Twice he vetoed bills that would have resurrected the Bank of the United States, causing most of his inherited Cabinet to resign in protest. And, of course, Tyler's pursuit of Texas annexation was not something Clay and his Whig cohorts in the Senate were in favor of, and they successfully postponed it until his term was almost over. By that point, however, admission of the Lone Star State had become a foregone conclusion with the election and incoming presidency of expansionist James K. Polk. Before he was through, Tyler had vetoed ten Whig bills, and his once-friendly relations with Clay were completely on the rocks—so much so, in fact, that the contemptuous Kentuckian was among those who sought to have him impeached in 1842, a move that never got out of the House of Representatives.[4]

Meanwhile, the first President Johnson's switch of his support from Democrat to Republican was less controversial than his notorious abandonment of his state and section at the opening of the Civil War. While simultaneous, one was merely a by-product of the other. With the Republican administration of Lincoln leading the North (or Union) and Tennessee joining its sister Southern states in secession, there were only two ways a Southern senator could go in 1861. Unlike most of the Southern political and military notables of his day, including most famously Robert E. Lee, who was offered command of the Union Army only to side with his home state, Virginia.... Andrew Johnson chose the Union.[5]

Ostracized as a result by his fellow Tennesseans and Southerners, Johnson would eventually accept as necessary the Republican policy of emancipation for the Southern slaves without relinquishing his own prejudices when it came to White supremacy. Later, like Tyler, he would find himself constantly at odds with the party that brought him to power as vice president. Once the war was over, Lincoln dead, and Reconstruction policy at stake, he would issue 29 vetoes as a Southern-sympathizing president (15 of which were overridden by the Republican Congress) in a return to his political roots. Finally, after being impeached by the House and coming within one vote of being removed by the Senate, he returned to the Democratic Party, remarkably being elected a Tennessee senator again in 1875, the same year he died.[6]

Perhaps no abandonment of party by a president or former president was more consequential to American political history than that of Theodore Roosevelt in 1912. Always a Republican and from a family of committed New York City Republicans, TR was also a conscientious reformer from the day he set foot in the New York State Assembly onward. One of the youngest assemblymen ever, it was also natural that he would grow into one of the country's leading "Progressives" when that new political brand began to manifest itself at the start of the twentieth century. Never one to turn his back on the party of his birth, however, he would remain a committed Republican as long as it added a progressive wing, and as both president and a hugely popular former president, it was his assumption that Republicans would follow his lead into a progressive future. When that did not happen under the leadership of his handpicked but more pliable successor, William Howard Taft, his loyalty became strained. That became especially true once the Republican Party, which he had led kicking and screaming towards reform in the new century, recoiled once he was out of office and the country in 1909.[7]

Although intending to continue the progressive agenda of his mentor and friend, Taft proved much less a patron reformer and much more a regular Republican, especially when doing anything else would have put him in conflict with the traditional party leadership. Unlike his predecessor, Taft was a committed reformer only to a point—the point at which the constant reformist pace of the Roosevelt years needed to be slowed somewhat—and he even said so upon being elected.[8]

Once Roosevelt was back from the "Dark Continent" of Africa and the bright lights of Europe, however, Taft's slower pace was obviously not something he wished to come home to. Upon discovering this reality on his return, he wrote:

> It was very bitter for me to see the Republican Party, when I had put it back on the Abraham Lincoln basis, in three years turned over to a combination of big financiers and unscrupulous political bosses.... My nomination would have meant putting the Republican Party definitely on an anti-boss and progressive basis. This was why the bosses preferred my defeat to Republican victory.[9]

The defeat he was talking about came when he and his progressive followers were denied his re-nomination at the 1912 Republican Convention thanks to the inner workings of the regular party leadership. They wound up walking out as a result. The resulting party split famously assured Democrat Woodrow Wilson's victory, with TR finishing second and the incumbent Taft a distant third. Conservatism has been in vogue in the Republican Party ever since, making it much more appropriately the Party of Coolidge or Reagan (and Trump) than the Party of Lincoln, and most certainly not the Party of Theodore Roosevelt.[10]

TR's defection was another classic example of party abandonment or abdication, depending on which side of the issue one is coming from.[11] There have undoubtedly been other party renouncements among our duly elected chief executives, but there's no doubt at least three of our accidental presidents were persona non grata in their elected parties by the time their presidential careers were over.

Did any of our accidental presidents find themselves personally at odds with any of the others in this select company party-wise? Not likely, you say, given the way they have been spaced out through history—at least one to two decades apart for the last century and three-quarters. On closer examination, however, there was one instance, when Chester Arthur and Theodore Roosevelt, both New York Republicans although a generation apart, were bequeathed a grudge not of their making.

It just so happened that when Arthur was collector for the Port of New York—that dream job he enjoyed as the result of political patronage, the one that President Rutherford B. Hayes intended to take away from him as an example of his crackdown on the Spoils System—the man initially positioned to be his replacement was TR's father, Theodore Roosevelt, Sr. The year was 1877, and TR would have been an idealistic college sophomore who witnessed his father becoming a political pawn in the ongoing struggle between Roscoe Conkling's Stalwarts and James Blaine's Half-Breeds within the Republican Party. Unfortunately, that also meant the younger Roosevelt had to endure exposure of the fact that his well-to-do father had avoided the Union Army and the Civil War by paying for a stand-in, an acceptable though somewhat demeaning personal choice that had always plagued TR's patriotism and martial spirit. That and other rumors were brought by the Conkling machine to undermine Hayes' selection and to keep Arthur in his prestigious post, which it did for another year. In the meantime, however, Theodore Sr.'s stressful candidacy combined with undetected colon cancer sentenced him to an early death at age 47, something historians believe resonated with the young TR, making him "a bitter enemy of the Stalwarts, including Arthur," at an early age.[12]

In addition, it turns out that John Tyler's very open disagreements with the party that accidentally brought him to power, the ill-fated Whigs, did initiate cross-purposes for the two accidentals whose presidential timelines were the closest and have been the most often connected. Following Tyler's opposition and veto of the Whigs' first legislation to come across his desk as president, their greatly anticipated return of the Bank of the United States that Jackson had so rudely done away with a decade before, the second item on their 1841 agenda was a new tariff. As fate would have it, the author of that economic protectionist legislation was none other than New York Congressman Millard Fillmore, then chairman of the House Ways and Means Committee, and just as accidentally, the last Whig president a decade later. As with the Bank, Tyler would veto Fillmore's original tariff bill.

A year later, however, in 1842, Fillmore managed to rewrite and steer through Congress a compromise tariff that surprisingly met with Tyler's approval, the one acquiescence by this anti-protectionist, free trade president that historians have found hard to explain given his vetoes on the rest of the Whigs' legislative agenda. Among their theories: (1) because of "desperate revenue needs" by the federal government at that time; (2) because of his desire to gain support among Northern commercial interests in hopes of a re-election bid in 1844; or (3) because he had grown weary of constant conflict with the Whigs, which had included calls for his impeachment.[13] Or perhaps the déjà vu of the two accidental Whig presidents actually connecting legislatively was just a coincidence of history that connects their sagas even more.

23

Racial Ramifications

"The Negroes are now Americans. Their ancestors came here years ago against their will, and this is their only country and only flag."
—William Howard Taft, 1909

Race and race relations, those related, overriding issues that have defined so much of our national story, were as much a factor for a few of our accidental presidents as anything that defined their presidential tenures. For at least four, it was a crucial component in judging their administrations and accomplishments, as well as in formulating their individual presidential rankings. After all, it has always been America's elephant in the room, so for Millard Fillmore and Harry Truman as well as both Johnsons, please consider how much it affected the way each was judged in his own time and how they have been remembered ever since.[1]

The product of a Southern-biased home in Border State Missouri, Harry Truman grew up in a family that had owned slaves in previous generations and one that actually reviled Abraham Lincoln. That's right, while most of the nation came to revere Honest Abe, Truman's mother and grandmother detested his memory while venerating Southern heroes like Robert E. Lee.

As a result, young Harry was bound to grow up with some racial prejudice. While never the outspoken defender of segregation that so many of his Southern contemporaries were, Truman no doubt had his bigoted moments throughout an early adulthood while tending his father's farm; during a series of failed business ventures and investments; when finally excelling as a sergeant in the segregated U.S. Army of World War I; and later while rising through the boss-driven, all-White world of Kansas City politics in the 1920s and 1930s.[2]

As recounted in several places in the 2005 book *The White House Looks South*, by William Leuchtenberg:

> Truman literally learned at his mother's knee to share the South's view of the "War Between The States" [Civil War]. He acquired from his family and the Jim Crow school he attended an abiding belief in White supremacy. He thought nothing of using words like darkies and once admitted, "I was raised amidst some violently prejudiced Southerners." He made no effort to conceal his racist convictions. He did not desire to mingle with Blacks and he resented efforts to compel integration. Nor did he see any reason to apologize for his views.[3]

And yet, in the same book Leuchtenberg admitted, "Despite Truman's Southern affinity, Blacks in Jackson County [Missouri] came to regard him as a just man," one who expanded job opportunities for African Americans, and one who received 88 percent of the African American vote in Kansas City in the 1934 Missouri Senate race. Candidate Truman was even opposed by the Ku Klux Klan, while politically astute enough to put aside acquired racial prejudices in order to build a staunchly pro-civil rights record by the time he succeeded Franklin Roosevelt as president in 1945.[4] That's when his most important action on behalf of racial equality took place—an action so profound, in fact, that it would become a major landmark in America's long struggle with civil rights.

While initially viewed as a friend of Southern White values much more than the liberal icon he replaced, Truman proved friendlier to African Americans than they expected. He re-funded the Fair Employment Practice Committee, started a President's Committee on Civil Rights, and even spoke at a huge NAACP rally at the Lincoln Memorial in 1947, a speech that Civil Rights Movement activist Walter White termed "the hardest hitting and most uncompromising speech on the subject of race" that any American president had delivered up to that time.[5]

It was all a precursor to what he would do on July 26, 1948, in the midst of his campaign for another term and despite the threat of a walkout by Southern Democrats at that summer's party convention, which did occur. On that day, President Truman issued Executive Order 9981, which abolished racial discrimination in the U.S. military and eventually ended segregation among all United States Armed Forces. By accepting the political risk of civil rights and integrating an institution as far-reaching as the U.S. military, Truman put the concept of racial equality on the national radar like never before.[6] With so much else going on during his presidency, especially the advent of the Cold War, it has been hard for historians to confer on him as much credit as he probably deserves for being the first modern president to truly address African American Civil Rights.[7]

One Black politician in South Carolina went so far as to state, "No American citizen has gone farther nor stood his grounds firmer on behalf of civil and other rights for Negroes than President Truman," and, indeed, it was Truman's intention to continue his proactive civil rights efforts in his second term until confronted by the Korean War. Most pundits now feel North Korea's surprise invasion of the South in 1950 inadvertently put a lot of those intentions on hold, forcing Truman to divert priorities almost totally to the Cold War and communism's global escalation. With his successor, Dwight Eisenhower, avoiding the issue, African American Civil Rights were put on hold until the late 1950s, when racial frustrations re-surfaced in Little Rock, Arkansas. That's where a group of nine African American students in 1957 legally integrated Little Rock Central High School over the objections of the Arkansas governor and the intimidation tactics of local White citizens, forcing President Eisenhower to send federal troops to ensure peace.[8]

Into this breach of simmering civil rights controversy, Senate Majority Leader Lyndon Johnson, a Texan with the same kind of Southern, biased ancestry as Truman, would surprisingly address the issue of civil rights that same year. Aiming for the presidency, LBJ knew that any Southern politician with designs on the White House would have to break away from the stereotype of race, "the barrier of opposition to civil rights legislation" that had made it virtually impossible for any Southerner, no matter how good his credentials, to be considered for the nation's highest office. There was simply no way he could ever become a national contender without distancing himself from his Southern political roots and voting record.[9]

To do so, Johnson would have to move against the likes of Georgia's Richard Russell, leader of the Senate's cadre of Deep South mainstays when it came to blocking civil rights legislation and one of his personal mentors. With only 25 percent of African Americans registered to vote nationwide and much less than that in the Deep South, LBJ backed an effort by the administration of President Eisenhower to protect Blacks' right to vote (minus the more volatile school desegregation issue) by ending such things as literacy tests and poll taxes designed to inhibit African American voter participation. Such practices had been prevalent in the South since the end of Reconstruction in 1877. As "architect" of the 1957 Civil Rights Act, the senior senator from Texas would be hailed as "the first Southern Democratic leader since the Civil War to be a serious candidate for his party's presidential nomination" by the *New York Times*, signaling his "arrival as a national political figure."[10]

Unfortunately for Johnson, his 1957 civil rights breakthrough (along with another pur-portedly strengthened civil rights bill less than three years later) would not propel him to the 1960 Democratic nomination as hoped, thanks to the efficiency, money, and charisma of Senator John F. Kennedy's campaign.[11] And in all honesty, the legislation proved not all that beneficial to African American voters either. Although the new legislation seemed to indicate a growing federal commitment to the cause of civil rights, the benefits were very limited, and by 1960, Black voting had only improved by three percent.[12]

But to LBJ's eternal credit, he didn't stop there. Although no longer tainted by the stigma of being merely a regional candidate following his 1957 and 1960 acts, he did not rest on those laurels when John Kennedy was assassinated in Dallas. While it might have been easy (or at least assumed) for a Southerner like Johnson to assume the presidency and largely ignore civil rights, especially after he had already stuck his neck out twice for Black progress, LBJ recommitted to the civil rights cause Kennedy had advocated before he was killed. Invoking the memory of his suddenly idealized predecessor, Johnson did

Lyndon Johnson, a Southerner, took up the challenge of racial equality when he became president. A year later, he rammed through Congress the first of two landmark civil rights bills, the signing of which was captured in this photograph with Civil Rights Movement icon Martin Luther King, Jr., directly behind the president (LBJ Library photograph by Cecil Stoughton).

what no other Southerner or normal politician would have dared by not only passing tougher civil rights legislation in 1964, but by upping the ante one year later when leaders of the Civil Rights Movement were still calling for stronger federal enforcement of voting rights. "In retrospect," he gave them what they wanted and our haunted nation required by 1965, but as he predicted at the time, the South has not voted Democratic since.[13]

Probably it only happened by evoking Kennedy's memory, but it nonetheless took guts to achieve. Who would have thought a Southern-born president would be second only to Abraham Lincoln when it comes to what he did for African Americans? Granted it was something that needed to be done and once-and-for-all removed from the 1960s' congressional plate, and there was no legislator better than Lyndon Johnson at passing legislation. And granted, it allowed LBJ to move on to the other social issues he really wanted to tackle as part of his Great Society program in hopes of replicating (or even surpassing) the Social Security and work-related legacy of his New Deal hero, Franklin Roosevelt. Regardless of why he got it done, Lyndon Johnson is the president on whose watch, 100 years after the Civil War and Black emancipation, finally got it done.[14] Actually, if Border State native Harry Truman and Texan LBJ are rightfully regarded as the first Southern presidents since Andrew Johnson, it is amazing how they were both able to overcome their lineage in order to take meaningful steps for racial equality.[15]

Meanwhile, no such ability or similar thoughts would have crossed the mind of our first president named Johnson. While both Truman and LBJ were obviously able to move past very prejudiced upbringings to initiate milestone advancements for African Americans, there's no way Andrew Johnson would have entertained such ideas in 1865, when he succeeded Lincoln. It was a reach for him just to acquiesce to the fact that slaves would be freed. For one of the poorest White Southerners, whose only social solace growing up was the knowledge that at least he would always be one step up the scale from Blacks, the idea of doing anything more for racial equality would have been unfathomable. There's no doubt Andrew Johnson was a bigot, as were all Southern-born presidents before him, each of whom owned slaves. His idea of Reconstruction had to include White supremacy and Southern Whites reassuming the roles of leadership throughout the Southern states as they re-entered the Union. In essence, that was the value at the heart of his problems with the Radical Republicans. While they were ready to enforce Southern compliance and even fealty to the notion of Black freedmen suddenly getting a fair shake and equal treatment throughout the unrepentant South, our first President Johnson had never bought into that kind of makeover. As he publicly stated, his was and always would be a White man's government.[16]

Such a concept, though unspoken, was probably imbedded in the persona of Millard Fillmore as well. How else to explain a Northern-born president who did not hesitate to lean South before the Civil War? We know President Fillmore consistently referenced Andrew Jackson's threat of armed force during the Nullification Crisis of 1832 to quell rebellious South Carolinians intent on declaring the Tariff of 1828 null and void in their state. Theirs was the states' rights doctrine of John C. Calhoun that would foreshadow that state's secessionist actions 28 years later. That would also be Fillmore's reasoning in demanding compliance by any would-be "nullifiers" of the new federal Fugitive Slave Law. With California entering the Union as a free state, another essential part of the Compromise of 1850, Fillmore's strict enforcement was viewed as a major concession to Southern voters for his re-election hopes. His unyielding adherence to the law, in fact, would prove anathema to Northerners not happy about being forced to help catch, incarcerate, and return runaway slaves seeking freedom.[17]

Rightly or wrongly, Fillmore's aggressive approach to the fugitive slave issue came to be regarded in the North as his endorsement of slavery. It rubbed his fellow Northerners the wrong way, setting him up to be the last lame duck incumbent of the ill-fated Whig Party. Known for being anti–Catholic and anti-immigrant, two beliefs he would later openly endorse as a third party candidate of the Know-Nothings, his unyielding support of stiff penalties for anyone abetting fugitive slaves along the aptly named "Underground Railroad" became a major theme in the spread of anti-slavery sentiment throughout the pre-war North.[18]

It was one more ramification on the road to war between the sections, a road that had twisted and turned with racial inequality ever since the nation's founding, and a road that would continue even after the bloodiest war in U.S. history. Unlike Harry Truman and Lyndon Johnson, Millard Fillmore and Andrew Johnson could never be accused of working to solve the racial divide, but there's no doubt they, too, had a primary role in the ongoing story of race in America. Like Truman and LBJ, they too brought the seemingly never-ending issue of race to the forefront of national debate. But unlike their twentieth-century counterparts, Fillmore and Johnson—one a hands-on Northerner, the other a hands-off Southerner—would approach it from the seamy side of their own prejudices and political experience, not based on what the nation needed.

24

Alternate Agendas

"This country needs and unless I mistake its temper, demands bold, persistent experimentation."—Franklin Delano Roosevelt, 1932

Following Woodrow Wilson and Warren Harding, Calvin Coolidge wanted a return to normalcy for his country in more ways than one when he unexpectedly became president with the news of Harding's death in San Francisco on August 2, 1923. On the other side of the nation—in the simplest of oath-taking ceremonies, in the wee hours of the next day—and by the light of an oil lamp in the parlor of his father's home, Coolidge became our 29th president in the tiny hamlet of Plymouth Notch, Vermont.[1] For those not used to Upper New England geographical jargon, a notch in New Hampshire or Vermont is a pass through the mountainous terrain of those states originally formed by glaciers. In the case of the Coolidge family, their notch was home to a tiny village of the same name, just off the beaten path of Scenic Route 100.[2]

Upon being sworn in by his father, a local justice of the peace, the new president set about rekindling the promises of normalcy that he and Harding had made as Republican running mates in the election of 1920. The country was coming off its first major excursion into international affairs after getting sucked into the wrongly named "War to End Wars" (World War I) under Wilson in 1917. Thousands of "doughboys," the informal name of the soldiers who made up the American Expeditionary Force, travelled across the Atlantic and brought about an Allied victory (including one Harry Truman) in what had otherwise become an unwinnable ordeal of trench warfare, the first major mechanized conflict in global history. When the Americans came home, it was no surprise that traditionally isolationist America was ready for a return to its good old days of "live and let live" without any further entanglements on foreign shores.[3]

Normalcy is what Harding first called it, and after agreeing to run as his vice president, Coolidge officially bought into it. Unfortunately, normalcy was not what the American electorate got from the scandal-prone Harding administration. Saddled with some less than honest associates from his Ohio days in what now might be termed a very "Trumpian Cabinet," Harding was ineffective and beset with controversy, including revelations of his two extramarital affairs (one with a neighbor and one with a minor). This was especially true when it came to getting things back to normal. That's the reason he was touring the Western United States, hoping to reconnect with the voting electorate, when sudden illness led to his totally unexpected death.[4]

Thus was Silent Cal, the man of few words, thrust into the unenviable position of still bringing the country back from the sacrifices and expenditures of World War I, while at the same time righting the ship of a scandal-riddled administration of which he was a part—and with just over a year to do so before another election. Honestly, he did so by backing away from federal programs and cutting taxes in the middle of a booming decade full of private economic growth. Coolidge did not like big government, and as Ken Burns and Lynn Novick recorded in their 2011 video history of "Prohibition," the new president "believed that government should keep its nose out of the lives of [its] citizens," a notion that obviously had appeal to a country engrossed in the Roaring Twenties, America's first decade of unabashed over-indulgence. If anything, the normalcy of doing away with constraints and spurring American finance is what Coolidge did.[5]

In much the same way, Gerald Ford, another Republican, had to return America to a level of decency when he became president in 1974. As recounted here and relived by America's "Baby Boomer" generation, the everyman from Michigan, the collegiate football hero who answered his party's call, sought a return to decency following the political and social upheaval of the Vietnam and the civil rights–dominated 1960s, and the unbelievable (and completely unnecessary) scandal foisted on the American democracy that became Watergate. Just getting past Vietnam, the Civil Rights Movement, and the administration of Richard Nixon strained American belief systems like not much else had (or at least not since the last world war, Great Depression, and Civil War). Ford's pardon of Nixon was the start of a healing process that continued with the election of Democrat Jimmy Carter in 1976,[6] but whether presidential decency will ever be achieved again remains much in doubt (now more than ever).

As for other presidential agendas that were value-driven, at least three of our other accidental chief executives should be lauded for their progressive efforts in the face of party or even historical backlash. Already we have recounted the surprising racial accomplishments of Lyndon Johnson despite his place of birth and in the face of almost 100 years of kicking our racial can down the road. Kudos were also due LBJ for his War on Poverty as part of his Great Society agenda. Although the idea of helping the nation's poorest people never gained the traction Johnson hoped, mainly because of his struggles with the Vietnam War, it at least got the nation debating programs to make things better for the poorest among us—programs conservatives have sought to abolish somehow ever since.[7]

It also begat Johnson's other signature legislation (other than civil rights), Medicare and Medicaid. Taking FDR's Social Security System a couple of steps further in 1965, the former program provided health insurance at a low monthly premium for senior Americans 65 and older, while the latter provided a safety net of hospital benefits for the poorest and disabled of any age. The tall, forceful Texan also became the first American president to address our worsening environmental problems through such things as the Water Quality and Air Quality Acts of 1965 and the Clean Water Restoration and Air Quality Acts of 1966.[8]

In similar progressive fashion, Theodore Roosevelt rather obviously went against the grain of Republican politics at the turn of the twentieth century, moving the country away from the wealth-driven age of domination by business and industry at the expense of the less fortunate mass of workers to one of reform, conservation, and anti-trust. His was a new energy and way of approaching the presidency that must have been anathema to the Rockefellers, Carnegies, and J. P. Morgans of the American financial landscape, the tycoons who were finally forced to back down when it came to the resident in the White House.[9]

In addition, TR's determined pursuit and fulfillment of the Panama Canal has to rate as one of the most beneficial developments of modern mankind, a boon not only to American interests but to the whole world. While achieved through less than ethical means, it more than justified TR's means to an end. On a more intimate level, Americans would also come to prize his advocacy and stewardship for what became our National Parks System, what documentarian Ken Burns called "America's Best Idea."[10]

Finally, what of the surprising progressivism of Chester Alan Arthur, one of our least known chief executives? To be the first to take on civil service reform in an era when to-the-victor-went-the-spoils was an accepted part of American government was an amazingly admirable goal for a system politician. To step out of his comfort zone once he ascended to the presidency and support a reformed civil service system must have shocked political friends and foes alike, and to do so knowing that such a bipartisan agenda would likely end any chances he had for re-election, should memorialize his efforts on behalf of governmental fair play. Named for Ohio Democrat George Pendleton, the Pendleton Act has since been called the "Magna Carta of U.S. civil service reform."[11]

But alas, our 21st president also signed into law the Chinese Exclusion Act of 1882 after initially vetoing its passage. Under congressional pressure, he finally agreed to a reduced version (from 20 to ten years), but once signed into law, it was renewed repeatedly through 1943—one of the longest-running acts of racist legislation in American history. Arthur would have been better served historically if he had stuck to his guns and refused to sign the Exclusion Act, which was an embarrassment by the time it was repealed during World War II with Nationalist China as an ally.[12] Maybe he would have been better remembered if he had.

25

Lasting Accomplishments and What Ifs

"There is nothing wrong with America that cannot be cured by what is right with America."—Bill Clinton, 1993

If building the Panama Canal should be viewed as Theodore Roosevelt's greatest achievement in the way it made worldwide transportation and logistics forever better, what can be viewed as the greatest accomplishments of our other accidental presidents? In LBJ's case, most Americans would assume his advancement of civil rights, but for senior citizens, both now and in the future, the social safety net of his Medicare legislation, as well as his consumer and environmental protection laws (such as cigarette labeling about the risks of tobacco and automobile safety standards), might be just as important, especially considering their impact on the nation's overall health.[1]

As for John Tyler, our first accidental chief executive whose precedent-setting assertion of vice presidential ascension was itself a milestone, Texas would have to rate as his crowning achievement, even though its admission came at the very end of his administration. Chester Arthur's initial modernization of our civil service system through the Pendleton Act undoubtedly topped his charts, as did Harry Truman's Marshall Plan, Truman Doctrine, and North American Treaty Organization (NATO), the interwoven Cold War outtakes of his extraordinarily eventful, seven-plus years in the White House. At the same time, some would argue that Truman's use of atomic bombs had more lasting implications—and based on the fact that a nuclear weapon hasn't been used since, the argument of their presence as deterrent seems plausible.[2]

As for the others, Millard Fillmore, Andrew Johnson, Calvin Coolidge, and Gerald Ford, the what-ifs of presidential power might deserve more consideration than their accomplishments. For instance, what if Fillmore had felt the same about the Compromise of 1850 as his predecessor, Zachary Taylor, the running mate whose administration had granted him national prominence but who openly opposed the Compromise? California statehood (as a free state), which occurred under Fillmore as part of the Compromise, might have earned him more lasting prestige if not for the fact that it was accompanied by a new and tougher fugitive slave concession to the South, which Fillmore embraced and determinedly executed even though it proved unpopular and threatened the very existence of his Whig Party.[3]

By the same token, what if Andrew Johnson, a Northern hero after disavowing his home state's secession by remaining in the U.S. Senate when all other congressional Southerners where heading home to support the Confederacy, had chosen not to buck and very publicly ridicule the Republican Party during Reconstruction, choosing instead to appease returning Southern states following the Civil War? Certainly he would not have faced impeachment by the House of Representatives, but would he ever have been accepted by his home state and region, where he was considered a traitor during the war? As it was, he assured himself of never being re-elected president in the reconstructed Union, but remarkably, he was re-elected to the Senate from Tennessee in 1875, a vindication of sorts that he relished.[4]

In the case of Coolidge, what if the master conservative, who slashed taxes and oversaw the elimination of deficits during boom times, had run again in 1928 instead of Herbert Hoover? Would Silent Cal have been able to avoid the pitfalls of excessive speculation as the Roaring Twenties came to a close? Would his no-nonsense approach have made any difference in stabilizing the ship of state as the nation careened towards the stock market crash of 1929 and the resulting Great Depression? Some have since blamed Coolidge as much as Hoover, but at the time it was hard to assign fault to a former president in retirement.[5]

Then there's Ford, who had credits and/or debits only touched on here, such as the Helsinki Agreement of 1975 (designed to ease U.S.–Russian tensions) and the financial bailout of New York City in 1975, and whose late charge from way behind in the 1976 presidential election almost overtook Jimmy Carter. What if Ronald Reagan had not challenged Ford's incumbency in the Republican Party that year? We can only surmise what might have happened if Ford had not pardoned President Nixon for the sins of Watergate, as well as Ford's clemency for thousands of Vietnam War draft dodgers. What would have been the effect on the electorate (and national mood) without those pardons?[6]

Other more obscure but world-shaping what-ifs were Theodore Roosevelt's pledge not to seek another consecutive term as president in 1908 (what would have been his third), a decision he regretted and rationalized by indeed running again, non-consecutively, four years later as a third party candidate, and one he undoubtedly took to his grave in 1919 at just 60 years of age.[7] Some of his descendants even believe his presence in the White House in the years preceding World War I might have forestalled the carnage of that massive and seemingly avoidable conflict. In their opinion, he was already a world-famous peacemaker and Nobel Prize winner for his successful mediation of the Russo-Japanese War in 1905, and he was on excellent terms with most of the crown heads of Europe, whose various alliances led to the dominoes of mass mobilization and war in 1914. Certainly he had far more international and diplomatic experience than the presidential winner of 1912, Woodrow Wilson, a relatively inexperienced, reform-minded governor of New Jersey, who even admitted being ill-prepared for foreign affairs.[8]

Also, what if Lyndon Johnson had not chosen to escalate the war in Vietnam? Bound by the Cold War containment doctrine to confront communism in the world whenever and wherever it reared its head, Johnson continued Kennedy's policy of support for the government of South Vietnam with material and advisers, but he also made the mistake of lying to the American people about the Gulf of Tonkin incident and of sending more and more American troops to Southeast Asia to engineer the same kind of divided stalemate that Truman and later Eisenhower had orchestrated on the Korean Peninsula.[9] The thought of being the first American president to accept wartime defeat was just not something LBJ could tolerate on his resume, so he over-escalated, looking for capitulation by the North Vietnamese in the face of overwhelming American force. Unfortunately, such capitulation never materialized, and as the jungle war dragged on, its opposition at home grew to protest levels never before seen in this country.

Bottom line: it was never winnable, as even trusted TV anchor Walter Cronkite surmised by February 27, 1968, and Johnson's image, which he had worked so assiduously to cultivate, finally came crashing down, forcing his momentous announcement the next month that he would not seek another term, just four years after cruising to landslide victory as the stand-in for John Kennedy. Just for the sake of argument, if only for a moment, take Vietnam out of LBJ's equation. In other words, allow his ledger to show only his accomplishments for civil rights, the environment, and health care, and his unfinished War on Poverty. Who knows, minus Vietnam such accomplishments might have even moved him into contention for an upper berth in our presidential pantheon.[10]

But perhaps the greatest foreign policy what-if among our accidental presidents might belong to Harry Truman—his interminably impactful 1948 decision to recognize the new nation of Israel. If surprised, don't be, because the biblical homeland of the Jews before centuries of their relocation throughout the world, and especially to Europe prior to World War II, has been a place of war and global conflict ever since. Actually, everything changed for Judaism with the rise of Germany's Adolf Hitler, a madman aiming for not only world domination in the 1930s but also elimination of the Jewish race. Eventually, it took the combined Allied power of the U.S., Great Britain, and Soviet Union to deny Hitler's goals, but his sinister genocide of the European Jews was already well underway by the time the Allied armies overran the German "Fatherland." These unspeakable atrocities, which were appropriately labeled the Holocaust, gave rise to a European exodus of Jews from their war-torn countries, many of whom understandably undertook a move back to the Middle Eastern "Holy Lands" their prophets had promised before many of their ancestors left centuries before. What they found there were more Arabs than remaining Jews, an entrenched Muslim population that had co-existed, multiplied, and also been there for centuries—the Palestinians—in a land known as Palestine.

When World War II ended, the British Protectorate that had governed Palestine was ended as the result of Great Britain's enormous war debts. Into this governmental void, the returning Jews were anxious to establish a nation of their own, despite the presence and total opposition of the Arabs who lived there and the neighboring Muslim nations throughout the region. Infighting between the incoming Jews and Palestinian Arabs started almost immediately and has been going on ever since. In addition, wars with the neighboring Muslim nations were threatened and have since come to pass, repeatedly. None of that, however, could stop Israel from forcibly being formed by the determined Jewish settlers, who immediately sought recognition from the newly constituted United Nations in 1948. Taking the worldwide lead in favor of the new Zionist kingdom, in complete disregard of the complaints of the surrounding, oil-rich nations of the Muslim world, was President Truman, who did indeed recognize the new Jewish state over the objections of his secretary of state, George Marshall, his under-secretaries, Robert Lovett and Dean Acheson, Secretary of Defense James Forrestal, and his top American diplomats, George Kennan and Charles Bohlen. Only White House Counsel Clark Clifford among the president's inner circle advocated recognition over the national security concerns of the others. But ever mindful of the political ramifications of not supporting the Jewish state in his upcoming, uphill re-election bid that fall, Truman opted for Clifford's arguments, and the Middle East has been the world's most volatile region ever since.[11]

Hypothetically, whether the Jews would have ever considered relocating their new homeland in another, less problematic corner of the globe, where they might have been accepted in peace, is doubtful, but one thing's for sure, their nation has been the target of controversy and conflict on the world stage ever since Truman's fateful recognition—so much so, in fact, it is now safe to assume Middle East peace may never happen. So far, the promise of the Promised Land has included ceaseless conflict for Jews, Muslims, and the world for over 70 years.[12]

26

Political Pros
or System Politicians

*"The people are responsible for the character of their Congress. If that body
be ignorant, reckless, and corrupt, it is because the people tolerate it."*
—James Garfield, 1877

Nowadays, with all the talk of illegitimate presidencies, it is interesting to consider this new terminology in the context of our accidental presidents. "Not in accordance with accepted standards or rules" is one definition of the word illegitimate, and at least one way to examine by what means these nine men were able to attain the nation's highest office. Obviously fate and the circumstance of constitutional succession was their eventual vehicle to ultimate national leadership, but their individual capacity to play the game also had to be evident for each to be in position to ascend when fate intervened. In other words, politics, that all-encompassing ritual of democracy, had to be in each of their personal DNAs even to have a chance at being president. As with all chief executives, some were better at the song and dance of politics than others, but all were products and beneficiaries of the same, two-party system.

Some were quite obviously political pros, even if that meant bending rules to achieve political ends. At the same time, their political proficiency was no guarantee of presidential success.[1] Both Johnsons should legitimately be remembered as political pros who rose steadily through statewide ranks no matter the ethical roadblocks, prominent opponent, or opposition constituency they faced. LBJ lost to a former Texas governor in Pappy O'Daniel his first time as a U.S. Senate candidate, but took steps to make sure that didn't happen again against an even more popular former governor, Coke Stevenson, eight years later. That's when he earned the reputation for playing the system—the Texas system whereby the predominantly Hispanic South Texas counties were for years the suspect home of questionable vote counts that determined more than their share of statewide elections. In other words, the Johnson campaign supposedly arranged support in South Texas and quite remarkably, so it seemed, came from way behind to capture a close (and to this day controversial) contest.[2]

By the same token, our other President Johnson was just as good at state politics in Tennessee over 100 years earlier. Despite being from a heavily Republican side of the state, East Tennessee, he became a dominant, go-to Democratic voice. While constantly having to contend with the opposition of Upper East Tennessee newspaper editor Parson Brownlow, their ongoing rivalry only served to strengthen Johnson's visibility and viability among Democrats throughout the state. It solidified his base and made him a statewide contender in an era when Tennessee's other designated "Grand Divisions," Middle and West Tennessee, were solidly Democratic. As a result, after a long and distinguished tenure as a representative at both the state and national levels, it was only natural that he was in position to be selected one of Tennessee's two U.S. senators at a time when the Democratically controlled state legislature still determined those seats. That next career step, in turn, along with his stalwart Union loyalty when all those around him were choosing states over country, managed to keep his national career alive by earning him a place as Abraham Lincoln's military governor of Tennessee and eventually the Republican Party's choice for vice president in 1864, despite his history as a Democrat. In essence, this Johnson was both a political pro and a political survivor.[3]

For another political pro among our accidental presidents, look no farther than Theodore Roosevelt. Above and beyond the exuberant style and charisma that made him one of the most popular Americans ever, he also knew his way around public opinion and how to influence it to get what he wanted, including reluctant legislative support. Otherwise he would never have been able to introduce so many progressive reforms at the end of the predominantly stand-pat, big business-dominated 19th century. Challenging the traditional powers of his party and the country's economic leaders, TR utilized the media in ways not previously employed, including the constant use of the presidency's high profile to make his message and opinions known, something he called his "Bully Pulpit," now commonplace for American presidents (regrettably, some more so than others). Sometimes he even engaged in political gambles, as with acquisition of the narrow neck of land that became the Panama Canal, but whatever the ploy, TR was more than willing to do whatever was necessary to aid the prospects of his own agenda.[4]

Despite his sullied, secessionist reputation in later years, John Tyler would also have to rate as a political pro by the way he rose through the Virginia states' rights ranks, becoming a regular legislative and statewide seat holder until the precise moment when a change in affiliation did him and his career the most good. How else to explain a descendant of Jeffersonian republicanism and an early proponent of Jacksonian democracy suddenly becoming a Whig senator, vice president, and president, all in a relatively short amount of time? Like Andrew Johnson, he proved not only a political pro but also a political opportunist. Unfortunately, again like Johnson, he never changed his political spots in terms of believing in White supremacy, leaving him no room to re-enter the U.S. political mainstream.[5]

As for the other four accidental presidents, history would judge them as system politicians—that is, beneficiaries of machine organizations or mainline party politics. Or, using a current college football analogy, they were more like spread or system quarterbacks than pure drop-back passers.[6] As previously established, Millard Fillmore was a product of New York State politics and the long-standing rival of William Seward. Both rose with the rise of the Whig Party, with Fillmore becoming a convenient vice presidential choice (the second-fiddle role the more ambitious Seward would not accept) as the result of his party loyalty, offsetting the celebrity-driven appeal of General Zachary Taylor, the Whig presidential nominee and political neophyte.[7] In much the same way, Gerald Ford was the steady Republican mainstay who just wanted to be Speaker of the House when he was called to step into the Spiro Agnew mess and later to clean up after the Nixon-Watergate scandal. Loyal to a fault, Ford stepped up when his party and country called and, needless to say, never got his coveted speakership as a result.[8]

Other system similarities can be drawn from the careers of Chester Arthur and Harry Truman. Certainly, Arthur's reliance on the machine-driven, partisan politics of his era and the corrupt Spoils System that resulted has been well-documented. Add the fact that Arthur never held an elected office before becoming a vice presidential candidate, and you have proof positive of the illogical results our national politics have often had. Arthur as president made no sense (still doesn't), but in the political climate and system of the time, the illogical happened.[9] On the other hand, Truman probably warrants the political pro tag for his eventful years in the White House, but not the way he got there. After all, he was deemed the senator from Pendergast for a reason, and to his dying day he would remain indebted to Tom Pendergast, the crooked boss of Western Missouri politics who made Truman, a popular local Army captain, a significant player in his well-oiled political machine between the world wars. To his credit, Truman never bent to Pendergast's corrupt wishes, but he also never withdrew entirely from his rather seedy political roots, a legacy he would have to overcome in Washington.[10]

Among our accidental presidents, there have been four Republicans, three Democrats, and two Whigs, as well as three party crossovers—Tyler from early Democrat to supposedly Whig by 1840, Andrew Johnson from Democrat to make-believe Republican in 1864 (before shifting back to the Dems by impeachment), and TR when he and the Progressives famously abandoned the Republicans to run their third party, "Bull Moose" campaign in 1912.[11] Politics aside, however, the personalities of these men were about as diverse as conceivably possible for a group ultimately bound by a common, overwhelmingly historic thread. While the variety of their backgrounds played a meaningful role in their individual development, such factors as physical appearance, character traits, and personal outlook all contributed to distinct personality differences.

As might be expected of an aristocratic Virginian, Tyler has been described as "tall and courtly," and "the perfect picture of a Southern gentleman planter." At the same time, at least one of his political contemporaries and another U.S. president, John Quincy Adams, caustically described him as "not above mediocrity."[12]

Even taller, Lyndon Johnson had a physical presence—an imposing, sometimes crass, and at times even ruthless presence. Though more and more recognized as his career progressed, LBJ could never tame his unbridled ambition, which constantly provoked him to action. He never wanted to leave a political stone unturned or an advantageous "means of ascent" off his radar.[13]

Arthur was also a big man, a fastidious dresser, trendsetter, and amiable host. But in political terms he was really no gentleman boss at all. Instead, he was a ranking political loyalist, a committed follower and willing subordinate until fate gave him the chance to step out of the shadows of others and into the limelight of a vice presidential candidate. Used to elite New York society and a lofty standard of living, he was described as a "procrastinator" and "sluggish," some of which may be attributable to his declining health.[14]

Almost exactly the opposite, Theodore Roosevelt was not tall, but he was, in his own way, physically imposing. He was charismatic, energetic, and driven, a personal force seldom seen in American politics. A descendant of New York City's old money social elite, he chastised his own class for not being more concerned and active in the elevation of those less fortunate, and he was driven to make his city, state, and country a better place for all, regardless of one's origin or station in life. Smart enough to be a published author 36 times and virile enough to be an enthusiastic hunter and outdoorsman known for his frequent forays into the wilderness, one TR historian has even contended that his constant fist-clinching was a sign of Attention Deficit Hyperactivity Disorder, way before such traits were accepted or identified.[15]

Equally surprising as TR's suspected ADHD would be Truman's previously mentioned childhood self-evaluation of being "sissified." This from a president whose often "salty" approach to the English language while in the White House would seem in stark contrast. But perhaps not so much for someone who never got to go to college despite a promising aptitude; for someone relegated to keeping the family afloat during his young adult years; and someone who for years had no luck with numerous financial investments. Or perhaps his direct approach and self-deprecating honesty came later in life, from his time in the Army and World War I. That's when he apparently became a true man's man in the way he led and spoke—the way he is remembered from his White House years.[16]

Certainly, Truman was at times blunt in his expressions, opinions, and Missouri-bred, show-me attitude, but not nearly so stubborn as his fellow accidental Andrew Johnson, who as previously noted, "was stubborn to the point of inflexibility." Unyielding in his beliefs with a dark, "swarthy" countenance that obscured his chances for compromise, this Johnson was a self-made politician, a loner with a lifelong aversion to the South's wealthy planter class as well as an ingrained racism that colored his thinking. His was a strict interpretation of the Constitution without leeway for reconstructed values.[17]

Surprisingly, Fillmore had been equally unwilling to reconstruct the slavery debate and Fugitive Slave Law a decade earlier, despite his roots being in the North every bit as much as Johnson's were in the South. Another tall chief executive with "striking blue eyes," he had an impressive appearance and usually made a dramatic first impression, but the substance of the man was apparently not so enduring. Since described as "modest, unassuming, and merely amiable," he was obviously a more pragmatic politician than revered statesman, an undeniable factor in the sustainability (and longevity) of most U.S. presidential administrations.[18]

So we see in many instances, these nine accidentally elevated presidents were soulmates of one stripe or another and not just in the common bond of how they got to the White House. Perhaps an incident in 1965, in fact, speaks to the type of connection all former presidents in retrospect generally feel and speak of regarding one another (at least until recent times). The fact that this event involved two of our accidental presidents was pure coincidence, but it still embellished their similar paths to power and common values. The moment in question was Lyndon Johnson's landmark achievement of government-financed healthcare for all of America's senior citizens—Medicare.

Normally such major legislation would be the subject of a celebratory signing ceremony at the White House, but for this special moment, LBJ chose to share it with Harry Truman, who 20 years before, in 1945, had first called for national health insurance. In recognition of that vision, Johnson had the signing moved to Independence and the Truman Presidential Library, where the man who used atomic power to end a world war also became the first person to receive a Medicare card.[19]

Epilogue
It Will Happen Again

Sooner or later, fate will again intervene and a tenth accidental president will find his or her way to the White House. With nine already among our first 45 chief executives, the odds of another one are about one in five. If presidential history has taught us anything, it's that we should never assume a vice president will not become president without being elected.

Despite much greater presidential security; improvements in healthcare, with many of our presidents serving at older ages; and technology that should make governing easier, America has rarely been a more divisive place than it is today. As a result, it would be foolish to think another presidential death in office, an assassination, or dismissal of some sort will not happen again.

Remember the Kennedy assassination? Baby Boomers certainly do, including where they were when they first heard the news that fateful fall. The outpouring of national resolve that followed those funeral-filled days was only possible because our system worked, as it has worked since the days of Tippecanoe and Tyler, too—without the threat of civil unrest so common in many other countries. In that regard, we have been blessed.

Chapter Notes

Chapter 1

1. Edward Crapol, *John Tyler: The Accidental President* (Chapel Hill: University of North Carolina Press, 2006).
2. Kenneth Davis, *Don't Know Much About the American Presidents* (New York: Hyperion, 2012), 187.
3. *Ibid.*, 191.
4. William DeGregorio, *The Complete Book of U.S. Presidents* (Fort Lee, NJ: Barricade Books, 2013), 156.
5. Michael Holt, *The Rise and Fall of the American Whig Party: Jacksonian Politics and the Onset of the Civil War* (New York: Oxford University Press, 1999), 127.
6. Edward Crapol, *John Tyler*, 8–9; Kenneth Davis, *Don't Know Much About the American Presidents*, 190–191.
7. *Ibid.*, 156–157.
8. Robert Remini, *Henry Clay: Statesman for the Union* (New York: W. W. Norton, 1991), 251–272.
9. Michael Holt, *The Rise and Fall of the American Whig Party*, 7–8.
10. Kenneth Davis, *Don't Know Much About The American Presidents*, 173.
11. Robert Remini, *Henry Clay*, 479–480; William DeGregorio, *The Complete Book of U.S. Presidents*, 141–143.
12. *Ibid.*, 154.
13. *Ibid.*, 149; Kenneth Davis, *Don't Know Much About the American Presidents*, 189.
14. *Ibid.*, 190; William DeGregorio, *The Complete Book of U.S. Presidents*, 153.
15. *Ibid.*, 158; Kenneth Davis, *Don't Know Much About the American Presidents*, 188.
16. *Ibid.*, 127; William DeGregorio, *The Complete Book of U.S. Presidents*, 154.
17. *Ibid.*, 115.
18. *Ibid.*, 154.
19. *Ibid.*, 156; Kenneth Davis, *Don't Know Much About the American Presidents*, 191–193; Michael F. Holt, *The Rise and Fall of the American Whig Party*, 127–137.
20. *Ibid.*, 140, 147; Kenneth Davis, *Don't Know Much About the American Presidents*, 191.
21. William DeGregorio, *The Complete Book of U.S. Presidents*, 156–157; Kenneth Davis, *Don't Know Much About the American Presidents*, 194.
22. William DeGregorio, *The Complete Book of U.S. Presidents*, 157.
23. *Ibid.*; Edward Crapol, *John Tyler*, 176–222.
24. Kenneth Davis, *Don't Know Much About the American Presidents*, 194; William DeGregorio, *The Complete Book of U.S. Presidents*, 157.
25. Edward Crapol, *John Tyler*, 278–280.
26. *Ibid.*, 16–17.
27. Kenneth Davis, *Don't Know Much About the American Presidents*, 191.
28. *Ibid.*, 19–20; Kenneth Davis, *Don't Know Much About the American Presidents*, 189; William DeGregorio, *The Complete Book of American Presidents*, 158.
29. *Ibid.*; Kenneth Davis, *Don't Know Much About the American Presidents*, 192; Edward Crapol, *John Tyler*, 261–265.

Chapter 2

1. William DeGregorio, *The Complete Book of U.S. Presidents*, 190; Michael Holt, *The Rise and Fall of the American Whig Party*, 521–523; Kenneth Davis, *Don't Know Much About the American Presidents*, 214.
2. *Ibid.*, 208, William DeGregorio, *The Complete Book of U.S. Presidents*, 178–179.
3. *Ibid.*, 171; Robert Remini, *Henry Clay*, 687, 750–751; Kenneth Davis, *Don't Know Much About the American Presidents*, 210;
4. *Ibid.*; Paul Finkelman, *Millard Fillmore* (New York: Times Books, 2004), 1–2.
5. William DeGregorio, *The Complete Book of U.S. Presidents*, 192; Kenneth Davis, *Don't Know Much About the American Presidents*, 215; Robert Remini, *Henry Clay*, 751–752.
6. Kenneth Davis, *Don't Know Much About the American Presidents*, 219.
7. William DeGregorio, *The Complete Book of U.S. Presidents*, 192; Michael Holt, *The Rise and Fall of the American Whig Party*, 551–552; Stephen Oates, *With Malice Toward None: The Life of Abraham Lincoln* (New York: Harper & Row, 1977), 139, 206.
8. William DeGregorio, *The Complete Book of U.S. Presidents*, 193.

9. *Ibid.*, 193–194; Paul Finkelman, *Millard Fillmore*, 3.

10. Robert Remini, *Henry Clay*, 762.

11. Michael Holt, *The Rise and Fall of the American Whig Party*, 981.

Chapter 3

1. H. W. Brands, "If Johnson Survived Impeachment, Anyone can—even Trump," *The Hill*, June 12, 2017.

2. Stephen B. Oates, *With Malice Toward None*, 13, 106, 196, 202–203, 211–212, 430–431, 451–452; Richard Carwardine, *Lincoln: A Life of Purpose and Power* (New York: Alfred A. Knopf, 2006), 310–321.

3. Kenneth Davis, *Don't Know Much About the American Presidents*, 269.

4. William DeGregorio, *The Complete Book of U.S. Presidents*, 252, 254.

5. *Ibid.*, 253–254; Kenneth Davis, *Don't Know Much About the American Presidents*, 273, 275.

6. Hans Trefousse, *Andrew Johnson: A Biography* (New York: W. W. Norton, 1989), 216–218.

7. Philip Dray, *Capital Men: The Epic Story of Reconstruction Through the Lives of the First Black Congressmen* (Boston: Houghton Mifflin, 2008), 24–27; Kenneth Davis, *Don't Know Much About the American Presidents*, 274; William DeGregorio, *The Complete Book of U.S. Presidents*, 253–254.

8. *Ibid.*

9. Eric Foner, *Reconstruction: America's Unfinished Revolution, 1863–1877* (New York: Harper & Row, 1988), 176, 273–275, 342–345, 421–425, 537–539.

10. Hans Trefousse, *Andrew Johnson*, 234–235, 251–252; Kenneth Davis, *Don't Know Much About the American Presidents*, 271, 275.

11. William DeGregorio, *The Complete Book of U.S. Presidents*, 248–249, 250–252; David Donald, *Lincoln* (London: Random House, 1995), 503–506, 529–531.

12. Walter Stahr, *Seward: Lincoln's Indispensable Man* (New York: Simon & Schuster, 2012), 525–526.

13. William DeGregorio, *The Complete Book of U.S. Presidents*, 255.

Chapter 4

1. Kenneth Davis, *Don't Know Much About the American Presidents*, 312, 313; Kyle Cheney, "No, Clinton Didn't Start the Birther Thing, This Guy Did," *Politico* magazine, September 16, 2016.

2. Mike Donovan, *The USA in the Time of Chester Alan Arthur* (Sun Valley, CA: CreateSpace, 2011), 11; Kenneth Davis, *Don't Know Much About the American Presidents*, 311, 405.

3. *Ibid.*, 314, 450; William DeGregorio, *The Complete Book of U.S. Presidents*, 310–311, 511–512.

4. *Ibid.*, 310; Candice Millard, *Destiny of the Republic: A Tale of Madness, Medicine, and the Murder of a President* (New York: Anchor Books, 2011), 96; Mike Donovan, *The USA in the Time of Chester Alan Arthur, 1881–1885*, 6.

5. William DeGregorio, *The Complete Book of U.S. Presidents*, 310; Kenneth Davis, *Don't Know Much About the American Presidents*, 314; Zachary Karabell, *Chester Alan Arthur* (New York: Times Books, 2004), 29–31.

6. William DeGregorio, *The Complete Book of U.S. Presidents*, 309, 311; Mike Donovan, *The USA in the Time of Chester Alan Arthur*, 13–14.

7. Kenneth Davis, *Don't Know Much About the American Presidents*, 297–298, 306–308; William DeGregorio, *The Complete Book of U.S. Presidents*, 284–285, 299–300; David Jordan, *Winfield Scott Hancock*, 96–100.

8. William DeGregorio, *The Complete Book of U.S. Presidents*, 300.

9. *Ibid.*, 302–303; Candice Millard, *Destiny of the Republic*, 54, 64, 152–153, 161, 225–226, 249–251, 269.

10. Zachary Karabell, *Chester Alan Arthur*, 19, 22, 26; Candice Millard, *Destiny of the Republic*, 192–193.

11. *Ibid.*, 193–195; Kenneth Davis, *Don't Know Much About the American Presidents*, 314.

12. Candice Millard, *Destiny of the Republic*, 269, photo caption.

13. *Ibid.*, 240–242.

14. *Ibid.*, 269–270; Kenneth Davis, *Don't Know Much About the American Presidents*, 316.

15. Candice Millard, *Destiny of the Republic*, 289–290.

16. *Ibid.*, 290–291; Kenneth Davis, *Don't Know Much About the American Presidents*, 317.

17. William DeGregorio, *The Complete Book of U.S. Presidents*, 313.

18. *Ibid.*, 313–314.

19. Zachary Karabell, *Chester Alan Arthur*, 88–89; William DeGregorio, *The Complete Book Of U.S. Presidents*, 313.

20. *Ibid.*, 313; Kenneth Davis, *Don't Know Much About the American Presidents*, 315–316; David Bain, *Empire Express: Building the First Transcontinental Railroad* (New York: Viking, 1999), 205–209; H. W. Brands, *American Colossus: The Triumph of Capitalism, 1865–1900* (New York: Anchor Books, 2010), 285, 286.

21. Kenneth Davis, *Don't Know Much About the American Presidents*, 317.

22. David McCullough, *The Great Bridge: The Epic Story of the Building of the Brooklyn Bridge*, Audio Book (Disc Nine); Kenneth Davis, *Don't Know Much About the American Presidents*, 317; William DeGregorio, *The Complete Book of U.S. Presidents*, 314.

23. *Ibid.*, 325; Kenneth Davis, *Don't Know Much About the American Presidents*, 317.

Chapter 5

1. Geoffrey Ward, "The Roosevelts: An Intimate History," Ken Burns Video; Doris Goodwin, *The Bully Pulpit, Theodore Roosevelt, William Howard Taft, and the Golden Age of Journalism* (New York: Simon & Schuster, 2013), 2; H.W. Brands, *T.R.: The Last Romantic* (New York: Basic Books, 1997), 669.

2. Edmund Morris, *Theodore Rex* (New York: Random House, 2001), 3–15, 17–18; Kenneth Davis, *Don't Know Much About the American Presidents*, 360; Edmund Morris, *The Rise Of Theodore Roosevelt*, 516–521.

3. H. W. Brands, *TR*, 9–11, 26–27, 31–32, 90, 92–93, 173; Douglas Brinkley, *The Wilderness Warrior: Theodore Roosevelt and the Crusade for America* (New York: HarperCollins, 2009), 68, 348–351, 429, 544, 603, 614, 795, 808, 813.

4. Doris Goodwin, *The Bully Pulpit*, 1–2, 301, 564; Kenneth Davis, *Don't Know Much About the American Presidents*, 360, 369.

5. George Mowry, *The Era of Theodore Roosevelt and the Birth of Modern America* (New York: Harper & Row, 1958), 110; H. W. Brands, *T.R.*, 434–435, 479–491, 523, 525, 527–528, 528–541, 548–551, 578–579, 586–587, 621–625; William DeGregorio, *The Complete Book of U.S. Presidents*, 384–386; Kenneth Davis, *Don't Know Much About the American Presidents*, 367–368.

6. Edmund Morris, *Theodore Rex*, 124–125, 137–149, 251–253, 419–420.

7. Doris Goodwin, *The Bully Pulpit*, 301, 663–665, 693–717.

8. William DeGregorio, *The Complete Book of U.S. Presidents*, 388; James Chace, *1912: Wilson, Roosevelt, Taft and Debs—The Election that Changed the Country* (New York: Simon & Schuster, 2004), 3, 8, 115–120.

9. H. W. Brands, *T. R*, 517–518, 546.

10. *Ibid.*, 720–723.

11. *Ibid.*, 234–235, 353, 355–358, 405–406, 641–659, 738–744.

12. William DeGregorio, *The Complete Book of U.S. Presidents*, 376, 378, 388–389.

13. James Chace, *1912*, 6–7.

14. George Mowry, *The Era of Theodore Roosevelt and the Birth of Modern America*, ix–x.

Chapter 6

1. Amity Shlaes, *Coolidge* (New York: HarperCollins, 2013), 7–8, 68, 73–74; William DeGregorio, *The Complete Book of American Presidents*, 442, 451–452.

2. *Ibid.*, 452; Kenneth Davis, *Don't Know Much About the American Presidents*, 408.

3. *Ibid.*; William DeGregorio, *The Complete Book of U.S. Presidents*, 437, 452.

4. Kenneth Davis, *Don't Know Much About the American Presidents*, 408, Samuel Adams, *Incredible Era: The Life and Times of Warren Gamaliel Harding* (New York: Capricorn, 1939), 366; William DeGregorio, *The Complete Book of U.S. Presidents*, 442.

5. Andrew Sinclair, *The Available Man: The Life Behind the Masks of Warren G. Harding*, 144, 187–189, 196, 265; Samuel Adams, *Incredible Era*, 260, 378–384; Laton McCartney, *The Teapot Dome Scandal: How Big Oil Bought the Harding White House and Tried to Steal the Country* (New York: Random House, 2008), 156–158; Michael Kazin, *A Godly Hero: The Life of William Jennings Bryan*, 285.

6. *Ibid.*, 155–156; Kenneth Davis, *Don't Know Much About the American Presidents*, 407.

7. *Ibid.*, 408.

8. *Ibid.*, 409, 410; Laton McCartney, *The Teapot Dome Scandal*, 260; Amity Shlaes, *Coolidge*, 6, 337–340.

9. *Ibid.*, 11, 450; James MacGregor Burns and Susan Dunn, *The Three Roosevelts: Patrician Leaders who Transformed America* (New York: Grove Press, 2001), 170, 208; David Pietrusza, *1920: The Year of Six Presidents* (New York: Carroll & Graf, 2007), 434 435; Kenneth Davis, *Don't Know Much About the American Presidents*, 411.

10. *Ibid.*, 406, 411; Amity Shlaes, *Coolidge*, 8; William DeGregorio, *The Complete Book of U.S. Presidents*, 457, 459; Laton McCartney, *The Teapot Dome Scandal*, 158.

11. Kenneth Davis, *Don't Know Much About the American Presidents*, 410.

12. William DeGregorio, *The Complete Book of U.S. Presidents*, 457–458.

13. *Ibid.*, 459; Amity Shlaes, *Coolidge*, 456.

Chapter 7

1. Kenneth Davis, *Don't Know Much About the American Presidents*, 426, 448; David McCullough, *Truman* (New York: Simon & Schuster, 1992), 349–350; William DeGregorio, *The Complete Book of U.S. Presidents*, 508, 511.

2. *Ibid.*, 479; Kenneth Davis, *Don't Know Much About the American Presidents*, 447.

3. William Leuchtenburg, *The White House Looks South: Franklin D. Roosevelt, Harry S. Truman, Lyndon B. Johnson* (Baton Rouge: Louisiana State University Press, 2005), 159.

4. William DeGregorio, *The Complete Book of U.S. Presidents*, 512; David McCullough, *Truman*, 270–271.

5. Anthony Summers, *Official and Confidential: The Secret Life of J. Edgar Hoover* (New York: G. P. Putnam's Sons, 1993), 153–154; Kenneth Davis, *Don't Know Much About the American Presidents*, 450–451; William DeGregorio, *The Complete Book of U.S. Presidents*, 511–512.

6. *Ibid.*; Kenneth Davis, *Don't Know Much About the American Presidents*, 451.

7. William DeGregorio, *The Complete Book of U.S. Presidents*, 512; William Leuchtenburg, *The White House Looks South*, 157–158.

8. Doris Goodwin, *No Ordinary Time*, 524, 530, 547.

9. David McCullough, *Truman*, 355–356; Kenneth Davis, *Don't Know Much About the American Presidents*, 451.

10. *Ibid.*, 448; David McCullough, *Truman*, Book Cover; McWilliam DeGregorio, *The Complete Book of U.S. Presidents*, 523.

11. Kenneth Davis, *Don't Know Much About the American Presidents*, 458.

12. William DeGregorio, *The Complete Book of U.S. Presidents*, 518; Walter Isaacson and Evan Thomas, *The Wise Men: Six Friends and the World They Made—George Keenan, Dean Acheson, Charles Bohlen,*

Robert Lovett, Averell Harriman, John McCloy (New York: Simon & Schuster, 1986), 310–313.

13. *Ibid.*, 516; William DeGregorio, *The Complete Book of U.S. Presidents*, 518–519.

14. *Ibid.*, 519; Kenneth Davis, *Don't Know Much About the American Presidents*, 456–457, 459.

15. *Ibid.*, 519–520; Kenneth Davis, *Don't Know Much About the American Presidents*, 456–457.

16. William DeGregorio, *The Complete Book of U.S. Presidents*, 520–521; Anthony Summers, *Official and Confidential*, 155.

17. Kenneth Davis, *Don't Know Much About the American Presidents*, 458; William Leuchtenberg, *The White House Looks South*, 191, 197–201, 206; William DeGregorio, *The Complete Book of U.S. Presidents*, 513–514.

18. *Ibid.*, 511, 522.

Chapter 8

1. Jon Meacham, *The Soul of America: The Battle for Our Better Angels* (New York: Random House, 2018), 212: Brion McClanahan: *Nine Presidents Who Screwed Up America and Four Who Tried to Save Her* (Washington: Regnery History, 2016), 119.

2. Kenneth Davis, *Don't Know Much About the American Presidents*, 498; William DeGregorio, *The Complete Book of U.S. Presidents*, 565.

3. *Ibid.*, 566, 567.

4. Robert Caro, *Means Of Ascent: The Years of Lyndon Johnson* (New York: Alfred A. Knopf, 1990), xxviii; William DeGregorio, *The Complete Book of U.S. Presidents*, 567–568.

5. *Ibid.*, 568–569.

6. *Ibid.*; Robert Caro, *Master of the Senate: The Years of Lyndon Johnson* (New York: Alfred A. Knopf, 2002), xx–xxii, 608.

7. *Ibid.*, 822; Robert Caro, *The Passage of Power: The Years of Lyndon Johnson* (New York: Alfred A. Knopf, 2012), 107–108; William DeGregorio, *The Complete Book of U.S. Presidents*, 535–536, 569.

8. *Ibid.*, 551–553, 569; Robert Dallek, *An Unfinished Life: John F. Kennedy, 1917–1963* (New York: Little, Brown, 2003), 250, 255, 257, 264, 269, 273–274.

9. David Grubin, "LBJ," American Experience Video; Kenneth Davis, *Don't Know Much About the American Presidents*, 490, 496.

10. *Ibid.*, 496; William DeGregorio, *The Complete Book of U.S. Presidents*, 558–560.

11. Kenneth Davis, *Don't Know Much About the American Presidents*, 496.

12. Robert Dallek, *An Unfinished Life*, 708; Michael Beschloss, *Presidential Courage* (New York: Simon & Schuster, 2007), 276; Kenneth Davis, *Don't Know Much About the American Presidents*, 496.

13. *Ibid.*, 504–505; Sarah-Jane Stratford, "Referring to JFK's Presidency as 'Camelot' Doesn't Do Him Justice," *The Guardian*, November 21, 2013; William DeGregorio, *The Complete Book of U.S. Presidents*, 555–557, 574–576.

14. *Ibid.*, 574–576; Jon Meacham, *The Soul of America*, 249; Kenneth Davis, *Don't Know Much About the American Presidents*, 500–502.

15. *Ibid.*, 501; Kenneth Walsh, "The Politics of Medicare and Medicaid, Fifty Years Later," *U.S. News and World Report*, July 30, 2015.

16. Brenda Glazzar, "How The Civil Rights Act of 1964 Changed America," *Los Angeles Daily News*, July 1, 2014; William Leuchtenburg, *The White House Looks South*, 397–398; Kenneth Davis, *Don't Know Much About the American Presidents*, 500–502.

17. Laura Kalman, *Right Star Rising: A New Politics, 1974–1980* (New York: W. W. Norton, 2010), xix; William Leuchtenburg, *The White House Looks South*, 307, 309, 325; Toni Monkovic, "Fifty Years of Electoral College Maps: How The U.S. Turned Red and Blue," *New York Times*, August 22, 2016.

18. Kenneth Davis, *Don't Know Much About the American Presidents*, 498; Osagie Obasogie, "Was Loving vs. Virginia Really About Love," *The Atlantic*, June 12, 2017; Nancy Cash and Terry Spohn, *Today In History: A Day-By-Day Review of World Events*, 579.

19. Kenneth Davis, *Don't Know Much About the American Presidents*, 503, 508; Jon Meacham, *The Soul of America*, 244; William DeGregorio, *The Complete Book of U.S. Presidents*, 567, 577.

Chapter 9

1. Henry Kissinger, *Diplomacy* (New York: Simon & Schuster, 1994), 744; Douglas Brinkley, *Gerald R. Ford* (New York: Times Books, 2007), 64.

2. Kenneth Davis, *Don't Know Much About the American Presidents*, 529; William DeGregorio, *The Complete Book of U.S. Presidents*, 592, 599, 609.

3. Jonathan Aitken, *Nixon: A Life* (Washington: Regnery, 1993), 505–506; Kenneth Davis, *Don't Know Much About the American Presidents*, 528, 530, 531.

4. *Ibid.*, 531; William DeGregorio, *The Complete Book of U.S. Presidents*, 608–609.

5. Laura Kalman, *Right Star Rising: A New Politics, 1974–1980* (New York: W. W. Norton, 2010), 5; Douglas Brinkley, *Gerald R. Ford*, 17–18.

6. William DeGregorio, *The Complete Book of U.S. Presidents*, 609.

7. *Ibid.*, 615.

8. Kenneth Davis, *Don't Know Much About the American Presidents*, 528.

9. Laura Kalman, *Right Star Rising*, 14; Douglas Brinkley, *Gerald R. Ford*, 67.

10. Laura Kalman, *Right Star Rising*, 98–107.

11. William DeGregorio, *The Complete Book of U.S. Presidents*, 613.

12. *Ibid.*, 614–615.

13. Douglas Brinkley, *Gerald R. Ford*, 140–141; William DeGregorio, *The Complete Book of U.S. Presidents*, 607, 623–624; Kenneth Davis, *Don't Know Much About the American Presidents*, 530, 534.

14. *Ibid.*, 527, 528, 530.

Chapter 10

1. Edward Crapol, *John Tyler*, 3, 22–23; Brion McClanahan, *Nine Presidents Who Screwed Up America and Four Who Tried to Save Her*, 209.

2. Edward Crapol, *John Tyler*, 3, 22–23; Glyndon Van Deusen, *The Jacksonian Era, 1828–1848* (New York: Harper & Row, 1959), 143; Margaret Coit, *John C. Calhoun: American Portrait* (Boston: Houghton Mifflin, 1950), 348–349.

3. Edward Crapol, *John Tyler*, 18.

4. Kenneth Davis, *Don't Know Much About the American Presidents*, 187, 192; Brion McClanahan, *Nine Presidents Who Screwed Up America and Four Who Tried to Save Her*, 211–212.

5. Michael Holt, *The Rise and Fall of the American Whig Party*, 41.

6. William DeGregorio, *The Complete Book of American Presidents*, 149; Brion McClanahan, *Nine Presidents Who Screwed Up America and Four Who Tried to Save Her*, 210–211; Edward Crapol, *John Tyler*, 30–31.

7. *Ibid.*, 31–34.

8. *Ibid.*, 35–36.

9. *Ibid.*, 37.

10. David Donald, *Lincoln*, 122.

11. Edward Crapol, *John Tyler*, 38–39.

12. David Clary, *Eagles and Empire: The United States, Mexico, and the Struggle for a Continent*, 57.

13. Edward Crapol, *John Tyler*, 39.

14. William DeGregorio, *The Complete Book of American Presidents*, 149, 154.

15. *Ibid.*, 97, 111.

16. Robert Remini, *Henry Clay*, 413.

17. Robert Remini, *Andrew Jackson* (New York: W. W. Norton, 1997), 258; Edward Crapol, *John Tyler*, 47–48.

18. *Ibid.*, 49–50.

19. *Ibid.*; Robert Remini, *Andrew Jackson*, 405.

20. *Ibid.*, 315–316.

21. *Ibid.*, 406.

22. Michael Holt, *The Rise and Fall of the American Whig Party*, 128.

23. Edward Crapol, *John Tyler*, 51.

24. *Ibid.*, 53–54; Brion McClanahan, *Nine Presidents Who Screwed Up America and Four Who Tried to Save Her*, 213–214; Robert Remini, *Henry Clay*, 299.

25. Edward Crapol, *John Tyler*, 59–65.

26. *Ibid.*, 17–18, 58.

27. Glyndon Van Deusen, *The Jacksonian Era*, 143; Margaret Coit, *John C. Calhoun*, 345.

28. Walter Borneman, *Polk: The Man Who Transformed the Presidency and America* (New York: Random House, 2008), 45; Kenneth Davis, *Don't Know Much About the American Presidents*, 182.

29. Robert Owens, *Mr. Jefferson's Hammer: William Henry Harrison and the Origins of Indian Policy* (Norman: University of Oklahoma Press, 1974), xiii–xx; Michael Holt, *The Rise and Fall of the American Whig Party*, 41; Robert Remini, *Henry Clay*, 75; Edward Crapol, *John Tyler*, 8.

30. *Ibid.*, 8–9; Michael Holt, *The Rise and Fall of the American Whig Party*, 41; Walter Borneman, *Polk*, 54–55.

31. *Ibid.*, 56; Edward Crapol, *John Tyler*, 10–11.

32. William DeGregorio, *The Complete Book of U.S. Presidents*, 156; Kenneth Davis, *Don't Know Much About the American Presidents*, 187; Edward Crapol, *John Tyler*, 10–12.

33. *Ibid.*; Kenneth Davis, *Don't Know Much About the American Presidents*, 187, 190–192, 215.

34. Margaret Coit, *John C. Calhoun*, 348–349; Glyndon Van Deusen, *The Jacksonian Era*; 156–159; Brion McClanahan, *Nine Presidents Who Screwed Up America and Four Who Tried to Save Her*, 213, 215–222.

35. Michael Holt, *The Rise and Fall of the American Whig Party*, 128–136; Robert Remini, *Henry Clay*, 581–583, 590, 593, 596, 602–604.

36. Walter Borneman, *Polk*, 173–174; William Freehling, *The Road to Disunion: Secessionists at Bay, 1776–1854* (New York: Oxford University Press, 1990), 364; Edward Crapol, *John Tyler*, 74–77.

37. *Ibid.*, 80–87; Robert Remini, *Henry Clay*, 299.

38. Walter Stahr, *Seward* (New York: Simon & Schuster, 2012), 76–77, 79; Edward Crapol, *John Tyler*, 91–92.

39. *Ibid.*, 96–97; Glyndon Van Deusen, *The Jacksonian Era*, 173–176; William DeGregorio, *The Complete Book of U.S. Presidents*, 156–157.

40. Glyndon Van Deusen, *The Jacksonian Era*, 175; Robert Remini, *Andrew Jackson*, 484; Edward Crapol, *John Tyler*, 97–104.

41. *Ibid.*, 106; Michael Holt, *The Rise and Fall of the American Whig Party*, 149.

42. *Ibid.*, 135; Edward Crapol, *John Tyler*, 106–107.

43. *Ibid.*, 114–115; David Clary, *Eagles and Empire* (New York: Bantam Books, 2009), 58–59; Robert Remini, *Daniel Webster: The Man and His Time*, 535–564.

44. Edward Crapol, *John Tyler*, 118–121; Walter Borneman, *Polk*, 173–174.

45. Brion McClanahan, *Nine Presidents Who Screwed Up American and Four Who Tried to Save Her*, 226–227; Michael Holt, *The Rise and Fall of the American Whig Party*, 170; Robert Remini, *Henry Clay*, 630.

46. Glyndon Van Deusen, *The Jacksonian Era*, 177; Robert Remini, *Daniel Webster*, 583–584; Edward Crapol, *John Tyler*, 126–127.

47. *Ibid.*, 130.

48. *Ibid.*, 132–136; Martin Harmon, *The Roosevelts and Their Descendants: Portrait of an American Family* (Jefferson, NC: McFarland, 2017), 86; Robert Remini, *Henry Clay*, 297.

49. Robert Remini, *Daniel Webster*, 579–581; William DeGregorio, *The Complete Book of American Presidents*, 100; Edward Crapol, *John Tyler*, 136–153.

50. Robert Remini, *Daniel Webster*, 581–582; Edward Crapol, *John Tyler*, 155–158.

51. *Ibid.*, 158–162.

52. William DeGregorio, *The Complete Book of American Presidents*, 155.

53. Margaret Coit, *John C. Calhoun*, 359; William DeGregorio, *The Complete Book of American Presidents*, 152–153.

54. Edward Crapol, *John Tyler*, 164–169; William DeGregorio, *The Complete Book of U.S. Presidents*, 157.

55. *Ibid.*; Edward Crapol, *John Tyler*, 171–172; Robert Remini, *Daniel Webster*, 710.

56. Kenneth Davis, *Don't Know Much About the American Presidents*, 191; Edward Crapol, *John Tyler*, 176; Michael Holt, *The Rise and Fall of the American Whig Party*, 170; Walter Borneman, *Polk*, 67–75.

57. *Ibid.*, 69; David Clary, *Eagles And Empire*, 11–12; Robert Remini, *Henry Clay*, 170–171, 175–176.

58. *Ibid.*, 303–305, 484–485; David Clary, *Eagles and Empire*, 31–36, 49–50.

59. *Ibid.*, 44; Robert Remini, *Andrew Jackson*, 360–364, 367–368; Walter Borneman, *Polk*, 73–74; Edward Crapol, *John Tyler*, 177.

60. *Ibid.*; Robert Remini, *Daniel Webster*, 464.

61. Michael Holt, *The Rise and Fall of the American Whig Party*, 168–170; Edward Crapol, *John Tyler*, 178–180.

62. *Ibid.*, 182.

63. *Ibid.*, 183–184; Robert Remini, *Daniel Webster*, 584; David Clary, *Eagles and Empire*, 58; Glyndon Van Deusen, *The Jacksonian Era*, 177.

64. Michael Holt, *The Rise and Fall of the Whig Party*, 150, 161; Edward Crapol, *John Tyler*, 184–185.

65. *Ibid.*, 194; David Clary, *Eagles and Empire*, 58.

66. *Ibid.*, 59–60; Edward Crapol, *John Tyler*, 195–19; Walter Borneman, *Polk*, 85, 87–88, 150–169.

67. *Ibid.*, 75; Edward Crapol, *John Tyler*, 196–198.

68. Glyndon Van Deusen, *The Jacksonian Era*, 178–179; Margaret Coit, *John C. Calhoun*, 358–359; Edward Crapol, *John Tyler*, 201–203, 213.

69. *Ibid.*, 207–209; William DeGregorio, *The Complete Book of American Presidents*, 157.

70. Robert Remini, *Henry Clay*, 635; Margaret Coit, *John C. Calhoun*, 361–362; Walter Borneman, *Polk*, 78.

71. Edward Crapol, *John Tyler*, 214.

72. *Ibid.*, 215.

73. Margaret Coit, *John C. Calhoun*, 371–372; Edward Crapol, *John Tyler*, 215.

74. Robert Remini, *Henry Clay*, 640–641.

75. Edward Crapol, *John Tyler*, 217.

76. Robert Remini, *Henry Clay*, 646–647, 656–657; Robert Remini, *Andrew Jackson*, 504–505.

77. Edward Crapol, *John Tyler*, 218–219; Walter Borneman, *Polk*, 117–119.

78. William Freehling, *The Road To Disunion*, 433, 448; Brion McClanahan, *Nine Presidents Who Screwed Up America and Four Who Tried to Save Her*, 228–229; Kenneth Davis, *Don't Know Much About the American Presidents*, 191; Edward Crapol, *John Tyler*, 220–221.

79. *Ibid.*, 225–230.

80. Walter Borneman, *Polk*, 356.

81. *Ibid.*, 135, 173–174, 190, 191.

82. Edward Crapol, *John Tyler*, 233–237.

83. *Ibid.*, 244–247; Stephen Oates, *With Malice Toward None*, 195.

84. Edward Crapol, *John Tyler*, 249, 253; William Davis, *Look Away: A History of the Confederate States of America*, 11.

85. David Donald, *Lincoln*, 297, 306; William Davis, *Look Away*, 113–115; Edward Crapol, *John Tyler*, 262, 264, 268.

Chapter 11

1. Paul Finkelman, *Millard Fillmore*, Cover; Kenneth Davis, *Don't Know Much About the American Presidents*, 220.

2. *Ibid.*, 2; Steve Times, *Zachary Taylor: The Life and Death of the Twelfth President of the United States*, 24–25; William DeGregorio, *The Complete Book of U.S. Presidents*, 178–180.

3. Robert Remini, *Daniel Webster*, 683; Paul Finkelman, *Millard Fillmore*, 2.

4. *Ibid.*, 4–5.

5. *Ibid.*, 6; William DeGregorio, *The Complete Book of U.S. Presidents*, 187–189.

6. *Ibid.*, 226–228, 188–189; Paul Finkelman, *Millard Fillmore*, 6–8.

7. *Ibid.*, 7–8.

8. *Ibid.*; Kenneth Davis, *Don't Know Much About the American Presidents*, 216; Walter DeGregorio, *The Complete Book of U.S. Presidents*, 193; Walter Stahr, *Seward*, 24, 146–147.

9. Michael Holt, *The Rise and Fall of the American Whig Party*, 299, 911; "List of Presidents of the United States who were Freemasons," wikipedia.org; Paul Finkelman, *Millard Fillmore*, 10–12.

10. *Ibid.*, 12–13.

11. *Ibid.*, 12–13; "Erie Canal," wikipedia.org.

12. Paul Finkelman, *Millard Fillmore*, 13–14; Robert Remini, *Daniel Webster*, 263, 649.

13. Walter Stahr, *Seward*, 33, 41–44, 52–57, 67–71, 93.

14. William DeGregorio, *The Complete Book of U.S. Presidents*, 190; Paul Finkelman, *Millard Fillmore*, 14.

15. Walter Stahr, *Seward*, 109, 116.

16. Paul Finkelman, *Millard Fillmore*, 15; Walter Stahr, *Seward*, 3, 65, 69, 74.

17. Michael Holt, *The Rise and Fall of the American Whig Party*, 124; Paul Finkelman, *Millard Fillmore*, 15–16.

18. *Ibid.*; Walter Stahr, *Seward*, 60–61.

19. Paul Finkelman, *Millard Fillmore*, 16–17.

20. Robert Remini, *Henry Clay*, 48, 251–252, 486, 737; William Freehling, *The Road To Disunion*, 355–356.

21. Paul Finkelman, *Millard Fillmore*, 18–19.

22. *Ibid.*, 20; Walter Stahr, *Seward*, 65, 109, 116.

23. Paul Finkelman, *Millard Fillmore*, 20.

24. *Ibid.*, 21; Robert Remini, *Henry Clay*, 645; Michael Holt, *The Rise and Fall of the American Whig Party*, 188–89.

25. William DeGregorio, *The Complete Book of U.S. Presidents*, 167–168; Kenneth Davis, *Don't Know Much About the American Presidents*, 216–219.

26. Paul Finkelman, *Millard Fillmore*, 22.

27. *Ibid.*, 23–24; William DeGregorio, *The Complete Book of American Presidents*, 190.

28. Paul Finkelman, *Millard Fillmore*, 24–25.

29. Kenneth Davis, *Don't Know Much About the American Presidents*, 200; Robert Remini, *Henry Clay*, 677, 679–680; Paul Finkelman, *Millard Fillmore*, 27.

30. Walter Borneman, *Polk*, 71–72.

31. *Ibid.*, 73–74, 82.

32. Robert Remini, *Henry Clay*, 634–635, 658; Paul Finkelman, *Millard Fillmore*, 28–29.

33. *Ibid.*, 29–30; Michael Holt, *The Rise and Fall of the American Whig Party*, 176–177; Walter Borneman, *Polk*, 74–75; David Clary, *Eagles and Empire*, 49–50.

34. Kenneth Davis, *Don't Know Much About the American Presidents*, 200–201; Paul Finkelman, *Millard Fillmore*, 30–31; David Clary, *Eagles and Empire*, 68–73.

35. *Ibid.*, 93–95, 99; Walter Borneman, *Polk*, 202–207.

36. Michael Holt, *The Rise and Fall of the American Whig Party*, 224–226; Paul Finkelman, *Millard Fillmore*, 34–35.

37. *Ibid.*, 35–37.

38. William Freehling, *The Road To Disunion*, 449–452, 493.

39. Paul Finkelman, *Millard Fillmore*, 41.

40. Robert Remini, *Daniel Webster*, 632–633; Robert Remini, *Henry Clay*, 706–707; Paul Finkelman, *Millard Fillmore*, 41, 42–43.

41. *Ibid.*, 43–44; David Donald, *Lincoln*, 126–129; Stephen Oates, *With Malice Toward None*, 88–91.

42. Michael Holt, *The Rise and Fall of the American Whig Party*, 323–325, 360–361.

43. *Ibid.*, 327–329; Paul Finkelman, *Millard Fillmore*, 47–49.

44. Michael Holt, *The Rise and Fall of the American Whig Party*, 334, 339–345, 368; Paul Finkelman, *Millard Fillmore*, 50–52.

45. *Ibid.*, 53.

46. *Ibid.*, 52–58; Michael Holt, *The Rise and Fall of the American Whig Party*, 505; Walter Stahr, *Seward*, 121.

47. Robert Remini, *Henry Clay*, 714, 728; Paul Finkelman, *Millard Fillmore*, 57.

48. *Ibid.*, 58; Kenneth Davis, *Don't Know Much About the American Presidents*, 217–219.

49. Paul Finkelman, *Millard Fillmore*, 57.

50. *Ibid.*, 58; Michael Holt, *The Rise and Fall of the American Whig Party*, 414, 506.

51. *Ibid.*, 535, 538; Walter Stahr, *Seward*, 121; Paul Finkelman, *Millard Fillmore*, 59.

52. *Ibid.*, 60–63; Walter Stahr, *Seward*, 122–124.

53. *Ibid.*; Paul Finkelman, *Millard Fillmore*, 63.

54. Michael Holt, *The Rise and Fall of the American Whig Party*, 437–439.

55. Robert Remini, *Henry Clay*, 728–729.

56. *Ibid.*, 752–753; Paul Finkelman, *Millard Fillmore*, 63–64; Walter Stahr, *Seward*, 121–127.

57. Robert Remini, *Henry Clay*, 731–732; Robert Remini, *Daniel Webster*, 665; Paul Finkelman, *Millard Fillmore*, 64.

58. *Ibid.*, 64–65; William DeGregorio, *The Complete Book of U.S. Presidents*, 192.

59. Paul Finkelman, *Millard Fillmore*, 65–66.

60. *Ibid.*, 69.

61. Robert Remini, *Daniel Webster*, 669; Robert Remini, *Henry Clay*, 735–737; Margaret Coit, *John C. Calhoun*, 487–488; Walter Stahr, *Seward*, 124–125.

62. *Ibid.*, 126; Michael Holt, *The Rise and Fall of the American Whig Party*, 478–479.

63. Paul Finkelman, *Millard Fillmore*, 70–71; Fergus Bordewich, *America's Great Debate: Henry Clay, Stephen A. Douglas, and the Compromise That Preserved the Union* (New York: Simon & Schuster, 2012), 220–221.

64. *Ibid.*, 279–283; Michael Holt, *The Rise and Fall of the American Whig Party*, 522; Paul Finkelman, *Millard Fillmore*, 71.

65. *Ibid.*, 72–73; Michael Holt, *The Rise and Fall of the American Whig Party*, 524–525.

66. Robert Remini, *Daniel Webster*, 683–687.

67. Paul Finkelman, *Millard Fillmore*, 74.

68. Michael Holt, *The Rise and Fall of the American Whig Party*, 526–527.

69. Paul Finkelman, *Millard Fillmore*, 75; Robert Remini, *Daniel Webster*, 687.

70. Michael Holt, *The Rise and Fall of the American Whig Party*, 527–528; Paul Finkelman, *Millard Fillmore*, 76–78.

71. *Ibid.*, 78–80; William Freehling, *The Road To Disunion*, 88, 496, 508–509.

72. Robert Remini, *Henry Clay*, 752–757.

73. *Ibid.*, 753–761; Fergus Bordewich, *America's Great Debate*, 303–305.

74. Paul Finkelman, *Millard Fillmore*, 81–86; Fergus Bordewich, *America's Great Debate*, 314–315.

75. *Ibid.*, 85.

76. Kenneth Davis, *Don't Know Much About the American Presidents*, 217–219; William DeGregorio, *The Complete Book of American Presidents*, 192; Fergus Bordewich, *America's Great Debate*, 364–365.

77. Paul Finkelman, *Millard Fillmore*, 86.

78. Fergus Bordewich, *America's Great Debate*, 363–366; Michael Holt, *The Rise and Fall of the American Whig Party*, 554; Paul Finkelman, *Millard Fillmore*, 87.

79. *Ibid.*, 89–90; Fergus Bordewich, *America's Great Debate*, 366–367.

80. Michael Holt, *The Rise and Fall of the American Whig Party*, 579–580; Paul Finkelman, *Millard Fillmore*, 91; Robert Remini, *Daniel Webster*, 764.

81. Michael Holt, *The Rise and Fall of the American Whig Party*, 687; Walter Stahr, *Seward*, 54; Paul Finkelman, *Millard Fillmore*, 92–93.

82. *Ibid.*; Kenneth Davis, *Don't Know Much About the American Presidents*, 221.

83. Paul Finkelman, *Millard Fillmore*, 94–98; William DeGregorio, *The Complete Book of U.S. Presidents*, 193.

84. Rhonda Blumberg, *Commodore Perry in the Land of the Shogun*, 17–26; Paul Finkelman, *Millard Fillmore*, 98.

85. Michael Holt, *The Rise and Fall of the American Whig Party*, 602–603; Paul Finkelman, *Millard Fillmore*, 98–100.

86. *Ibid.*, 102–115; William Freehling, *The Road To Disunion*, 500–502.

87. *Ibid.*, 126–132; Robert Remini, *Daniel Webster*, 723–724, 726–727, 729–740.

88. *Ibid.*, 132–137; Michael Holt, *The Rise and Fall of the American Whig Party*, 963–965, 974, 983; William DeGregorio, *The Complete Book of U.S. Presidents*, 229.

Chapter 12

1. Richard Carwardine, *Lincoln A Life of Purpose and Power*, 243–244; Philip Dray, *Capitol Men*, 23.

2. Hans Trefousse, *Andrew Johnson*, 378–379.

3. *Ibid.*, 13.

4. Eric Foner, *Reconstruction*, 176–177, 221–224, 260, 269, 334.

5. Hans Trefousse, *Andrew Johnson*, 17–21.

6. William DeGregorio, *The Complete Book of U.S. Presidents*, 248–249; Kenneth Davis, *Don't Know Much About the American Presidents*, 271; Jay Winik, *April 1865: The Month That Saved America* (New York: HarperCollins, 2001), 268–269.

7. Hans Trefousse, *Andrew Johnson*, 27, 29.

8. *Ibid.*, 30–31.

9. *Ibid.*, 32–33; William DeGregorio, *The Complete Book of U.S. Presidents*, 250.

10. *Ibid.*; Hans Trefousse, *Andrew Johnson*, 36–37.

11. Hans Trefousse, *Andrew Johnson*, 46–48.

12. *Ibid.*, 48; Noel Fisher, *War at Every Door*, 11.

13. *Ibid.*, 53–54.

14. *Ibid.*, 57–58; Robert Remini, *Henry Clay*, 663–665, 668; *Polk*, 133–135; William DeGregorio, *The Complete Book of U.S. Presidents*, 250.

15. Hans Trefousse, *Andrew Johnson*, 73–76.

16. *Ibid.*, 78–79; Robert Remini, *Daniel Webster*, 463, 636.

17. Walter Stahr, *Seward*, 177; Hans Trefousse, *Andrew Johnson*, 80–81; William DeGregorio, *The Complete Book of U.S. Presidents*, 202.

18. *Ibid.*, 250; Robert Corlew, *Tennessee: A Short History* (Knoxville: University of Tennessee Press, 1981), 275–278; Mary Caldwell, *Tennessee: The Volunteer State* (Chicago: Richtext Press, 1968), 108; Hans Trefousse, *Andrew Johnson*, 85–88.

19. *Ibid.*, 92–93, 95; Robert Corlew, *Tennessee*, 236–237, 280–281; Mary Caldwell, *Tennessee*, 108–109.

20. Hans Trefousse, *Andrew Johnson*, 105–108; Robert Corlew, *Tennessee*, 282.

21. Walter Stahr, *Seward*, 117; Stephen Oates, *With Malice Toward None*, 144, 150, 151–153.

22. Hans Trefousse, *Andrew Johnson*, 111–112.

23. Hans Trefousse, *Andrew Johnson*, 119.

24. *Ibid.*, 120–122; Walter Stahr, *Seward*, 249.

25. Hans Trefousse, *Andrew Johnson*, 122–124; William DeGregorio, *The Complete Book of U.S. Presidents*, 233; Stephen Oates, *With Malice Toward None*, 176–177.

26. *Ibid.*, 199–200; David Donald, *Lincoln*, 253; Hans Trefousse, *Andrew Johnson*, 125–127.

27. David Donald, *Lincoln*, 256; Kenneth Davis, *Don't Know Much About the American Presidents*, 253–254.; Hans Trefousse, *Andrew Johnson*, 128–129.

28. Hans Trefousse, *Andrew Johnson*, 129–132; Robert Corlew, *Tennessee*, 290–294; Mary Caldwell, *Tennessee*, 109.

29. *Ibid.*; Hans Trefousse, *Andrew Johnson*, 132.

30. *Ibid.*, 133–136; Robert Corlew, *Tennessee*, 294; Stephen Oates, *With Malice Toward None*, 307.

31. Kenneth Davis, *Don't Know Much About the American Presidents*, 270–271; Phillip Paludan, *The Presidency of Abraham Lincoln* (Lawrence: University of Kansas Press, 1994), 83.

32. Hans Trefousse, *Andrew Johnson*, 138–139; Richard Carwardine, *Lincoln*, 137, 157, 171.

33. Noel Fisher, *War at Every Door*, 49; Hans Trefousse, *Andrew Johnson*, 139–143; William DeGregorio, *The Complete Book of U.S. Presidents*, 251.

34. Robert Corlew, *Tennessee*, 296; David Donald, *Lincoln*, 327; Jay Winik, *April 1865*, 269; Hans Trefousse, *Andrew Johnson*, 143.

35. *Ibid.*, 144–146; Noel Fisher, *War At Every Door*, 107.

36. William McFeely, *Grant: A Biography*, 97–101; Benjamin Cooling, *Forts Henry and Donelson: The Key to the Confederate Heartland*, 66, 238, 242.

37. Kenneth Davis, *Don't Know Much About the American Presidents*, 272; William DeGregorio, *The Complete Book Of U.S. Presidents*, 251; Stephen Ash, "Sharks in An Angry Sea: Civilian Resistance and Guerrilla Warfare in Occupied Middle Tennessee, 1862–1865," *Tennessee in the Civil War*, 177; Hans Trefousse, *Andrew Johnson*, 151.

38. *Ibid.*, 152–156; William McFeely, *Grant* (New York: W. W. Norton, 1982), 143; Mary Caldwell, *Tennessee*, 113–114; Robert Corlew, *Tennessee*, 319–323; Charles Elder, *The History of Nashville*, 194. Bobby Lovett, "Nashville's Fort Negley: A Symbol of Blacks' Involvement with the Union Army," *Tennessee in the Civil War*, 124.

39. James McDonough, *Shiloh: In Hell Before Night*, v–viii; Peter Cozzens, *No Better Place to Die: The Battle of Stones River*, ix–xi; James McDonough, *Chattanooga: A Death Grip on the Confederacy*, xiii–xv; Jack Hurst, *Nathan Bedford Forrest: A Biography*, 71–76, 80–106, 112–117, 127–144, 157–82; James Ramage, *Rebel Raider: The Life of John Hunt Morgan*, 111–118, 128–133, 144–145, 150–151.

40. Stephen Ash, "Sharks in An Angry Sea: Civilian Resistance and Guerrilla Warfare in Occupied Middle Tennessee, 1862–1865," *Tennessee in the Civil War*, 181–182; Hans Trefousse, *Andrew Jackson*, 155–157.

41. Hans Trefousse, *Andrew Johnson*, 164–165.

42. *Ibid.*, 165–166; Stephen Oates, *With Malice Toward None*, 360.

43. Hans Trefousse, *Andrew Johnson*, 166–167; Noel Fisher, *War At Every Door*, 166.

44. Phillip Paludan, *The Presidency of Abraham Lincoln*, 273–274; David Donald, *Lincoln*, 506.

45. Hans Trefousse, *Andrew Johnson*, 176.

46. *Ibid.*, David Donald, *Lincoln*: 530–531.

47. William McFeely, *Grant*, 137; Phillip Paludan, *The Presidency of Abraham Lincoln*, 210–211.

48. David Donald, *Lincoln*, 505–506; Stephen Oates, *With Malice Toward None*, 422.

49. Hans Trefousse, *Andrew Johnson*, 180–182; Eric Foner, *Reconstruction*, 44.

50. William DeGregorio, *The Complete Book of U.S. Presidents*, 236.

51. John Fowler, "The Finishing Stroke to the Independence of the Southern Confederacy: Hood's Tennessee Campaign," *Tennessee in the Civil War*, 140–155; Noel Fisher, *War at Every Door*, 166; Hans Trefousse, *Andrew Johnson*, 185–186.

52. *Ibid.*, 187–192; David Donald, *Lincoln*, 165; Walter Stahr, *Seward*, 428.

53. *Ibid.*, 447; Hans Trefousse, *Andrew Johnson*, 192; Michael Kauffman, *American Brutus: John Wilkes Booth and the Lincoln Conspiracies* (New York: Random House, 2004), ix–x.

54. *Ibid.*, xi, 22–27, 61, 73; Stephen Oates, *With Malice Toward None*, 468–471; David Donald, *Lincoln*, 596; Walter Stahr, *Seward*, 1, 434; Hans Trefousse, *Andrew Johnson*, 193–196.

55. *Ibid.*, 195–196; Michael Kauffman, *American Brutus*, 261, 262–263; William McFeely, *Grant*, 225–226.

56. Kenneth Davis, *Don't Know Much About the American Presidents*, 269, 272; Eric Foner, *Reconstruction*, 44.

57. *Ibid.*, 177–178; Hans Trefousse, *Andrew Johnson*, 197–198.

58. *Ibid.*, 207–213; William McFeely, *Grant*, 230–231.

59. Hans Trefousse, *Andrew Johnson*, 215.

60. Walter Stahr, *Seward*, 447, 452, 458, 459, 460–461; Hans Trefousse, *Andrew Johnson*, 216–218.

61. William McFeely, *Grant*, 240–242; Walter Stahr, *Seward*, 447–448, 458.

62. Hans Trefousse, *Andrew Johnson*, 225–228; Eric Foner, *Reconstruction*, 190–191, 250.

63. *Ibid.*, 176–184, 187–189, 192–193, 199–201; William DeGregorio, *The Complete Book of U.S. Presidents*, 253; Kenneth Davis, *Don't Know Much About the American Presidents*, 274; Hans Trefousse, *Andrew Johnson*, 229–231.

64. *Ibid.*, 234–235, 237; Kenneth Davis, *Don't Know Much About the American Presidents*, 275.

65. *Ibid.*; Hans Trefousse, *Andrew Johnson*, 240–241, 244, 245–246; Eric Foner, *Reconstruction*, 250–251.

66. *Ibid.*, 247–251; William DeGregorio, *The Complete Book of U.S. Presidents*, 253–254; Hans Trefousse, *Andrew Johnson*, 247–251.

67. *Ibid.*, 252–253; Eric Foner, *Reconstruction*, 260–261.

68. Hans Trefousse, *Andrew Johnson*, 255–257, 272; Walter Stahr, *Seward*, 459–461.

69. *Ibid.*, 463, 469, 470–471; Eric Foner, *Reconstruction*, 229, 261–264; Jay Winik, *April 1865*, 211; Philip Dray, *Capitol Men*, 32, 53.

70. *Ibid.*, 32–35; Walter Stahr, *Seward*, 471–473; Eric Foner, *Reconstruction*, 249; Hans Trefousse, *Andrew Johnson*, 262–263.

71. Hans Trefousse, *Andrew Johnson*, 263, 267, 270, 272; Walter Stahr, *Seward*, 480; Eric Foner, *Reconstruction*, 333.

72. Philip Dray, *Capitol Men*, 35–36; Hans Trefousse, *Andrew Johnson*, 272–275.

73. *Ibid.*, 276–277; Eric Foner, *Reconstruction*, 333; Walter Stahr, *Seward*, 479–480.

74. Eric Foner, *Reconstruction*, 276–277; Hans Trefousse, *Andrew Johnson*, 280–281.

75. *Ibid.*, 282; Eric Foner, *Reconstruction*, 333–336.

76. *Ibid.*, 334–335.

77. Michael Kauffman, *American Brutus*, 379–380; Hans Trefousse, *Andrew Johnson*, 284.

78. *Ibid.*, 273, 288; Walter Stahr, *Seward*, 485, 486–487.

79. *Ibid.*, Hans Trefousse, *Andrew Johnson*, 291–293.

80. *Ibid.*, 293–295.

81. *Ibid.*, 295–296; William McFeely, *Grant*, 262.

82. *Ibid.*, 262–265; Walter Stahr, *Seward*, 507–509.

83. Hans Trefousse, *Andrew Johnson*, 298–299.

84. *Ibid.*, 300–301, 303, 304–305.

85. *Ibid.*, 306–307, 308–310; William McFeely: *Grant*, 262–268.

86. *Ibid.*, 274–275; Eric Foner, *Reconstruction*, 335–336; Walter Stahr, *Seward*, 507–508.

87. Hans Trefousse, *Andrew Johnson*, 311–315.

88. *Ibid.*, 316; William DeGregorio, *The Complete Book of U.S. Presidents*, 254.

89. Walter Stahr, *Seward*, 512–513; Hans Trefousse, *Andrew Johnson*, 319.

90. *Ibid.*

91. *Ibid.*, 324–326.

92. *Ibid.*, 326–327; Walter DeGregorio, *The Complete Book of U.S. Presidents*, 265.

93. Walter Stahr, *Seward*, 515; Hans Trefousse, *Andrew Johnson*, 331.

94. *Ibid.*, 332–334.

95. Eric Foner, *Reconstruction*, 338–339; Hans Trefousse, *Andrew Johnson*, 336–338.

96. *Ibid.*, 346–347; William DeGregorio, *The Complete Book of U.S. Presidents*, 253.

97. Hans Trefousse, *Andrew Johnson*, 351.

98. William DeGregorio, *The Complete Book of U.S. Presidents*, 255.

Chapter 13

1. Kenneth Davis, *Don't Know Much About the American Presidents*, 312.

2. Zachary Karabell, *Chester Alan Arthur*, 2.

3. *Ibid.*, Cover flaps.

4. *Ibid.*, 3.

5. H. W. Brands, *American Colossus*, 5–8; David McCullough, "The Congress: History and Promise of Representative Government," PBS Home Video.

6. Zachary Karabell, *Chester Alan Arthur*, 3.

7. Candice Millard, *Destiny of the Republic*, 102.

8. Zachary Karabell, *Chester Alan Arthur*, 6, 7.

9. Mike Donovan, *The USA in the Time of Chester Alan Arthur*, 15–16.

10. William DeGregorio, *The Complete Book of U.S. Presidents*, 310; Zachary Karabell, *Chester Alan Arthur*, 12–13.

11. *Ibid.*, 14–15; Mike Donovan, *The USA in the Time of Chester Alan Arthur*, 12–13.

12. Zachary Karabell, *Chester Alan Arthur*, 16.

13. Candice Millard, *Destiny of the Republic*, 40–43; Kenneth Davis, *Don't Know Much About the American Presidents*, 314.

14. Zachary Karabell, *Chester Alan Arthur*, 25–26.

15. H. W. Brands, *American Colossus*, 378–383.

16. Shanthi Rexaline, "Every President Who Won the Election, but Lost the Popular Vote," Benzinga.com, December 6, 2016.

17. Candice Millard, *Destiny of the Republic*, 72–

73; Kenneth Davis, *Don't Know Much About the American Presidents*, 297–298.

18. *Ibid.*; William DeGregorio, *The Complete Book of U.S. Presidents*, 288, 310.

19. Zachary Karabell, *Chester Alan Arthur*, 29; David Bain, *Empire Express*, 452.

20. *Ibid.*, 28.

21. Candace Millard, *Destiny Of The Republic*, 40–41; Zachary Karabell, *Chester Alan Arthur*, 30–32; H. W. Brands, *American Colossus*, 394.

22. Zachary Karabell, *Chester Alan Arthur*, 32–33.

23. *Ibid.*, 34–35, 38; Mike Donovan, *The USA in the Time of Chester Alan Arthur*, 13.

24. *Ibid.*; Zachary Karabell, *Chester Alan Arthur*, 39.

25. Candice Millard, *Destiny of the Republic*, 40–53; William DeGregorio, *The Complete Book of U.S. Presidents*, 284–285.

26. Zachary Karabell, *Chester Alan Arthur*, 40–41.

27. *Ibid.*, 41–42.

28. *Ibid.*, 42–43.

29. Candice Millard, *Destiny of the Republic*, 67–68.

30. Zachary Karabell, *Chester Alan Arthur*, 46–51; William DeGregorio, *The Complete Book of U.S. Presidents*, 300.

31. Zachary Karabell, *Chester Alan Arthur*, 51–52, 57, 59, 62, 65; Candice Millard, *Destiny of the Republic*, 153, 194, 197–198, 207–208, 264–265.

32. Zachary Karabell, *Chester Alan Arthur*, 62.

33. Kenneth Davis, *Don't Know Much About the American Presidents*, 314.

34. Zachary Karabell, *Chester Alan Arthur*, 63, 64.

35. Candice Millard, *Destiny of the Republic*, 192, 213–216.

36. Zachary Karabell, *Chester Alan Arthur*, 65–66.

37. Mike Donovan, *The USA in the Time of Chester Alan Arthur*, 15; Zachary Karabell, *Chester Alan Arthur*, 66–67.

38. *Ibid.*, 67–68.

39. Mike Donovan, *The USA in the Time of Chester Alan Arthur*, 16.

40. Zachary Karabell, *Chester Alan Arthur*, 68.

41. *Ibid.*, 68–69.

42. *Ibid.*, 69; Candice Millard, *Destiny of the Republic*, 241, 289; Mike Donovan, *The USA in the Time of Chester Alan Arthur*, 26.

43. *Ibid.*, 26–27; Zachary Karabell, *Chester Alan Arthur*, 72–74.

44. *Ibid.*, 74.

45. *Ibid.*, 81.

46. Kenneth Davis, *Don't Know Much About the American Presidents*, 315–316; Zachary Karabell, *Chester Alan Arthur*, 83; Ric Burns and Li-Shin Yu, "The Chinese Exclusion Act," American Experience Video.

47. *Ibid.*

48. H. W. Brands, *American Colossus*, 285; Kenneth Davis, *Don't Know Much About the American Presidents*, 316; Zachary Karabell, *Chester Alan Arthur*, 85–86.

49. Ric Burns and Li-Shin Yu, "The Chinese Exclusion Act," American Experience Video.

50. Candice Millard, *Destiny of the Republic*, 273–280; Zachary Karabell, *Chester Alan Arthur*, 86–87; Mike Donovan, *The USA in the Time of Chester Alan Arthur*, 17–19.

51. *Ibid.*; Zachary Karabell, *Chester Alan Arthur*, 87–88.

52. *Ibid.*, 88–89.

53. *Ibid.*, 90; William DeGregorio, *The Complete Book of U.S. Presidents*, 156, 253–254, 313.

54. *Ibid.*, 314; Mike Donovan, *The USA at the Time of Chester Alan Arthur*, 50; Zachary Karabell, *Chester Alan Arthur*, 92.

55. Mike Donovan, *The USA in the Time of Chester Alan Arthur*, 26–28; Zachary Karabell, *Chester Alan Arthur*, 95.

56. *Ibid.*, 95–98.

57. William DeGregorio, *The Complete Book of U.S. Presidents*, 313; Kenneth Davis, *Don't Know Much About the American Presidents*, 312; Mike Donovan, *The USA in the Time of Chester Alan Arthur*, 28.

58. Zachary Karabell, *Chester Alan Arthur*, 104–107.

59. Jason Emerson, *Giant in the Shadows* (Carbondale: Southern Illinois University Press, 2012), 259–260; Zachary Karabell, *Chester Alan Arthur*, 113–114.

60. *Ibid.*, 114.

61. *Ibid.*, 115–120; Mike Donovan, *The USA in the Time of Chester Alan Arthur*, 20–21; William DeGregorio, *The Complete Book of U.S. Presidents*, 313–314.

62. Zachary Karabell, *Chester Alan Arthur*, 120–121.

63. *Ibid.*, 122.

64. *Ibid.*, 123.

65. David McCullough, *The Great Bridge*, Audio Book (Disc Nine); Nancy Cash and Terry Spohn, *Today in History*, 292.

66. Jason Emerson, *Giant in the Shadows*, 245–248.

67. Zachary Karabell, *Chester Alan Arthur*, 126–127.

68. Paul Jeffers, *An Honest President: The Life and Presidencies of Grover Cleveland*, 57, 96–97, 111.

69. *Ibid.*, 113–117; Kenneth Davis, *Don't Know Much About the American Presidents*, 322; Zachary Karabell, *Chester Alan Arthur*, 133.

70. *Ibid.*, 134; William DeGregorio, *The Complete Book of U.S. Presidents*, 326.

71. *Ibid.*, 314; Jason Emerson, *Giant in the Shadows*, 288–289; Zachary Karabell, *Chester Alan Arthur*, 137, 139.

Chapter 14

1. Edmund Morris, *Theodore Rex*, 3; Kenneth Davis, *Don't Know Much About the American Presidents*, 363, 364.

2. *Ibid.*, 3–11, 43; Edmund Morris, *The Rise of Theodore Roosevelt*, 654.

3. William DeGregorio, *The Complete Book of U.S. Presidents*, 379–381.

4. H. W. Brands, *T.R.*, 518; Edmund Morris, *Theodore Rex*, 10, 430, 431.

5. *Ibid.*, Book Jacket.

6. *Ibid.*; Michael Kazin, *A Godly Hero: The Life of William Jennings Bryan*, 113–114; Brion McClanahan, *Nine Presidents Who Screwed Up America and Four Who Tried to Save Her*, 35–36, 52–53.

7. Edmund Morris, *Theodore Rex*, 13–40; H. W. Brands, *T.R.*, 416.

8. Edmund Morris, *Theodore Rex*, 43–45.

9. *Ibid.*, 47–51.

10. *Ibid.*, 52–58; H. W. Brands, *T.R.*, 421–424; George Mowry, *The Era of Theodore Roosevelt and The Birth of Modern America, 1900–1912*, 165–166; Brion McClanahan, *Nine Presidents Who Screwed Up America and Four Who Tried to Save Her*, 47.

11. Edmund Morris, *Theodore Rex*, 59–60.

12. *Ibid.*, 62–65; George Mowry, *The Era of Theodore Roosevelt and The Birth of Modern America*, 131.

13. William DeGregorio, *The Complete Book Of U.S. Presidents*, 389; Edmund Morris, *Theodore Rex*, 89–90.

14. *Ibid.*, 91–94; George Mowry, *The Era of Theodore Roosevelt and The Birth of Modern America* (New York: Harper & Row, 1958), 132–133; H. W. Brands, *T.R.*, 437.

15. *Ibid.*, 424–425; Edmund Morris, *Theodore Rex*, 94–95.

16. *Ibid.*, 131; George Mowry, *The Era of Theodore Roosevelt and The Birth of Modern America*, 134–136.

17. Edmund Morris, *Theodore Rex*, 136–137.

18. *Ibid.*, 137, 139.

19. *Ibid.*, 142–143, 150–152; H. W. Brands, *T.R.*, 452–454.

20. Edmund Morris, *Theodore Rex*, 155, 156, 158; H. W. Brands, *T.R.*, 454–455.

21. *Ibid.*, 455; Edmund Morris, *Theodore Rex*, 159–161.

22. *Ibid.*, 162, 164, 165; Brion McClanahan, *Nine Presidents Who Screwed Up America and Four Who Tried to Save Her*, 43.

23. *Ibid.*, 163–169; James Morris, *Pulitzer: A Life in Politics, Print, and Power*, 1; George Mowry, *The Era of Theodore Roosevelt and The Birth of Modern America*, 137–140; William DeGregorio, *The Complete Book of U.S. Presidents*, 386.

24. *Ibid.*, 385; H. W. Brands, *T.R.*, 463–471.

25. Edmund Morris, *Theodore Rex*, 67–68, 201–202, 241; David McCullough, *The Path Between the Seas: The Creation of the Panama Canal, 1870–1914* (New York: Simon & Schuster, 1977), 333–341, 384; Brion McClanahan, *Nine Presidents Who Screwed Up America and Four Who Tried to Save Her*, 51–52.

26. Edmund Morris, *Theodore Rex*, 202.

27. *Ibid.*, 208, 215–219; H. W. Brands, *T.R.*, 471–475.

28. *Ibid.*, 477–486; Edmund Morris, *Theodore Rex*, 238–240.

29. *Ibid.*, 242–243.

30. *Ibid.*, 85–86, 243; George Mowry, *The Era of Theodore Roosevelt and the Birth of Modern America*, 150–152; H. W. Brands, *T.R.*, 479–491; William DeGregorio, *The Complete Book of U.S. Presidents*, 385.

31. Edmund Morris, *Theodore Rex*, 272–283.

32. *Ibid.*, 264, 285–294.

33. *Ibid.*, 293, 295–296; James Morris, *Pulitzer*, 417–418.

34. Kenneth Davis, *Don't Know Much About the American Presidents*, 368–369.

35. Edmund Morris, *Theodore Rex*, 387–414, 433–435, 437–438, 447–448; William DeGregorio, *The Complete Book of U.S. Presidents*, 385.

36. *Ibid.*, 382, 385, 387; Kenneth Davis, *Don't Know Much About the American Presidents*, 369; Doris Goodwin, *The Bully Pulpit*, 422.

37. *Ibid.* 1; George Mowry, *The Era of Theodore Roosevelt and the Birth of Modern America*, 180; Edmund Morris, *Theodore Rex*, 364; H. W. Brands, *T.R.*, 514.

38. *Ibid.*, 528–541; Edmund Morris, *Theodore Rex*, 311, 399–400, 414, 415.

39. *Ibid.*, 387, 397; H. W. Brands, *T.R.*, 528.

40. Edmund Morris, *Theodore Rex*, 376, 396–397.

41. *Ibid.* 377–378, 387; H. W. Brands, *T.R.*, 528–535.

42. Edmund Morris, *Theodore Rex*, 312–313, 387, 393, 396–397.

43. H. W. Brands, *T.R.*, 536–540; Edmund Morris, *Theodore Rex*, 414; William DeGregorio, *The Complete Book of U.S. Presidents*, 385.

44. George Mowry, *The Era of Theodore Roosevelt and the Birth of Modern America*, 199–205; Edmund Morris, *Theodore Rex*, 422–423.

45. *Ibid.*, 427.

46. *Ibid.*, 430–431.

47. *Ibid.*, 431, 433; George Mowry, *The Era of Theodore Roosevelt and the Birth of Modern America*, 203.

48. *Ibid.*, 203–206; Edmund Morris, *Theodore Rex*, 433–436, 445.

49. *Ibid.*, 437–438; H. W. Brands, *T.R.*, 548–549.

50. *Ibid.*, 549–551; Edmund Morris, *Theodore Rex*, 448.

51. Douglas Brinkley, *The Wilderness Warrior*, 642–647, 663–665; Brion McClanahan, *Nine Presidents Who Screwed Up America and Four Who Tried to Save Her*, 46.

52. Edmund Morris, *Theodore Rex*, 498–499, 507.

53. Doris Kearns Goodwin, *The Bully Pulpit*, 511–515; Edmund Morris, *Theodore Rex*, 511.

54. *Ibid.*, 535; Doris Goodwin, *The Bully Pulpit*, 515; George Mowry, *The Era of Theodore Roosevelt and the Birth of Modern America*, 214.

55. *Ibid.*, 2–3, 708–741, 732–735, 744; H. W. Brands, *T.R.*, 785–786, 797–798.

56. *Ibid.*, 797, 802, 814.

57. *Ibid.*, 808, 811, 812.

Chapter 15

1. Kenneth Davis, *Don't Know Much About the American Presidents*, 409; Amity Shlaes, *Coolidge*, Book Cover.

2. William DeGregorio, *The Complete Book of U.S. Presidents*, 447; Amity Shlaes, *Coolidge*, 5–12.

3. *Ibid.*, 5–6; Brion McClanahan, *Nine Presidents*

Who Screwed Up America and Four Who Tried to Save Her, 252.

4. Amity Shlaes, *Coolidge*, 7–8; Brion McClanahan, *Nine Presidents Who Screwed Up America and Four Who Tried to Save Her*, 267–270.

5. David Pietrusza, *1920: The Year of Six Presidents*, 90, 98–100, 224–234, 239–240, 315.

6. Amity Shlaes, *Coolidge*, 202.

7. David Pietrusza, *1920*, 312–313.

8. Samuel Adams, *Incredible Era*, 167.

9. Andrew Sinclair, *The Available Man*, 158, 173; William DeGregorio, *The Complete Book Of U.S. Presidents*, 437–438, 486.

10. Amity Shlaes, *Coolidge*, 214.

11. Samuel Adams, *Incredible Era*, 221; Amity Shlaes, *Coolidge*, 226.

12. *Ibid.*, 227; Andrew Sinclair, *The Available Man* (Quadrangle Books, 1965), 181–197, 261–263; Samuel Adams, *Incredible Era*, 196–208; Kenneth Davis, *Don't Know Much About the American Presidents*, 400–401.

13. Laton McCartney, *The Teapot Dome Scandal*, 110, 147, 158–159; Amity Shlaes, *Coolidge*, 233, 242.

14. *Ibid.*, 233, 245.

15. *Ibid.*, 249–251; Samuel Adams, *Incredible Era*, 366; Warren DeGregorio, *The Complete Book of U.S. Presidents*, 442.

16. *Ibid.*, 452–453; Amity Shlaes, *Coolidge*, 251.

17. *Ibid.*, 251–253.

18. *Ibid.*, 256; James Burns and Susan Dunn, *The Three Roosevelts: Patrician Leaders Who Transformed America* (New York: Grove Press, 2001), 62–63.

19. Amity Shlaes, *Coolidge*, 257; William DeGregorio, *The Complete Book of U.S. Presidents*, 257–258; Kenneth Davis, *Don't Know Much About the American Presidents*, 408.

20. Amity Shlaes, *Coolidge*, 261, 267; Kenneth Davis, *Don't Know Much About the American Presidents*, 409–410; Brion McClanahan, *Nine Presidents Who Screwed Up America and Four Who Tried to Save Her*, 256.

21. *Ibid.*, 251; Amity Shlaes, *Coolidge*, 269, 271, 272, 273.

22. Laton McCartney, *The Teapot Dome Scandal*, 158–159; Amity Shlaes, *Coolidge*, 280–282.

23. *Ibid.*; William DeGregorio, *The Complete Book of U.S. Presidents*, 457.

24. Amity Shlaes, *Coolidge*, 292, 294.

25. James Burns and Susan Dunn, *The Three Roosevelts*, 189.

26. Amity Shlaes, *Coolidge*, 302–303, 308–311.

27. *Ibid.*, 315, 318, 319; William DeGregorio, *The Complete Book of U.S. Presidents*, 455.

28. Amity Shlaes, *Coolidge*, 330–331, 335.

29. William DeGregorio, *The Complete Book of U.S. Presidents*, 457.

30. *Ibid.*, 337.

31. *Ibid.*

32. Robert Sobel, *Coolidge: An American Enigma*, 311; Amity Shlaes, *Coolidge*, 339–340.

33. *Ibid.*, 344–347.

34. Brion McClanahan, *Nine Presidents Who Screwed Up America and Four Who Tried to Save*

Her, 264; William DeGregorio, *The Complete Book of U.S. Presidents*, 458; Amity Shlaes, *Coolidge*, 348–350.

35. *Ibid.*, 350.

36. *Ibid.*, 344, 352–353; James Burns and Susan Dunn, *The Three Roosevelts*, 247; Brion McClanahan, *Nine Presidents Who Screwed Up America and Four Who Tried to Save Her*, 364.

37. *Ibid.*, 265–266; Amity Shlaes, *Coolidge*, 357.

38. *Ibid.*, 357–360; Brion McClanahan, *Nine Presidents Who Screwed Up American and Four Who Tried to Save Her*, 266–267.

39. Amity Shlaes, *Coolidge*, 359–360.

40. *Ibid.*, 360–366; Nancy Cash and Terry Spohn, *Today In History*, 287.

41. Amity Shlaes, *Coolidge*, 367–371, 372–374.

42. *Ibid.*, 375–376, 381.

43. *Ibid.*, 381–382, 384; Brion McClanahan, *Nine Presidents Who Screwed Up America and Four Who Tried to Save Her*, 270.

44. Amity Shlaes, *Coolidge*, 388, 389.

45. *Ibid.*, 390; Brion McClanahan, *Nine Presidents Who Screwed Up America and Four Who Tried to Save Her*, 258–259.

46. Amity Shlaes, *Coolidge*, 397–398.

47. *Ibid.*, 398–402.

48. *Ibid.*, 402–403.

49. William DeGregorio, *The Complete Book of U.S. Presidents*, 458; Amity Shlaes, *Coolidge*, 408–412.

50. Brion McClanahan, *Nine Presidents Who Screwed Up America and Four Who Tried to Save Her*, 267, 269.

51. William DeGregorio, *The Complete Book of U.S. Presidents*, 459; Amity Shlaes, *Coolidge*, 435–436, 441.

52. *Ibid.*, 446, 450; William DeGregorio, *The Complete Book of U.S. Presidents*, 473–474; Nathan Miller, *F.D.R., An Intimate History*, 282–283.

53. Amity Shlaes, *Coolidge*, 450–453.

54. *Ibid.*, 452, 454; Brion McClanahan, *Nine Presidents Who Screwed Up America and Four Who Tried to Save Her*, 270; William DeGregorio, *The Complete Book of U.S. Presidents*, 389, 459.

Chapter 16

1. David McCullough, *Truman*, Book Cover, 9–10, 340–342; David McCullough, *John Adams*, Book Cover; Walter Isaacson and Evan Thomas, *The Wise Men: Six Friends and the World They Made, George Kennan, Dean Acheson, Charles Bohlen, Robert Lovett, Averell Harriman, John McCloy*, 255–256.

2. William DeGregorio, *The Complete Book of U.S. Presidents*, 509, 511–512; David McCullough, *Truman*, 349, 352.

3. *Ibid.*, 353; Walter Isaacson and Evan Thomas, *The Wise Men*, 255–257; Robert Ferrell, *The Dying President: Franklin D. Roosevelt, 1944–1945*, 151.

4. David McCullough, *Truman*, 357–358.

5. *Ibid.*, 358–359.

6. Brion McClanahan, *Nine Presidents Who*

Screwed Up American and Four Who Tried to Save Her, 100–101; David McCullough, *Truman*, 378–379, 390–397, 454–457, 457–458.

7. *Ibid.*, 382–384, 403–404, 409–410.

8. *Ibid.*, 410–412, 416; Walter Isaacson and Evan Thomas, *The Wise Men*, 303–305.

9. Richard Overy, *The Dictators: Hitler's Germany, Stalin's Russia*, 20; David McCullough, *Truman*, 417–418.

10. *Ibid.*, 418.

11. *Ibid.*, 420–426, 432–433, 445.

12. Richard Overy, *The Dictators*, 650; Walter Isaacson and Evan Thomas, *The Wise Men*, 291.

13. *Ibid.*, 302–305; Forest Pogue, *George C. Marshall: Statesman, 1949–1959*, 20–21; David McCullough, *Truman*, 430–439.

14. *Ibid.*, 435–437.

15. *Ibid.*, 438–439.

16. *Ibid.*, 442–443; Winston Churchill, *Memoirs of the Second World War*, 982, 983.

17. Ronald Spector, *In The Ruins of Empire: The Japanese Surrender and the Battle for Postwar Asia*, 3; Forest Pogue, *George C. Marshall*, 21–22; David McCullough, Truman, 447, 449, 451.

18. *Ibid.*, 453–455.

19. *Ibid.*, 455, 457, 459, 461; Forrest Pogue, *George C. Marshall*, 22–23.

20. David McCullough, *Truman*, 463.

21. David Grubin, "Truman," American Experience Video (Part 2).

22. David McCullough, *Truman*, 525.

23. David Grubin, "Truman," American Experience Video (Part 2).

24. Forrest Pogue, *George C. Marshall*, 145–146; David McCullough, *Truman*, 532–534, 539–541.

25. *Ibid.*, 545–547, 548–549, 554, 565; Walter DeGregorio, *The Complete Book of U.S. Presidents*, 519; Kenneth Davis, *Don't Know Much About the American Presidents*, 453–454.

26. David McCullough, *Truman*, 585.

27. William Leuchtenburg, *The White House Looks South: Franklin D. Roosevelt, Harry S. Truman, Lyndon B. Johnson*, 163–192.

28. Michael Beschloss, *Presidential Courage*, 197–203, 207–209, 214–232; David Pietrusza, *1948: Harry Truman's Improbable Victory and the Year That Transformed America* (New York: Union Square Press, 2011), 109, 114, 115–117.

29. David McCullough, *Truman*, 584, 624, 629, 663; David Pietrusza, *1948*, 362–364; William DeGregorio, *The Complete Book of U.S. Presidents*, 514.

30. David McCullough, *Truman*, 723–724.

31. *Ibid.*, 725, 726, 731, 733.

32. Walter DeGregorio, *The Complete Book of U.S. Presidents*, 519; Forest Pogue, *George C. Marshall*, 300, 302–303, 333, 335; David McCullough, *Truman*, 734–735, 742.

33. *Ibid.*, 743–744, 747–749.

34. *Ibid.*, 751–757; Forrest Pogue, *George C. Marshall*, 413–415; Walter Isaacson and Evan Thomas, *The Wise Men*, 464–466, 480–481.

35. *Ibid.*, 486–489; David McCullough, *Truman*, 761–764.

36. *Ibid.*, 759–760; Jonathan Aitken, *Nixon: A Life*, 150, 176; David Pietrusza, *1948*, 297.

37. David McCullough, *Truman*, 764.

38. *Ibid.*, 765–766, 770; Walter DeGregorio, *The Complete Book of U.S. Presidents*, 520–521.

39. David McCullough, *Truman*, 770–771.

40. Walter Isaacson and Evan Thomas, *The Wise Men*, 505–507; David McCullough, *Truman*, 773–776.

41. *Ibid.*, 777–778; Forrest Pogue, *George C. Marshall*, 448–449.

42. David Halberstam, *The Coldest Winter: America and the Korean War* (New York: Hyperion, 2007), 54–55, 94, 101, 166–168, 293–295, 306–309, 381–383, 388, 390.

43. David McCullough, *Truman*, 808–811; William DeGregorio, *The Complete Book of U.S. Presidents*, 521.

44. David McCullough, *Truman* 813–815.

45. David Halberstam, *The Coldest Winter*, 407–424.

46. David McCullough, *Truman*, 816–817.

47. *Ibid.*, 820.

48. *Ibid.*, 820–822.

49. David Halberstam, *The Coldest Winter*, 477–482.

50. *Ibid.*, 482–483; David McCullough, *Truman*, 823–824.

51. *Ibid.*, 824–825, 826, 832, 835; David Halberstam, *The Coldest Winter*, 591, 593.

52. *Ibid.*, 588, 593–594; David McCullough, *Truman*, 833, 834–835.

53. *Ibid.*, 836–837, 838; David Halberstam, *The Coldest Winter*, 597–601.

54. David McCullough, *Truman*, 837–838; David Halberstam, *The Coldest Winter*, 603–604.

55. *Ibid.*, 605–606; David McCullough, *Truman*, 840–844.

56. *Ibid.*, 844–845, 846, 850–852.

57. *Ibid.*, 849, 852–854, 856; *David Halberstam, The Coldest Winter*, 610–617.

58. William DeGregorio, *The Complete Book of U.S Presidents*, 520, 538; Forrest Pogue, *George C. Marshall*, 488–490; David McCullough, *Truman* 860–861.

59. *Ibid.*, 886–891.

60. *Ibid.*, 895, 896–897; William DeGregorio, *The Complete Book of U.S. Presidents*, 520.

61. Noah Feldman, *Scorpions: The Battles and Triumphs of FDR's Great Supreme Court Justices*, 356–368; Brion McClanahan, *Nine Presidents Who Screwed Up America and Four Who Tried to Save Her*, 116–117; David McCullough, *Truman*, 899–903.

62. *Ibid.*, 903–904, 913; William DeGregorio, *The Complete Book of U.S. Presidents*, 534–535.

63. David McCullough, *Truman*, 928, 930, 932, 936.

64. *Ibid.*, 947–949, 952, 958, 960, 974; William DeGregorio, *The Complete Book of U.S. Presidents*, 522.

65. "Harry S. Truman National Historic Site," wikipedia.org.

Chapter 17

1. David Grubin, "LBJ," American Experience Video (Part 1).

2. Anthony Summers, *Official and Confidential: The Secret Life of J. Edgar Hoover*, 273; Robert Caro, *The Passage Of Power*, 21, 74, 82, 95, 113–114.

3. *Ibid.*, 7, 8–9, 48, 112, 114–115, 118–120; William Leuchtenburg, *The White House Looks South*, 281–282; Robert Dallek, *An Unfinished Life*, 269–271.

4. Robert Caro, *The Passage of Power*, 22–23; Robert Caro, *Master of the Senate*, 521–523, 540–541, 601.

5. Robert Caro, *The Passage of Power*, 119–120.

6. *Ibid.*, 140–141; Robert Dallek, *An Unfinished Life*, 26, 239, 254, 257, 264; David Nasaw, *The Patriarch: The Remarkable Life and Turbulent Times of Joseph P. Kennedy*, 720.

7. David Grubin, "LBJ," American Experience Video; Robert Caro, *The Passage of Power*, 242–245, 263–265.

8. *Ibid.*, 135–138, 246–249, 264–270, 294–295; William DeGregorio, *The Complete Book of U.S. Presidents*, 552–553.

9. David Grubin, "LBJ," American Experience Video; Robert Caro, *The Passage of Power*, 270–271, 272, 273, 301–302, 307.

10. *Ibid.*, 309, 311, 312–313; William Leuchtenburg, *The White House Looks South*, 295–296; Robert Dallek, *An Unfinished Life*, 691–695.

11. Robert Caro, *The Passage of Power*, 317, 319–326.

12. John Williams, "Robert Caro Nearing the End of His Epic LBJ Bio, Eyes a Trip to Vietnam," *New York Times*, June 2, 2017.

13. *Ibid.*; Jacqueline Trescott, "Obama Honors Leaders in Arts and Humanities," *Washington Post*, February 26, 2010.

14. Nancy Cash and Terry Spohn, *Today In History*, 657; Robert Caro, *The Passage of Power*, 319–336.

15. Hans Trefousse, *Andrew Johnson*, 193–196; Zachary Karabell, *Chester Alan Arthur*, 63, 64; Edmund Morris, *Theodore Rex*, 3–11, 43; David McCullough, *Truman*, 357–358.

16. Robert Caro, *The Passage of Power*, 313–317, 323–324, 328–336, 339–345.

17. *Ibid.*, 319.

18. *Ibid.*, 324.

19. Edmund Morris, *The Rise of Theodore Roosevelt*, 738–741; Candice Millard, *Destiny of the Republic*, 253–254; Nancy Cass and Terry Spohn, *Today In History*, 213–214, 657.

20. Robert Caro, *The Passage of Power*, 344–351, 358, 411, 603; Robert Caro, *Means of Ascent*, 10.

21. Robert Caro, *The Passage of Power*, 341–343, 364–365, 386.

22. *Ibid.*, 344, 349, 376, 399–400, 409–414.

23. *Ibid.*, 419–421.

24. Jonathan Aitken, *Nixon*, 321; Jon Meacham, *The Soul of America*, 229; Brion McClanahan, *Nine Presidents Who Screwed Up America and Four Who Tried to Save Her*, 120.

25. Robert Caro, *The Passage of Power*, 345–349;

William Leuchtenburg, *The White House Looks South*, 294–295, 300; Jon Meacham, *The Soul of America*, 222.

26. *Ibid.*, 229–232; William Leuchtenberg, *The White House Looks South*, 302–303; Robert Caro, *The Passage of Power*, 348–349.

27. William Leuchtenburg, *The White House Looks South*, 303–309.

28. Robert Caro, *The Passage of Power*, 430–431.

29. *Ibid.*, 433; Jon Meacham, *The Soul of America*, 229–230.

30. Robert Caro, *Means of Ascent*, xix–xx, xxi.

31. *Ibid.*, xxi; Robert Caro, *The Passage of Power*, 604; William DeGregorio, *The Complete Book of U.S. Presidents*, 569–571, 574–575.

32. Robert Caro, *Means of Ascent*, xxiii–xxvi; Kenneth Davis, *Don't Know Much About the American Presidents*, 502–503.

33. Robert Caro, *Means of Ascent*, xxv–xxvi; Robert Caro, *The Passage of Power*, 604.

34. Robert Caro, *Means of Ascent*, xxvi; Anthony Summers, *Official and Confidential*, 272–273.

35. Robert Caro, *Means of Ascent*, 4–7.

36. *Ibid.*, 6–7.

37. *Ibid.*, 8; William DeGregorio, *The Complete Book of U.S. Presidents*, 565, 567.

38. Robert Caro, *The Path of Power*, 737–740.

39. William DeGregorio, *The Complete Book of U.S. Presidents*, 567–568; Robert Caro, *Means of Ascent*, 20, 26, 35–36, 39–43, 141.

40. *Ibid.*, 141, 175, 177, 180.

41. *Ibid.*, 180–191; Robert Caro, *Master of the Senate*, 116.

42. Robert Caro, *The Passage of Power*, 3–8; Kenneth Davis, *Don't Know Much About the American Presidents*, 504–505; William DeGregorio, *The Complete Book of U.S. Presidents*, 577.

Chapter 18

1. Douglas Brinkley, *Gerald R. Ford*, Book Cover.

2. *Ibid.*, 2–3, 5–6, 13; William DeGregorio, *The Complete Book of U.S. Presidents*, 605, 608.

3. Douglas Brinkley, *Gerald R. Ford*, 5–13.

4. *Ibid.*, 13.

5. *Ibid.*, 15, 17–18, 20–21, 23; David Halberstam, *The Fifties*, x–xi; Laura Kalman, *Right Star Rising*, xix–xxi.

6. Douglas Brinkley, *Gerald R. Ford*, 26, 30–31; Laura Kalman, *Right Star Rising*, 5.

7. Kenneth Davis, *Don't Know Much About the American Presidents*, 531; Douglas Brinkley, *Gerald R. Ford*, 32.

8. *Ibid.*, 34–35, Kenneth Davis, *Don't Know Much About the American Presidents*, 518–519.

9. Jonathan Aitken, *Nixon*, 503–504, 505–506; William DeGregorio, *The Complete Book of U.S. Presidents*, 592.

10. Douglas Brinkley, *Gerald R. Ford*, 52, 53–54.

11. *Ibid.*, 54–58.

12. *Ibid.*, 58–59.

13. *Ibid.*, 59, 71–74; Laura Kalman, *Right Star Rising*, 14–17.

14. William DeGregorio, *The Complete Book of U.S. Presidents*, 613.

15. *Ibid.*, 613–614; Kenneth Davis, *Don't Know Much About the American Presidents*, 537; Laura Kalman, *Right Star Rising*, 152, 153.

16. *Ibid.*, 126–127; Douglas Brinkley, *Gerald R. Ford*, 118–119, 122; Jon Meacham, *The Soul of America*, 260; Kenneth Davis, *Don't Know Much About the American Presidents*, 549, 562.

17. Douglas Brinkley, *Gerald R. Ford*, 139–140, 145–146, 150, 152–153.

18. *Ibid.*, Book Cover.

19. Jonathan Aitken, *Nixon*, 472–480; Robert Caro, *Means of Ascent*, xxiv–xxv; Robert Dallek, *An Unfinished Life*, 359–366, 439–440; Stephen Kinzer, *The Brothers: John Foster Dulles, Allen Dulles, and Their Secret World War*, 3, 133, 159, 248; David Pietrusza, *1948*, 51.

20. Andrew Sinclair, *The Available Man*, 21; Amity Shlaes, *Coolidge*, 255; Laura Kalman, *Right Star Rising*, 7, 203.

21. Jon Meacham, *The Soul of America*, 266–271.

22. Adam Clymer and James Naughton, "Gerald Ford, Thirty-eighth President Dies at Ninety-three," *New York Times*, December 27, 2006; Jill Vejnoska, "Celebrate Jimmy Carter's Birthday and Other Things to Do in Atlanta on Monday," *Atlanta Journal-Constitution*, September 30, 2018; Rachel Siegel, "George H. W. Bush Makes History by Celebrating His Ninety-fourth Birthday," *Washington Post*, June 12, 2018.

23. William DeGregorio, *The Complete Book of U.S. Presidents*, 614; Douglas Brinkley, *Gerald R. Ford*, 150, 157.

24. *Ibid.*, 151.

25. *Ibid.*, 151–153.

26. *Ibid.*, 154–155, 157–158, 159.

Chapter 19

1. Ann-Marie Imboroni, "How Do The Presidents Rank?" Infoplease.com, October 19, 2018; Brion McClanahan, *Nine Presidents Who Screwed Up America and Four Who Tried To Save Her*, xii.

2. Brennan Weiss, "Ranked: The Greatest U.S. Presidents According to Political Scientists," *New Haven Register*, February 20, 2018; Jackie Bischof, "The Best U.S. Presidents, as Ranked by Presidential Historians," *Quartz* February 19, 2017.

3. *Ibid.*

4. *Ibid.*; Brennan Weiss, "Ranked: The Greatest U.S. Presidents According to Political Scientists," *New Haven Register*, February 20, 2018; George Mowry, *The Era of Theodore Roosevelt and the Birth of Modern America*, 1900–1912, x.

5. Jackie Bischof, "The Best U.S. Presidents as Ranked by Presidential Historians," *Quartz* February 19, 2017; Brennan Weiss, "Ranked: The Greatest U.S. Presidents According to Political Scientists," *New Haven Register*, February 20, 2018.

6. Jackie Bischof, "The Best U.S. Presidents as Ranked by Presidential Historians," *Quartz* February 19, 2017.

7. Kenneth Davis, Don't Know Much About the American Presidents, xiv–xvi; Elizabeth Nix, "Which States Have Produced the Most Presidents," History Channel (September 10, 2014); Aline Cain, "Twenty-nine Presidents Who Served in the Military," *Business Insider*, February 19, 2018.

8. Brion McClanahan, *Nine Presidents Who Screwed Up America and Four Who Tried to Save Her*, 35–54, 99–118, 119–140, 209–230, 251–272.

9. William DeGregorio, *The Complete Book of U.S. Presidents*, 382, 454–455, 514–515, 570–571, 623–624; Kenneth Davis, *Don't Know Much About the American Presidents*, 192, 219, 275, 317, 533.

10. *Ibid.*, 192, 219–220, 316–317, 369–370, 411–412, 458–459, 504–505, 532–533.

Chapter 20

1. William DeGregorio, *The Complete Book of U.S. Presidents*, 151, 188, 248, 308, 374, 449, 509, 565, 605.

2. *Ibid.*, 188, 248, 565; Kenneth Davis, *Don't Know Much About the American Presidents*, 214.

3. William DeGregorio, *The Complete Book of U.S. Presidents*, 449, 509.

4. *Ibid.*, 605.

5. Kenneth Davis, *Don't Know Much About the American Presidents*, 189, 313–314, 362–363.

6. Zachary Karabell, *Chester Alan Arthur*, 10, 129; David McCullough, *Truman*, 308, 585, 708–709; Douglas Brinkley, *Gerald R. Ford*, 33, 118–119, 144; Amity Shlaes, *Coolidge*, 187, 302, 319.

7. *Ibid.*, 183–185, 222, 245, 337–340.

8. *Ibid.*, 202; David McCullough, *Truman*, 314.

9. *Ibid.*, 356, 359, 468; Brion McClanahan, *Nine Presidents Who Screwed Up America and Four Who Tried to Save Her*, 99–100; Walter Isaacson and Evan Thomas, *The Wise Men*, 395–399, 404–408, 450, 507–509.

10. Mike Donovan, *The USA in the Time of Chester Alan Arthur: 1881–1885*, 26–28; Candice Millard, *Destiny of the Republic*, 289; Zachary Karabell, *Chester Alan Arthur*, 131; H. W. Brands, *American Colossus*, 397–406.

11. Laura Kalman, *Right Star Rising*, 126–127, 165–171, 172, 178–179; Douglas Brinkley, *Gerald R. Ford*, 144–145.

12. *Ibid.*, 17, 53–61; Jon Meacham, *Destiny and Power: The American Odyssey of George Walker Bush*, 170.

13. H. W. Brands, *T.R.*, 419–421, 426–430, 433; Robert Caro, *The Passage of Power*, xix, 3–8, 602, 603.

14. Edward Crapol, *John Tyler*, 9–11; Doris Kearns Goodwin, *The Bully Pulpit*, 259, 260, 278; Robert Caro, *The Passage of Power*, 3–5, 312–317.

15. Hans Trefousse, *Andrew Johnson*, 109, 176, 335–339; Walter Stahr, *Seward*, 109, Paul Finkelman, *Millard Fillmore*, 3, 126–131.

16. Hans Trefousse, *Andrew Johnson*, 367–374; Paul Finkelman, *Millard Fillmore*, 133–135; "Maryland," wikipedia.org.

Chapter 21

1. Douglas Brinkley, *Gerald Ford*, 120–121; Kenneth Davis, *Don't Know Much About the American Presidents*, 529; Erin Blakemore, "These Two Female Assassins Tried to Kill Gerald Ford," *Smithsonian*, June 3, 2015.

2. *Ibid.*, 449; David McCullough *Truman*, 810–812; Rachel Lewis, "Is Puerto Rico Part of the U.S.? Here's What to Know" *Time*, September 26, 2017; Edmund Morris, *Theodore Rex*, 215–216.

3. James Chace, *1912*, 230–231; James Burns and Susan Dunn, *The Three Roosevelts*, 138–139.

4. Michael Kauffman, *American Brutus*, 3–9, 22–27, 61, 214–215, 320–322, 332–333, 373–374; Hans Trefousse, *Andrew Johnson*, 196.

5. Candice Millard, *Destiny of the Republic*, 194, 196–197; Zachary Karabell, *Chester Alan Arthur*, 61–66.

6. Robert Caro, *The Passage of Power*, 320–321, 440, 574; Anthony Summers, *Official and Confidential*, 316, 325–333.

7. George Mowry, *The Era of Theodore Roosevelt and the Birth of Modern America*, ix–xii; Terry Kinney, "Murder At The Fair: The Assassination of President McKinley," History Channel Video (Ten Days That Unexpectedly Changed America); Kenneth Davis, *Don't Know Much About the American Presidents*, 360, 411, 458, 504.

8. *Ibid.*, 533.

9. Zachary Karabell, *Chester Alan Arthur*, 123–125; Amity Shlaes, *Coolidge*, 370–386; Douglas Brinkley, *The Wilderness Warrior*, 20–21.

10. Paul Finkelman, *Millard Fillmore*, 132; William DeGregorio, *The Complete Book of U.S. Presidents*, 193; H. W. Brands, *T.R.*, 661–663; David McCullough, *Truman* 952–959.

11. Edward Crapol, *John Tyler*, 273, 281–283; Hans Trefousse, *Andrew Johnson*, 136, 139–140, 141–143; William DeGregorio, *The Complete Book of U.S. Presidents*, 158–159, 251.

12. Amity Shlaes, *Coolidge*, 269, 280–281; Douglas Brinkley, *Gerald R. Ford*, 1, 146–147; Andrew Sinclair, *The Available Man*, viii, 296; Jonathan Aitken, *Nixon*, 467, 472; Zachary Karabell, *Chester Alan Arthur*, 106–111.

13. Amity Shlaes, *Coolidge*, 151–172; Hans Trefousse, *Andrew Johnson*, 128–151.

14. David McCullough, *Truman*, 256–280, 159–161, 211–213; William DeGregorio, *The Complete Book of U.S. Presidents*, 511, 512.

15. Zachary Karabell, *Chester Alan Arthur*, 21–22, 31–33, 140; Kenneth Davis, *Don't Know Much About the American Presidents*, 314.

16. Edward Crapol, *John Tyler*, 19–20, 75, 127; Hans Trefousse, *Andrew Johnson*, 234, 251–252, 293; Zachary Karabell, *Chester Alan Arthur*, 84–85, 88–90, 132; William DeGregorio, *The Complete Book of U.S. Presidents*, 156–157, 253–254, 313.

17. Edward Crapol, *John Tyler*, 177–222; H. W. Brands, *T.R.*, 479–491; Kenneth Davis, *Don't Know Much About the American Presidents*, 191, 368–369, 471, 484–486, 552–554.

18. William DeGregorio, *The Complete Book of U.S. Presidents*, 157.

19. H. W. Brands, *T. R.*, 449–450.

20. George Mowry, *The Era of Theodore Roosevelt and the Birth of Modern America*, 105, 292; William E. Leuchtenburg, *The White House Looks South*, 309, 325, 327–330.

21. Fergus Bordewich, *America's Great Debate*, 355–356, 359, 370, 373–374; Eric Foner, *Reconstruction*, 225–239, 333–336; Niraj Chokshi, "U.S. Partisanship Highest In Decades," *New York Times*, June 23, 2016; Rich Rubino, "Democratic and Republican Ideologies Undergo Dramatic Role Reversal," huffpost.com, August 13, 2013.

22. William DeGregorio, *The Complete Book of U.S. Presidents*, 188–189, 249.

23. *Ibid.*, 141, 144, 151, 178, 191, 297–298, 309, 311, 381, 452–453, 606.

24. Kenneth Davis, *Don't Know Much About the American Presidents*, 214, 271.

25. David McCullough, *Truman*, 355–356.

26. William DeGregorio, *The Complete Book of U.S. Presidents*, 150, 261, 375, 411, 564; "East Room," wikipedia.org.

27. William DeGregorio, *The Complete Book of U.S. Presidents*, 152, 309, 449.

28. "Ten U.S. Presidents Have Suffered Strokes," newswise.com (February 15, 2015); "Curse of Tippecanoe," wikipedia.org; Robert Owen, *Mr. Jefferson's Hammer*, 217–218; Jennifer Rosenberg, "Reagan Assassination Attempt," thoughtco.com (April 11, 2018).

Chapter 22

1. Edward Crapol, *John Tyler*, 16–17; Hans Trefousse, *Andrew Johnson*, 243, 251; Edmund Morris, *Theodore Rex*, 427.

2. William DeGregorio, *The Complete Book of U.S. Presidents*, 154; Kenneth Davis, *Don't Know Much About the American Presidents*, 189–190; Michael Holt, *The Rise and Fall of the American Whig Party*, 104, 127–136.

3. Robert Owens, *Mr. Jefferson's Hammer*, 248–249; William DeGregorio, *The Complete Book of U.S. Presidents*, 141–142, 145.

4. Kenneth Davis, *Don't Know Much About the American Presidents*, 191; Michael Holt, *The Rise and Fall of the American Whig Party*, 137–150, 168, 218–219, 221–222.

5. David Donald, *Lincoln*, 313, 327; Hans Trefousse, *Andrew Johnson*, 133–143; William DeGregorio, *The Complete Book of U.S. Presidents*, 251; Stephen Oates, *With Malice Toward None*, 249–250.

6. Hans Trefousse, *Andrew Johnson*, 145, 165–172, 335, 367–374; Walter Stahr, *Seward*, 461, 478, 480; William DeGregorio, *The Complete Book of U.S. Presidents*, 253, 254, 255.

7. Edmund Morris, *The Rise of Theodore Roosevelt*, 195–196, 227–240, 248–251; Edmund Morris, *Theodore Rex*, 427, 547; James Burns and Susan Dunn, *The Three Roosevelts*, 66–67; James Chace, *1912*, 32; Doris Goodwin, *The Bully Pulpit*, 2, 11, 532, 533, 585–599, 637–643.

8. *Ibid.*, 605–606, 627–633, 645; William DeGregorio, *The Complete Book of U.S. Presidents*, 399.

9. Kenneth Davis, *Don't Know Much About the American Presidents*, 379.

10. Doris Goodwin, *The Bully Pulpit*, 697–712; H. W. Brands, *T.R.*, 717–719; James Burns and Susan Dunn, *The Three Roosevelts*, 131.

11. Kenneth Davis, *Don't Know Much About the American Presidents*, 379.

12. Edmund Morris, *The Rise of Theodore Roosevelt*, 93–94, 251; H. W. Brands, *American Colossus*, 394.

13. Michael Holt, *The Rise and Fall of the American Whig Party*, 135, 147, 242; Edward Crapol, *John Tyler*, 106–107.

Chapter 23

1. Kenneth Davis, *Don't Know Much About the American Presidents*, 216–220, 273–277, 458, 459, 501, 504–506.

2. David McCullough, *Truman*, 26–34, 53–54; William Leuchtenburg, *The White House Looks South*, 147–161.

3. *Ibid.*, 150, 151, 152.

4. *Ibid.*, 156–158; David McCullough, *Truman*, 170–171.

5. *Ibid.*, 569–570; William Leuchtenburg, *The White House Looks South*, 163–172.

6. David McCullough, *Truman*, 651; David Pietrusza, *1948*, 224, 288.

7. Brion McClanahan, *Nine Presidents Who Screwed Up America and Four Who Tried to Save Her*, 107–118.

8. William Leuchtenburg, *The White House Looks South*, 207, 219; David McCullough, *Truman*, 667, 672, 677; Kenneth Davis, *Don't Know Much About the American Presidents*, 469–471.

9. Robert Caro, *The Path of Power*, 5–6; William Leuchtenburg, *The White House Looks South*, 267.

10. Robert Caro, *Master of the Senate*, 779, 863–872; Eric Foner, *Reconstruction*, 593; William Leuchtenburg, *The White House Looks South*, 260–265, 267.

11. Robert Caro, *The Passage of Power*, 76–78; Robert Dallek, *An Unfinished Life*, 259–269.

12. William Leuchtenburg, *The White House Looks South*, 263, 268–271; "Civil Rights Act of 1957," wikipedia.org.

13. Robert Caro, *The Passage of Power*, xiv–xvi; William Leuchtenburg, *The White House Looks South*, 325 327.

14. Robert Caro, *The Passage of Power*, 550, 569–570; William Leuchtenburg, *The White House Looks South*, 375–376.

15. *Ibid.*, 365–366, 382–383.

16. Eric Foner, *Reconstruction*, 179–181, 191, 250; Hans Trefousse, *Andrew Johnson*, 225, 236, 279, 299, 345, 379; Kenneth Davis, *Don't Know Much About the American Presidents*, 268.

17. Fergus Bordewich, *America's Great Debate*, 83; Paul Finkelman, *Millard Fillmore*, 105–107.

18. *Ibid.*, 116–129; William DeGregorio, *The Complete Book of U.S. Presidents*, 192.

Chapter 24

1. Amity Shlaes, *Coolidge*, 251–252, 255–259; Samuel Adams, *Incredible Era*, 374–377.

2. W. D. Wetherell, "Notches: Rock Carved By Glaciers," *New York Times*, May 8, 1994; Michael Blanding, "Best Foliage Drive in VT/Vermont's Route 100," *Yankee* magazine, August 19, 2009.

3. Amity Shlaes, *Coolidge*, 253; David Pietrusza, *1920*, 25; David McCullough, *Truman* 138; Kenneth Davis, *Don't Know Much About the American Presidents*, 390; John Cooper, *Woodrow Wilson: A Biography*, 6–7, 452, 459.

4. Andrew Sinclair, *The Available Man*, 28, 150, 182–183, 187–189, 261–263, 280, 285–286, 293; Amity Shlaes, *Coolidge*, 196, 204.

5. *Ibid.*, 255–259, 261, 262; Geoffrey Ward, "Prohibition," Ken Burns Video; Kenneth Davis, *Don't Know Much About the American Presidents*, 409–411.

6. Laura Kalman, *Right Star Rising*, 6–9, 63, 153–154, 203; Douglas Brinkley, *Gerald R. Ford*, 146–149.

7. Kenneth Davis, *Don't Know Much About the American Presidents*, 500–502, 504; William DeGregorio, *The Complete Book of U.S. Presidents*, 574–575.

8. *Ibid.*, 575; Brion McClanahan, *Nine Presidents Who Screwed Up America and Four Who Tried to Save Her*, 122–123.

9. George Mowry, *The Era of Theodore Roosevelt and the Birth of Modern America*, 131–134, 210–211, 214–216, 222; Edmund Morris, *Theodore Rex*, 20, 28, 29, 91–92, 205–207.

10. H. W. Brands, *T.R.*, 479–491; David McCullough, *The Path Between the Seas*, 327; Kenneth Davis, *Don't Know Much About the American Presidents*, 368–369; Dayton Duncan, "The National Parks: America's Best Idea," Ken Burns Video.

11. William DeGregorio, *The Complete Book Of U.S. Presidents*, 313; Mike Donovan, *The USA in the Time of Chester Alan Arthur*, 26–28.

12. *Ibid.*, 31–32; Kenneth Davis, *Don't Know Much About the American Presidents*, 315–316; Ric Burns and Li-Shin Yu, "The Chinese Exclusion Act," American Experience Video.

Chapter 25

1. Kenneth Davis, *Don't Know Much About the American Presidents*, 368–369, 501; Jon Meacham, *The Soul of America*, 249.

2. Kenneth Davis, *Don't Know Much About the American Presidents*, 190–191, 451–455; Candice Millard, *Destiny of the Republic*, 289–290; Walter Isaacson and Evan Thomas, *The Wise Men*, 325, 489–490.

3. Fergus Bordewich, *America's Great Debate*, 207, 239–240, 355–356; Kenneth Davis, *Don't Know Much About the American Presidents*, 216–218.

4. Eric Foner, *Reconstruction*, 239, 264–265; Hans Trefousse, *Andrew Johnson*, 336–340, 370–372.

5. Kenneth Davis, *Don't Know Much About the American Presidents*, 411; Amity Shlaes, *Coolidge*, 423–425, 438.

6. Douglas Brinkley, *Gerald R. Ford*, 67–69, 106–

112, 116, 127–128, 139–145; William DeGregorio, *The Complete Book of U.S. Presidents*, 612–613, 623.

7. Edmund Morris, *Theodore Rex*, 364, 490; H. W. Brands, *T. R.*, 514–516, 628, 673, 697–700.

8. Martin Harmon, *The Roosevelts and Their Descendants*, 52; Edmund Morris, *Theodore Rex*, 473; James Chace, *1912*, 39–41, 63, 243–244.

9. William DeGregorio, *The Complete Book of U.S. Presidents*, 520, 538, 575–576; Kenneth Davis, *Don't Know Much About the American Presidents*, 502–503.

10. Henry Kissinger, *Diplomacy*, 656–658; 659, 662–663, 671; Kenneth Davis, *Don't Know Much About the American Presidents*, 496–497, 504–505.

11. Michael Beschloss, *Presidential Courage*, 196–234; Forrest Pogue, *George C. Marshall*, 362–377; Walter Isaacson and Evan Thomas, *The Wise Men*, 451–453.

12. Zvi Dor-Ner, "The Fifty Years War: Israel and the Arabs," PBS Home Video.

Chapter 26

1. David Graham, "What Happens When a President Is Declared Illegitimate?" *The Atlantic*, January 18, 2017; "Illegitimate," *Webster's Seventh New Collegiate Dictionary*; Jon Meacham, *The Soul of America*, 17–18.

2. Hans Trefousse, *Andrew Johnson*, 165–166; Robert Caro, *The Path of Power*, xx–xxii, 266–268, 285–292, 333–334, 340, 361, 389–436, 734. Robert Caro, *The Passage of Power*, xxx–xxxi, 13, 384.

3. Hans Trefousse, *Andrew Johnson*, 13, 35–50, 51, 52–53, 69, 82–85, 107–108, 138, 151, 176–179, 378–379.

4. Edmund Morris, *Theodore Rex*, 116–117, 216, 238, 430, 431; Doris Goodwin, *The Bully Pulpit*, xi–xii, 1, 11–12, 138, 217, 243–244, 321, 657–658; David McCullough, *The Path Between the Seas, 1870–1914*, 269, 360, 379–386.

5. Edward Crapol, *John Tyler*, 3, 30–40, 41, 248–249, 277, 283; Michael Holt, *The Rise and Fall of the American Whig Party*, 99, 104.

6. William Shannon, "The Political Machine I: Rise and Fall—The Age of the Bosses," *American Heritage*, June 1969; Kevin Babb, "Quarterbacks in Spread Offenses Have Big Adjustment," *Washington Post*, September 15, 2015.

7. Paul Finkelman, *Millard Fillmore*, 8, 14, 15, 46–49, 55–56.

8. Douglas Brinkley, *Gerald R. Ford*, 15, 17–18, 23–28 33, 49, 51–52.

9. Zachary Karabell, *Chester Alan Arthur*, 3, 4–9; Candice Millard, *Destiny of the Republic*, 96.

10. David McCullough, *Truman*, 151–161, 185, 208, 214, 215–216, 300, 336.

11. William DeGregorio, *The Complete Book of U.S. Presidents*, 153–155, 156, 190–191, 250–252, 254, 310–311, 379–381, 416–417, 451–452, 511–512, 567–568, 607–609.

12. *Ibid.*, 159; Kenneth Davis, *Don't Know Much About the American Presidents*, 189.

13. *Ibid.*, 499; Robert Caro, *Means of Ascent*, xxxiv.

14. Zachary Karabell, *Chester Alan Arthur*, 20–22; Kenneth Davis, *Don't Know Much About the American Presidents*, 312, 314, 317.

15. James Chace, *1912*, 6, 11, 20; James Burns and Susan Dunn, *The Three Roosevelts*, 9, 19, 26; Martin Harmon, *The Roosevelts and Their Descendants*, 170; Geoffrey Ward, "The Roosevelts: An Intimate History," Ken Burns Video.

16. William DeGregorio, *The Complete Book of U.S. Presidents*, 507–508, 509, 511; Kenneth Davis, *Don't Know Much About the American Presidents*, 458–459; David McCullough, *Truman*, 990–991.

17. *Ibid.*, 496, 967; Kenneth Davis, *Don't Know Much About the American Presidents*, 271, 275; William DeGregorio, *The Complete Book of U.S. Presidents*, 247; Hans Trefousse, *Andrew Johnson*, 21–22, 235, 305.

18. Paul Finkelman, *Millard Fillmore*, 3, 4, 16, 74, 85–86 137; Kenneth Davis, *Don't Know Much About the American Presidents*, 215, 219; William DeGregorio, *The Complete Book of U.S. Presidents*, 187.

19. Michael Beschloss, "LBJ and Truman: The Bond That Helped Forge Medicare," *New York Times*, February 28, 2015; David McCullough, *Truman*, 990.

Bibliography

Adams, Samuel Hopkins. *Incredible Era: The Life and Times of Warren Gamaliel Harding.* New York: Capricorn, 1939.

Aitken, Jonathan. *Nixon: A Life.* Washington: Regnery, 1993.

Bain, David Howard. *Empire Express: Building the First Transcontinental Railroad.* New York: Viking, 1999.

Beschloss, Michael. *Presidential Courage: Brave Leaders and How They Changed America, 1789–1989.* New York: Simon & Schuster, 2007.

Bordewich, Fergus M. *America's Great Debate: Henry Clay, Stephen A. Douglas, and the Compromise That Preserved the Union.* New York: Simon & Schuster, 2012.

Borneman, Walter R. *Polk: The Man Who Transformed the Presidency and America.* New York: Random House, 2008.

Brands, H. W. *American Colossus: The Triumph of Capitalism, 1865–1900.* New York: Anchor Books, 2010.

_____. *T. R.: The Last Romantic.* New York: Basic Books, 1997.

Brinkley, Douglas. *Gerald R. Ford.* New York: Times Books, 2007.

_____. *The Wilderness Warrior: Theodore Roosevelt and the Crusade for America.* New York: HarperCollins, 2009.

Burns, James MacGregor, and Susan Dunn. *The Three Roosevelts: Patrician Leaders Who Transformed America.* New York: Grove Press, 2001.

Caldwell, Mary French. *Tennessee: The Volunteer State.* Chicago: Richtext Press, 1968.

Caro, Robert. *Master of the Senate: The Years of Lyndon Johnson.* New York: Alfred A. Knopf, 2002.

_____. *Means of Ascent: The Years of Lyndon Johnson.* New York: Alfred A. Knopf, 1990.

_____. *The Passage of Power: The Years of Lyndon Johnson.* New York: Alfred A. Knopf, 2012.

Carwardine, Richard. *Lincoln: A Life of Purpose and Power.* New York: Alfred A. Knopf, 2006.

Chace, James. *1912: Wilson, Roosevelt, Taft and Debs—The Election That Changed the Country.* New York: Simon & Schuster, 2004.

Clary, David A. *Eagles and Empire: The United States, Mexico, and the Struggle for a Continent.* New York: Bantam Books, 2009.

Coit, Margaret L. *John C. Calhoun: American Portrait.* Boston: Houghton Mifflin, 1950.

Corlew, Robert. *Tennessee: A Short History.* Knoxville: University of Tennessee Press, 1981.

Crapol, Edward P. *John Tyler: The Accidental President.* Chapel Hill: University of North Carolina Press, 2006.

Dallek, Robert. *An Unfinished Life: John F. Kennedy, 1917–1963.* New York: Little, Brown, 2003.

Davis, Kenneth C. *Don't Know Much About the American Presidents.* New York: Hyperion, 2012.

DeGregorio, William A. *The Complete Book of U.S. Presidents.* Fort Lee, NJ: Barricade Books, 2013.

Donald, David Herbert. *Lincoln.* London: Random House, 1995.

Donovan, Mike. *The USA in the Time of Chester Alan Arthur, 1881–1885.* Sun Valley, CA: CreateSpace, 2011.

Dray, Philip. *Capitol Men: The Epic Story of Reconstruction Through the Lives of the First Black Congressmen.* Boston: Houghton Mifflin, 2008.

Emerson, Jason. *Giant In The Shadows: The Life of Robert T. Lincoln.* Carbondale: Southern Illinois University Press, 2012.

Finkelman, Paul. *Millard Fillmore.* New York: Times Books, 2004.

Foner, Eric. *Reconstruction: America's Unfinished Revolution, 1863–1877.* New York: Harper & Row, 1988.

Freehling, William W. *The Road To Disunion: Secessionists at Bay, 1776–1854.* New York: Oxford University Press, 1990.

Goodwin, Doris Kerns. *The Bully Pulpit: Theodore Roosevelt, William Howard Taft, and the Golden Age of Journalism.* New York: Simon & Schuster, 2013.

Halberstam, David. *The Coldest Winter: America and the Korean War.* New York: Hyperion, 2007.

Harmon, F. Martin. *The Roosevelts and Their Descendants: Portrait of an American Family.* Jefferson, NC: McFarland, 2017.

Holt, Michael F. *The Rise and Fall of the American Whig Party: Jacksonian Politics and the Onset of the Civil War.* New York: Oxford University Press, 1999.

Isaacson, Walter, and Evan Thomas. *The Wise Men:*

Six Friends and the World They Made, George Kennan, Dean Acheson, Charles Bohlen, Robert Lovett, Averell Harriman, John McCloy. New York: Simon & Schuster, 1986.

Kalman, Laura. *Right Star Rising: A New Politics, 1974–1980.* New York: W. W. Norton, 2010.

Karabell, Zachary. *Chester Alan Arthur.* New York: Times Books, 2004.

Kauffman, Michael W. *American Brutus: John Wilkes Booth and the Lincoln Conspiracies.* New York: Random House, 2004.

Kissinger, Henry. *Diplomacy.* New York: Simon & Schuster, 1994.

Leuchtenburg, William E. *The White House Looks South: Franklin D. Roosevelt, Harry S. Truman, Lyndon B. Johnson.* Baton Rouge: Louisiana State University Press, 2005.

McCartney, Laton. *The Teapot Dome Scandal: How Big Oil Bought the Harding White House and Tried to Steal the Country.* New York: Random House, 2008.

McClanahan, Brion. *Nine Presidents Who Screwed Up America and Four Who Tried to Save Her.* Washington: Regnery, 2016.

McCullough, David. *The Path Between the Seas: The Creation of the Panama Canal, 1870–1914.* New York: Simon & Schuster, 1977.

_____. *Truman.* New York: Simon & Schuster, 1992.

McFeely, William S. *Grant: A Biography.* New York: W. W. Norton, 1982.

Meacham, Jon. *The Soul of America: The Battle for Our Better Angels.* New York: Random House, 2018.

Millard, Candice. *Destiny of the Republic: A Tale of Madness, Medicine, and the Murder of a President.* New York: Anchor Books, 2011.

Morris, Edmund, *Theodore Rex.* New York: Random House, 2001.

Mowry, George E. *The Era of Theodore Roosevelt and the Birth of Modern America, 1900–1912.* New York: Harper & Row, 1958.

Oates, Stephen B. *With Malice Toward None: The Life of Abraham Lincoln.* New York: Harper & Row, 1977.

Owens, Robert W. *Mr. Jefferson's Hammer: William Henry Harrison and the Origins of American Indian Policy.* Norman: University of Oklahoma Press, 1974.

Paludan, Phillip Shaw. *The Presidency of Abraham Lincoln.* Lawrence: University of Kansas Press, 1994.

Pietrusza, David. *1920: The Year of the Six Presidents.* New York: Carroll & Graf, 2007.

_____. *1948: Harry Truman's Improbable Victory and the Year That Transformed America.* New York: Union Square Press, 2011.

Pogue, Forrest C. *George C. Marshall: Statesman, 1945–1959.* New York: Penguin Books, 1987.

Remini, Robert. *Daniel Webster: The Man and His Time.* New York: W. W. Norton, 1997.

_____. *Henry Clay: Statesman for the Union.* New York: W. W. Norton, 1991.

Shlaes, Amity. *Coolidge.* New York: HarperCollins, 2013.

Sinclair, Andrew. *The Available Man: The Life Behind the Masks of Warren G. Harding.* Chicago: Quadrangle Books, 1965.

Stahr, Walter. *Seward: Lincoln's Indispensable Man.* New York: Simon & Schuster, 2012.

Summers, Anthony. *Official and Confidential: The Secret Life of J. Edgar Hoover.* New York: G. P. Putnam's Sons, 1993.

Trefousse, Hans. *Andrew Johnson: A Biography.* New York: W. W. Norton, 1989.

Van Deusen, Glyndon G. *The Jacksonian Era, 1828–1848.* New York: Harper & Row, 1959.

Winik, Jay. *April 1865: The Month That Saved America.* New York: HarperCollins, 2001.

Index